W9-BMP-210

Chernobyl

Chernobyl

Crime without Punishment

Alla A. Yaroshinskaya

Transaction Publishers
New Brunswick (U.S.A.) and London (U.K.)

The author wishes to express her thanks to Rosalie Bertell and Lynn Ehrle for their voluntary editing of the translation of this volume and also the Nuclear Age Peace Foundation and Engineers and Scientists for Global Responsibility for their financial support of the translation.

This book is printed on acid-free paper that meets the American National Standard for Permanence of Paper for Printed Library Materials.

Library of Congress Catalog Number: 2011017274
ISBN: 978-1-4128-4296-9
Printed in the United States of America

Library of Congress Cataloging-in-Publication Data

Yaroshinska, Alla.
    [Chernobyl 20 let spustia. English]
    Chernobyl : crime without punishment/Alla A. Yaroshinskaya; [translated from Russian by Sergei Roy].—North American ed./ edited by Rosalie Bertell and Lynn Howard Ehrle.
        p. cm.
    ISBN 978-1-4128-4296-9
1. Chernobyl Nuclear Accident, Chornobyl, Ukraine, 1986—Environmental aspects.   2. Chernobyl Nuclear Accident, Chornobyl, Ukraine, 1986—Social aspects.   3. Radioactive pollution—Ukraine—Chornobyl Region.   4. Soviet Union—Politics and government—1985–1991.   I. Bertell, Rosalie, 1929– II. Ehrle, Lynn.   III. Title.
    TK1362.U38Y36513 2011
    363.17'99094777—dc23

2011017274

Contents

Introduction

On April 26, 1986, about seven years after the Three Mile Island nuclear accident, the nuclear reactor at Chernobyl experienced an explosion, meltdown, fire, and massive release of radioactivity. The International Atomic Energy Agency (IAEA) had been poised to begin a concerted public relations effort to market nuclear power in the developing countries. It had been mandated by the United Nations, when it was founded in response to President Eisenhower's Peaceful Atom Program, to promote nuclear technology to the whole world. Imagine its consternation when the Swedish government proclaimed that the then Soviet Union had experienced a nuclear reactor accident! It had waited patiently until it thought the world had forgotten Three Mile Island!

The first time I visited the failed Chernobyl reactor site, I saw that it was in prime agricultural and orchard land. In fact, it was even called the breadbasket of the Soviet Union. Prypiat, the nearest city to Chernobyl, was a place where the ancient art of icon painting had begun, and its library contained many priceless icons from the Middle Ages. Prypiat was a modern city prior to the disaster. It had high-rise apartment buildings, a new school with a large playground, and a public library. Looking in through the library windows, I could see the precious icons strewn on the floor together with books and other debris—now all radioactive waste. The school swings and slides stood waiting for children and the apartment buildings were empty, all of the windows closed against the spring air, and the streets were empty.

This area was inside the exclusion zone. We had driven from Kiev to the border of the exclusion zone and then transferred to buses that only operated within the zone. Surrounding the city of Prypiat and the failed reactor were blooming apple and cherry trees and even a few elderly people who refused to leave the land they knew so well.

I learned that the people of Prypiat were country people with a volunteer fire department that was first on the scene when the accident occurred. Like other rural fire departments, the wives relieved their husbands in the early days of the fire so they could have a meal and take some rest. Because of years of indoctrination by radiation experts who claimed nuclear reactors posed no risk, children played in the yards or went to the store and people stood out in the street watching the fire. When buses finally arrived to remove them from harm's way, many refused to leave their farms and farm animals. The Soviets had to round up the animals (and kill them later when the farmers were gone) before people would evacuate.

There was a forest, heavily contaminated, which had been cut down and buried. There was one tree still standing, one with a branch that had grown strong and lay parallel with the ground. The people told me that this tree was used during the Nazi occupation of Ukraine in World War II as the hanging place for patriots. There were wreaths of flowers around the base of this tree and remembrance candles. It would not be buried like the rest of the trees!

We saw the burying ground for the large trucks and diggers that had been brought in to fight the blaze. We also met the young men who were running the other nuclear reactors on the site—walking every day by the failed reactor, (which was) still fissioning and spewing out radioactive materials. As we neared the reactor, my Geiger counter registered quite a high reading, and my camera film was overexposed so that none of the pictures I took turned out.

The following account, by reporter Paul Hofheinz in Moscow, appeared in the July 20, 1987 issue of *Time* magazine.

Soon after the Chernobyl meltdown, Soviet officials ordered the permanent evacuation of villages within 30 km (19 miles) of the power plant, but heavy nuclear fallout covered a much broader area. In some parts of Narodichi, a Ukrainian agricultural district whose boundaries lie some 60 km (37 miles) from the reactor, levels of radioactivity are still nine times as high as the acceptable limits, according to the local Communist Party chief.

Vladimir Lysovsky, a doctor at Narodichi District Central Hospital, contends that in the past 18 months, there has been a dramatic rise in cases of thyroid disease, anemia and cancer. Residents also have begun complaining of fatigue and loss of vision and appetite—all symptoms of radiation sickness. Worst of all, there has been a startling drop in the immunity level of the entire population. "Healthy people are having trouble getting over their illnesses," Lysovsky notes. And children are the most affected.

Farmers, meanwhile, are seeing an explosion of birth defects among livestock. Colts have appeared with eight limbs, deformed lower jaws and disjointed spinal columns. Photographer Kostin reports that 197 freak calves have been born at the Yuri Gagarin collective farm in Vyazovka. Some of the animals had no eyes, deformed skulls and distorted mouths. At a farm in Malinovka, about 200 abnormal piglets have been born since the accident.

Later, I met the woman doctor who had been in charge of the emergency medical tent set up for the so-called "liquidators" of the fire. She decided who would be sent to Hospital 10 in Moscow for special treatment for radiation sickness. She was upset when I first met her because a young woman, a well-trained laboratory technician, whom she chose to take with her to help in the clinic, had just died. She was twenty-eight years old and had been in good health prior to the disaster. I asked about her death, and the doctor told me she died of "adult sudden death," adding, "I never thought I was giving these young people a death sentence. I chose the best we had!"

The doctor told me that she had autopsied some of these sudden deaths and found that the person's internal organs had been severely damaged. The victims looked healthy externally, just as they had looked before the accident, but their vital organs had been damaged. She said that their internal organs looked like those of very elderly people.

I only stayed in Kiev for a week, but I visited the hospitals and saw the former "liquidators" and so many children bearing signs of unusual sickness with internal digestive, neurological, blood, and heart problems. There was also an almost immediate increase in cancers, contrary to current belief that cancer would not occur for ten to twenty years. At first, the local physicians were calling the people's complaints "radio-phobia," but they soon learned to respect the true sickness, especially in children, and became ashamed of that term.

Being a cancer scientist, I recognized the early cancers as those promoted by the radiation. In a large population, many people have developing malignancies which are subclinical and with which their immune system is successfully coping. These malignancies may not ever become clinically detectable, but the body may successfully destroy them. When someone experiences a sudden exposure to radiation, it is a blow to the immune system. The cellular immune system can no longer cope with the developing malignancy, and what was subclinical becomes an overt diagnosable cancer. The governments and people of Russia, Ukraine, and Belarus never received an outpouring of aid from the global community that has been customary after other major disasters. This was because of the government secrecy that silenced most victims and kept their accounts of radiation sickness within a close circle of local friends and relatives. The author recounts case after case of official denials, blame for the accident on operator error, and refusal to relate radiation illnesses to the disaster. International experts minimized the extent and danger posed by the spreading clouds of radioactivity across much of Russia and Europe. This was in no small measure due to the fact that Soviet officials invited the IAEA, rather than the World Health Organization, to investigate and report on the disaster, harking back to an unfortunate 1959 agreement made during the cold war.

It is now twenty-five years since the event. Few of the professional papers describing the aftereffects of the disaster have been translated from Russian into English and distributed in the West. The sarcophagus has not yet been secured because the reactor is still releasing radioactive gases. The people are still waiting to be heard!

The official paper prepared by the IAEA for the twentieth anniversary was released in the fall of 2005, and it continued to minimize the effects, presenting a relatively benign picture of the disaster. Although the World Health Organization's (WHO's) name was attached to this IAEA press release, a spokesperson for WHO told a reporter for *New Scientist* that the IAEA had dropped five thousand deaths for political reasons. This reduction does not begin to cover the full extent of the suffering experienced by those who were witnesses and recipients of the radioactive debris in the air, water, and food.

Alla Yaroshinskaya is herself a Ukrainian whose town was showered with fallout from the accident. From her writing, it is obvious that she loves her land and its people. She did not merely collect official information in a short time period and then publish an official understated press release about the disaster. Instead, she has produced a book giving the human side of the disaster, with firsthand accounts by those who lived through the world's worst public health crisis. It has now been translated into English from the original Russian, with graphic descriptions of what has really happened to the people and their land.

Unlike the IAEA, Yaroshinskaya is not burdened by trying to promote nuclear power or official attempts to hide the consequences of the accident and the suffering of the people. She hopes that we will see the strength of the people whose patience has endured under the yoke of Communist Party repression; their ancient culture and productive lifestyle; the beauty of the land and its defilement brought on by the disaster and its subsequent cover-up.

This book is a unique account of events by a courageous woman who defied the Soviet bureaucracy in her quest for truth. The author presents an accurate historical account of events and quotations from all the major players in the Chernobyl drama. We appreciate her grant of editorial license and trust that our efforts are in accord with her intent. On a personal note, the editing of Yaroshinskaya's book has given me another opportunity to extend and deepen our friendship that developed after the Chernobyl debacle.

Rosalie Bertell, PhD
Yardley, PA
April 2011

Prologue: Life Weighed on Chernobyl Scales

The cozy little Ukrainian town of Chernobyl had been known in Europe almost two hundred years before the fatal nuclear blast that shook both Europe and the entire world, and ultimately speeded up the disintegration of that mighty Communist empire, the Soviet Union. Chernobyl, it appears, also had a role to play in the French Revolution of 1789. One of the more active participants in those historic events was a twenty-six-year-old Chernobyl lady, Rosalia Lubomirska, née Chodkiewicz. Her fate was not unlike that of thousands of others. For her connection with Marie-Antoinette and the royal family she was guillotined in Paris on June 20, 1794. As wars spread throughout France and Europe, the pretty young blonde with china-blue eyes became known as "Rosalie of Chernobyl."

This sleepy provincial town was under Rzecz Pospolita, the unified Polish-Lithuanian state. Since the end of the seventeenth century, it was owned by Lithuanian magnate Chodkiewicz. Until the 1917 October revolution in Russia, his descendents owned 20,000 *desyatinas*, or 54,000 acres of land there. One of the Chodkiewicz family estates was also located in that area. I obtained an interesting bit of history about Rosalie of Chernobyl from Nikolai Lacis, the one-time chief editor of the local Chernobyl daily *Prapor peremohi* (Banner of Victory). He and his entire staff, like myself, had to leave our native town ten days after the explosion. Apparently, one of the Chernobyl buildings that used to belong to the Chodkiewicz family still contains a tile with a small neat likeness of Rosalie, a defender of the Bourbons in the turbulent times of the French Revolution. Previously, the building housed the main district hospital of Chernobyl, and the sculpted likeness of Rosalie of Chernobyl happened to grace one of its neurology wards.

And so, barely 200 years later, Chernobyl again reminded the world of its existence but could not have imagined what was to follow.

Chernobyl today is arguably the most notorious town on the planet. For years Ukraine was associated with this name, which had taken on a sinister meaning. It should be noted that hundreds of journalists and writers worldwide who covered that nuclear disaster still fail to realize, twenty years on, that the accident actually occurred in the town of Pripyat but was christened the Chernobyl disaster after the district center of that name. Pripyat it was, the town of power plant engineers, that was evacuated on April 27, 1986, while the district center of Chernobyl was not evacuated until ten days later, though it, too, got more than its fair share of nuclear contamination. And it was that hospital with Rosalie's sculpted head that, in the first days after the worst nuclear disaster in human memory, was chock-full of casualties. The terrified and sick people would be unaware of the lovely finely chiseled head of a young stranger whose beauty was in marked contrast to the radiation madness around us. The locals tell stories of a young woman's ghost with a severed head in her hands seen on the outskirts of town on the eve of the tragic blast. They insist it was the spirit of Rosalie of Chernobyl, trying to warn her fellow townspeople and possibly guard them against the impending doom.

Today, thanks to another Orange Revolution that occurred in Ukraine at the end of 2004, some of my American friends finally stopped asking me where exactly Ukraine was situated. Is it in the south of Russia, by any chance, they asked? Now the whole world knows that Ukraine is more than just Chernobyl. It is also a newly independent state in the heart of Europe. But that has not made Chernobyl disappear. Indeed, Chernobyl is still with us. When the "best" Soviet nuclear reactor blew up, I lived with my family in Zhitomir, a city of about 300,000, situated in the wooded area called Polesye, 140 kilometers southwest of Chernobyl. This is ancient Slavic land. The first settlements here appeared way back in the second millennium b.c. My ancestors trod its soil in the Bronze Age and in the early Iron Age, as attested to by burial mounds and remnants of an Old Rus ancient settlement site. But the first mention of Zhitomir is to be found in the chronicles of 1392. The name, say historians and students of local lore, was the gift of the town's founder, Prince Zhitomir. It consists of two parts—*zhito* and *mir*. Those are perhaps among the simplest and most essential ideas in any language. *Zhito* translates from Ukrainian as *rye*, and *mir* is *peace*. These are not just words but fundamental truths—rye and peace. A philosophy of life built upon the rich traditions of peasant families who struggled to make the land productive and villages that would be safe havens in which children could grow and prosper.

Right in the center of the city is Castle Mountain. Legend has it that this is where the town originated. There on the mountain, washed on either side by the rivers Kamyanka and Teterev, the ancient Zhitomir castle was built to fend off enemies. Around it the town itself grew and flourished. Living in it were craftsmen—blacksmiths, potters, hunters, peasants, merchants. The pristine forests that hugged Zhitomir abounded in game, berries, mushrooms, and edible roots. Fish filled the rivers on whose banks the town was laid. Ah yes, our ancestors did know, uncannily, how to choose the most magic, wonderful places on earth to erect their towns and churches, built to last through the ages.

Whenever I could find time for an outing with my family or friends we would go to the outskirts of town to admire the spectacular views, never tiring of their beauty. Within a few kilometers of Zhitomir flows the strikingly primeval river, Teterev, its clear waters running between huge circular boulders, with the ancient forest on either bank and naked rocks bashfully covered with moss. Here and there a tree seemed to cling to a precarious existence. There are gorges, too. And somewhere, far away in the distance, among the dark-green pine tops—sky-blue, and light as children's hearts, rise the domes of a modest village church. Perfect peace, as if one were in the presence of Eternity, safe in the knowledge that we were part of an unbroken chain, whose forefathers lived in harmony with the fertile land, this forest, this river, and this church, in whose gleaming sun-lit cross brought comfort to the sick and hope to those who had fallen on hard times. Don't break the spell, just yet, with this unnecessary question. What comes later will do that.

At any rate, those were the thoughts that occurred to me that time, too, when our family managed to go there yet again. It was spring. The air was mellow with the sense of liberation and renewal. Timid blue petals of the spring came peeping out from under the carpet of last year's dead leaves. My two-year-old son, Sasha, squatted by each tiny bloom. We did not know, nor did anyone else, I suppose, that just a few hours later something would happen to change us forever, destined to alter this beautiful ancient land with its lush forests, fields and meadows, transforming our way of life in ways unimaginable. Life on Earth from then on would be divided not only into epochs, eras, cultures, religions, social and political structures. It would be divided into the age before and after, pre and post-Chernobyl. (Before. And after.) This planet would never again be as it had been before 26 April, 1986, at 01:24 p.m. At precisely that moment a blanket of fog drifted over us, "on little cat feet." Silently, with no warning, harboring its deadly ^{137}cesium and ^{90}strontium. Nothing to break the quiet of a peaceful afternoon, except—did no one notice—the birds stopped singing.

Zhitomir is 130 kilometers west of Ukraine's capital Kiev. Once in a while my husband and I allowed ourselves the treat of a theater visit in Kiev. By a quirk of fate precisely on April 27, in the afternoon, we set off for Kiev, unsuspecting, because no one, whether on the radio, television or in newspapers, had reported the blast at the Chernobyl nuclear power plant. That night a Japanese group, Shyotiku, were doing a show at the Ukraine arts center. We left the car at a nearby parking lot. The Shyotiku show became something of an occasion. It was real art. I still remember the flowing white robes of the actors, their graceful movements as they danced. We were returning home rather late in a festive mood. The road from Kiev to Zhitomir passed through lush, spring woods coming into leaf. Having covered just over half of the distance, we pulled up by the roadside and got out for a breath of the heady green fragrance. It was very quiet. Bright cold stars glittered overhead. Distant galaxies were sending us greetings. The Big Dipper was clearly visible in the clear sky and the moon flooded the countryside with its even light. It seemed as though one could hear buds on the fruit trees bursting into bloom.

Even though the Soviet media still reported no news of the nuclear explosion, rumors soon spread panic in the cities closest to Chernobyl—Kiev, Zhitomir, and Chernihiv. No one knew what had happened, but table talk soon turned to suspicion and distrust, as though some evil monster had suddenly overtaken us. When news of escaping radiation from the reactor reached our ears, the pharmacies quickly sold out of iodine. A lot of the people, believing that it was some cure against radiation, drank pure iodine, burning their throats and intestines. The official medical establishment uttered nary a word. Finally, after ten days, Ukraine's health minister, Anatoly Romanenko, deigned to dispense dubious advice. Keep your windows shut and wipe your shoes well on a wet rag before entering home. Wash the floors and wipe the furniture with a damp cloth. And that was that, as far as anti-radiation measures went. This incoherent counsel only served to whip up the panic. We first learned that there had been an explosion at Reactor Unit No.4 of the Chernobyl nuclear power plant and that background radiation levels were rising, this from Western broadcasters. As for our own Soviet leadership, they did not inform us of the accident until three days later. (The Swedish authorities, when they were still unaware of the exact location of the radiation leak, removed the entire staff of their own nuclear power station even before they had learned the particulars; only then did they proceed to find out what had happened and where).

Meanwhile, the May Day celebrations were approaching, and apparently no one wished to believe that something truly monstrous and desperate had happened. On May 1, millions of people all over the country—in Zhitomir, in Kiev, and in Chernihiv, as in virtually every Soviet village and town in the Ukraine, Belorussia, Russia, the Baltic republics, and everywhere else, went out to join the festive parade, as they had done annually. It was hot. Not just warm, but scorching. In Kiev children in national dress danced on Kreshchatik, the main street of the Ukrainian capital, breathing in radioactive fumes to please the eye of Ukraine's Communist leaders who waved to the public from the stands. Almost at that precise moment their own children were being dispatched in a hurry to the Borispol airport, to board the planes that would take them far away from the disaster. It was the children of duped workers and intellectuals who entertained the government and so created an illusion before the world community that everything was ok. Even as celebrations were going on, crowds of Party functionaries several thousand strong were lining up for plane and train tickets in the exclusive Ukrainian Communist Party booking offices, according to eyewitness accounts.

My friend from university years, journalist Nina Smykovskaya, who had to wait till the age of forty to be blessed with children, did not manage to leave Kiev for Odessa until May 7, to stay there with her relations. Ukraine's capital had by then been engulfed by panic. Nina gave birth to premature twins, two tiny girls. They were named Diana and Inna in honor of those who had given the family shelter in their hour of trial. The babies were born weak and anemic. Their mother, naturally unaware of any danger, had been feeding them radioiodine and cesium until her departure. A month later doctors in Odessa told her that the babies had to have an urgent blood transfusion to replace all of their blood. The girls were saved by a miracle, although their health remained something of a problem afterwards. Now these children of the nuclear disaster are old enough to be married.

I clearly remember the days in early May of that fatal year. A dazzlingly blue sky. Snow-white clouds. It is warm. Very warm. Warmer than one might expect. Rumor and misinformation became the order of the day. After May 1, all of that started snowballing. The newspapers and the radio told us one thing, but people who came "from there" said something very different. Kiev's booking offices were sold out a month in advance. Tickets to any place at all were not to be had for love or money. High strung people, scared by the uncertainty, stormed railway stations, booking offices and trains. They were glad to leave for just about any place, as long as they could put some distance between themselves and Chernobyl.

On May 7, my husband Alexander phoned me from work and said firmly, "Take the kids and leave—at once." (Several of his friends had been sent to Chernobyl, to pump away water from under the death-breathing reactor). Easier said than done. Where could I go? How? At the time I worked as a correspondent with the industry and capital construction section of the district Party daily, *Radyanska Zhitomirshchina* ("Soviet Zhitomirland"). I hastened to apply for short leave. My boss made it conditional on my writing an article on the construction of a new plant at Kroshnya. The next morning the piece was lying on his desk. It opened with a line about the riot of flowers at Zhitomir's outskirts, and the exquisite fragrance of apple blossoms wafting over to the building site from nearby orchards. We could not buy a ticket to Armavir in the Caucasus where our relations lived. There were none to be had. There were no tickets to any other city either. With enormous difficulty we contrived to leave for Moscow, to stay at our friends' place.

The farewell at the Zhitomir railway station was not unlike an evacuation routine. My elder son, Milan, who was then twelve, did not have the time to complete his school year, but all the parents who had the slightest chance to do so were allowed to take their children away from school. My whole family came to the station, including my mother, my sister, and my husband's parents, all of them choking back tears. The grandmothers kept talking to my youngest Sasha, heaping on him sweets and toys. They showered me with advice and instructed the elder boy, Milan, to always do as he was told and help me on the train. It is an eighteen-hour train ride from Zhitomir to Moscow. That day, May 8, was my younger son's birthday; he turned two. His big day was spent in a crowded car of the Zhitomir-Moscow train, among equally upset people crushed by the disaster.

We had no relations in Moscow. Previously, I only rarely went there—once as an undergraduate and afterwards as a journalist sent to write a report about the USSR Exhibition of Economic Achievements. On my first trip to Moscow I saw hardly anything of the city because my thoughts were on the man I loved who stayed behind in another city. The second time Moscow enchanted me with its churches and quaint crooked streets in Zamoskvorechye, beyond the Moskva River, that bore lovely ancient names. There are lots of them here. And it is these streets and their names that make the capital so irresistible. But this time we were immune to Moscow's charms. At the station we were met by a family of friends—Faina Alexandrovna and her son Misha. They used to live in Zhitomir once, and every year came over to stay with us on vacation. Faina Alexandrovna taught German at a school. Misha was a university student. They are singularly kind and decent people.

As soon as we got to their place, we stripped off all our clothes and I washed them at once. Not because I had been told that this was the right thing to do, nor because I knew what levels of radiation our garments emitted. It was an intuitive feeling of self-preservation. I only knew that all vegetables bought at the Zhitomir market had to be washed to reduce radiation levels—to remove radioactive dust. I am still deeply grateful to Faina Alexandrovna and Misha for their heroic hospitality. Meanwhile, I know of families escaping radiation that were (and still are) ostracized in the places to which they had fled, from fear of contamination. This is simply unimaginable.

We stayed several days with that family in Moscow. Their apartment was a very small apartment, and the inconvenience we were causing to these kind people made me buy tickets to the Caucasus where my own relations lived. Buying tickets in Moscow was no problem. Over there in the Caucasus, we were welcome. So on May 14, after a harrowing day and night in a dusty third-class railroad car of the Moscow-Adler train, we finally arrived in Armavir. The Caucasus was already in the midst of a gorgeous spring. Beside the house of the Miklashevsky family where we nervously hoped to weather the atomic winter, (who could have known that it was for good!) the first May cherries had ripened. All around was bloom and fragrance. Life seemed to be on its normal course. Chernobyl was seldom mentioned. It was as if it had nothing to do with Armavir residents. (Eventually, three years later, I learned that parts of Krasnodar Territory, with its famous health resorts, had also been contaminated with Chernobyl radiation).

The first thing I did was take the children to the local radiology lab. Our clothes emitted some 0.025 milliroentgen (mR). Such, the doctors said, was the background radiation level there. In pre-Chernobyl Zhitomir the background level did not exceed 0.017 mR. In spite of the warmth and spring blossoms, Armavir did little to assuage our anxieties. My youngest, Sasha, fell ill. Here, too, we found quite a few kindly folk. Larisa Ivanovna, the local GP summoned to attend to the child, on learning that we were from the Chernobyl zone, took us to her bosom. That's how it should be, is it not? However, knowing what our Soviet medical establishment was like, we fully appreciated Dr. Ivanovna and her attitude. Sasha, it turned out, not only had a sore throat but also the first symptoms of bronchitis. When he recovered, my leave came to an end. In June we had to go back to Zhitomir. I could not possibly leave the kids behind in the Caucasus. There was simply no one to look after them. And I had to report for work. Nor could I quit my job because a Soviet family could not possibly get by on a single salary.

A long sultry summer laden with anxiety lay ahead. The main Communist daily, *Pravda*, served up a daily diet of platitudes and disinformation, hoping to tranquilize the population into thinking that all was well, all the while telling us there was nothing to worry about. I still have a deep sense of indignation when recalling the headlines my Moscow colleagues used for their stories. "Nightingales over the Pripyat" or "Souvenirs from under the Reactor," and such. Twenty years on, the people living in affected areas—and there are nine million of them—still pay much too high a price for those souvenirs. But more of that later.

Not one drop of rain, it seemed, fell on the city in the whole of that tense summer of 1986. The sky was a bottomless faded blue from the demented sun. The reactor's fiendish innards, having gulped down unholy amounts of sand, lead and some other stuff, had finally clogged up. It was laid to rest in a special "sepulcher," since christened The Sarcophagus. We still do not now how much radiation still leaks each day from the tangled fuel rods. Families no longer wailed over the zinc-plated coffins of firemen killed by radiation and buried a long way from home, at the Mitino cemetery in Moscow.

Now the team of nuclear physicists, selected by the bureaucrats as Chernobyl scapegoats, have already served time and left prison, and some of them have even died. So, the whole thing is over and done with? No, decades after the disaster, we are beginning to see it in proper perspective, to fathom the hopelessness and despair, with the Chernobyl genes carried by our children and grandchildren on into the future. As we learn about this global malignancy, figuratively and literally, we are learning more about ourselves and about our diseased society. We are coming to grips with our past that is not unlike the Andromeda nebulae. Although anxious about the future, we understand that Hope is the last thing to die.

Deafened by ideological incantations in the brutal cavern of Communism, we have only just broken through the encirclement, after battles with heavy losses. Just look at what Chernobyl has wrought! We still haven't shaken off all of the clinging mud and falsehood, the pack of lies we were fed about the accident. But already, a post-Chernobyl veil of secrecy and scientific deception is spread over us as the bureaucrats and their lap dogs try to smother us under layers of misplaced optimism and doubletalk.

Chernobyl is a measure of time, government duplicity, and death. So let us weigh life and power, truth and falsehood on the Chernobyl scales—and demand some measure of accountability and justice.

1

Rudnya-Ososhnya:
A Deception Zone

The year was 1986, April 27, a day after the Chernobyl accident, and I was a reporter working for the regional party daily *Radyanska Zhitomirshchina*, in the town of Zhitomir. We received information that four villages in the Narodichi District of our region had been evacuated because of lethal radiation levels registered there. The Central Party press, radio, and television assured us that people had been resettled in safe areas. Everything humanly possible had been done for them. Our daily paper always followed the party line. I had no evidence at all that anything untoward was happening in the affected areas. But intuitively I felt that things were *not well* there (a journalistic trait?). Apparently, what had put me on guard was the fact that the new houses for these people were being built in the immediate vicinity of Chernobyl, right next to the fenced-off villages that recently had been evacuated. Would these poor peasants suffer in silence?

Our paper reported that the builders from all over the region were doing a splendid job, quickly constructing accommodations for the people being rehoused and to the best standards. Yet not a word was said about what these new houses were doing next to the crippled reactor. Was that place really safe, being so close? I decided to find out.

When I went to chief editor Dmitry Panchuk to share my misgivings, he, a party functionary of many years' standing, heard me out and rather brusquely and stonily replied, "We did not make the decision. It's nothing to do with us." I asked to be sent to the old Narodichi District, now evacuated, to observe firsthand the new settlement only a few miles away. (But my request was flatly turned down. I then decided to dissemble; I came to my superiors with a plan for a trip to Malin, to a local experimental pilot plant, to write about science and technology progress. That request was OK with my boss, so I went. Sorting out the matter of science and technology progress

1

took me a day and a half, and I also contrived to make a detour to the out-of-bounds Narodichi District (it borders the Malin District, and that had been my journalistic ruse). It turned out that a construction team from the Malin plant was building a kindergarten in the village of Rudnya-Ososhnya.

The plant manager let me use a decrepit bus with a driver. For a couple of hours we rattled on to the facility in question. The hot summer was drawing to a close. The bus was going through luxuriant forests ringing with bird song. Mushrooms grew almost under the bus's wheels. The sun could barely filter through the dense tree crowns. The elderly driver—I forget his name—was telling me, with anguish in his voice, how terribly Chernobyl had defiled the land and what a wonderful mushroom and berry country this had been. It still was, in fact, except that now one could not enter a forest, plump down on the lush grass, or pick a wide variety of delicacies, including strawberries, bilberries, and mushrooms. Everything was contaminated. However, the locals were unable to comprehend a danger they could not see, feel, or taste. They ignored all talk of danger and made forays into the woods to fill their baskets with berries or mushrooms for their own tables or to take to the Kiev and Zhitomir markets.

Rudnya-Ososhnya is a typical Polesye village. In spring, when orchards give off heavenly fragrance, it resembles a big flowerbed wedged between fir forests. We drove up to a group of workers who, it turned out, were building a public bathhouse right next to the woods. The conversation was sticky. The five men were morose and taciturn. Besides, it started to drizzle unpleasantly. But I still did not abandon attempts to understand what was going on, why they were building precisely at this spot, and what the radiation levels were. At long last they warmed to the subject and became more forthcoming. It transpired that the bathhouse was being built on that site because of high radiation levels. How high they did not know. No one told them anything about these things. "The army chaps come, take the readings, and say nothing to us." The work was taking longer than originally planned. At first they hoped to have the bathhouse built in two months. But as was usually the case under the Soviets, something went wrong. There was no crane. No one could explain why a bath-house that could service ten people at a time should be built beyond the village green—when each homestead had one anyway. Besides, the project cost fifty thousand rubles.

But back to the kindergarten construction. I found the team of eight workers somewhat more cooperative. The foreman, Yuri Grishchenko, told me that the kindergarten would cost the state 120,000 rubles. They had been working there for over a month, and the locals were already laughing at them. Who would use it? There were practically no toddlers or preschool kids in Rudnya-Ososhnya, and the kindergarten was for twenty-five children. It was then that I heard for the first time the terrifying phrase "coffin money." That was how people referred to the measly monthly sum of thirty rubles for the villagers and construction workers building the bathhouse and the kindergarten—to pay for a "high-caloric diet," if you please. It worked out at just one ruble over their daily wages. The victuals at their disposal included peas, vermicelli, and beef. Chicken meat was not for them because, I was told, it would come to more than the mandatory three rubles a day for food.

The workers complained that they felt sick and weary and suffered from persistent headaches. They blamed it on increased radiation levels. And today, years after the Chernobyl explosion, I can say this. They were dead right. Just four years after the nuclear disaster, the village with the unusual name of Rudnya-Ososhnya was evacuated, after all. Staying in it had proved to be life-threatening. But it was not till four years later that the villagers were told about it by the authorities. That time, however, I had to keep my trip to Rudnya-Ososhnya secret from my own bosses and colleagues.

Having talked to the builders, we set out across the village to look for the foreman's house. The village, it appeared, lacked a village Soviet or a kolkhoz management. Rudnya-Ososhnya, its inhabitants informed us, was a village "without a future," as the phrase went. It did not even have a secondary school. There were countless such villages "without a future" in the country, forsaken by God and Soviet power. Some of them did not boast even a shop or a post office, let alone telephones or other amenities of civilization. And yet, there were human beings living in them, needing all sorts of things—bread, clothing, matches, electricity, books, radio. The people were left without any of those "luxuries." Today the government condemns the policy of "futureless villages." But it is much too late. The harm has been done. The countryside is dying out. The once sound houses stand boarded up and paths and cemeteries are overgrown with weeds. People are leaving the countryside for cities, to be closer to civilization.

3

Here is what I heard (told bitterly and half-mockingly) then from the head of a kolkhoz team, Valentina Ushchapovskaya, who was also a member of the regional Soviet of People's Deputies:

Our village has ninety homesteads. It is a limited-access village (contaminated by radiation). There are twenty-seven children between the ages of 7 and 14, and two senior graders of 15–16 plus six preschool kids. The elementary school has been closed because rooms inside the building registered 1.5 mR. There were thirteen children attending school. The premises consisted of just two rooms. Now water here registers 0.2 mR, and soil, 0.4 mR. The level is higher at the other end of the village and a bit lower over here. I personally measured the levels with a dosimeter. I have a DOS-5 device, so I use that to measure radiation, though it's a liar of a device. It shows about one third of the actual level. Last year a special lab came over and measured 1.1 mR here. The place was "habitable," they said. They issued me with the dosimeter at the district Soviet executive committee. Army chaps also come now and then to take measurements, but they do not tell us anything.

Did you see the kindergarten they are building? What for? Oh, all right, let it stand. We have a lot of young guys but too few lasses. It will make a good old people's home for them eventually. Also, there are no proper roads here. You can't get from Rudnya-Ososhnya to Lesser Minky. I spoke at the district Soviet session in Narodichi about that—about the roads and about the children. For ten years our children have been walking to a school ten kilometers away. After the radiation, the dirt road got completely impassable from heavy trucks. We have to travel seventeen kilometers to reach the flax field, and if there was a road here, it could be just three. For six years they have been promising us to fix the road. True, they've laid asphalt in the village.

We wrote to the Ukrainian council of ministers, to Masol (council of ministers chairman). After that we had visitors from the regional Soviet executive committee. We were promised a road in the fourth quarter. We were instructed as to how we should behave and what to eat when we had already eaten our fill of all the right and wrong stuff in the periodic table.

The team head went on, wiping her earth-stained hands on her dress.

When we had come up, she was digging up potatoes on her vegetable plot. Not far from her, other women were picking potatoes out of the soft earth. Next to them children were playing in the sand. Some distance away someone was burning the leafy tops of potato plants. And radioactive ash showered down on the vegetable plots and orchards, and on children's heads. . . . They had intended to remove the top soil around the village right after the accident, but they must have thought better of it and simply plowed the land. The village itself had been "washed." As for limestone decontamination, that had to wait until the fall of 1987. Dozens of the villagers, having survived the first radiation shock and having been exposed to radiation inside and outside their bodies, drank radioactive milk from their cows for almost three months following the disaster and ended up in the district hospital. Some had done several stints there.

The women who worked on the plots also came over. Hearing what we were talking about, they joined in with their own disheartening life stories. It transpired that sixty-three cows had been taken away from the village, and the owners had been paid 1.92 rubles per kilo of live weight. The cows were taken to a kolkhoz nearby, in the village of Bazar in the same district. (It was not until four years later that Bazar was chalked up for total evacuation). Why there? They said Bazar was "clean" and the cows could be fattened there and sold for meat later. The cows were removed on July 17, 1986. The heifers were left behind. But later they, too, were taken away. The only animals allowed on homesteads were pigs and chickens. "In the first days after the blast," the women told us, "we all went hoarse. This year we have been forbidden to eat currants and strawberries. Apples were allowed, but they said we had to wash them in running water. The same for tomatoes and cucumbers." I also learned that the village had a dairy farm of 86 cows, and a cattle-fattening farm of 113 head. The Krasnoye Polesye ("Red Polesye") collective farm had fulfilled its annual production plan in the first half-year by 113 percent. While previously the cereal yield here had been ten to thirteen hundredweight per hectare, now the figure was 18.

The more the women told me, the more I was convinced that crimes were being committed, crimes against the people. Wasn't that the reason why my request to be sent here had been denied? It turned out that the newly built kindergarten in Rudnya-Ososhnya was a stone's throw from the evacuated and barbed wire–fenced villages of Bober and Vladimirovka in the Kiev region. As for the fields, they positively hugged the barbed wire. Not far off was the village of Golubievichi. There, the women told me new houses had been built, but people from evacuated villages refused to settle there. For a while the houses stood empty, but eventually some of the locals moved in. It was just sixty kilometers from there to the Chernobyl reactor, and just thirty kilometers to the thirty-kilometer exclusion zone. At present, the village of Rudnya-Ososhnya does not exist. Four years after the blast the government decided to have it urgently evacuated. Urgently—after years of deception! Criminal deception.

I vowed then that I would go on with my journalistic investigation at whatever cost to myself and would write about everything I had seen and heard. Publicity alone could save those people. Despite the fact that glasnost had been declared in this country in 1985, when Mikhail Gorbachev came to power, there was no sign of it in those parts. My trip to radioactive Rudnya-Ososhnya was kept secret from the newspaper staff. My husband and I drove to various villages in the Narodichi District in our Lada. Those were heartrending encounters with bewildered, crushed, and deceived people. Twenty years on, I still remember every one of those meetings because they are impossible to forget. I keep in my Chernobyl archives the writing pads from those trips. The memory of very old people who expect nothing but death from life, living out their remaining days in quiet desperation, remains with me forever.

2

"Halt! Life Hazard!"

Here it lies, autumnal land strewn with crimson and golden leaves, too beautiful for words. On the left are the fields, and beyond those, pastures with herds grazing in them. Against the haze of the forest melting away behind them, this looks like a painting. Could this be Provence? Hardly. Provence would fall well short of this scenery. Polesye! Wide open spaces and woods give one a poignant sense of eternal affinity with them. Over there lies Khristinovka like a precious brooch in the unvaryingly rich green setting. Was it named after Christians? After Christ? Or could it be related to the Ukrainian *khrest*, that is, cross? So what was that special cross which Providence gave this village to bear? On its right, in the distance, Polesye wooden cottages and newly built good houses of white firebricks are barely discernible for the cherry and apple orchards. That is Old Sharneh. And right in front . . . a warning sign on the swing-beam barrier, screaming, "Halt! No Passage! Life Hazard!" There is another sign on the barbed wire of the gate with a heavy padlock.

Impossible. It simply can't be. It's inconceivable. It doesn't make sense. There's a cottage, isn't there, not a hundred yards away, this side of the barbed wire? An apple drops in the orchard off a tree by the fence and rolls away in the grass. A tiny tot of five or so comes out of the house and waddles happily among the riot of fall flowers. He stretches out his small hand to reach for the apple, and then the hand goes back to his mouth, apple juice running down his chin, dripping on his little boots and on the grass. The boy is laughing about something, oblivious to the gathering ash.

The houses beside the meadow on the other side of the barbed wire are the village of New Sharneh, sprawling along the river Uzh. After the Chernobyl disaster, it ceased to exist. It is dead. The same sad lot befell three more local villages—Dolgy Les, Motyli, and Omelniki. I knew from the press that in the summer of 1986, two hundred and fifty-one families were evacuated from them, a total of five-hundred-odd people. Where did they go? How were they faring now? This is what interested me above all else. How do people adjust psychologically to a new and terrifying situation? That Saturday, when I came to Narodichi for the first time since the Chernobyl explosion, I failed to comprehend the scale of the calamity and deception, even as far as our region was concerned. This being a day off, the district executive committee building was deserted. I simply talked to people in the streets or in shops and knocked on people's doors. I was advised to go, first of all, to the outskirts of Narodichi, to the township of Mirny. It was there that fifty new houses had been built for resettled families. People did not want to live in them. What was their complaint? I would soon find the answer, and much more, as I talked with New Sharneh villagers rehoused in Mirny. And here is what the evacuees told me.

Adam Pastushenko, a World War II invalid, found a job at the Narodichi District finance department on resettlement:

> They should never have built those houses here, for two reasons. First, this place is not much better than the one we were evacuated from. Second, years ago there was a pesticide store here for agriculture aircraft. The air is simply not fit for breathing.

As word got around of the arrival of a journalist, evacuees started flocking to the shop where I was talking to the victims of the "peaceful atom," to share their grievances and ask for help. And every one of them, literally everyone, asked me the same question: Who had given the orders? Who had decided to build new houses for resettling here, next door to dangerous contaminated areas—houses for people who had already had more than their fair share of suffering by the Chernobyl walls? I did not have an answer then, but I was determined to explore Chernobyl's impact in the entire region. The villagers suggested taking me on a tour along the two streets of the new settlement. Many of the houses stood empty. In four new buildings workers were ripping up the floorboards and throwing pesticide-laden earth clods out of the window. One of my interlocutors joked, "We don't even have flies around here. They're all dead." The nauseating stench of ammonia permeated the air. It wouldn't be a bad trade-off if it could wash away the radioactive ash.

In some houses it was quite cold. The steam boilers had blown up. "The bosses say," people complained, "that old grannies don't know how to handle steam heating, so the boilers have exploded." In

Zhukov Street, the locals told me, all the earth in eight houses had to be removed after the floorboards had been pried off. One of the new settlers, Fyodor Zaichuk, invited me in and showed me his three rooms. The ceilings were black from damp and cold. He kept asking me wearily and dejectedly, "How can one live here?" After examining the houses, we returned to the shop. I wanted to know how the evacuees were supplied with "clean" food. The shop manager, Lyudmila Pastushenko, complained that they were sent terrible loaves of bread, burnt and altogether inedible. There was no mineral water. Quite often they were short of meat. Those at work could not buy it in the daytime, and after working hours, meat was usually sold out. No smoked fish or chicken meat. Sometimes they got duck. Fruit juices were usually in stock, but generally, the food rations prescribed by the authorities were only a meager kilo of buckwheat a month per settler, a kilo of millet, plus a couple of cans of stewed meat and condensed milk.

The greatest concern, though, was for their health. War veteran Adam Pastushenko discovered he had absorbed 17 µCi of cesium. For twenty-four days he received treatment in a hospital in Zhitomir. On discharge, they told him his cesium level had dropped to 9 µCi.

Nina Mokhoid:

> I have two girls—Olya, twelve, and Lyuda, nine. Olya spent some time in the district children's clinic a while ago. Lyuda, too, is sickly. We have been given some tablets to take for two months. Both children have enlarged thyroids—first and second degree.

Valentina Kavka, a worker at the district culture center: "My two kids, Bohdan (aged six) and Svetlana (fourteen), were sent to Zhitomir and Kiev. Bohdan has an enlarged liver and cholecystitis."

Over and over again they reverted to the one basic question: What was the point of taking us away from the hazardous contaminated zone and resettling us here, of all places, within miles of our own village of New Sharneh, now fenced off by barbed wire? Wasn't it obvious that this was a case of taking us from the frying pan and into the fire? I searched in vain for an answer. In the late afternoon I left Mirny with a heavy heart. The people walked me to the center of Narodichi and showed me a shortcut across potato plots. Again, the heavy scent of ammonia filled the air, blending with the acrid smell of wilting potato tops. Here and there small fires went up as children burned the discarded potato tops just like their peers in Rudnya-Ososhnya had done. One persistent fact remained—the deadly radioactive mist continued to drift down on all living things.

On Sunday we set off in a different direction. We were heading again for villages in which new houses for evacuees had been built. The village of Mezhileska, which translates from Ukrainian as "among the woods," indeed turned out to be true, located as it is among the woods. The soil next to the school had been removed, six ramshackle houses had been knocked down, the radioactive earth from under one house had been taken away, and seven homesteads had all the soil around them removed. Even though scientists and government officials knew radiation was ubiquitous, the village was pronounced safe. "Clean." People here did not get any extra pay, as in other "classified" villages, or a 25 percent in extra wages or the 30 rubles of monthly "coffin money." The party had even installed telephone lines (every cloud does have a silver lining). A first-aid post was hastily constructed, except it did not function. In summer, after the Chernobyl explosion, fifteen houses were built for the evacuees who were being resettled. On the day of my arrival one third of these houses were still unoccupied. Here is what eyewitnesses said.

Nadezhda Osadchaya, accountant with the village Soviet:

> The cottages were poorly constructed, not the kind the villagers could live in. Our grannies did not budge from the village Soviet premises all winter. They needed a stove, and there aren't any in the newly built houses. If they had installed central heating, it would be different. But now it's useless—our grannies don't know how to handle boilers, hot-water heating. They want their stoves.

Antonina Adamovna Kondratenko, born in 1912, and Olympia Mikhailovna Zhovnirchuk, born in 1905, were also present and nodded in agreement. Tears slowly ran from their faded eyes down their wrinkled cheeks. (I doubt that these old ladies are still alive today.) The houses that were lived in were chiefly occupied by old-age pensioners. No more than two or three people of working age were present. "When the settlers were being rehoused, they were given two piglets per family, a few boxes of cabbages, cucumbers, canned tomatoes, three sacks of grain, and a dozen chickens," said the locals.

"And what a torment it was to leave your own home, your village. You couldn't hear yourself think for the wailing. How we sobbed! A truck would drive over to the house, and you had to get all your things on to the truck in two shakes. And our houses were much better than these. Warm, too! We did not want for anything. The only thing we had to buy was bread. Now, anything you need, you go and buy it," ancient grannies were complaining. "One oldie lost her husband. Well, she took him back home to Dolgy Les to be buried next to their own. Luckily, she got permission to do that." In this village of Mezhileska, the authorities, eager to show their caring attitude, purchased three more houses for the settlers in addition to the fifteen new ones, at twenty thousand rubles each. But radiation victims would not live in those houses either. Two of the three houses were eventually taken by two newlywed couples from the kolkhoz, while the third remained empty.

Anatoly Konotovsky, Communist Party cell secretary on the Mayak collective farm:

> The houses have been redecorated and refurbished. It will not be cold this winter. The ceilings have been insulated against the cold; the doors have been carefully fitted to exclude drafts. The regional executive committee has given orders for firewood deliveries from the Ovruch timber facility. We are not allowed to take firewood from the Narodichi facility, because timber there is contaminated. The settlers, though, bring wood from their abandoned villages—Omelniki, Motyli. They mustn't do that, you know. Radiation levels are too high there. We have installed stoves in houses for the old grannies, ordinary village stoves. We'll let them have five to seven cubic meters of firewood, and they are welcome to heat the place all they want, throughout the winter. Our village is not on the danger areas list, but children keep falling ill; doctors have given them a checkup, and quite a few are now on those special lists. All children have enlarged thyroid glands; they were examined at school. That village next door is Osoka. It also belongs to our kolkhoz. There, radiation levels are higher than, say, in Golubievichi. But the people in Osoka are not getting any extra pay. And the village is not on the danger list, either, though we are not allowed to use our own milk, meat, and poultry. But there is a dairy farm in the village. We sell the milk to the state, and it goes on for processing to Ovruch—while we are getting milk for consumption from the Korosten District.
>
> Four years later it would be discovered that there, too, radiation levels were too high!

Vladimir Rudnitsky, village Soviet chairman:

> The Osoka farm employs eleven people. They tend three hundred and fifty head of cattle. The farms both in Mezhileska and in Osoka have been decontaminated. Next to the school building, radiation

11

levels were six times the tolerance average, so they removed the soil from there. Although the settlers have food cards, there are no deliveries for them, except when we manage to browbeat the authorities into bringing a consignment of something. We in Mezhileska have been given condensed milk twice. And some cans a few times.

The dairymaids in Osoka refused to go to work. In the village of Golubievichi, where settlers were also offered twenty newly built houses, all the cows had been taken away on August 6, 1986 because their milk was radioactive. The children are kept at school all day. They are given three "clean" meals a day—free.

Maria Konotovskaya, accountant with the village council of Golubievichi:

> For two or three months we were getting 25 percent extra wages plus thirty rubles for food. Then it stopped abruptly. We were told they had made a mistake. A mix-up, if you please. The extra pay was intended not for us but for another village, Buda-Golubievichi. A while ago they lifted the land tax. We are not allowed to eat our own food, yet they would not pay us that thirty rubles of food money. People don't want to live in the new houses. They see how we are struggling here. The houses are too cold, to cap it all. Take our granny Yuzefa. She's been begging to go back to her village all winter. "I'll return after that," she says. Born in 1914, she is still helping some with the kolkhoz work. And we here prepared such a grand welcome for the settlers, complete with the bread-and-salt ritual and flowers. We were told to expect them in July or August. A day was specially set off for that. Narodichi District party committee secretary Muzgorin came and said the settlers were not coming. And we here had laid the tables, bunches of flowers, and all. School kids turned up, too, and the whole village had come out to welcome them. But they never arrived. The houses stood empty until the local villagers were finally allowed to live there. And till then we had been waiting and waiting.
>
> A similar thing happened in the village of Guto-Maryatin.

Nina Volokh, post office manager:

> Twelve of the fifteen houses were occupied by our own new families, the locals. We received just three settler families. There were flowers and the bread-and-salt welcome. We have a brass band of our own. The first secretary of the district party committee, Anatoly Melnik, arrived for the occasion. We gave a concert for the settlers right in the street.

Victor Tereshchenko, tractor driver:

> We came here from the Brovary District of the Kiev region. No, that part of the country is not radioactive. It was just that we were recently married, our baby Masha is now eleven months old, and we had nowhere to live. So we decided to come here, because we knew that there were vacant houses and a shortage of work force. My wife, Valentina, stays at home with the baby, and I have taken a job on the Mayak collective farm. I'm a tractor driver. The house is cold. When it rains, the roof leaks in the bedroom and in the corridor. In winter I get up at three in the morning to get the heating going. It is so cold your breath is steaming. In six weeks I have used up three cartloads of firewood. We get natural liquefied gas in cylinders. You have to wait six weeks for a replacement. In winter there is no water in the pump—it freezes solid. It is two kilometers to the nearest well in the village. And the baby has to be bathed every day.

The setters in no. 7 moved out for the same reasons. Old-age pensioner Nikolai Kharchenko and his wife from the evacuated village of Omelniki left for Tychkov. There he bought a proper warm house.

But the most memorable confession for me was the bitter account of an old lady, Maria Stepanovna Kozyrenko, from the village of Dolgy Les:

> They moved us at once to the small village of Rozsokhovsky. We had nowhere else to go. Those who had any relations went to live with them. And people like us were taken to Rozsokhovsky. We spent about a week there. I also had with me my son's little boy. He's two-and-a-half. We had spent the summer at my son's, but in the fall, on September 15, we came here. We miss our village, something awful. There are four families of the Dolgy Les folks here, almost all of us retired. Very few young people. And we had been told that this rehousing business would last just a few weeks, a month at the most. The bus came for us on May 27, at seven in the morning, and at ten we already left the village. In the morning people had started to drive the cows out to pasture but the militia drove them back. We had been thinking of slaughtering the pig, too. It is cold here, away from the village, on the edge of the village.

Kozyrenko could not hold back the tears any longer and started wiping her gaunt face on the ends of her black-and-white polka-dot kerchief.

To complete my document collection, I had to talk to the Narodichi District authorities, whatever the cost. I had to learn how they felt about the issue and piece together the overall radiological picture of the district, and perhaps of the whole region as well. By then I had already realized that we knew absolutely nothing of the real state of affairs in the wake of the nuclear blast. We knew nothing about the scale and the aftermath of the disaster. The mass media just churned out brazen lies and misinformation.

I could only meet officials during working hours, but I had to spend those hours at my place of employment. I had not been authorized to visit the contaminated areas. In search of a means to get away to the district center for at least one day during office hours (Narodichi is a five-hour bus ride from Zhitomir; it is in the north of the region), I applied for an unpaid day off, "owing to the circumstances that have arisen." What sort of circumstances had arisen I obviously could not specify. But the chief editor turned down my request anyway. Section head Grigory Pavlov kept pestering me for an explanation. But I held firm. Some time later I handed in one more application to that effect. I simply had no alternative. The editor did not have the nerve to refuse me a second time. After all, I was not the only one to turn to him with a personal problem, and he never refused anyone. For that day off, I undertook to work on a Saturday, doing duty for the newspaper in the printing shop. But section head Pavlov, apparently instructed by the boss, kept asking me why I wanted a day off. Unable to think of any other convincing explanation, just to shut him up, I informed him that I intended to have an abortion.

Now free for the day, I instantly left for Narodichi and the district executive committee. Valentin Semyonovich Budko, chairman of the Narodichi District executive committee, turned out to be an unaffected and friendly person. Normally, people in similar positions, heads of Soviets, Communist Party secretaries, do as they are told by their higher-ups without a murmur. Quite possibly, before the nuclear explosion, Budko may have been the same kind of functionary. But the terrible accident had shattered him, affecting as it had his own family and relatives, and the injustice and hushing up of facts had changed him into the man I encountered—a normal human being. His thoughts were no longer of his high post. His thoughts were about the people in his district.

I told him about my rounds of the villages in the district, living and dead ones. I asked him for information about people's health and radiation levels in the area and indicated I wished to help by making these facts public. Valentin Budko agreed, observing, however, that there had been quite a few journalists coming over. All of them gathered information and left with the promise of publishing their articles as a matter of course. Yet no one had ever published anything anywhere. The only piece of information about the local children appeared in the *Vecherny Kiev* ("Evening Kiev") newspaper, where G. I. Razumeev, head of the medical aid and disease prevention for children and mothers board of the Ukrainian Health Ministry, wrote, "The children of Pripyat and Chernobyl have been unharmed; but as for a certain category of youngsters in the Narodichi District, their thyroids registered increased doses of radioiodine. They were hospitalized in time, and now the children's health is not at risk." In short, all is well, nothing to worry about.

We got in the chairman's jeep and went, first of all, to the closed village of New Sharneh. On the way—it is eight kilometers from the district center—Valentin Budko told me the story of that tragic day:

> I learned of the accident at Chernobyl in the morning of April 27. No, not from any official report. That day the first party secretary and I, we held a fair in the district. Well, so that was where we were going. Suddenly, we saw a convoy of vehicles moving toward Polessky, Kiev region. A black Volga sedan. The Volga braked. Out climbed Kolbasenko (head of the regional automobile directorate) and said that there had been a serious accident at the Chernobyl nuclear power plant.... What kind of accident and how serious no one explained. So that fatal day we did hold the fair in Narodichi in a big way. People had brought over stuff from all the villages in the district—lard, meat, cucumbers, tomatoes, cabbages, milk, curds, butter, all sorts of vegetables, mushrooms—in short, everything our Polesye could boast in the "developed socialism" era. Meanwhile, according to the data of district civil defense head, I. P. Makarenko, on April 27, 1986, at 1600 hours, dosimeters registered 3 R/h in Narodichi. The next day, April 28, the reading at nine in the morning said 0.6 R.

As we were passing through the village of Nozdrishche, Valentin Budko pointed to the right, toward the end of the village: "Over there was the most contaminated radioactive spot in the whole district—160 Ci/km^2." I looked where he was pointing. A magnificent green meadow extended as far as the horizon. It was there that a liberal amount of cesium-137 had fallen. Grazing on the meadow were a number of cows, lazily nibbling radioactive grass, without a care in the world. Ahead, some two hundred or three hundred yards away, rose a barbed wire fence—New Sharneh. Our car pulled up, and the driver asked if it wouldn't be better to stay in. Odd, I thought, that people

15

lived there, right next door, and I was being warned that it might be better not to venture out of the car. Nonetheless, we got out. Beside the gate secured with a heavy padlock and signs saying NO ENTRY, there was a wooden shed. Through the window one could see telephones, a desk, some chairs. From the shed emerged a policeman. I asked him to let us through the gate to the other side of the barbed wire. The gate opened, and we drove into the restricted area. An autumn orchard next to the nearest cottage was shedding worthless radioactive fruit into the lush grass. The branches sagged under its weight. The last of the marigolds and chrysanthemums were blooming by the boarded houses. They had run wild and reached up almost to the windows. Here and there pots with dry flowers stood on windowsills. In the yard of one of the houses a white rag was fluttering in the wind. Fence poles were topped with large glass jars, and clay pots were washed with rain and snow. No earthly use to anyone. "The cats and dogs in the village were shot down on the third day after evacuation," the chairman said absent-mindedly.

That village is a monument. It is a monument to Chernobyl. A criminal monument. The peasants who used to live in that village had to pay dearly, much too dearly for it. And nearby, on the other side of the barbed wire, is Nozdrishche. Not far off, a new kindergarten was built a while ago. It is proudly shown off to every visitor. The kindergarten is within spitting distance of that radioactive meadow. On the way back to Narodichi the chairman told me how the villages had been evacuated:

> I personally oversaw the evacuation of all four villages. Frankly, I felt uneasy about everything I saw and heard there. I remember the neighbors locking up an old woman at her own request. She flatly refused to leave. But we could not possibly let her stay behind in that inferno. We found her and took her with us. The first village we evacuated was Dolgy Les. It was a bright sunny day. We arrived at six in the morning to be in time for the peasants taking their cattle out to pasture. On May 27, we evacuated New Sharneh. Everything was done in a hurry. We, too, believed that it was temporary, just for a few weeks. We went from house to house, trying to reassure the people. But everyone was on edge, very jittery. The women wailed as they left their homesteads, as though they were leaving them for good.

And it had been for good, it turned out. Forever. They say those who have not been through it will never understand. Polesye natives for generations, they had lived there for thousands of years, on the banks of pristinely pure rivers, Ukraine's most beautiful rivers—the Uzh, the Zherev, the Noryn, the Rudenka.

Every house was a work of art, each one more striking than the next: carved wood casings on the windows outside, woven rugs and embroidered towels inside. For countless centuries people on this ancient land tilled, sowed, and harvested. There had never been any industry to speak of. The air seemed pure, and the forests pristinely beautiful and rich in mushrooms, berries, and game. Such a resplendent countryside, and now so wantonly, irresponsibly, and utterly destroyed. Is it too much to be hoped that some day it will be restored to its unsullied state?

Back in his office, the district executive committee chairman unlocked the safe and spread before me a map of the whole district, with radiation levels marked on it. Nearly the entire surface of the map was splashed with red, like a wounded human being. Only in places about the edges some green was showing through—hardly a clean patch anywhere. I hurriedly copied radiation level statistics into my writing pad. On one side of the map a note said, "maximum permissible rem total per sq km—40 Ci; lower limit—15 Ci." Later it transpired that in some areas the maximum had reached 1,200 Ci and more. I saw that new houses for resettlement had been built in eight other villages, close to the danger zone, and half of them had already been listed among villages where strict radiation monitoring had to be carried out. Moreover, the district center itself, with the new township of Mirny on its outskirts, and the village of Lesser Kleshchi, had been included in those "black lists" almost immediately after the accident, as it turned out. But the authorities, fully aware of that, cheerfully started building there—next door to the ruined ancestral homes—new cottages, bathhouses, kindergartens, and water-supply systems. Indeed, out of the frying pan into the fire.

By the time I started my investigation, some 105 million rubles had already been sunk in new construction, chiefly within the restricted contaminated area. And it seemed no one was going to stop it. Rather, the reverse happened as the building activity was stepped up. Every Thursday, deputy chairman of the Zhitomir regional executive committee, Georgy Gotovchits (now deceased), conducted an emergency meeting in Narodichi. There, behind closed doors, the future and very life of the wretched deceived people was decided. Why did they have to build there of all places? Couldn't they find a "clean" spot in the whole region, the enormous Soviet Empire, for the people hit by radiation, who had suffered enough by the walls of Chernobyl? It is difficult—nay, impossible—to find a reasonable explanation for that unjust and deadly decision.

What I then heard in the Narodichi children's hospital and clinic shocked me even more. Testimony of the doctors, October 1987:

Lyubov Golenko, head of the children's clinic, the Narodichi district hospital:

> We did swallow a dose of radioiodine, that's for sure. I'd say the incidence of thyroid complaints has grown by some 60 percent. We mark extraserious cases as T and D. These children Kiev took away for treatment. Is this area entirely safe for children's health? I couldn't say. Visiting experts tell us that it will become clear in three to five years.

Leonid Ishchenko, head physician of the Narodichi district hospital:

> We have repeatedly examined all the children in the district. Eighty percent have enlarged thyroid glands. And the normal proportion is 10 percent. Previously we had, say, 10 percent of kids with an enlarged thyroid, fifteen at the most. We put this down to the accident; there could be no other reason.

Alexander Sachko, manager of the Narodichi district hospital:

> No one will convince me that our kids have no health problems and that what thyroid enlargement there may be has nothing to do with the accident. It's no use pretending that all is well. Some time ago, I looked at all children's analysis results for a week. In 180 cases out of 500 there was evidence of changes in their blood.

"Are the authorities in Zhitomir, in Kiev, and at the republic's health ministry aware of that?" I asked. "They are indeed," the doctors told me. "We have lots of experts coming over; they take blood samples. Admittedly, they do not always send back the results of their analyses. They assure us that we suffer from nothing more serious than radiophobia, that our children's health is okay, and there is nothing to worry about."

The doctors handed me the results of the children's and adults' medical examinations across the district that checked the levels of cesium-137 in the body. Two brief but hand- and mind-scorching papers. They said that all five thousand children in the district had been exposed to radioactive iodine-131. Of that number, 115 children had been "classified," meaning they ran an increased risk of developing such thyroid diseases as tumors, goiter, excessive or deficient thyroid activity, which could cause mental retardation and have other grave consequences. Armed with that shattering information, I returned to Zhitomir. The following day I went to the regional health administration to get some explanation. For a very long time I was shunted from expert to expert. No one could offer a coherent comment of any sort. Or they did not want to, apparently from fear. It became abundantly clear to me that the authorities had classified as secret all information about the real state of affairs in the affected parts of the district. They had done that at once, and securely. Although I managed to talk to the head of the childhood and motherhood protection sector of the regional health committee, Victor Shatilo, his words merely confirmed my initial belief:

> There have been no registered cases of radiation-induced sickness. When we compare the statistics of the previous four years, there is no increase. The thing is that liver enlargement is caused by other, additional factors. . . . There has been no evidence of thyroid malfunction. The people who ought to know say with one voice that no bad consequences can possibly ensue.

There, you see. Nothing had been discovered. Nothing had been registered. What I was talking about was impossible. In short, the children's health was not in jeopardy.

I wrote an article about everything I had heard and observed. Despite my best efforts, I could not get it published in my own newspaper. The matter of "her being seen in the villages of the Narodichi District" was raised at the staff party meeting (incidentally, I was the only nonparty person on the staff of the Communist Party daily). Another correspondent, Vladimir Bazelchuk, was promptly dispatched to the district. And he it was who wrote a piece on the settlers the way he had been ordered to write it. His article was instantly sent to the presses. My colleague could think of nothing better than to reproach those unfortunate people. The leitmotif of his huge half-page creation was this: *They have been given new houses, and still they whine and complain!*

I decided to go to Moscow at once to offer my article to national papers and do my damnedest to get it accepted. Again I had to concoct a request for a day off. I promised to work on a Saturday to compensate for that day off. It was the same thing all over again. Again, a second attempt did the trick, and I secretly left for Moscow. There I made the rounds of at least six newspapers, but not one of them wanted to hear a thing about Chernobyl. At long last the best perestroika daily, *Izvestia*, agreed to prepare it for publication. But my joy was premature. Some time later I had a phone call from *Izvestia*, and they told me frankly that my piece would not appear after all because the subject was classified. It was already January 1987.

Unexpectedly, six months after I had sent my article to *Pravda*, its own correspondent in Kiev, Semyon Odinets, phoned me, and we had the following conversation:

"Vladimir Gubarev asked me to tell you that your material would not be printed."

"Why not?"

"Because there is already a similar piece by another author ready for publication."

However closely I perused every issue of *Pravda*, I failed to detect anything remotely similar on its pages. It must have been infinitely safer to write an abstract-art play about the "sarcophagus" over the Chernobyl reactor than risk publishing an article on the subject banned by the authorities. And that was an article which, if published at the time, could have helped stop the madness of more and more new construction projects in contaminated areas and preserve the people's health. Who will pay for this? Vladimir Gubarev, author of *The Sarcophagus* and Communist Party journalist on the staff of *Pravda*, to whom I had forwarded my long-suffering request for publication in the name of rescuing thousands of people from the radioactive inferno, did not even dignify my request with a written reply. But perhaps it is more convenient that way, through a third person, by word of mouth, leaving no written evidence?

However, Vladimir Gubarev was not alone in his zeal. Unappeased, I once more went to Moscow to the weekly *Ogonyok*, which at the time was in the forefront of perestroika propaganda and tremendously popular. It published daring articles that debunked much of the Soviet mythology. Out there in the provinces we admired its editor's courage. Alas, years later I learned that this courage had been sanctioned by a Communist Party Central Committee secretary and by Gorbachev himself in person. I did not manage to get an audience with editor Vitaly Korotich. I was sent to the political journalism section, to its head Panchenko. He proved to be an elderly, nervous man. The telephone in his office was ringing virtually nonstop, but he did not pick up the receiver. Or if he did, he instantly replaced it. Having read my article, he promised that the weekly would publish it. Section head Alexei Panchenko lied to me. Time and time again, I phoned him from Zhitomir, wrote letters, and sent telegrams. Finally, I went to Moscow once more. I was determined to fight my way through to *Ogonyok* editor Vitaly Korotich. After all, he also came from Ukraine—from Kiev. Surely he would not fail to see the importance of that material. He also seemed to be a man with a conscience.

I caught up with the *Ogonyok* editor in the corridor. And right there, perched on a settee, we had a talk. The talk turned to Ukraine. Just then the republic's press unleashed an anti-Korotich campaign, and he was interested enough in that. True, I did not have any of the newspapers on me. And my own interest lay elsewhere. I wanted to know if and when my piece on radiation in Narodichi would be published. Vitaly Korotich assured me that he knew about it; Panchenko had my article, and asked me to let him prepare it for publication. I got yet another promise from Panchenko. And again I phoned him from Zhitomir, not to have my article published, not any longer, but at least to get it back. On my last visit to *Ogonyok*, Panchenko, in my presence, rummaged long and thoroughly through the contents of his desk drawers but never found my article. While he was at it, he informed me in passing that it could not be published, anyway, because "Dolgikh [Communist Party Central Committee secretary] was 'there' [in Chernobyl, on May 2, 1986]" and nothing like what my article said appeared in the press after his Chernobyl visit. Then Panchenko told me, again in passing, that he knew personally Zhitomir region first secretary Vasily Kavun. He had written an essay about Kavun way back during his days as a *Pravda* journalist. I finally saw the light. I realized now that my piece would never be published in *Ogonyok*. Never. That was all over and done with.

My last letter to the *Ogonyok* staff remained unanswered. However, I no longer expected it would be. Instead of my article in *Ogonyok*, our *Radyanska Zhitomirshchina* suddenly ran a piece from the Narodichi District to the effect that all was well there. That looked like cynical mockery of the people, and it defied common sense. The author, it transpired, was none other than my section head, Grigory Pavlov. It was a sort of response or greeting to me from *Ogonyok*. I have not the slightest doubt that my critical article, gone astray in the depths of

Panchenko's desk, had ended up on a different desk, in the Zhitomir region's party committee. Really efficient workers, that lot!

After that I decided to storm the *Literary Gazette*. At the time it was one of the most liberal periodicals in the Soviet Union. But there, too, things did not go beyond the offered promises. No one apparently wanted us, not me nor that wretched Chernobyl of ours. As for our children, they could wait out their fate. Both Ukrainian and Moscow press and television pretended nothing much had happened. A while ago, as I was going through my archives, I leafed through my diary for that year and came across this entry:

> August 31, 1986. "International Panorama" television program. Political observer Stanislav Kondrashov. He covered every issue under the sun, that political observer. He talked about Ethiopian separatists and about Ethiopian children flying over to their relations on board an Aeroflot plane. About a Nazi anthem introduced in Nuremberg schools. Correspondents asked a few Japanese what they thought of the Soviet moratorium. He described a trip down the Mississippi. Especially thorough was his discourse on "new thinking." Me, I was waiting to hear something about Chernobyl— the introduction had briefly mentioned Chernobyl and the IAEA. But the relevant sequence was never shown. It was as if a German anthem and Ethiopian separatists were much more of a priority to me now than the health of my own children. This program casts doubt on Stanislav Kondrashov's professional integrity.

Alas, he was not alone in that.

Many of the former "talking heads" and media moguls have slid into obscurity, without sometimes realizing what had happened. Knowledge is power, particularly when government officials control the media.

And when these representatives of the public decide they don't like the message, they go after the messenger by adopting the age-old tactic of shunning or, worse, imprisonment.

During one of my Moscow visits, despairing in my utter helplessness, I went to the central post office and sent one more registered letter, with my article enclosed, to the address of a famous poet Yevgeny Yevtushenko. I got no reply. In the spring of 1989, at the request of his Moscow friends, I arrived in Kharkov to work in his campaign for the USSR Congress of People's Deputies (I had completed my own election campaign by then and got a brief respite). I asked him why he had not even bothered to answer me. The poet said he had never received my letter. "Though, truth to tell," he remarked, "if you sent it to my Moscow address, it might easily have gone astray. You see, I stay almost exclusively at my dacha in Peredelkino. I only go to my Moscow apartment once in a while to collect my mail."

So let us take it that that time my scream for help got lost somewhere among Moscow apartments and country residences. The post service's fault, that. The communications minister's.

3

Brainwashing in Zhitomir

I decided to add this chapter because I realized that unless I explained what occurred in my life in the wake of my numerous vain attempts to make public what had been happening to us in the contaminated areas, my account would be incomplete, one-sided. As we pieced together from various unofficial sources the real state of affairs in the affected zone and beyond it, the issue of Chernobyl ecology became increasingly politicized.

Since there was no earthly chance of publishing everything I had seen and heard in the contaminated areas in the north of the region, I typed dozens of copies of my Chernobyl article (at the time there were no photocopiers or establishments offering these services in the Soviet Union), and handed them round among my friends and acquaintances. They read them and passed them on to other people. That was a perestroika version of *samizdat* (lit. "self-publishing"). Let me explain. I had managed to publish in the national dailies, *Pravda* and *Izvestia*, two extremely critical pieces on the suppression of glasnost by the local press, the pressure the regional party authorities exerted on the newspaper, and the double standards exercised by the party leaders in the region and the republic. Let me stress this again. This was the beginning of perestroika. People who for decades had kept their innermost feelings and thoughts well concealed, people who had turned into meek slaves over the years of dictatorship, suddenly, on reading those articles, became my ardent supporters. After the first piece appeared in *Izvestia*, under the heading "Confessions of a Provincial Journalist," the telephone in my editorial office kept ringing for several days. Some of the more emotional women sobbed into the receiver. In the provincial town of Zhitomir many named that day Liberation Day. My fellow countrymen saw proof that freedom was indeed possible, that the truth could be uttered, and that good could not be conquered by evil.

That was how most of the ordinary Zhitomir folk saw my freedom manifesto. Among the disgruntled were the corrupt regional party bosses, the venal, ham-fisted *nomenklatura* who had for decades been making fools of the people. They rushed to do battle with me, defending their exclusive feeding trough, sensing for the first time in the seventy years of their rule that the very foundation of their way of life was now threatened by a provincial journalist's article. Obeying orders from the top, nearly all of my colleagues, having recovered from the shock, hastened to hold me up to shame, as had been the Soviet practice of dealing with dissenters. (That, despite the fact that only a short while before they had been heartily partying in my house on the occasion of my second son's birth.) The Communist Party met where they did a hatchet job on that article in the presence of the second secretary of the regional party committee, Vasily Kobyliansky. It lasted six hours. The whole thing was basically a case of prosecution of me personally even though I was not a party member and thus not officially accountable to the party committee. Only a few people at the meeting gave me tacit support. And just one person, a former prisoner at a Nazi concentration camp, a journalist on the agriculture section of the paper, Grigory Stolyarchuk, was at another meeting, undaunted by the presence of the chief editor and the regional party committee secretary. He stood up and said, "If you had a gun you'd have shot down that woman by now!" Apparently, the people persecuting me were quite comfortable with authorized glasnost within permitted limits. After all, each of them had a party membership card in their pocket but they were all hostage to their own lack of inner freedom for various reasons, not least because of ordinary philistine envy of someone who, to quote Dostoevsky, was not a "quivering creature."

Then nineteen journalists of *Radyanska Zhitomirshchina* sent a letter denouncing me to the Communist Party Central Committee, and not just to any petty official, but to Yegor Ligachev in person, a Central Committee secretary and the most odious figure among the almighty gerontocracy. (Among those who signed the smear letter was even my friend, Alina Tyshkovskaya, who used to come to my place to spend the night with her married boyfriend. Either she lacked the moral scruples to abstain or the browbeating had been too much for the poor lass.) The letter was sent to Ligachev, although the man in charge of ideology in the Central Committee at the time was Alexander Yakovlev, habitually referred to as the architect of perestroika. Presumably, Yakovlev's views were not quite to the liking of my opponents.

They sought their own kind in the Central Committee. Out of habit, they assumed that in response to their letter orders would instantly arrive from the top of the party hierarchy and that would be the end of my career.

But no such "happy ending" occurred, although working at the editorial office became altogether impossible for me. Unceasing faultfinding and bullying forced me to switch to a part-time job on the pretext of having a young child. I was now working a three-day week. I simply could not face turning up in the office more often. Triumphant mediocrity had saturated every pore in the building. Stifling everything, it splashed out onto the pages of our newspaper.

The workers of the car spares factory sent a letter to the regional party committee demanding a meeting with the journalist who had fallen out of favor with the authorities. They welcomed and shared criticism of party bosses contained in my articles and were critical of the way things were done. The letter had some 500 signatures. (In the years of Communist rule you could not budge without a blessing from the regional party committee.) They wanted to know what I thought about various issues, the facts of abuse by senior local party functionaries when distributing apartments in the town, and the classified data on the aftermath of the Chernobyl disaster, which many of them had already read in my illegally disseminated typescript. But I was not allowed to meet the workers. The regional party committee simply chickened out. Three times a meeting with the discredited journalist was announced at the factory, and every time the newspaper sent over other persons.

As for me, I could not leave the office during working hours without authorization. Editor Panchuk had warned me in private that if I went to the meeting with the workers he would at once fire me for absenteeism. Second secretary of the regional party committee Vasily Kobylyansky, deputy chief editor of the newspaper Stanislav Tkach, and district party committee secretary Nikolai Galushko were sent to pacify the workers. On the last occasion I asked colleague Yakov Zaiko, also in disgrace with the bosses, to go to the meeting with the workers and explain to them why I could not come myself during working hours. Zaiko, editor of the regional news agency *Novosti Zhitomirshchiny*, did not succeed, however. The factory manager, backed by several unscrupulous party and trade union activists, shut the door of the factory club in his face where the workers were waiting for me.

Passions were running high in the town. Besides, I had succeeded for a second time in breaking through to the central press with a scathing critique of the regional party leadership in my piece, titled, "A Feuilleton . . . in the Wastepaper Basket." In it I made public some documents that proved abuse of authority on the part of the region's top party bosses in the distribution of state-owned apartments. To them this was nothing short of calamitous. The article had appeared in the country's number one party daily, *Pravda*. I became the most famous journalist not just in my region and in the Ukraine, but nationwide. I have to admit the instant fame was most gratifying. After those two publications in the national dailies, I got several thousand letters from all over the country. People addressed the envelopes simply "Journalist Yaroshinskaya, Zhitomir." Those were letters of sincere support. Several dozen old party members, still not disenchanted with Communist ideals, sent over letters of reference for me, to recommend me for party membership. But I had other plans. The party had long been disintegrating and its foul corruption was poisoning the political and social life of the entire country.

What the workers at the Zhitomir car spares factory had failed to achieve was uncannily accomplished by Ivan Ivanovich Korolev, an engineer at the large plant Promavtomatika. His deep knowledge of the psychology in the party upper echelons (he was himself a lecturer with the Marxist–Leninist educational society Znanie) must have helped him quite a bit. He used that guise to convince the bosses that the meeting would not harm them in any way. And so, in the late summer of 1988, I managed for the first time to meet a sizeable body of workers face to face. It was there, at that factory, that I had my first chance to talk publicly to workers. People wanted to see me, wanted to hear what I was fighting for and against, what I thought of the situation in the country. It was a long talk, lasting some three hours, and it was also frank and detailed—a talk about everything that concerned the public. After all, it had been several years since perestroika was declared, but the waves breaking against the walls of our city of Zhitomir were of another kind—the waves of falsehood, deception, and party corruption. I told the people about the big lie in which we all as well as the rest of the whole country had been living under for almost three years since the explosion at the Chernobyl nuclear power station. I also told them about censorship that continued during the years of perestroika and about my helplessness as a journalist. I was not allowed to make public any of what I had seen in the restricted-access areas. This was the first time that the facts about the aftermath of the Chernobyl disaster were publicly spoken of in Zhitomir. The country, meanwhile, still endured a barrage of falsehood and misinformation. I then appealed to the workers for joint action—that was the only way to achieve anything at all.

That was the period in the run-up to the election of people's deputies of the Soviet Union, that is, Soviet parliament. That was the first relatively free election campaign in all the Soviet years; it was totally unlike the usual sham and shameless simulation by the party nomenklatura of a nationwide approval of the party's doings. Several working collectives at industrial enterprises and universities nominated me as their candidate. It had never crossed my mind that I could run for the Supreme Soviet. I am first and foremost a journalist. My job, I thought, was to write articles, not make laws. But before long I had to change my plans. On learning about the support from the town's working collectives for me, the party apparatchiks launched a whirlwind anti-Yaroshinskaya campaign. They were past masters at that sort of thing. They would leave all comers simply nowhere when it came to besmirching and belying a person the regime did not favor.

It so happened that two big plants, Promavtomatika and an automatic machine-tool manufacturer, scheduled my nomination for the same day and hour—after the morning shift. Out of my office window I saw two "teams" of my colleagues packing into the black Volga sedans that belonged to the newspaper. I realized that they were going to the plants where some time later the meetings were to begin and candidates for Supreme Soviet deputies would be nominated.

Obviously, I could not be present in two places at once, so I decided to go to Promavtomatika. It was one of its workers, Leonid Boretsky, who had come to visit me at home and see for himself what sort of person I was, what I was fighting for, and what principles I subscribed to. It must be said that when he came, I noticed that he was deeply upset. It turned out that before arriving at my doorstep he had gone to the *Radyanska Zhitomirshchina* editorial office, and there he had been treated to all the carefully assembled sleaze about Alla Yaroshinskaya. That was the cause of Boretsky's concern. For if everything he had been told at the office happened to be true, I would merit a spell behind bars, not an election nomination. But then we started to talk. I showed him the documents I had relied on when writing my critical articles about abuse by senior officials (you see, the newspaper was writing, on behalf of the regional party committee, that I had slandered squeaky clean party functionaries). In the end the worker saw for himself who it was the party newspaper was protecting, and who and what I was defending.

When I came to Promavtomatika, the hall was already packed. People were standing in the aisles, crowding in the doorways and even in the corridors.

I also saw the same familiar glowering faces full of hatred for me that belonged to my fellow journalists from *Radyanska Zhitomirshchina*—Galina Pronina, Mikhail Pyekh, Lyudmila Natykach, and Ivan Gotsalyuk. The editor's pets, as it were; his faithful heralds, so to speak. The chief striking power of the foursome was Ms. Pronina, head of the section of the paper that covered the work of the Soviets. Pugnacious and hard line, garish as usual, with her mop of hair dyed an indescribable hue and chubby fingers sporting four gold rings, Ms. Pronina stood at the lectern and delivered a withering diatribe against me. I was accused of dishonesty and failing to report at party meetings (I have said a couple of times already that I was not a party member). But she was not destined to finish her speech. Suddenly, a worker who gave his name as Vladimir Manheim stood up and said something to this effect: "What sort of person Yaroshinskaya is we know from her articles in the central press in defense of the likes of us, but who you are we have no idea. And although you too work as a journalist, we do not recall either you or your articles. We do not know you, nor wish to." With that, he sat down. His words were received with thunderous applause. Ms. Pronina bore up heroically.

Later the workers asked her what proof she could cite to back her accusations of me. But Ms. Pronina could not come up with anything specific. The audience started to rumble. She wanted to leave the platform, but the public would not have it. The workers would not let her. They went on questioning her. I was sitting with the meeting organizers at the table on the platform. The lectern was next to the table. I feared that Ms. Pronina might collapse (God forbid!), for I knew that she had only just recovered from a stroke and had spent four months on sick leave. I could see her hands tremble and the tremor waves passing all the way to her legs. I felt sorry for her.

The next person to take the floor was Ivan Gotsalyuk. If I remember rightly, he was then head of the paper's agriculture section. But having witnessed the signal failure of the previous act, he toned down his fervor, though he was playing the same role. He was there to stop the workers electing me as their candidate. The carefully planned and well-conceived tactic of the loyalist brigade from my newspaper flopped with equal efficiency. I was voted in almost unanimously, with only the plant manager and the party cell secretary abstaining. This is humanly understandable, after all; because of me they had to withstand enormous pressure from the regional party bodies.

At the Promavtomatika meeting for candidate nomination I expounded for the first time on my election program. One of its sections was called "Health Services and the Environment." I described my vision of the situation in radiation affected areas and the concrete plan for countering the consequences of the Chernobyl disaster in our region. At the time I could only guess at the real scale of the calamity.

The powerful vilification against me on the part of my own newspaper and party bodies at all levels, from Ukraine's Communist Party Central Committee down, was running out of steam. Despite tremendous pressure, three working collectives with multi-thousand work force, Promavtomatika, Avtozapchast, and Elektroizmeritel, managed to get me, a disgraced journalist, registered as their candidate for people's deputies of the Soviet Union. Four more collectives, the Vibroseparator and automatic machine-tools factories, plus the Polytechnic Institute and a research center, failed to do so, in spite of their representatives going to Moscow to the Central Electoral Commission, and despite the commission chairman coming to Zhitomir from Moscow.

My enemies got their last chance of having my name struck off the list at the district meeting in the run-up to the election. By then a new cunning election law regulating the elections to the USSR Congress of People's Deputies had come into force. Though more democratic than the previous law, it was intended not so much to ensure equal rights to candidate nomination and registration but to let the populace play at democracy for a start, to convene, at the end of the "heat," a district session of local collectives' representatives with the express purpose of weeding out undesirable candidates.

The venue for tackling the issue was the enormous hall of the Zhitomir House of Political Education, the domain of the regional party committee. In all there had been eight candidacies nominated. Some of those people had withdrawn their candidacy of their own accord. The Partocracy insisted on leaving no more than two or three names on the list, and enter only these in the secret-ballot papers. My supporters, the workers and engineers, saw clearly what was happening.

They told me later that the audience had been selected in such a way that my candidacy, if a separate vote was taken on it, had little chance of passing. To begin with, the front rows were filled with smug party watchdogs from the city and the district. However, the plan did not work. Yuri Oleinik, a worker of the local wood-working association, took the floor to read out the texts of several statements by working collectives to the effect that they had not held an election of representatives to the district meeting. Their party cell secretaries and managers had appropriated the right to represent the collectives' interests at those district meetings. The workers protested against this manner of usurping their lawful rights and denying them a chance to make their will known.

The workers' statement proved to be a minor bombshell for the meeting. As a result, almost at two in the morning, it was decided to include all the candidates' names on the list. All of them, apart from me, were party members, and nearly all were members of the city and district party committee bureaus. The list as a whole, not the individual names on it, was put to the vote. Thus the working class of Zhitomir won yet another small victory.

But looming ahead were more harrowing, exhausting battles with the powers that be at pre-election meetings with the voters at factories, research centers, colleges, and especially on collective farms. For it was there that the foundations of the existing order of things were more unshakeable than anywhere else. The browbeaten kolkhoz peasantry did not dare say a word against the authorities. Kolkhoz chairmen and party secretaries intimidated their slaves, telling them that if they voted for me they would not be given a horse to plow their vegetable plots nor get coal or firewood deliveries. There were lots of other things they could be deprived of. The Soviet collective farmer was utterly dependent on his boss, the chairman. The kolkhoz chief was lord and master and could do as he pleased.

And yet, collective farmers, too, displayed newfound courage by supporting, mostly tacitly, the candidate so unwelcome to the authorities. Many of them had read my second article in *Izvestia* published during the election campaign, "Barefoot on Broken Glass." In it I described my attempts at defending in my newspaper, *Radyanska Zhitomirshchina*, a collective farmer, Antonina Oborskaya, hounded by Zaria kolkhoz chairman Vladimir Galitsky. I also wrote how after that article of mine a fellow newspaperman, Ivan Ilchenko, unencumbered by moral scruples, carried out the party's orders, not only whitewashing the tarnished image of the chairman whose hothouses kept up a steady supply of fresh tomatoes and cucumbers at all seasons for the table of the party chiefs, but also smearing as much as he could that rank-and-file farmer, Antonina Oborskaya, and me too for good measure.

The people, only too well aware of the way things were done on collective farms, just as easily saw through Ivan Ilchenko's article in defense of the kolkhoz chairman, a favorite of the Zhitomir regional party committee first secretary Vasily Kavun; that chairman had kicked the recalcitrant serf out of the hothouse where she was working for a pittance. And that was far from the only episode. First the newspaper published a critical piece of mine. Then the characters denounced in the article sent letters of complaint to the editor and to the regional party committee, and after that a specially selected journalist was tasked by the editor with writing a piece in refutation of my article. In that way they hoped they were discrediting me, but in fact the only persons discredited were themselves.

Naturally, I was not sure of victory in the election. There was one weighty reason for that. We all feared rigging and fraud. After all, there were lots of polling stations and there were countless party secretaries, venal trade union leaders, village council chairmen, and party activists of every hue. But, it turned out, honest people still outnumbered those. Rallies 20,000 to 30,000 strong gathered to support me. On election day, March 26, 1989, we decided to post our own checkers at every polling station to prevent large-scale election rigging.

Publication of classified data on the health of the people in contaminated areas and on radiation levels would have been an excellent opportunity of instantly drawing the country's attention to the Chernobyl problem. But it never took place—the subject was made strictly taboo by the party bosses. And I decided to use my own election campaign to bring into the open everything I had learned and seen in the strict radiation monitoring zones. Within eight weeks I had some 160 meetings with various collectives. And each time I talked about the public being bamboozled at the highest state level—about the danger of further hushing up the Chernobyl aftereffects, about misinformation concerning the state of affairs in the northern parts of our region, and also in the Kiev and Chernihiv regions of the Ukraine, and in Belorussia, where they had likewise been liberally sprinkled with radioactive cesium and strontium. I still did not know then that the black cloud of radiation had swept through another sixteen regions in Russia, as well as some other parts of the country and even other countries around the world. I did not learn these facts till later, when, despite the frenzied resistance of the Partocracy, I became a people's deputy of the Soviet Union and got access to classified documents. But more of that later.

At that time, in the spring of 1989, vigilant colleague Irina Golovanova, a KGB "liaison officer" in our newspaper, even crossed out of my official election program, which *Radyanska Zhitomirshchina* had reluctantly published, the crucial words about the aftermath of the Chernobyl explosion. Let me here quote that section of my program in the form in which it appeared in the paper on March 1, 1989:

> It is imperative to make public the consequences of radioactive contamination in the Narodichi District, hitherto carefully concealed from the people. There are numerous villages under super-strict radiation regulations. New construction is vigorously pursued on contaminated land. 50 million rubles has already been invested in construction projects there. The expediency should be thoroughly looked into.

Deleted from the text had been bits about the growing number of villages under strict radiation control schemes (to be replaced with the noncommittal phrase ". . .there are numerous villages . . ."), and about the deteriorating health of Narodichi children. I also pointed the finger at the culprits—the local authorities. But that too had been ruthlessly cut out of the text by the party hatchet men.

The big guns of the party, indoctrinated during the seventy years of Communist rule, now were pointed directly at me. In the words of the party anthem, this was their "final big fight" and they were determined not to lose. The authorities heaped abuse upon me in the local and central party press, on radio and TV in the Ukraine. I would report for work at my editorial office, open my newspaper, and read absolutely unbelievable news about myself. For instance, the other day I had called for all Communists to be hanged on lampposts. A cameraman from Kiev TV, acting on instructions from his bosses, would leap from behind a bush next to the flax-mill and later produce some dirty footage of me to be shown within days of the election. I was charged with defaming party functionaries who bombarded me daily with subpoenas. They dragged almost forty of my supporters, including some disabled World War II veterans, into court and indicted them. They were prepared to shoot at people who were preparing to storm the regional party headquarters. They demanded that my husband divorce me. My oldest son was even harassed at school. They threatened me over the telephone and sent threatening hate mail. I could list other similar incidents.

Poor things! Their efforts were all in vain. I won with over 90 percent of the votes. That was the best showing in the Soviet Union; the second best result was Boris Yeltsin's in Moscow.

I resolved to use my deputy's mandate primarily to tell the public, from the rostrum of the Congress of People's Deputies of the USSR in Moscow, about the cocoon of lies that officials had woven over the Chernobyl nuclear explosion and its aftermath with the help of corrupt journalists. Also, I wanted to obtain access to classified material, making that public, too, and to help the people being swindled. Naturally, I had suspected that the falsehood was enormous. But when I later started investigating, I was appalled. The lies about Chernobyl proved to be as vast as the disaster itself.

4

Voices Crying in the Parliamentary Wilderness

On May 25, 1989, the first Congress of People's Deputies of the USSR opened in Moscow. Those were the heady days of euphoria and cheerful anticipation. The whole country put business aside and sat glued to television screens and radios. People placed their most fervent hopes on the people's deputies and their first congress. They saw it as an escape from totalitarianism, a breakthrough toward glasnost and democracy, which one of the people's deputies lovingly called a "young girl." The deputies, still feeling the heat of the election battles recently won, had brought a whole avalanche of problems from every corner of the vast country, and that avalanche started rolling from the land's chief rostrum as from a high peak, reaching, via radio and TV, the most godforsaken outback.

Frequently the Congress turned into a stormy rally. Speakers queued before the microphones waiting for their turn. Four thousand and five hundred deputies could not wait to show to their voters and the world at large that they had arrived. Talking of the most acute regional problems mentioned below, they often failed to hear what the others were saying. Each imagined that his or her local problem was more important than all the others. There was the pollution of the Black Sea, the dying Aral Sea, the rescue of unique Lake Baikal, appalling air pollution in Zaporozhye, tens of thousands of people living below the poverty line—the Soviet paupers, hidden unemployment, shoddy goods and their increasingly glaring shortage, the mounting scarcity of all conceivable items, inflation . . . . The litany could be continued indefinitely. Furthermore, shedding the tyrannical shroud imposed by seventy years of a one-party dictatorship would stretch the limits of our power and abilities.

Against the backdrop of this inconceivable economic and moral crisis, some people might deem the Chernobyl issue rather too local, a disaster that only the Ukrainians and Belorussians were feeling most acutely—so vague was the public's idea of the scale and implications of the accident. The deceitful propaganda was yielding its bitter fruit. The people had been duped.

Ukrainian parliamentarians were asking to be heard by the Congress. A Kiev people's deputy of the USSR, Yuri Shcherbak, and I agreed that if he was not given the floor—and he too wished to talk about Chernobyl—I would try to fight my way to the microphone. Both our names were on the list of prospective speakers but Shcherbak had the advantage of also being a member of the Congress secretariat, which naturally improved his chances. Yet, as day after day passed in debate, clashes, and political discussions, neither of us was given the floor. We intended to not just inform those present of the state of affairs in Ukraine's affected areas, but we were also going to publicly hand over to Gorbachev a videocassette with the documentary *Zapredel* ("Outrage"). It had been shot in our long-suffering Narodichi District. To many of us who had been there, who had seen and talked to the local people, Narodichi was a symbol of the system that was destroying everything that lived.

Now, this is how the cassette plan had been conceived. A USSR people's deputy for Kiev, chairman of the republic's Cinematographers Union, Mikhail Belikov, called on me in the Hotel Moskva. He said he had some footage filmed in the contaminated areas of our administrative region, and asked me to give it to Gorbachev, should either Shcherbak or I get the floor. The cassette was in Shcherbak's briefcase. On one of the last days of the Congress, I realized that we were not going to be allowed to speak to the assembled deputies, neither Shcherbak nor I. And then I made up my mind to stand up and speak, whatever it took, and say at least a few words about Chernobyl. I could not fail. I had no moral right to return home without making that speech from the Congress platform. My voters simply would not understand that. Besides, a speech from the Congress rostrum was an all-Union event; in those days the attention not just of the country but of the world was riveted to that rostrum. Even a couple of words about Chernobyl broadcast live worldwide might undo the entire three-year flow of lies about the disaster. So I resolved to risk it.

At the end of one of the last days of the Congress's work, I walked up to Gorbachev in the presidium from my row forty-nine, in full view of the audience. Frankly, I was shaking—either with fear or with excitement, I could not say which. I gave my name and firmly requested to have the floor to speak about Chernobyl. Obviously taken aback by my nerve, he said: "Sit down here, in the front row. Anatoly Lukyanov will give you the floor after the next speaker." Shcherbak was sitting quite close, in row three or four. I remembered all the time that he had that "radioactive" cassette in his briefcase. I dashed to him at once, telling him that I was about to speak, and asked for the cassette, but Shcherbak must have misunderstood me. The last seconds were ticking out, and I decided that I would speak just as I was, without the cassette—the next best thing.

Anatoly Lukyanov, first deputy chairman of the USSR Supreme Soviet, Gorbachev's personal friend and comrade-in-arms, soon to be one of the leaders of the August 1991 coup attempt, called my name, and I stepped toward the rostrum. At that point I felt someone shove into my hand what I took to be a book—but it turned out to be the cassette. I assumed that Shcherbak had passed it on at the last moment.

The audience, weary after a difficult day, was noisy and it was a struggle to speak. But I said: "I have a big request to make of our president, and of you all. What I am going to say concerns not only my constituency and myself. This is a problem that affects the entire human race. The matter is that a large portion of our Zhitomir region is included in the extra-strict radiation-monitoring zone. I am referring to the Narodichi District, an area engulfed in absolute silence. As a journalist, I have been vainly trying to make public the facts about what is going on there. While right after the explosion we had eighteen villages in the extra-strict radiation-monitoring zone, now, three years on, there are ninety. If previously the Narodichi District alone was contaminated with radiation, now four more districts have joined it on the list. Meanwhile, Ukraine's Health Minister Romanenko tells us, the people living in that zone, that we have a sort of Swiss health resort there. This is simply scandalous! If you watch the footage made by documentary filmmakers, you will see what is really taking place there. This is something that directly concerns you and me, all of us. The events in Tbilisi are important, too, granted, and so are all the other events as well. But what is happening over there is tremendously important. And I appeal to the presidium with a big request: I have here a videocassette. I would very much wish the presidium to give all the people's deputies a chance to see it. It shows the truth about the Narodichi District after the Chernobyl disaster."

Although under the Congress regulations I was entitled to three minutes, Lukyanov was already ringing his bell barely into my second minute at the lectern. Having completed my confused speech—for what can one say in a minute or two?—I showed to the audience the cassette with the footage that in itself was an accusation, and handed it to Gorbachev right there and then.

In the evening, the floor attendant at the Hotel Moskva brought to my room dozens of thank-you express telegrams not only from my own constituency in the Ukraine, but also from Belorussia. That was the first major dent in the rock-solid barrier of falsehoods about the nuclear disaster and its aftermath.

Later, at other Congress sessions, several more people's deputies from contaminated areas managed to fight their way to the microphone. Words of truth about the consequences of the Chernobyl accident were uttered at the highest possible level for the first time in three years. Here are some of the speeches.

Z. N. Tkacheva, head of department at the Slavgorod Central Clinic, Mogilev region:

> At present we, the people living in these areas, have been deprived of clean soil, pure air, uncontaminated forests and meadows, all the vital ingredients of the human environment whose lack makes life a misery. The press, the health ministry's official reports, the daily *Pravda* of May 29, 1989, convey none of the proper concern about people's health and the fate of future generations. After all, a disaster of this magnitude has never happened before, and the international community has therefore no experience of observation of similar events.
>
> It is my opinion that scientists have proved unequal to the task assigned to them. This refers to doctors and biophysicists alike. So hadn't we better turn to foreign scientists for help—they have more reliable equipment and more experience. After all, what is at stake today is the destiny not of any one region but of the entire Belorussian nation.
>
> It must be said that the medical practitioners' opinion of the people's condition in contaminated areas is increasingly divergent from that of medical scholars and top health-care authorities in the country. I can compare the difference between then and now, as I have lived for years on this territory and I see the changes occurring in people's health in the wake of the disaster. Visiting experts, particularly the more senior officials, after a few hours or days spent in our parts try to convince us that human health is not deteriorating. The changes that are in evidence they explain by every conceivable reason—high-nitrate food, low-calorie diet, lack

of breast-feeding, anything but the radioactivity factor. But we have had all those things before. And we could have told them that those faults could only enhance the damaging effect of radiation, but they cannot explain it away.

Like the other people's deputies, I am afraid that it is impossible to say with certainty today that living in contaminated areas is safe.

I cannot forget my voters' eyes at our meetings when they demanded to be resettled at once. We offer them free sausage, personal dosimeters, and tractors with hermetic driver cabs. They don't want any of that. They asked to be resettled as soon as possible, so that they could live a normal life, work on their vegetable plot, breed cattle . . . . I shudder to think about all that.

B. I. Oleinik, secretary of the Ukrainian Writers' Union Board, Kiev:

I must tell you that the radioactivity situation is acute, for all the assurances to the contrary by the atomic energy ministry and the health ministry. In areas where radiation levels exceed 15 Ci/km^2 there are still people living, and if the maps that appeared in *Pravda* [on the eve of the Congress] are anything to go by, in Belorussia and in parts of the Bryansk region [of the Russian Federation] contamination is even worse. So I give my full backing to the appeal to this Congress by the staff of the Geology Institute of the Ukrainian Academy of Sciences. It demands, in particular, that we consider information about the environmental situation, including radiation, in every region and district, in every locality. [Health] departments must be forbidden to revise effective standards [of permissible contamination] to keep up with the changing situation, and the temporarily admissible radioactive contamination levels (TARCL) adopted by the health ministry for the post-accident period must be published. We should demand that the government find the money and the means for urgently resettling the people outside the strict radiation-monitoring areas.

Proceeding from the universal principles of humanism and mercy and taking into account the immediate danger to the genetic pool of the people of the Ukraine, Belorussia, and several areas in Russia caused by the nuclear disaster, a national program of child protection must be worked out, with mandatory establishment of clinics-cum-sanitariums for mothers and children to improve the health of children in affected areas.

A law must be devised and approved on the legal responsibility of officials who conceal and distort information about the ecological, including radiation, situation and its health effects, because by their actions such officials blatantly violate human rights and jeopardize man's very existence. Until such a law is adopted, the

41

professional competence of senior officials in various departments and commissions responsible for the present state of affairs should be examined.

I appeal to individuals under Hippocratic oath: do not blaspheme accusing people of radiophobia. What radiophobia there may be is caused by the radio which falsely deceived the masses and lulled them by false information. This is as unpardonable a sin as furtively installing reactors and setting up burial grounds for dangerously harmful substances.

Unexpectedly, several party functionaries of Belorussia and the Ukraine also shed their inhibitions. It was hard to believe that they were saying *this*. What had been stopping them before? From their speeches, the country was gradually learning the Chernobyl secrets of the Kremlin court.

First Secretary of the Belorussian Communist Party Central Committee Ye. Ye. Sokolov:

Time will not ease the pain in the hearts of Belorussians; in our republic 18 percent of farmland has been radioactively contaminated. Whereas initially the matter was considered by a Union-level government-appointed commission, now its efforts are almost nil. In three years the commission failed to come up with a convincing and well-considered conception of safe residence that would guarantee health to future generations as well. In our view the stand to be taken on this issue should be perfectly unambiguous. People mustn't live where it is impossible to use the produce of their own homesteads. This is not the place or time for skimping.

Chairman of Ukraine's Council of Ministers V. A. Masol, on the other hand, in his lengthy fifteen-minute oration talked about anything at all, down to some "positive results achieved," except Chernobyl, the sore that tormented (and still does, decades later!) various parts of Ukraine!

Gorbachev remembered Chernobyl; Ryzhkov (USSR Premier) said a few words about it; Professor Alexei Yablokov, a people's deputy from Moscow, talked about it, but Ukraine's leader forgot all about it. Would you believe it—not a word did he say about Chernobyl!

Amazingly, not one doctor, not one government member said anything in reply to the people's deputies' charges. That too was indicative; a kind of barometer measuring the attitude of official structures to *vox populi*, to the voice crying out in the wilderness. Or were they simply afraid to touch that subject?

For a long time I thought that the cassette I had given to Gorbachev had been given me at the last moment by Shcherbak. But, as people's deputy Belikov told me later, he had had another copy in his briefcase. Belikov was sitting in the front row at the Congress. And it was he who thrust it into my hand when my name was called.

The next day I approached Lukyanov to ask him about arranging a viewing of the cassette. After all, the Congress was to close in a day or two. Lukyanov said he was not sure if the footage viewing could be organized at such short notice. The only problem, according to him, was lack of time. (The people's deputies had by then already seen several video recordings of the bloodshed in Tbilisi.)

The Congress was over, and the time to show the people's deputies footage of how people were living in contaminated areas, in the nuclear war zone in the heart of Europe, was never scheduled. After a while the first session of the USSR Supreme Soviet was convened again. I approached Lukyanov with the same question: Why hadn't the people's deputies been shown the "radiation footage"? Lukyanov sincerely assured me that it had been shown to the USSR Council of Ministers and the Politburo. I suppose it had.

What did their faces look like, what were they feeling, those who watched *Outrage*, when a nurse at the Narodichi district hospital said on the screen: ". . . In the first few days, when children were being examined, I worked the apparatus called GVM and saw all the doses. It was a nightmare! . . . We were told then, all these copies you are making, destroy every one so that not a single copy leaves this room . . ."? Or when the hospital's chief surgeon A. B. Korzhanovsky said: "Of the five thousand children we have tested for radioiodine, 1,478 kids registered between 0 and 30 rad; 1,177, between 30 and 75 rad; 862, between 75 and 200 rad; 57, between 200 and 500 rad; 467, from 500 rad upwards. That's just their thyroid glands . . .. We obtained these figures nearly two years after the event"? Did their conscience prick the people who had kept criminal silence in high government offices and posts while in a position to tell the truth? Did the individuals who had known but never warned the public of the danger feel any pangs of conscience? I doubt it.

5

"Top Secret: Ban Chernobyl Theme!"

After the First Congress of the USSR People's Deputies, the flood-gates of glasnost opened at last and crowds of journalists from various periodicals, both Soviet and foreign, rushed to the Narodichi District. Not infrequently, they turned for assistance to the working group on environmental safety at my public consultation office headed by Dr. Yuri Reznik. Every time we implored them not to go to Narodi-chi, not to go there *now*. The whole country and the entire world had already learned about that long-suffering area. After the Congress, I finally managed to get published a series of articles on the life and suffering of people in the strict radiation-monitoring areas, in the popular weekly *Nedelya* ("Week") and in the journal *Selskaya nov'* ("Country Novelty"—here, my Chernobyl essay was named the article of the year). The Paris-based *Russkaya mysl* ("Russian Thought") also published my article. (The editor of *Ogonyok* had come up to me after my emotional outburst at the Congress, saying, "So, why don't you give us your article; we'll print it right away," but I no longer wanted to have anything to do with that magazine.)

It turned out that in our region there were six more contaminated administrative districts besides Narodichi—the Ovruch, the Luginy, the Korosten, the Olevsk, the Emilchino; even in the Malin District there were patches of radioactivity. Four years later, the Novograd-Volynsky District was added to the list. In short, almost half the ad-ministrative region (*oblast*) was a danger zone. But the country and the world were largely unaware of that. The press ignored the issue. That was why we asked journalists to go to these districts that were total silence zones. Slowly but surely the secret was being divulged; we got to know the individuals who were responsible for imposing the secrecy and thus responsible for several years of radiation hell for the local people. I even contrived to obtain a few documents marked

"SECRET." Let me talk, in this chapter, about the Chernobyl disaster publicity.

Consider the instructions issued on June 27, 1986, by the USSR Health Ministry's main directorate: "On Tightening Secrecy Regulations While Carrying Out Work on Eliminating the Consequences of the Accident at the Chernobyl Nuclear Power Plant." Here are the three fatal paragraphs:

> (4) Classify as secret all information about the accident. (8) Classify as secret all information about the results of medical treatment. (9) Classify as secret all information about the degree of radioactive injuries to the personnel taking part in the liquidation of the consequences of the accident at the Chernobyl Nuclear Power Plant. Head of Main Directorate 3 of the USSR Health Ministry Shulzhenko.

And another document, this time made available by the government commission itself: "List of Data on Issues of the Chernobyl Accident Not to Be Circulated by the Press, Radio and Television," no. 423, dated September 24, 1987. It ordered the following subjects to be classified as secret: "(1) Information about radioactive contamination levels in separate localities in excess of the maximum permissible concentrations. (2) Information about the indices of physical deterioration in work capacity and loss of professional skills by the operative personnel working in special conditions at the Chernobyl nuclear power plant, or by persons employed in eliminating the consequences of the accident."

Those were not mere pieces of paper. All of those instructions were put into force, striking fear in people in charge of newspapers, magazines, the radio, television, and the cinema. While no one ever replied to me in writing, explaining the real reason for denial of publication, the vigilant officials had no qualms about issuing the appropriate orders. Chairman of the group of experts with the USSR State Committee for Atomic Energy, P. M. Verkhovykh, informed USSR State Cinematography Committee chairman A. I. Kamshalov and the Ukrainian documentary film board manager in his letter no. dd 142, dated February 1, 1989: "The commission of experts on Chernobyl, having watched the documentary film *The Microphone*, . . . deems it necessary to point out that the tendentious and one-sided selection of facts, many of which are, according to specialists, dubious, can do political harm to the Soviet State." A curious brand of solicitude for our country's welfare on the part of the atomic energy committee head, wouldn't you say? Let our own Soviet folk quietly take in their fill of radionuclides, as long as the public worldwide is happily unaware of the fact. The maker of *The Microphone* was Ukrkinokhronika director Georgy Shklyarevsky. The film was shot in the Narodichi District.

Another film, *The Knell of Chernobyl* by Rollan Sergienko, was minutely examined for five months by the authorities until the ministry of medium engineering industry (for which read atomic industry—the Soviets' way of misleading the foe) allowed it to be released. The same fate befell a second film by Sergienko, *The Threshold*. It took the authorities seven months to dissect it. But even after it was declassified, it gathered dust on the shelf for several more months. Our bureaucrats' supervigilance and their permanent readiness to exercise it have always been of the highest order. It seems that whatever else might have been in short supply, supervigilance was always plentiful.

The Soviet Ministry of Defense, too, had a hand in throttling glasnost after the Chernobyl disaster. Here is yet another document, "Explanation by the Central Military Medical Commission of the USSR Ministry of Defense," no. 205, dated July 8, 1987, sent out to recruiting centers:

> (1) Among the long-term consequences of exposure to ionizing radiation and induced by the latter should be listed: (1) Leukemia or leukosis five to ten years after exposure to radiation doses in excess of 50 rad. (2) Evidence of acute somatic disorders, and also signs of chronic complaints entering an acute stage in persons who were recruited to eliminate the consequences of the accident and are not suffering from ARS [acute radiation sickness], must not be linked to the effects of ionizing radiation. (3) When issuing medical certificates to persons previously engaged in work at the Chernobyl nuclear power plant and without ARS in their anamnesis, the fact of their recruitment for the said work and the total dose below the radiation sickness level are not to be mentioned in Point 10. Head of military control commission No. 10, Colonel Bakshutov, Medical Service.

A very special role in this big lie was reserved for the Soviet State Hydrometeorology Committee. Here is a paper marked "SECRET." It is dated June 12, 1989. That means that it was issued after the First Congress of People's Deputies, when, it seemed, the shroud of secrecy covering the accident ought to have been lifted. No such luck! This is what the paper says, in part:

> In accordance with the orders from the USSR state hydrometeorology committee, we are forwarding information about the radioactivity situation in the Luginy district of the Zhitomir region based on the findings of the latest examinations. Appended: Information about radioactive contamination in the Luginy district. SECRET.

The paper was signed by Ukrhydromet (the Ukrainian Hydrometeorology Committee) deputy head, P. V. Shendrik.

When sometime later a meeting of residents of contaminated areas and the state commission members took place in Narodichi, and I, as a people's deputy of the USSR, found myself, by a quirk of fate, sitting next to deputy head of the USSR State Committee for Hydrometeorology, Yuri Tsaturov, I asked him about the meaning of that. His reply was, "It cannot be!" So either I had to disbelieve my own eyes and the imposing stamps with signatures by high officials at the Ukrhydromet, or the right hand, the USSR State Committee, was unaware of what the left hand, its republic branch, was doing. Later still, when I had to fight with the USSR State Committee for Hydrometeorology officialdom to obtain information about contamination levels in Russia's Krasnodar Territory, I phoned Yuri Tsaturov. It transpired that the Big Man was nursing a grudge against me because I had quoted that document marked "SECRET" in the weekly *Moscovskie novosti* (*Moscow News*). He said somewhat brusquely into the telephone: "Not our fault. We can't be held responsible, can we, for some fool in the Ukraine writing a paper like that." Since Ukrhydromet was a branch of the USSR State Committee, I could only commiserate with Mr. Tsaturov over the kind of personnel he had to put up with.

Meanwhile, on the third anniversary of the Chernobyl disaster, a month before the First Congress of People's Deputies was convened, I learned about another classified official document—the order by A. I. Mayorets, the USSR minister for power engineering and electrification. The orders were to classify and keep secret from the public all data concerning accidents and fires at the ministry's power and construction facilities, environmental pollution, failures of major equipment, and levels of material damages, casualties, and so on. The minister sternly instructed his subordinates thus: "Ensure control in order to rule out divulging the said information in open official documents and telegraph correspondence, as well as in material intended for publication in the public press." This looks like a diagnosis of an incurable disease.

One more interesting thing that happened to me, something of a detective story, is of interest. In early May 1989, we, newly elected USSR people's deputies from Ukraine, were assembled in Kiev, in the magnificent Mariinsky Palace (the very same that was so deftly blockaded by "orange revolutionaries" in 2004). The object was to appoint those who would work in the USSR Supreme Soviet and whose names would be suggested for ballot lists over there in Moscow. (It must be pointed out that the act was a complete party-nomenklatura farce aimed at barring the disloyals from sneaking in. But even that did not help the Communists.) During one of the breaks, an official from the Ukrainian Supreme Soviet I knew came up to me with a furtive glance over his shoulder and, having beckoned me behind a column, took out of his inside coat pocket a package, which he surreptitiously handed to me with a whisper: "I never gave this to you. And you must not mention the names of the people who signed the document. Please." Quite a cloak-and-dagger mystery, the reader will say. A cloak-and-dagger mystery from necessity, I will concede. That episode shows that even three years after the disaster and declarations of perestroika and "new thinking," people at the top still feared coming into the open for fear they might call down upon themselves a lot of unpleasantness. Today I can disclose the name of that man— he was an official with the Ukrainian Soviet parliament's *apparatchik*, Yevgeny Bay. Someone told me that he was now an ambassador to some country or other.

Inside the packet was a largish, twelve-page report on research into the health of Ukrainian children and adults resident in the republic's affected areas. The first page was missing, so I do not know exactly what kind of letterhead the document had originally, of which institution, and who its addressee was. But since I had received the document in that mysterious fashion, it was obvious that it was not intended for the general public, nor for the press either. There were also a number of appendices—research tables and charts that described the various illnesses afflicting the residents of contaminated areas in Ukraine.

What I read there horrified me. I will not cite here the whole of that document (it would take too much space, and the text is far too specialist, anyway). But quote the most frightening bits that show up the system's whole disgusting core I must. Well then:

> None of the medical institutions (except in the Chernigov region) have papers registering the deceased, while the death certificates lack the date and cause of death.... There are no registration papers on dead children. . . . Radiation monitoring teams (that include dosimeter operators) regularly fail to record the measuring results in medical documents and have not drawn up a single exposure dose data chart for any of the patients examined.

A terrible crime, that, not only against the living but also against the dead. The system was trying to cover its tracks, afraid to leave documentation that might become an indictment—medical examination results, death causes in children and adults.

And further, verbatim:

> In the Zhitomir and Kiev regions not all persons previously exposed to radiation have been discovered and registered, in particular among those that had been evacuated (resettled) from the affected areas. The records related to the persons arriving from interior ministry offices remain in regional departments (second sectors thereof); they are not used in the work of the departments and are not sent on to health care institutions in whose territories they reside. It has been established that in the township of Polesskoe and the villages attached to it there live 206 evacuees, while the special file of the All-Union Research Center for Radiation Medicine has been notified of a mere 54 persons.
>
> As far as the persons taking part in eliminating the consequences of the accident are concerned, the health care system has no reliable information about their numbers, and the records on them are kept only when medical personnel discovers them accidentally. No data about their migration reach the health care system.

Now, here are some curious instructions: "As of 1988, on the orders of the USSR ministry of health, it is forbidden to enter in registers the names of persons who took part in eliminating the consequences of the accident after January 1, 1988." Meanwhile, work on rebuilding reactor unit no. 4, decontamination, and elimination of the disaster's consequences went on even after 1990. Thousands of people had their health ruined while working there.

And here is further horrendous evidence of crime found in the secret document:

> In the Kiev region (the Polesskoe and Ivankovo districts) autopsy is not performed on the deceased and stillborn because these areas do not have autopsy (pathoanatomical) facilities. Of the

353 persons who died in Polesskoe and Vilcha in 1987, autopsy was
not performed on a single one. Nor is postmortem performed on
the deceased in the town of Slavutich. In the Zhitomir region, in
Ovruch, an inter-district pathoanatomical center has been set up,
but it performs postmortem only on those who died in hospitals.

The tables and charts enclosed with the document suggest that as
a result of medical checkups in the Zhitomir region, 43.7 percent of
the patients were pronounced healthy; in the Kiev region, the figure
was 39.7 percent; and in the Chernihiv region, 66.3 percent.

The secret document was signed by—and now I can speak about
it openly—V. A. Buzunov, MD, director of the Research Institute for
Epidemiology and Prevention of Radiation Damage under the All-
Union Research Center for Radiation Medicine of the USSR Academy
of Medical Sciences; V. N. Bugaev, MD; B. A. Ledoshchuk, candidate
of medicine; Prof. N. I. Omelyanets, MD; A. K. Cheban, candidate
of medicine—all of them laboratory heads at the same center; and
N. I. Ivanchenko, section head at the Ukrainian republic's data-
processing computer center of Ukraine's Health Ministry.

Such was the truth that was classified as secret. As for the official
medical establishment, it accused all of us of being sick, yes, indeed,
sick with radiophobia. Meanwhile, the medical professors who made
these allegations would always bring with them, on their visits to the
affected areas, chicken meat sealed in cellophane and mineral water,
which they used even to wash their hands. And these people assured
the locals that there was no danger whatever. They only advised the
locals to wash the firewood before feeding that radioactive stuff into
village stoves! This is no joke, but a solid fact.

The secret Chernobyl information was "contraindicated" not only
to the common public and journalists; it was even withheld from
some of the medical experts. Although, as USSR State Committee
for Hydrometeorology chairman, Yuri Izrael, assured the deputies,
"all Chernobyl data were fully available to those ministries and departments that could contribute to the elimination of the disaster's
consequences, the secrecy was intended just for the public" (there,
he admitted it, after all!).

But here is the testimony of Dmitry Grozdinsky, corresponding
member of the Ukrainian Academy of Sciences:

> Instead of explaining to us, radiobiologists, what had happened,
> so that we could counsel the public about safe behavior in the first

hours after the accident, they sealed our counters. What had happened at Chernobyl is top secret, we were told. That was done by people who had no specialist knowledge but who did their best to protect the authorities; people like that always think that it is better to turn a blind eye to everything happening around, and they pass off illusion for reality. They can say that all that was the result of the "stagnation period." But how can one explain then that those same people (four years on), while no longer sealing up the counters, still render secret any information about the consequences of the accident? What for? Where does it come from, this wave of instinctive imposition of secrecy?

The laboratories that possessed dosimeters and radiometers were simply sealed so that no one could measure anything in those days. . . . And instead of explaining in sober, comprehensible, clear terms the situation as it objectively was, there was strange silence, hushing up, statements to the effect that by such and such a date we had fully regained control—all that at a time when the reactor was on fire and each second brought any amount of unexpected changes, unpredictable behavior from that reactor! I can find very little justification for the administrative bodies responsible for keeping the public informed.

And here is what a group of researchers under Prof. Ye. B. Burlakova, doctor of biology, wrote several years after the disaster:

To make a scientifically substantiated forecast of radiobiological consequences in those areas, it is essential to have specific dosimetric data on every kind of ionizing radiation in the contaminated areas of the Ukraine, Belorussia, and Russia. However, the existing data are inaccessible not only to radiobiologists, but even to most scientists at the health ministry and the USSR Academy of Medical Sciences.

No more need be said.

There was another type of slipknot with which to strangle the truth about Chernobyl: instead of the SECRET stamp, papers were marked "FOR OFFICIAL USE ONLY." This bashful tag I saw, for instance, on a statement by O. I. Voloshchenko, deputy director of the center for hygiene of the Ukrainian Health Ministry. A resolution by the Zhitomir region Communist Party Committee Bureau of February 1, 1990, sported the same stamp. The document signed by first secretary V. G. Fedorov was named "On the Current State and Additional Measures to Eliminate the Consequences of the Accident at the Chernobyl Nuclear Power Plant."

So what was there in the bureau resolution that the people, allegedly unanimously supportive of the Communist Party, had better be kept in ignorance of? Lots of stuff, but mostly this, presumably: "The tardiness and inconsistency displayed by Party and Soviet bodies, lack of glasnost, failure to inform the public promptly and convincingly are causing resentment, social tension, and coupled with various rumors and conjectures, sows panic." That was really rich! Imagine deploring a lack of glasnost under the FOR OFFICIAL USE ONLY stamp. Would you believe it—glasnost for official use only! Most of us learned of the terrible disaster at the Chernobyl reactor from Western radio broadcasts. The first to raise the alarm was a Swedish nuclear power plant.

The other day I was going through my Chernobyl archives and stumbled across a TASS report at the May 6, 1986, press conference at the USSR Foreign Ministry Press Center, "On Events at the Chernobyl Nuclear Power Plant," published in every Soviet newspaper. Here is what the then deputy foreign minister of the Soviet Union A. G. Kovalev said there: "Our approach aims at ensuring that information is responsible, objective, reliable, balanced, in a word—honest. . . . As soon as we obtained reliable data we released them at once. . . . We do not go in for crystal gazing, we rely on facts and data supplied by the best experts and instruments." Today it is only too well known what officials did then; no, they did not engage in crystal gazing, of course; they just told lies, pure and simple—as ever. They lied without giving it a second thought. That was part of their official duties, their lifestyle and second nature.

The alarming news from Chernobyl that the Soviet public learned from "hostile radio stations" in those early days the deputy minister dismissed as "yet another bout of hysterics" that had been "organized by and directed from the same center, the United States, and clearly followed the usual pattern. And it is not really about the nuclear power plant at all," he pontificated. "Certain militarist circles feel that under pressure from world public opinion the ground is giving way under them." So that's what it was! Those bloody imperialists again!

The deputy minister continued, "Such are the real springs that activated this massive eruption of lies, falsification, fact juggling, pretence, shoddy shows . . ." Oh, what a shame! Especially now that we know the real falsifiers and stagers of "shoddy shows" of deception that nine million people had for decades been paying for with their own health and that of their children. Halloo, Comrade Kovalev, where are you today?

It was not until 1990 that the chairman of the USSR State Committee for Hydrometeorology, Yuri Izrael, announced to the people's deputies and experts, "The government commission and the Politburo task group have decided to declassify certain technical data that were forwarded to the IAEA in August and published. In particular, our brochure was issued in Russian and English." Where was it issued? What was the print run? Whoever saw it? And whom was the English version for? Scottish sheep? In May 1986, the Finns put out a second brochure for their compatriots, "Internal Report on the Radiation Situation in Finland. May 1986," in Finnish. It offers detailed advice as to how a person ought to behave in a contaminated area, where children can play outside their homes, and for how long. There is advice to farmers on where and how to graze cattle, and what to eat and what to drink.

In Ukraine, however, it took Ukraine's health minister, A. Ye. Romanenko, ten days to make a television appearance. Here is how he counseled his audience to fight radiation: "Do not go for outings in the country, keep your windows shut, and clean your floors with a wet mop." Only after May 20, that is, nearly a month after the accident, were people in some of the areas finally instructed to stay off milk from local cows. But then look at this admirable concern expressed by our good old USSR Hydrometeorology Committee apropos of "dirty" milk, in Poland: "[O]ur proposals regarding a ban on milk consumption in Polish territory: 0.1 mR/h—[Premier] Ryzhkov has been informed." Very touching solicitude for our Slavic brethren abroad, is it not? It is particularly so if you recall that it was shown at a time when thousands of their own compatriots living in monstrously contaminated areas that registered 170–200 Ci/km^2 went on sipping radioactive milk fresh from the cows. There had been no "proposals" about them to Premier Ryzhkov.

Paradoxically, after the First Congress of People's Deputies, when a lot of facts had surfaced, the provincial mass media suffered a new bout of the secrecy disease. This time round there weren't any written instructions. The names of Chernobyl secret holders were struck off or simply concealed. In my own city of Zhitomir, for instance, this censor job was voluntarily performed by the regional daily *Radyanska Zhitomirshchina* and the local radio. In one of the speeches at a meeting of residents in contaminated areas that had attracted thousands of victims of the Chernobyl disaster and of bureaucratic abuse of power, I directly accused the first secretary of the regional Communist Party Committee, V. M. Kavun, naming him personally responsible for the sorry plight of those people and their children. Also present at the meeting were journalists of *Radyanska Zhitomirshchina* and the regional radio. Knowing that the meeting would be covered by radio correspondent Grigory Shevchenko, I asked him not to cut out those words of mine from the tape. Grigory told me that the report was ready but that those words were not in it, on orders of his boss Pyotr Smolyar. So I went to Smolyar. He said that on the whole he was for reproducing my speech in full, but it was now too late to make any changes. And if it was all the same to me, the radio station would do it a few days later.

Time passed, but the radio was still silent. Again I paid a visit to Smolyar. He informed me, without batting an eyelid, that the tape with my speech was at the regional party committee, where, he said, they would furnish it with a commentary. OK, I agreed to that, too. After all, the important thing to me was that people (nearly a million of them in the region; that's practically half of Lithuania) should hear who had known the truth but kept silent, hiding it from them. I would not be intimidated by any sort of commentary. But the tape was not released, with or without the commentary. Then I sent an official deputy's question to the chairman of the regional television and radio committee V. Ya. Boiko and received a staggering reply: apparently, I myself had asked Smolyar to take the tape with my speech to the regional party committee! In short, the first secretary was saved, both on the radio and in the daily *Radyanska Zhitomirshchina*, which had pointedly ignored that part of the meeting.

Some time later, there was a big green rally in Zhitomir. Predictably, people spoke about Chernobyl. I, too, was given the floor. By then, working as I did on the state expert commission on Chernobyl, I had gathered a fair amount of documents that enabled me to reveal certain names of regional and Ukrainian republic's leaders who had known the truth about the accident's consequences but kept it from the public. In front of the twenty-thousand-strong rally I asked the regional daily's correspondents working there to print that speech of mine. Alas! The newspaper was not so much interested in the disaster as it wished to kick yet again the people in disfavor with the party apparatchiks, the people who were at that time running for seats in Ukraine's parliament, my former election agents and persons of independent views—journalist Yakov Zaiko and economist Alexander Sugonyako. Of course, that was infinitely safer than naming party bosses invested with power as the main culprits. This was only to be expected. The party press had always been and remained, regardless of any perestroika, the well-greased party reprisal machine (its "drive belt") aided by their lapdog journalists who were nothing more than trusted party hirelings. Rest assured, they lost no sleep over the whole affair.

My speech was published in the very first issue of the independent newspaper *Golos* ("Voice"), edited by Yakov Zaiko, member of the freshly elected Ukrainian parliament. (Incidentally, its first issue did not come out until several thousand people had gathered in Zhitomir on Lenin Square, in front of the regional party committee premises, demanding that the newspaper be released from attachment imposed on it by instructions from the regional party bureau.)

The first official document ever, in the whole post-Chernobyl period, to clearly state that there indeed were secrecy regulations for the consequences of the accident came in the form of a resolution, overwhelmingly adopted in a joint session of three USSR Supreme Soviet committees—for public health, for the environment and rational use of resources, and for issues related to women, protection of motherhood and children. That happened three years after the explosion. The resolution said, among other things, "During the first two years following the accident, generalized medical and dosimetric information was classified." And right there the document gave these instructions: "The USSR ministry of health and the USSR Academy of Sciences shall ensure glasnost on the radioactivity situation in all areas affected by the accident, and declassify materials on general morbidity in contaminated areas." But even in that breakthrough document there is a grave inaccuracy, which, I am sure, party-apparatus-related deputies of the Soviet parliament managed to work in. It was not for two but for three years that information had remained fully classified. Only on the eve of the First Congress of the USSR People's Deputies, on May 24, 1989, did the government pass a resolution to have it declassified. I do not doubt that it was done for fear that the people's deputies might express righteous indignation during the Congress session (which they did!).

The flames have been beaten down, but the coals are still smoldering.

6

Crime without Punishment

As soon as the Congress of the USSR People's Deputies was over, a public assembly was called in Narodichi, where I was handed an appeal to the USSR Supreme Soviet:

> We are appealing to the country's parliament as the last resort, in the hope and faith that we may be heeded and understood. The shadow of the Chernobyl disaster has closed any prospects for the future that we had. For a fourth year running we have been living in constant anxiety about our children's and our own fate. Nearly the whole of our district happens to be within the strict radiation-monitoring zone. Anything we grow on our "dirty" and is unfit for human consumption. Radiation levels exceed the maximum amounts permissible for human habitation.
>
> Our greatest grief is our children, the health of our children. It causes us the most serious concern. Most of our children have thyroid problems. Chronic complaints have become much more common; there is plentiful incidence of eye pathology. The children are sleepy and unresponsive in class; they suffer from headaches and pain in the legs, which worries their parents greatly. Adults display an increase in cancer incidence, which is also cause for concern.
>
> Our appeals to various authorities at the [Ukrainian] republic and Union levels meet with lack of understanding and support. We have no one else to turn to. We trust in the fairness of people's power and ask for our demands to be considered.
>
> Provide guarantees for preserving the health and social protection for the population of the Narodichi district in conditions that have emerged in the wake of the Chernobyl nuclear accident. To this end, resettle the residents of localities where the levels of radioactive contamination exceed maximum permissible levels; give families (first of all those with children) the right to move to uncontaminated areas and obtain accommodation there; provide clean food for the entire population of the district with a proper extra pay ratio introduced for all, including old age pensioners; extend annual leave for the working population of the district. Appeal approved at the residents' assembly on June 17, 1989.

I took this appeal with me to the first USSR Supreme Soviet session and handed it to first deputy chairman, Anatoly Lukyanov, together with my question on the issue in my capacity as people's deputy. Let me take the liberty of quoting it in full, for this is important.

> While the [first] Congress [of People's Deputies] was in session, I publicly handed to the Congress presidium a videotape with footage showing the state of affairs in the radiation-affected zone of the Zhitomir region, and asked that it be shown to all the people's deputies. Unfortunately, the presidium did not deem it possible to heed my request.
>
> In the meantime, the radiation situation in the Narodichi district (and partly in four more districts—Luginy, Korosten, Ovruch and Olevsk) has been growing increasingly difficult. (I was unaware at the time that half the region had been badly contaminated by the Chernobyl fallout.) According to official documents, the incidence of various diseases in the district, including instances of cancer, has increased. Monsters are being born on collective farms. In some places, radiation levels exceed natural background levels 100 to 160 times. And people have to live there.
>
> A considerable proportion of farmland lies in areas containing between 40 and 200 Ci/km^2 of radioactive cesium. The human tolerance level is 40 curies. According to experts' reports, at least twelve villages in the district need to be resettled. At the same time more and more money is being sunk in the extra-strict radiation-monitoring regime. People should be moved out of the newly built houses for evacuees in the radiation zone. Yet over 100 million rubles has already been invested in new housing construction there.
>
> After the Congress, Narodichi district residents invited me to their assembly. There they approved an appeal to the USSR Supreme Soviet. The assembly authorized me to deliver it to its destination, and also to make the following people's deputy's inquiry: (1) Who made the decision to build new houses, schools, kindergartens, etc., in the hard-radiation zone? (2) Who will be personally accountable for the fact that tens of thousands of people have lived for three years in ignorance of radioactive contamination and that the real state of things has been kept secret to this day? (3) When exactly and which villages in the Narodichi and other districts will be finally resettled in ecologically "clean" areas? (4) Given that 4,000 children in the Narodichi district, as well as children in other districts affected by radiation, require medical examination, treatment, and recuperation in a "clean" area, I request the Supreme Soviet of the USSR to take a decision on making available to these long-suffering children all medical and sanitarium facilities of directorate No. 4 of the USSR ministry of health in the Ukraine, including and primarily in Zhitomir. (Those medical facilities of directorate No. 4 belonged to the

Communist Party at the time; it provided free medical treatment for the top functionaries.) (5) Considering that my question in my capacity as people's deputy handed to the Congress presidium about the showing of the videocassette with the film *Outrage* has remained unanswered, I am appealing again, this time to the Supreme Soviet, requesting that the documentary video be shown for USSR Supreme Soviet deputies during the current session. (6) I also request the USSR Supreme Soviet to reply to my question as people's deputy, the response to be read out in the course of this session.

Although under the USSR law on the status of people's deputies their questions were to be read out at a session of the Soviet, which was not done. My question was simply passed on to the USSR Council of Ministers, to its chairman, Nikolai Ivanovich Ryzhkov. Two weeks later, Nikolai Ryzhkov gave the following orders as per my inquiry: "To Comrade V.V. Maryin. Please talk to people's deputy Yaroshinskaya, consider the issues raised in her letter, and prepare the requisite proposals." And that was that. This episode epitomized the attitude of our powers that be to the victims of the Chernobyl explosion. They were already thoroughly fed up with our letters, requests, entreaties, and appeals—and here I was thrusting on them my question, on top of everything. What infernal nuisance! The prime minister's reply, if you could call it that, reminded me of Vladimir Bazelchuk's article, made to order, that had appeared in *Radyanska Zhitomirshchina*. In it the journalist reproached the ungrateful settlers for finding fault with the free housing they had so generously been given. So the logic down below proved a perfect match for that among the top bosses. And that was the brace that had kept together the entire totalitarian system!

Still, I went to the fuel and energy resources bureau under the USSR Council of Ministers, to see deputy chairman Vladimir Vladmirovich Maryin, member of the government commission for eliminating the consequences of the Chernobyl disaster. He had also invited for the interview a section head at the bureau, V. Ya. Voznyak, and a senior expert Yu. V. Dekhtyarev. According to Maryin, it was the local authorities that had decided where houses for evacuees should be built and that people in twelve villages were to be rehoused in 1990–93. The three gentlemen assured me ardently that there had been—wait for it— no information bans or data classifying relative to the consequences of the accident. They were saying, perfectly straight-faced, that every collective farmer could obtain any information he or she wished at his local village council. That was a lie told by a high official. And when I cited prohibitive instructions (including some by the government commission whose member was that very V. V. Maryin), he said they were no longer in force! It was odd, to say the least, that I, a journalist, should have had to work hard to glean classified information and then could not get my Narodichi article published anywhere for nearly three years, when all the while it was a snap for any peasant to obtain whatever information he thought might interest him or her. Ah, well, Comrade Maryin was telling a lie, trying to fob me off. The decision to lift the confidentiality-imposing resolutions was taken (and then not nearly all of them) just days before the first Congress of People's Deputies convened under Gorbachev. And then the only reason it was done was fear of glasnost, whose spirit the new deputies were sure to bring with them.

My conversations in the lofty offices of the USSR Council of Ministers left me with a heavy heart. I realized that the delicate shoots of glasnost post-Chernobyl, sprouting in the wake of the Congress, would continue to be smothered for a long time to come. After all, no one was remotely interested in either the medical reports or the official documents I showed there. They had their own reports, the kind that made them feel comfortable. ("You have your documents," they told me, "and we have ours.") It was as if they were trying to mesmerize me with their mantra, "People's health is not in jeopardy." So the government's decision to have twelve villages in the Narodichi District resettled at once must have been taken precisely because the people's health was not in jeopardy. And they said that it was to be done immediately—three years after the accident.

On September 25, 1989, I sent a third question to the Soviet government about the whole picture of the radiation situation in the Zhitomir region, about the number of people marked down for resettlement, apart from the urgent evacuation of the said twelve villages. I also asked for additional amounts of "clean" food to be delivered to the contaminated areas. To the first two of my requests I received a reply from the chairman of the Zhitomir regional party committee, V. M. Yamchinsky! The government had instructed that man to reply to me. That beats anything for sheer hubris and cynicism! My "clean" food request yielded a note from the deputy chairman of the USSR Council of Ministers, Lev Alexandrovich Voronin—or rather a duplicate of his note. It was addressed to USSR trade minister Kondrat Terekh: "Please send a deputy minister to the Zhitomir region and, jointly with the

Ukrainian Council of Ministers, examine on-site the entire range of issues related to food provision for the residents of the radioactive disaster areas in the Zhitomir region. Report on the measures taken to people's deputy Comrade Yaroshinskaya before November 1 of this year, and to the USSR Council of Ministers." The same paper ordered my question to be sent to Ukrainian Council of Ministers chairman V. A. Masol and to V. V. Nikitin, chairman of the state committee for foodstuffs and procurement under the USSR Council of Ministers. I am still waiting for a reply from these worthies, twenty years on.

As for USSR deputy trade minister P. D. Kondratov, he sent me a classic travesty of a response, two weeks after the deadline specified in Voronin's letter. Instead of really trying to provide uncontaminated food for the region's residents, the deputy minister informed me of what deliveries the region had received in the past! In the final paragraph, he assured me that in 1990 the region's needs for canned baby food would be met in full—as if children fed exclusively on canned food would suffice. Enclosed was a list of foodstuffs supplied to the region in 1989. The deputy minister's reply spoke of the bureaucrat's total indifference to what the people's deputy had been writing about, imploring him to pay attention to the nuclear accident's victims and their children. As it turned out, the minister had no concern for the misery of citizens in his own country. With that worthless scrap of paper he brushed aside a mere people's deputy like a tiresome fly.

On August 10, 1989, the government commission for emergencies had yet another meeting in Narodichi with public representatives from contaminated areas. Against all the odds, the breakthrough toward glasnost on the part of Ukrainian and Belorussian deputies, the truthful articles that had by then appeared in the press, finally prodded the government into remembering its citizens in distress. The gathering was scheduled for eleven o'clock, but the hall of the district Palace of Culture was packed long before then. More people had assembled outside, where several loudspeakers had been installed. They were eagerly awaiting the arrival of government commission head V. Kh. Doguzhiev. What was he going to say? everybody wondered.

The commission was taking its time, raising the anxiety level of those in the hall. There were journalists from Zhitomir, Kiev, and Moscow, and lighting engineers from Ukraine's documentary film studio were putting up floodlights. Finally, a whisper swept across the rows that the helicopters had landed. Someone in the hall said that a take-off and landing strip had been expressly constructed nearby the day before. Waiting for the VIP visitors on the platform was a long table covered with a red cloth, and half a dozen chairs. But when the commission members started filing in through a side door and taking their places at the table, it turned out that the chairs were woefully short of demand. More chairs were promptly brought over and arranged in four rows, and still several of the newcomers had to take seats in the hall.

Presumably, the imposing turnout of officials was meant to imply extra solicitude for the disaster victims on the part of the government. However, not everyone in the hall was appreciative, and those on the platform were pelted with accusations and reproaches, which at times bordered on insult. I don't have it in me to censure those people. One can only sympathize with them. They had been cruelly deceived. Houses had been built for them on contaminated land, with gas and sewer facilities installed. In short, everything had been done to create an illusion of care and safe living. But it is not without reason that the popular saying goes thus: you can get anywhere in the world by deception, but you'll not come back. And that was exactly what happened on that occasion.

I had not planned to speak, but the audience demanded that I should. The meeting was chaired by V. N. Yamchinsky, head of the executive committee of the Zhitomir region's Soviet of People's Deputies. Next to him in the center sat Vasily M. Kavun, member of the Communist Party Central Committee and of the Ukrainian Communist Party Central Committee, twice Hero of Socialist Labor, holder of several Orders of Lenin, and first secretary of the regional party committee. When the meeting chairman announced the fact of his arrival, the audience booed. Someone yelled, "Well, at least he's come now—three years too late!"

As I spoke, I asked the first secretary a few questions: Why did the Narodichi children have to swallow radioactive dust and eat contaminated food for nearly a month? Why hadn't they been moved out of the area in time? Why hadn't he interrupted his vacation abroad and returned at once on hearing of the nuclear explosion to order the children to be moved out of the dangerous areas? Without him, the region's master, no one had ventured to do it. I also asked him who exactly had decided to build houses for the evacuees on radioactive soil, and why he, the first secretary, was saying that he had not seen the contamination map of the Narodichi District, if I, an ordinary journalist, had seen it at the regional executive committee.

The hall was seething. It must have been the first time V. M. Kavun was hearing such words about himself in public. He got up and, standing right where he was, started saying in a hushed voice that the decision on construction had been taken collectively, together with the government commission, that there had been no contamination maps, and that he had not known all the facts. When the explosion occurred, he was away and, it turned out, had not managed to "find transportation"; so he returned twelve days later, when construction had already begun without him. . . . The man was talking through his hat. Had his subordinates really failed to show the contamination map to the first secretary? Not likely. Or was that the way to cover his tracks? What the eye does not see, the heart does not get upset about. And who then was the liar—V. V. Maryin, that deputy chairman of the bureau for fuel and energy resources under the USSR Council of Ministers, who had explained in his reply to my inquiry that the decision on where to build houses for resettlement had been made exclusively by the local authorities? Or was first secretary of the Zhitomir Communist Party Committee, V. M. Kavun, a liar?

In the daily *Trud* of August 2, 1989, a piece entitled "The 'Strict Regimen' Villages" said the following:

> However, already the next spring the emergency commission of the USSR Council of Ministers, and regional executive committees of the Kiev and Zhitomir regions had at their disposal a detailed map of radioactive contamination in the northern areas of the Ukraine's Polesye. Marked on the map were the villages and fields where concentrations of health-destroying cesium-137 exceeded 40 to 100 curies (per sq km). It was clear then that people must not live and work there. Particularly not in the villages of Yasen and Shevchenkovo of the Polesye district in the Kiev region or in Lesser Minki, Shishalovka, Greater Kleshchi and Polesskoe of the Narodichi district in the Zhitomir region. Meanwhile, people are still living in those villages.

And lower down—

> However, even without the map officials at the regional civil defense HQ and the region leadership knew that on April 27–29, 1986, the gamma background level in the courtyard of the local district Party committee exceeded one roentgen per hour.

Let me explain. This is twenty times the amount that makes evacuation imperative!

When rereading a May 6, 1986, TASS report on the conference at the foreign ministry press center, I never tire of wondering at how they do it. The "comrades in authority" announced that "over the past day radiation levels have further gone down." B. Ye. Shcherbina, deputy chairman of the USSR Council of Ministers, informed those present that "increased radiation levels have been registered on the territory immediately bordering the accident site, where maximum radiation levels reached 10–15 mR/h. By May 5 (1986), radiation levels in these areas had decreased two to three times." Subsequently, according to official reports, those radiation levels continued to steadily diminish. At times it seemed to me that they disappeared altogether. Only why—the question keeps eating into my brain—three years after the accident, like a bolt out of the blue, is there suddenly a need to resettle people? Could it be that the "comrades in authority" were really unaware of the fact that in the town of Pripyat radiation in the streets kept at 0.5–1 R/h all day on April 26 and for several days afterwards? (See G. Medvedev, *The Chernobyl Notebook*.)

At that meeting in Narodichi, on August 10, 1989, when the entire government commission, headed by chairman V. Kh. Doguzhiev, arrived in the district, one of the speakers was deputy chairman of the Ukrainian Council of Ministers, Yevgeny V. Kachalovsky. It was impossible to listen to his remarks without feeling a deep sense of revulsion and utter disgust toward this man whose power was largely responsible for the suffering and death of our children. It was his boot heel, and those of other party leaders, that had left an indelible imprint on the hopes and dreams of our people.

For a start, Kachalovsky tried to shift the blame onto foreigners (I am quoting verbatim from a tape recording, leaving intact his style and phraseology): "And let me tell you, folks, it is no accident that foreigners are now begging to come over, for dollars, to study the knowledge we have gained in the matter, because . . ." His audience would have no more of that. Sheer blasphemy! To come to the worst hit district three years after the event and fail to find anything else to say than this nonsense! Only words of contrition, as well as concrete decisions about how these people were to live on, would have been right for the occasion. But the big boss never realized any of this. It just did not enter his thick skull. The audience was increasingly noisy, but he forged ahead, lecturing his audience on their lack of manners, without shame or any respect for good grammar or sense. The record speaks for itself:

> [Y]ou'd better behave, you lot. You don't want to listen, I can stop speaking. Now, shouting won't get you anywhere; this is not a fish market. You listen to me, now. If you don't like it, you can get the hell out. You don't fancy me speaking. I'll go back to my seat, and you come out here and speak yourselves! What's this buzz-buzz now? And yonder, there's a cheerleader, a woman by the mike, arms up—yell, then arms down—don't yell. It's wrong to create this atmosphere. What do you think you're doing?

Without doubting for a moment that he was infallible, that he had the right to talk in this manner to these deceived people, Kachalovsky went on to say this: "So we do not see an issue there that we then made the wrong decision and resettled as many as we did, the more so since it was the government commission that took decisions then, the Politburo of the CPSU Central Committee, the final decision, the numbers of people, was decided up there. We just sent in our proposals, though our proposals were cut down to a degree."

Kachalovsky read out a note someone had passed on to him from the audience:

> Our children were hit by the accident worse than any other children in the zone. They started moving our children out on May 24 and finished on June 9, 1986. The children spent the most dangerous days inside the zone and no one warned us of the danger. Who will be called to account for that?

No coherent answer was forthcoming.

Meanwhile, it was none other than Kachalovsky himself who was the Ukrainian head of the government commission for dealing with the accident at the Chernobyl Nuclear Power Plant. But it was not until Politburo members, chairman of the USSR Council of Ministers, Nikolai Ryzhkov, and Communist Party Central Committee secretary, Yegor Ligachev, arrived from Moscow in Chernobyl on May 2, 1986, that the Ukrainian leadership finally plucked up courage to visit the accident site and approach the reactor that radiated terror and death.

The audience asked Kachalovsky one more question, of a similar nature. "Why were our children moved out of the area later than children in Kiev, the Kiev region, than children in Belorussia, all of whom had been taken away in the first half of May 1986? Who personally took the decision on our district?" In reply they got more incoherent babble. Here is Kachalovsky's reply:

> I'll tell you that we were holding a May Day civil parade, and the whole Politburo was standing there. Our wives were standing there, our children and grandchildren, and some also asked this question in Kiev—who gave orders to hold the parade? There was no ban, and no one, not our scientists nor specialists, those comrades who eloquently spoke here three years later—a fireman comes when the house has burnt down. Look, comrades, what you have here. . . . A smart guy, that, and when he came yesterday before the fire, he did not know. Everyone is wise after the fire, so you see, you too could have been standing there then. . . . We did not know then yet . . . how it can . . . where that radiation was, in what amounts there was of it, you did not give any proposals, you did not come even half a year after the parade, only three years later, because, well, so that's how it happened with the parade then.

Listening to Kachalovsky's clumsy and incoherent oration, I recalled the events of a month earlier. On June 12, 1989, the first session of the USSR Supreme Soviet considered the candidacy of Yuri Izrael for the post of chairman of the state committee for hydrometeorology. Deputies from Ukraine and Belorussia asked Yuri Izrael the questions on Chernobyl that had already become a repetitive demand for answers. Why didn't anyone know of the radioactive contamination maps? Why was information absent about radiation levels? Who decided that the May Day civil parade throughout the republic should be held as usual? Why weren't the children moved out of Kiev in time? And many more issues that still await official response.

Then the Soviet parliament witnessed a veritable drama whose protagonists were Yuri Izrael, the weather committee chairman who sought reappointment; Valentina Semyonovna Shevchenko, member of the Ukrainian Communist Party Central Committee; and N. I. Ryzhkov, chairman of the USSR Council of Ministers and member of the CPSU Central Committee Politburo. The hot controversy unfolded in full view of the stunned people's deputies and the whole country (broadcast on live TV nationwide), ripping off the shroud of secrecy surrounding Chernobyl risks. As soon as Izrael, cornered by Shevchenko, started mentioning the names of the people he had sent information to since the first days of the accident, Shevchenko began flinging emotional accusations at Izrael, alleging that he and

Academician Ilyin had pronounced the radiation safe for residents in Kiev and the region, including children.

Shevchenko then addressed the hydrometeorology committee chairman from the parliament rostrum: "I'm sure you remember sitting across the table from me and my asking you how you would act if your own grandchildren were in Kiev. You did not answer. . . . Every other decision taken by the state commission was religiously carried out by Ukraine's political leadership that worked efficiently round the clock, taking absolutely every measure that was humanly possible and coordinating their actions with the political leadership of the country." So feeling that the day of retribution was nigh, they started betraying one another. Not just in any old place, either, but in parliament. Incidentally, Shevchenko was a USSR people's deputy precisely from the Kiev region, and the Chernobyl zone was her constituency. Here is what her voters wrote in a collective appeal to the USSR Supreme Soviet:

> We have our own deputy in the Supreme Soviet, Valentina Semyonovna Shevchenko, but she has not once come to communicate with us. Nor did we manage to meet her in Moscow. We notified her in advance that we were coming to meet her, but after waiting all day at 27, Kalinin Prospekt (the premises of Supreme Soviet committees) we discovered that she had gone to Kiev that very day. We no longer count on her for help.

At the conclusion of her rousing oration, without a word of repentance, Shevchenko announced, "In my view, Yuri Antonievich, holding as he does so high a post and being in charge of an extremely important section of work, would do well today to take a principled stand instead of compromise. And I will vote against your candidacy, Yuri Antonievich!" That statement was greeted with applause. Alas, the applause was for a person who bore quite a lot of the blame for the children's ruined health, for years of lying about the true state of affairs in contaminated areas, for the hush-up. (After the Soviet Union disintegrated, Ukraine's prosecutor general would find her guilty of all that, but there the matter would rest.) The whole thing looked too much like a farce.

After Shevchenko, the floor was given instantly, and out of turn, to Nikolai Ryzhkov, the USSR Council of Ministers chairman. Ryzhkov parried vigorously,

> There has been talk about the May 7 events. What Ukraine's Polit-
> buro did when in session I do not know. I was not there. But I do
> know that on the second of May I was in Kiev. On the second. Do
> you remember? Do you remember that the political leadership and
> I went to visit the zone? That was before May 7.

At the end of his emotional speech, Nikolai Ryzhkov declared himself firmly convinced that "he (Izrael) is not to be blamed for Chernobyl." I, and apparently other people's deputies, instantly wondered who
was. Whose fault was it then that information was withheld and that
the country was inundated with rumors? Who had given orders that
all information be classified? Finally, who would answer for the consequences of these secrets being withheld from the people? It turned
out that there were sick and deceived people, but no culprits. This is
the chief lesson of our entire history. Here, decisions had always been
taken by the Communist Party Central Committee, the Politburo, and
the person at the very top, yet no one would be called to account. And
if blame was placed, it was typically some small fry chosen to be the
scapegoat. Chernobyl fit the pattern and thus was no exception.

Some six years after the Chernobyl disaster, when the Soviet
Union had already collapsed, I managed to unearth a fair number of
top secret documents on Chernobyl issued by the Communist Party
Central Committee Politburo. Enclosed with the Politburo resolution
of May 22, 1986, that was marked "TOP SECRET" was an equally
secret memo by *Pravda* journalist Vladimir Gubarev. Here is what
he says, among other things:

> Within an hour of the accident, the radiation situation in the city
> was clear. No emergency measures had been provided for; people
> were at a loss. Under every instruction that had been in existence for
> 25 years, the decision to move people away from the risk zone rested
> with the local authorities. By the time the government commission
> arrived the entire population of the city could have been taken out of
> the affected area even on foot. But no one had the courage to assume
> responsibility.... The whole system of civil defense proved paralyzed.
> There were not even dosimeters in working order to be found.

In fact, this is a sentence passed on the local party elite, with
Ukraine's Communist Party first secretary, V. V. Shcherbitsky, and
Supreme Soviet chairperson Shevchenko at the head. But I ask the
reader to note that the journalist Gubarev does not report of this
criminal outrage on the pages of the main party daily. Instead, he

secretly informs the Central Committee. (The top secret Politburo resolution, with Gubarev's memo enclosed, bears the signature of Secretary General Mikhail Gorbachev.)

When I read that secret paper by journalist Gubarev, I saw why my article "By the Ravaged Nests," on similar outrage in Chernobyl zones, sent to *Pravda* had never been published. Gubarev had been the watchdog there. And such double-standard wizards (one thing for the newspaper, another for the Politburo) were ubiquitous then. In his report to the Central Committee the correspondent deplores the sluggishness of the local party authorities and, while he is at it, dispenses this advice: "Propaganda from abroad has had a powerful effect, but not one member of the republic's (Ukraine) leadership has appeared on the radio or television to say simple words to this effect. There are no grounds for panic and no threat to the health of children and adult residents." The journalist is telling scientists how they could have lied more artfully to keep the public happy!

Perestroika was well under way in the country by that time, at the very time these Chernobyl lies were being told. How could this be explained? How could these things go together?

Meanwhile, the discussion of Izrael's candidacy continued apace. Describing the incumbent's good sides, Academician Yablokov, people's deputy and deputy chairman of the committee for the environment, even cited the following unorthodox example of his unprecedented boldness:

> This is probably the first time you'll hear about this. The whale episode—three whales rescued near the Alaskan shores. Within three hours of a phone call from the American Greenpeace branch, our icebreakers, on orders from Izrael, changed course and sailed there to save the whales. Within three hours. The official decision by the government was not taken until three days later. I may be divulging a secret here. Perhaps Nikolai Ivanovich (USSR Council of Ministers chairman Ryzhkov) does not know that the icebreakers set off after three hours, three days before the government decision was taken. That was a risky thing to do, but done it was. The effect on the world public opinion, comrades, was incredible.

In saying these things in defense of Izrael, the people's deputy of the USSR apparently wished to sway the people's deputies' voting in his favor. The fact that he narrated there is unquestionably to Izrael's credit. Or it would have been, if there had not been the disgraceful Chernobyl page in that man's life. It is certainly exceedingly noble to save three whales, but what about thousands of children and adults whose health has been ruined? Yuri Izrael was elected to the high post of chairman of the USSR Committee on Hydrometeorology. Taking part in voting were 422 deputies; 294 voted in favor, 86 against, and 42 abstained.

Before announcing a break, first deputy chairman of the Supreme Soviet, Anatoly Lukyanov, gave three minutes to people's deputy S. N. Khajiev, director general of the R&D petrochemical association in the Chechen-Ingush Republic, to speak on their motivation for voting the way they had voted. His brief speech served as an epilogue to the drama that preceded the vote.

> So just now we approved Yuri Antonievich's appointment. . . . And we have effectively approved everything done to our people, our compatriots, our rivers, our lakes, our seas. We have okayed all that. He said, didn't he, that he had known what was going on, and we didn't, you and me. Speaking for myself, I learned the facts in 1988, but he had known them all along. And he thought it his duty to merely report things to his superiors. There he thought his duties ended, and we have just approved all that. . . . I don't know how you are going to look your voters in the eye. . . . So I for one think that we have actually forgotten our voters today, those millions of children who are ill because of the contaminated environment, those of our brothers and sisters who are in hospitals. We have forgotten them. We should have assessed the competence of Yuri Antonievich, but we should also have said, "Comrade Yuri Antonievich, you have no civic position; your heart does not bleed for our citizens. And has not bled throughout these fourteen years (of his previous work in that capacity), when you kept quiet [about disasters] and just reported things to your bosses."

But nothing could change the ignominious decision passed a minute earlier by the majority of the people's deputies in the tame USSR Supreme Soviet. (Remember my story about the way people's deputies in the Ukraine were appointed to the Soviet? The same thing happened in other republics as well.)

The militant if incoherent and inarticulate speech by deputy chairman of Ukrainian Council of Ministers and chairman of the government commission for Chernobyl accident elimination, Yevgeny V. Kachalovsky, at the meeting with Narodichi residents and bitter memories of the battle royal between party bosses in the country's parliament over disclaiming responsibility for the crime against Chernobyl victims did nothing to cheer me up.

7

The Cover-Up

The reader is already aware that one of the principal arias in the Soviet Chernobyl nuclear opera was performed by the USSR Goskomgidromet, an acronym that stands for the USSR State Committee for Hydrometeorology, which we will sometimes refer to here as simply the USSR weather committee. More specifically, the title role here was played by its chairman, Yuri Antonievich Izrael. His duties included reporting to the party and Soviet leadership of the country and its constituent republics how much of what the reactor's hellish crater had spewed out, where the wind had blown that stuff, and where it had fallen. In short, in this chapter, I will try to answer who Mr. Izrael reported to and, more to the point, what he was telling them. This is important for understanding the overall picture of the consequences of the disaster. Let us weigh the leaders who sat on the Chernobyl scale of injustice.

The first time the USSR people's deputies learned about some of the particulars was on June 24, 1989, when the Supreme Soviet committee for the environment discussed the candidacy of Izrael for chairmanship of the USSR State Hydrometeorology Committee. As he presented his program, Izrael tried to forestall awkward questions:

> I'll dwell on two issues in which we participated. The first such issue is our part in dealing with the accident at the Chernobyl nuclear power plant. There the committee was very active right after August 26, 1986. On the third or fourth day after the accident, there were already ten planes and helicopters working there. Every meteorological station in the country's European part was pressed into service. Over a thousand stations were involved. The data were *daily* [emphasis added] reported to the government commission stationed in Chernobyl and to the Politburo commission in Moscow. On the basis of that information, crucial decisions were taken.
>
> As you know, 116,000 people were evacuated. Subsequently, the health ministry and the state agricultural industry committee used the data, together with us, to calculate possible aftereffects. The

health ministry and the state agricultural industry committee took decisions on what was to be done in the contaminated areas.

Information about radioactive contamination was also reported regularly to the councils of ministers in the Union republics affected by the fallout, above all in Belorussia, the Ukraine, and the Bryansk region [of the Russian Federation], as well as to the relevant regional executive committees.

As for the data on the separate villages, I have all of them here in my folder, and they were passed on to councils of ministers and regional executive committees to keep the villagers informed. . . . Now I would absolutely like to assure those present that all the maps with a vast amount of data have been collected. All the relevant information, from May 1986 on, about radiation levels and about the isotope makeup—since June and July 1986—was reported to local authorities.

That was the first instance of an official forced to come up with confessions about where the readings on radiation levels and contamination maps had been forwarded. The next forced act of exposing those who had withheld the data they received from Izrael's organization was performed three weeks later, on July 12, 1989. This time it was in the hall where the session of the Supreme Soviet was held and where he again was nominated for the weather committee chairmanship on behalf of the Soviet government. On that occasion, Izrael, aware that he would have to bear the full brunt of the people's deputies' anger, was even more explicit: "Since the first day of the accident and to the present moment, the data were sent without fail to the Politburo commission headed by Nikolai Ivanovich Ryzhkov, to the government commission working in Chernobyl, to the CPSU Central Committee, to the councils of ministers in the Union republics, and to regional executive committees [of the relevant Soviets]. All of that information was available to the regional executive committees, and it must be made known to the residents."

In the lobby, some deputies demanded that a special parliamentary commission be set up to look into the causes of the Chernobyl accident and judge the actions of officials who had concealed the truth about the radiological situation for three years after the disaster. And the louder these demands grew, the more feasible it looked, the greater was the amount of information Izrael disclosed about the "efficiency" of the weather committee machine. Having started in 1989 with organizations and departments that received information since the first days after the accident, twelve months later, on April 12, 1990,

Izrael proceeded to divulge the names of the highest level officials. It was on that very day that the joint session of two USSR Supreme Soviet committees took place—the committees for the environment and for public health protection. It preceded the Chernobyl hearings in parliament.

Here is what Mr. Izrael said when the people's deputies demanded more of the truth: "On April 27, the State Committee for Hydrometeorology sent a report on the radiation situation in the Chernobyl accident area, complete with charts and inscription at the top 'To the CPSU Central Committee.' There were no specific names on the document. Is that clear?" In the perfect stillness, someone in the audience asked a very audible question: "Did you send it to the janitor, or what?" Izrael elucidated, "There is an accepted procedure. If I prepare a program on instructions from the Council of Ministers, I address it not to Comrade Ryzhkov, but to the USSR Council of Ministers. That's the form. Do you get my meaning or don't you?"

The minister was clearly nervous and annoyed. As well he might be. What was at stake was his cushy job, one that he had been doing for fourteen years and would dearly love to go on doing. That was the only reason why he fired a volley of dozens of VIP names—the recipients of classified information from day one. I am quoting from the official shorthand report on the hearings: "To the CPSU Central Committee and the Council of Ministers without names, on April 27 (here and further, 1986); on April 30, to Nikolai Ivanovich Ryzhkov; on May 3, to Nikolai Ivanovich Ryzhkov; on May 4, to Nikolai Ivanovich Ryzhkov; on May 7, to Murakhovsky—I am not naming the other ministries. On May 8, to Ryzhkov; on May 9, to Gusev, of the RSFSR Council of Ministers; on May 11, to Murakhovsky; on May 12, to Murakhovsky; on May 13, to Gusev; on May 15, to Kovalev; on May 18, to Shcherbina; on May 21, to Gorbachev; on May 21, to Ryzhkov; on May 27, to Kovalev; on May 24, to Murakhovsky; on May 26, to Ryzhkov, Ligachev, Dolgikh, Chebrikov, Vlasov, Sokolov, Vorotnikov, Murakhovsky, Shchepin. If necessary, I am willing to go on."

That was a day-by-day account. Meanwhile, there were also hour-by-hour accounts too. On the same night, at 3:00 a.m. (literally within an hour of the accident), V. V. Maryin was informed of the explosion. He was head of the nuclear power engineering sector at the CPSU Central Committee at the time. The same Maryin who was later given the chairmanship of the bureau for fuel and energy resources and who, you may recall, used to reply to me, a USSR people's deputy, that all was well in the Narodichi District and that I was making a fuss over nothing. All the persons named by Izrael were senior executives in the Soviet Union and Russian Federation governments, the KGB, members of the country's top political leadership—the CPSU Central Committee and the Politburo. As I listened to him in amazement, it dawned on me that it looked very much like a list of culprits guilty of concealing the truth about Chernobyl that the USSR prosecutor general's office should deal with at once. But this simple idea, it seemed, never occurred to the prosecutor general.

The more uncomfortable the people's deputies' questions got, the more names of various weather committee data recipients Izrael disclosed: ". . . here, if you please, to Sinegubov of the Tula regional executive committee, September 23, 1986." No less promptly, it transpired, the information had been supplied to the highest officials in the Ukraine and Belorussia. In a July 20, 1990 talk with USSR people's deputy Vitaly Chelyshev at the USSR Supreme Soviet committee for the environment, Izrael stated:

> Here we have assembled material for our Ukrainian and Belorussian branches—to whom, where, when, and which letters were written. Here you are—the Ukrainian folder . . . this sheet has records of which letter went to whom. To the Ukrainian Communist Party Central Committee, to the Council of Ministers, to the Supreme Soviet, to the Ukrainian KGB. Later a task group was set up in the Ukraine, and then we started forwarding information to them too, regularly, and to the civil defense headquarters that had joined in. Also the various departments, naturally. See? Ukraine's Academy of Sciences, Ukraine's health ministry, etc. Besides, these maps were sent to regional executive committees [of the relevant Soviets] or to party committees. We made no distinction between them at the time. We sent all the information we had to the councils of ministers in the Ukraine and Belorussia, and somewhat later—to the Russian Federation's Council of Ministers. On April 26, 1986—to the Ukrainian Communist Party Central Committee, to first secretary V. V. Shcherbitsky, to Central Committee Secretary Kachura, to V. S. Shevchenko, the chairperson of Ukraine's Supreme Soviet and member of the Ukrainian Communist Party Central Committee Politburo, and also to Bakhtin, to the Ukrainian Council of Ministers, to Lyashko, Boiko, Kachalovsky, Kolomiets. The documents forwarded to them said that on April 30, 1986, radiation levels in Kiev had shot up. For instance, on Prospekt Nauki they were known to have varied from 2.2 mR/hr (maximum) to 1.4 mR/hr (minimum). By nightfall, they had gone down.

Izrael explained further:

> On May 1, 0.62 mR/hr; on May 2, 0.85 mR/hr; on May 7, 0.7 mR/hr, etc. From then on it's been steadily downward. On the thirtieth [April, 1986], though, there was a sharp rise in radiation levels precisely at 13:00.

They had known it all. And knowing it all, they lied. Each at his or her level.

> We also sent this information to the Central Committee of the Ukrainian Communist Party and to Ukraine's Council of Ministers. And our information was available to the leadership . . . It was forwarded to Shcherbitsky and to Shevchenko . . . to several Central Committee secretaries.

And yet, the (Ukrainian) republic's leadership resolved to hold a May Day civil parade in Kiev—making merry under radioactive fallout. They invited children's song and dance groups there. Among the festive crowds filing past the stand were schoolchildren carrying flags, banners, flowers, and balloons. As for their own grandchildren, the party bosses had taken care to instantly pack them off to safety. This fact journalist Gubarev reported in his secret memo that reached Gorbachev and was added to the top-secret minutes of a Politburo session on May 22, 1986. Among other things, Gubarev had written, "The 'reticence' of the republic's leadership, however, rekindled the panic, particularly when it became known that the children and family members of the party functionaries were leaving the city. The ticket offices of the Ukrainian Communist Party Central Committee were stormed by a crowd a thousand strong."

Today, decades later, when the Soviet Union is no more, along with the Soviets and the CPSU Central Committee that were responsible for keeping millions of people ignorant of the danger and thus ruining their health, many of the former functionaries still move from one cushy job to another. They still occupy posts of importance—ministers and deputy ministers, members of republics' parliaments, party leaders, and heads of state corporations. Some have gone into well-earned retirement, as the Soviet cliché has it, and are drawing fabulous exclusive pensions (to say nothing of the fact that they all have been issued Chernobyl Accident Fighter cards and are now enjoying the attendant set of benefits). As ex-first secretary of the Zhitomir regional party committee, there is V. M. Kavun, to name just one. Almost as soon as

I managed to unseat him by my critical articles in the national press, the Communist Party transferred him from Zhitomir to Kiev, where he was promptly given an apartment at state expense and a special extra-large retirement pension. Incidentally, I learned this likewise in total confidence from N. I. Ignatovich, an investigator of cases of special importance (later he would be murdered in Belorussia under suspicious circumstances).

He told me what trouble his commission had trying to get the Council of Ministers to cough up the list of Union-level, special-category retirees. Apparently, with a 250-ruble maximum for ordinary mortals' pensions and a 300-ruble maximum for the military, there are also super-special pensions, presumably for some altogether outstanding merits. These came up to 500 and even 700 rubles. Among the names on the list of such pensioners was Kavun, holder of five Orders of Lenin, Orders of the Red Labor Banner, and of Friendship among Peoples Order, as well as of countless medals and various badges, including Hero of Socialist Labor. Incidentally, he got his fifth Order of Lenin two years after the nuclear accident. It looks like the Kremlin rewarded him for keeping mum about Chernobyl. After all, as chairman of the Zhitomir regional executive committee, A. S. Malinovsky wrote in reply to my deputy's inquiry, from the first days after the Chernobyl accident, a network of monitoring and laboratory control facilities was set up by the regional civil defense bodies to observe the radiation situation in residential localities in northern districts. The first data on the gamma radiation dosage rates in various localities started coming in to the regional executive committee from the civil defense headquarters on April 28, 1986 (and from Narodichi, on April 26). From the moment of the accident and throughout 1986–87, information about the radioactive contamination of individual localities, above all in the Narodichi, Ovruch, and Luginy districts, was sent by special delivery from superior bodies of the republic and were then returned. The Ukrainian committee for hydrometeorology kept forwarding research findings to the region's authorities since May 1988.

This is also confirmed by a reply to my question, asked in my capacity as people's deputy, from S. A. Lyashchenko, head of the radiology department of Ukraine's state committee for agricultural industry— "The Ukrainian state committee for agricultural industry forwarded the general report [on the degree of radionuclide contamination] to the Zhitomir regional executive committee on September 12, 1986, memo number 1231-C. In May 1987 . . . after repeat radiochemical analyses, the report was sent to the Zhitomir regional committee for agricultural industry on August 1, 1987, memo number 1319-C." So didn't the region's boss, the first secretary of the party, know that?

Another such special pensioner was first secretary of Ukraine's Communist Party Central Committee, Shcherbitsky. Now deceased, he shot himself on his birthday because none of his former party pals came to him to congratulate him on the event. Stripped of the "first secretary" title, he proved useless and unwanted. One more exclusive pensioner of the same sort is ex-chairperson of Ukraine's Supreme Soviet Presidium, Shevchenko. And V. A. Ivashko, who was then first secretary of the Ukrainian Communist Party Central Committee, moved to Moscow on orders from the then CPSU Central Committee General Secretary Mikhail Gorbachev to take the latter's place. In 1995, Chernobyl caught up with Ivashko too. He died of thyroid cancer.

Among other ex-leaders rewarded with higher posts were some at the regional level. G. A. Gotovchits, deputy chairman of the Zhitomir regional executive committee, went to head the ministry for Chernobyl affairs in the Ukrainian government. (He, too, died a few years ago.) Yu. P. Spizhenko, former head of the public health department at the regional executive committee, became health minister of Ukraine and eventually worked his way into parliament. And—amazing as it seems, dear reader—actually spent some time as chairman of the All-Ukraine Chernobyl Party for Welfare and Social Protection! Nor was A. Ye. Romanenko left in the lurch. The ex-health minister of Ukraine had staunchly kept silent during the first days after the accident, but then kept lying his head off. Owing to his criminal inaction, tens of thousands of people in Ukraine's affected areas now have severe health problems. Well, he became head of the radiation medicine center and afterwards was appointed director general of the radiation medicine research center of Ukraine's Academy of Medical Sciences. To cap it off, he was also made chairman of the commission for the health effects of the Chernobyl nuclear accident (another classic case of the fox guarding the henhouse, a common occurrence in these parts).

I was invited to participate in a talk show on Kiev television com-memorating the eighteenth anniversary of the Chernobyl explosion and discovered, much to my surprise, that the journalists of the private 1+1 TV channel in Kiev who anchored the *Double Proof* program had made some footage of Romanenko, where he acted no longer as the Chernobyl health information censor but quite the reverse—as a chief expert. There he was, confident and relaxed, telling us what had happened and what and how it should have been done! Unfortunately, the program never aired, as its editor, Vakhtang Kipiani explained, not very coherently, for a purely technical reason. But I am certain the reason was different. It must have been my severe criticism during the program recording of the incompetent anchors who simply did not know the first thing about Chernobyl and of the Ukrainian authorities who had done precious little for its victims in the years of independence. Then, after the program was recorded, it transpired that, "purely by accident," the same team recorded another program over it. Astonishing, this brand of journalism! And yes, they still call themselves "journalists."

All the Chernobyl antiheroes at first doggedly assured society and the world that "the children's health was in no way at risk," then complained that they "had no information and did not know the facts," and so on. Now they seem to be laboring under the delusion, judging by ex-minister Romanenko's smug haranguing, that much of their Chernobyl "heroism" has been forgotten and it is time to don white robes again. It has not!

When people's deputies asked Izrael about the May Day civil parade in Kiev in the wake of the explosion, Izrael said firmly, "I've said it before, and I'll say it again. Neither I, personally, nor a single member of the state committee for hydrometeorology took part in discussing the issue and did not know whether the parade was to be held."

Another three months later, on July 20, 1990, Izrael had one more talk with people's deputies and experts at the committee for the environment and continued his good work of declassifying, down-to-the-minute details on virtually every radioactive cloud released in the atmosphere, when and where it had drifted, who had been informed of the fact, and which documents had been presented:

> Here on this map are shown the main particulars . . . Yes, if we wish to be accurate, this is the authentic map. All authentic, accurate maps, or rather charts, we sent to the Central Committee and to the Council of Ministers . . . Surveys were made on a daily basis. Within three or four days, we already had eight planes and helicopters that measured both the overall gamma radiation, the dosage rates, and the gamma radiation spectrum. But the main thing was that we could already draw curves at ground level. This one is a unique map that was made at ground surface level, unaffected by atmospheric pollution . . . Next I would like to show you one of the maps that

was sent to the government commission. I have one left by chance, because Silaev, who succeeded Shcherbina as head of the commission . . . this is Silaev's hand—a souvenir map.

I have been showing here the very first maps. I began by displaying the charts that were presented to the leadership on the twenty-seventh [of April 1986]. Here, it was still difficult to distinguish between the mainstream effects and what was forming at surface level. We used aviation as our tool. This one here is probably the first plume. This is a surviving rough draft of May 1. It includes data from a whole series of planes and helicopters. I also showed the map that was *daily* [my italics] sent to the government commission. This map here is the most interesting . . . This one is very important. It did indeed play a serious role. It was made in early May. It was used since May 4, when the thirty-kilometer zone was being evacuated, and the map was readjusted till May 10 or thereabouts. After that, we released it. Here are the maps, dates, and figures. This is the November account.

We have two big folders with our daily reports. We wrote reports every day. Where they were sent I am going to say in a minute . . . and taking part in the work were the ministry of defense, the health ministry, the USSR Academy of Sciences, the Belorussian Academy of Sciences, the Ukrainian Academy of Sciences, the agricultural industry committee, the ministry of medium engineering industry [code name for the nuclear ministry] . . . The military reported through their own channels, including to the Politburo. The chemical warfare force kept up continuous reporting on the immediate zone.

Because I was in Chernobyl and in Kiev, I regularly cabled Ryzhkov (every other day) and CPSU Central Committee Secretary Dolgikh, but more rarely. I sent telegrams to Ryzhkov more often.

Finally, Izrael passed on the list to the Politburo task group and to the government commission, this time naming all the names:

> We reported to the Politburo task group. But that was in late July. There were three memos from each of the councils of ministers, I emphasize. The Council of Ministers worked on its own through its channels with regional executive committees in the Ukraine, in Belorussia, and in Russia. The Politburo group was headed by Ryzhkov, and its name was given as a task group . . . That commission sat extremely often and efficiently. In May, it sat, well, let me see, at least every other day, I suppose. Then the intervals lengthened a little. The government commission was headed by deputy chairmen of the Council of Ministers. The first one was Shcherbina, the second, Silaev, the third, Voronin, the fourth, Maslyukov, the fifth, Gusev, the sixth, Vedernikov, the seventh, Shcherbina.

They had known everything, all right. Everything! Why was the commission chairmanship taken in rotation? I think it was done to have all of them bound by collective responsibility for the cover-up. Izrael was trying hard to prove that he had been up to his job, that he was blameless, and that it was not his job to make the information public. This is what he said over and over again with minor alterations when answering questions.

> As for official information, we indeed supplied the councils of ministers with all the facts. And talking of regional committees, we sent those data to the Gomel Regional Party Committee. The Gomel committee, incidentally, was the most active of all. We sent the data to Mogilev [region's party committee]. I have that information. I even have the map. It is another matter that the isotope makeup, as such, reached them a bit later. They sent it out, and I have proof of that, even to district party committees, to district executive committees. They sent the lot . . .

One of the USSR People's Deputies asked the crucial question, "If everything had been so well-known from the first hours and days, why hadn't the public been informed?" Izrael countered, without batting an eyelid, "You go ask this of the republics' councils of ministers. Because our duty is to inform the leadership, which will then hand it down." Translated from officialese into plain-speak, this means roughly, "I see that my neighbor's house is on fire, and there are people asleep inside. I can dial 01, but whether or not this will fetch a fire brigade is none of my business. And don't expect me to rush over with a bucket of water to douse the flames. One may get burnt, you know." Charity begins at home.

I. N. Smolyar, at that time chairman of the commission for eliminating the consequences of the Chernobyl accident at the Belorussian Supreme Soviet, observed with reason, "You can talk a lot of the *top secret* mark and so on, but there is also your personal stand as a citizen . . . Why did not one member of the government commission that left for Chernobyl on April 27 appear on television to explain in so many words how things were?" Throughout the hearings and debates, Izrael seemed utterly unable to grasp what those malevolent people's deputies had against him. He could not (or would not) understand the simple truth that every conscientious person takes for granted. Warn about the danger! You knew, didn't you? You reported to your superiors. You knew that they were supposed to make the information public but did not. You realized how that jeopardized children's health. We did not know—because he did. And so did *they*. They knew and, criminally, kept silent. He knew and said nothing. For three years, he reported the facts to the people at the top without fail. He was awarded the Order of Lenin for Chernobyl.

He is a good man, is Izrael. He saved three whales—remember? Without authorization from the government, at that! Thank God for that! Otherwise, what would the world be thinking of us?

8

Byzantium in the Kremlin

"The children's health is at no risk whatsoever!" I have heard any number of times these comforting incantations in reference to Chernobyl victims that people in all kinds of jobs kept uttering by reflex. Most often these words came from high-ranking pro-Kremlin medicos as they attempted to damp down the mounting anxiety and apprehension. Every year since the accident this same phrase was repeated—on the radio and TV, newspapers, and magazines. But to those who even now live under the radioactive cloud, these words mean just one thing—undisguised mockery of themselves and their sickly children.

The reason for the growing skepticism can be readily understood when, in a single post-Chernobyl year, the official Soviet medical establishment, the USSR Ministry of Health headed by the academician Yevgeni Chazov, officially revised the human tolerance dose of radioactivity three times! Immediately after the accident, it was 70 rem over seventy years of life, then 50, and finally, 35 from 1987 to the present day. Meanwhile, prior to Chernobyl, it had been a mere 25 rem (rem, an acronym for Roentgen equivalent man). Translated from the language of physics into plain everyday terms, this norm means the maximum acceptable risk level beyond which human health will be impaired. Knowing the environment pollution levels and the radiation background, it is perfectly possible to calculate how long it will be before a person absorbs a critical dose (with one caveat from recent studies—there is no safe dose). Unlike chemicals, radiation, even at very low doses, is measurable. Therefore, it is possible to say which areas are dangerous for human habitation so that people can be moved out of them to an uncontaminated environment. This is a very serious and important index for human beings. So the flippant juggling with this hazardous or possibly fatal "safe" level is more than astonishing—it is alarming, or even criminal! Well then, was that figure research-based or off the top of some Russian medical mandarin's head?

The unscientific, arrogant, and highly subjective selection of the 35-rem exposure level in the Soviet Union is rightly attributed to Dr. and Academician L. A. Ilyin, the former head of the National Commission for Radiological Protection at the USSR Health Ministry. Anyone, including physicians, academics, and journalists, who dares question an official dictum is immediately branded "incompetent" or worse—"an enemy of the state" or "traitor." As for those who now suffer from one of the many radiation-induced diseases, they are accused of having a bad case of "radiophobia"—it's all in your head!

Here is what Ilyin announced to the media at a theoretical workshop, "The Medical Aspects of the Chernobyl Accident," that took place in Kiev in May 1988:

> We all must share the blame for the radiophobia syndrome. I would single out two aspects there—the overwhelming ignorance of the public in matters of radiation protection and the irrepressible desire of journalists to focus on the issues that never fail to excite excessive morbid interest of the man in the street.

Odd, to say the least. In the spring of 1988, when Ilyin was hurling his accusations at the media, journalists did not have a ghost of a chance to publish their impressions of life in affected areas as that subject was strictly taboo. And the medical community, including Ilyin, personally, did its part to conceal information about the health effects of the deadly exposures. At this point one feels tempted to remind the doctors who zealously carried out their bosses' orders that they had once taken the Hippocratic oath. But it would be no good in this particular instance, I am afraid, for they had long forgotten its mandate "to first, do no harm." That is item one. And item two. How can the man in the street be blamed for showing a "morbid interest" in his children's health, particularly if his child has been stricken with some rare disease?

Ilyin shouldn't have reproached *all* journalists in that wholesale fashion. After all, the closing sentence in a report about the conference entitled "Rumors...," penned by two journalists of the country's number one Communist daily, *Pravda*, gave us the official party line. "The assault on radiophobia is gathering pace." One of the journalists was Mikhail Odinets, *Pravda*'s special correspondent for Ukraine, the same Odinets who had phoned me to say that his newspaper would not publish my article. Later, right after the Soviet Union's disintegration, he printed a vitriolic piece about me—to add insult to injury, apparently. It was called "Presidential Ambitions." Just then Ukraine was witnessing its first ever presidential election campaign, and had I decided to run, I would have stood a pretty good chance of winning. But Providence decreed otherwise. The candidate on the democratic ticket was Vyacheslav Chornovil, a political prisoner of the Soviet Gulag of many years' standing, and he asked me to join his campaign headquarters. I could not refuse him. Unfortunately, for a number of reasons, Chornovil lost to ex-party secretary Leonid Kravchuk. The people elected as their first president a man who had for years stifled every sign of justice for all with party dogmas. That this should have happened is a mystery to me. As for Chornovil, he met with a fatal road accident some years later, under very strange circumstances. His son Taras, member of Ukraine's Supreme Rada (parliament), does not doubt that his father was assassinated. But that is a matter for a different investigation.

On October 19, 1989, at public hearings in USSR Supreme Soviet committees, Ilyin kept assuring the audience, "Thirty-five rem is not a dangerous level; it is one at which people in charge should begin to take decisions." Ilyin's view was shared and endorsed by his Moscow colleagues V. A. Knizhnikov, A. K. Guskova, Ye. I. Chazov, a group of Ukrainian scientists comprising I. A. Bebeshko, V. G. Likhtarev, A. V. Romanenko, the Ukrainian health minister, and others. It was that circle of Kremlin court physicians, whose 35-rem-over-70-years idea was used as the basis for crucial government decisions, that should now feel the weight of responsibility for those who, over a period of four long years, until glasnost had triumphed, went on living in contaminated areas. They are responsible for the plight of those children who within two years absorbed, in one short period, from 120 to 500 rem. It is those medical authorities, together with the Soviet Union's and the constituent republics' governments' political leadership, who should answer the question asked by anguished and heartsick mothers and disabled liquidators[1] of the disaster's consequences at all the meetings, rallies, and strikes that still convulse radiation-affected areas: Why?

---

[1] The term "liquidator" is used here and throughout the text for those servicemen and civilians who were mobilized to eliminate the consequences of the Chernobyl disaster. This usage appears to have been established in the relevant literature.—S.R.

At one such meeting in Narodichi Prof. V. A. Knizhnikov, laboratory head at the Biophysics Institute of the USSR Academy of Medical Sciences, said in all seriousness, "Nowhere in the world have scientists recorded a rise in the frequency of genetic disorders or cancer incidence at doses of 100 or 50 rem while exploring the consequences of radiation exposure. Not in Hiroshima, not in Nagasaki, nor yet in this country after the 1957 accident in the Urals, where the average dose was 52 rem, nor from the data on other population groups, such as miners, x-ray doctors, etc." This was countered with a resentful shout from the audience: "What's Hiroshima got to do with it if we had different kinds of radionuclides falling out?" The professor promptly parried, "Well, if old wives' tales are what really interests you . . ." But "old wives' tales" were precisely what did not interest the people angry at years of deception. Therefore, the audience clapped Prof. Knizhnikov into silence.

Indeed, are these comparisons legitimate? The A-bomb dropped on Hiroshima weighed a mere (if *mere* is the word) 4.5 metric tons. Let me remind the reader that unit 4 of the Chernobyl Nuclear Power Plant released into the atmosphere, in the form of tiny dispersed particles, all of 50 (!) tons of uranium dioxide, highly radioactive nuclides of iodine-131, plutonium-239, neptunium-139, cesium-137, strontium-90, and lots of other radioisotopes with varying half-life periods, plus some 70 tons of fuel emitted from the peripheral areas of the fissile core. Add to this nearly 700 tons of radioactive Chernobyl graphite scattered about the wretched reactor. Chernobyl equals three hundred Hiroshimas in terms of long-living cesium-137 alone that was thrown outside the reactor.

Didn't the venerable scholar know all that?

However, facts notwithstanding, the official medical establishment stuck to its guns, coming up with more new props for its stand. One of the "arguments" Prof. Knizhnikov put forward at the same Narodichi meeting was this. "In Argentina the government has approved the dosage of 100 rem over 20 years." So what? Apparently, people were supposed to draw comfort from this piece of news. One might think that it was in Argentina, not in this country, that people still lived in the midst of the aftermath of Europe's local nuclear war. In fact, this is exactly what Chernobyl is in terms of sheer scale. And that was how Central Committee members referred to the disaster at their exclusive get-togethers, as I managed to find out a couple of years after the meeting (I'll say more about that later). Chernobyl is simply beyond any comparison. It absolutely cannot be measured against Argentina or Hiroshima or the Urals. Could it be that they failed to see that—Profs. Knizhnikov and Ilyin and Guskova and Chazov, and a host of other professors?

The ordinary man in the street would like to know what the 35-rem dose might mean for his child's health. Is it too much, is it a minor dose, or is it just right? We want to know this because we no longer take for granted the word of the people who have for years deceived us and go on pulling the wool over our eyes. It was the "illuminati" who had assured us that "the children's health was not at risk," when suddenly, well into the fourth year after the accident, it turned out that dozens of villages had to be urgently evacuated. Was it because the villagers' health "was not at risk"? Given all that, can I trust those Kremlin court physicians and my government that sanctioned this deception, no less global than the disaster itself?

Let us open one of the most respectable information sources in this country—the Greater Soviet Encyclopedia. And here it is. "DOSE. The dose equivalent to 5 rem per year is considered to be the maximum permissible one in occupational exposure." Brief and utterly clear—even for the man in the street. So the residents in twelve Narodichi villages, in just one region, lived for over three years in total ignorance of the facts, in the kind of environment faced by the nuclear power plant's staff! And that, let me note, without any extra perks that such professionals would be entitled to, including long vacations, early retirement, medical checkups, free medical treatment and recuperation.

But let us go back to the speech delivered by Prof. Knizhnikov in front of the Chernobyl victims. "In the case of repeated exposure at 25 rem and less, some of the more sensitive persons can react with transient blood changes that will clear in three or four weeks. No health damage ensues," was his outrageous claim. Now let us read a little further from the Greater Soviet Encyclopedia: "The minimum dose of gamma radiation causing suppression of mitosis in some cells after a single exposure is 5 rem. Exposure to a daily dose of 0.02–0.05 rem continuing for a long time causes incipient blood changes, while a dose of 0.11 rem provokes tumor growth (You won't find these very low dose estimates in any official U.S. documents—Eds). Remote consequences of exposure to radiation are judged by increased incidence of mutations in the progeny." What is it about this statement that is not clear to the professor, who will take even 25 rem in his stride (not for himself, though, but for others)?

Alas, those remote consequences are already beginning to be felt. Over the last few years the number of malformed animals born on Narodichi farms has gone up sharply. Three years after the blast, 119 mutant piglets and 37 mutant calves were born in the countryside. Some lack limbs, others eyes, ribs, or ears, while others have deformed skulls. One of the farms witnessed the birth of an eight-legged foal. Its frightening photograph was printed by most of the world's papers. All those monsters were on display, preserved in alcohol in the special lab in my native city of Zhitomir. And the Oscar-winning 2002 documentary by Adi Roshe, *Chernobyl Heart,* leaves no hope even to the most passionate advocates of the Chernobyl nuclear benefits. I watched it in the packed hall of the UN General Assembly, every one of us in tears.

Let me cite two more very important conclusions made by scholars: "It may be pertinent to point out that in accordance with the linear no-threshold theory, the risk of remote radiological consequences can be present, however small the dosage." And here is the second: "Assuming the 2.15-rem dosage rate as the basis for calculating remote consequences of global fallout, the incidence of lethal tumors in the planet's population caused by the 2.15 rem exposure over 20 years per average human in the wake of a nuclear disaster would amount to 1,200,000, while the genetic defect total would be 380,000."

Some forecast, that! And who may the doomsayer be? Would you believe it, I have found all that in books by the same professors—Chazov, Ilyin, and Guskova. The titles of those learned treatises are *The Danger of Nuclear Warfare* and *Nuclear War: Medical and Biological Consequences.* So what's the problem here? The thing is that the books were written in 1982 and 1984 respectively—that is, before the Chernobyl era. Who could have thought then that all these risks would have to be applied to the nuclear victims in their own country?

So when were they honest? When writing their scholarly monographs a few years before the nuclear disaster in Ukraine, or after it, when they (and society at large) experienced unprecedented ideological pressure? We had to prove to those bloody imperialists, with some help from such scientists, that even a nuclear reactor meltdown in this country was the best in the world—without casualties or tragic consequences. I do not doubt for a moment, though, that several years before the accident those academic luminaries had justly cautioned the world, citing in their works scientifically, not ideologically, grounded data on acceptable risks and potential nuclear victims. As the same academicians rightly observed in their pre-Chernobyl books, according to the no-threshold theory, health might be impaired however small the radiation dosage. This I will discuss later, in a separate chapter.

After the Chernobyl disaster, Ilyin adduced the following arguments, not exactly scientific, in support of the half-baked 35-rem-in-70-years theory: "The issue of resettling hundreds of villages is a complicated act involving disruption of the accustomed way of life, when people will be deprived of the comfort they are used to." So let them live on in clouds of radiation—that must have been the implication. In her article "Outrage" published in the *Soviet Culture* weekly on November 18, 1989, prominent filmmaker Gemma Firsova, winner of the State Award and member of the state Chernobyl commission, quite reasonably asked what sort of comfort did the academician mean exactly, the thirty rubles of "coffin money"? Or the "dirty" milk that was more like liquid radioactive waste? Perhaps he was referring to the children's long-term illnesses. Was it not in compliance with the first edition of the Ilyin theory that kept the children in Kiev until two weeks after the accident, although it is now common knowledge that the city became one huge x-ray room precisely in those first days of May?

Yu. A. Izrael:

> On May 7 the Politburo of the Ukrainian Communist Party Central Committee convened an emergency session where I was invited as one of the experts, together with Academician Ilyin, and one more person from the Biophysics Institute, I cannot quite recall his name now, I'll check it later. At first we were asked to give our views on evacuating Kiev because some of the residents had already started to leave the city of their own accord. Not only children [were being moved out of the city] but adults, too, were leaving. The ticket offices were overcrowded. And I am not sure, but I suppose the mass exodus had prompted the Politburo to consider the matter. They consulted Ilyin and me. I said I could give information about the levels of radioactive contamination (which I did). Ilyin and I compared the dosages to the established evacuation criteria. As experts, we concluded that there was no reason to evacuate the Kiev population, given the radiation levels [at the time]. . . . And when [First Secretary of the Ukrainian Communist Party] Shcherbitsky told us to "put it down in writing," we sat down there and then and wrote for several hours. We were aware of fulfilling a responsible duty in our capacity as experts. We did it, we wrote the lot and Shcherbitsky put the document in the safe and locked it. . . . Very well, they said. So they made up their minds, they accepted the verdict of two experts, whatever it was. The decision to evacuate the city was not taken.

> I understand that if the leadership considered a decision inadequate or questionable, they could have called in experts in any other or the same field, from Kiev or from another part of the Ukraine (I am still wondering why they didn't do so, incidentally). Nevertheless, that was the decision they did take.

Those were the fatal conclusions of Ilyin and Yu. A. Izrael that are now used as a shield to protect the (already former) authorities in Ukraine: "The radiation situation in Kiev and the Kiev region (most particularly in the region!) does not currently constitute a health hazard for the residents, children included. It is within the normal limits recommended by the national and international, IAEA standards in case of an accident at the Chernobyl plant." And here are the recommendations of the two luminaries. "Analysis of the Kiev radioactive situation suggests an absence of indications at present for moving the people, including children, to other areas." Apparently, precisely because the "indications were absent," the authorities that very day decided, two weeks too late, to move Kiev's children of pre-school age out of the city, away from the dangerous place, starting from May 8. As for schoolchildren, they went on attending classes until May 15. Only then were they sent away to holiday homes, children's summer camps, and boardinghouses in resort areas—and not all of them, either, but only the under-fifteens. High-school students remained at home, to continue filling their livers with radioactive cesium and their bones with radioactive strontium, to add to the first radiation strike and the march through the May Day x-ray room in Kiev's main thoroughfare, Kreshchatyk Street.

After speeches of people's deputies at the congresses and Supreme Soviet sessions, after the first articles in the press telling the truth about the appalling examples of the state's indifference to millions of human lives, it became abundantly clear that Chernobyl was assuming far greater dimensions than a mere environmental problem. Chernobyl became a species of barometer gauging the intentions of the new leadership headed by Gorbachev. And when the lies about the disaster and the people hit by it exceeded all conceivable limits, Chernobyl buried the entire country, along with perestroika and the chief perestroika maker. It was obvious that Ukraine and Belorussia could not tame the nuclear ogre unaided. They quite simply did not have the money for that. Besides, the gap between what academicians in Moscow were saying and the reality in the affected areas became an ever-widening chasm.

In the spring of 1990, at the second Congress of the USSR People's Deputies, when the government program of reviving the Soviet economy was discussed, the democrats crossed swords with the partocrats so that sparks flew. As we were trying to get it approved or discarded, I found myself in a quandary. On the one hand, it was obvious to me that the Ryzhkov government's program in its present form would merely prolong the agony of our chronically ailing economy. But on the other, it was equally obvious that even if I voted against, the Congress would approve it anyway, and by a vast majority. Given the balance of forces among the deputies, it was as inevitable as sunrise. Meanwhile we, the people's deputies from the Ukraine and Belorussia, set great store by convincing Gorbachev and the Congress that it was essential to adopt a national program of dealing with the frightful consequences of the Chernobyl accident, even if it was three years later. We continued to be plagued by a shortage of building materials and money, but our overriding concern was always for our health and safety. Even the instant resettlement of those who were still suffering in the radioactive hell as prescribed by official Soviet medicine did little to allay our fears. We all felt vulnerable and powerless, trapped in the vortex of the unyielding machinery of the state.

For the sake of our fellow citizens and their children, I had to make a difficult compromise. Since the economic development program proposed by the government was bound to be approved by a majority vote anyway, I had no alternative but to accept it. I could then demand that the deputies add to it a national Chernobyl program as a special item. That was the only sensible decision. And that was the message of my appeal to the Congress from its main rostrum in the Kremlin. Other Ukrainian and Belorussian deputies who spoke at the Congress also backed my suggestion. And we had our way. The Congress included an entry to that effect in its resolution. A state expert commission was set up under Gosplan, the USSR State Planning Committee, to examine the state programs for eliminating the consequences of the Chernobyl nuclear disaster for the period between 1990 and 1995 in the Russian Federation, the Ukrainian Soviet Socialist Republic, and the Belorussian Soviet Socialist Republic. The person appointed to head the commission was Nikita Moiseev, a prominent academician and author of the "nuclear winter" theory. After years of the people and the government talking at cross-purposes, that was the first public expert examination of the Chernobyl aftereffects on a state level.

The expert commission comprised scholars of experience—scientists from the USSR Academy of Sciences, Moscow State University, staff members at research centers in Ukraine and Belorussia, sociologists, psychologists, lawyers, specialists in transport, communications, and public utilities, and in agriculture. Among the many working groups within the expert commission, there was also a group of public associations and people's movements, an absolute first at the time. The state commission also included nearly hundred experts, as well as several people's deputies, including me. Almost half of them had already busied themselves with Chernobyl issues, in one way or another; many had been to the affected areas and conducted their own research. All of that proved to be useful in our deliberations.

I worked on the commission headed by A. G. Nazarov, doctor of biology, deputy chairman of the Gosplan state commission. Here is his first testimony:

> You know, radiobiology has been my subject for quite some time. For twenty years I have been taking part in various expert examinations, both in this country and abroad. But what I encountered here simply stunned me. The most painful thing was to talk to the residents of the affected localities. I sometimes wished I could sink through the floor or dissolve in thin air. I just could not look those people in the eye. I felt ashamed for the helplessness, for the false promises high-ranking officials had given them. They made them promises by the cartload, then went away and forgot all about it. The scale of the disaster was impossible to conceive!

The commission faced an enormous task just to sort out the mass of lies and break through the shroud of departmental secrecy. Not all of the documents we were interested in could be obtained at the first try. Some we never saw at all. Radioactive contamination maps from the USSR State Committee for Hydrometeorology did not reach the environment committee until March 4, 1990, and we saw them for the first time on April 12 at the parliamentary hearings.

The experts and the people's deputies worked practically seven days a week, for within three months we were to submit a final report to the USSR Supreme Soviet on the three republics' programs for eliminating the consequences of the Chernobyl nuclear accident, to be presented to the Union government by the governments of Ukraine, Belorussia, and the Russian Federation. We had to scrutinize Ilyin's 35-rem-over-70-years concept and diagnose it for what it was—on the basis of documents, measurements, checkups, and consultations with foreign scientists. Millions of people's destinies depended on it, practically the health of entire nations. After all, in Belorussia alone 80 percent of the territory had been covered by the black wing of the radioactive cloud. We studied the experiences of West Germany, the United States, and Sweden. The volume of information was stupendous. Besides, the fourth anniversary of the accident was approaching. That, too, was a factor to be considered.

As we worked on program analysis, there arose quite a few problems, which I will touch upon a bit later. But as expected, it was the conception of safe living in contaminated areas that proved to be a major stumbling block in commission discussions. Was it widespread radiophobia, or was it something else, after all? Some experts argued that Ilyin was right because it was virtually impossible to detect "something at rustle level." By "rustle" they meant low radiation doses. Others countered with the following argument. Austrians register "rustles" of just 1 rem. To do their research, they used our nuclear accident! In Salzburg, where radioactive fallout had also occurred, they kept up permanent monitoring of the people whom they had observed before the accident. And they managed to register changes in their condition at just 1 rem. Reliable results were obtained at 5 rem. At that level they already registered a definite "disintegration" of people's health. It was amazing, unbelievable. And we felt hurt on account of ourselves; we felt cheated on account of Soviet medicine and science. And our hearts bled for the Chernobyl victims.

The majority of the experts were in favor of dropping the 35-rem-over-70-years theory as unscientific and inhumane. Unexpectedly, we discovered that the whole world had long been talking of the no-threshold radiation risk prediction model. That means, quite simply, that any radiation dose affects a person's health. Admittedly, the human body also contains radionuclides, but those are our very own, so to speak, not introduced from the outside. This is what prominent scholar Ernest J. Sternglass wrote on this issue: dose sensitivity obeys the logarithm or fractional-power law; that is, sensitivity increases faster at low radiation dose as compared with those at higher levels. Dr. Sternglass wrote that post-Chernobyl examination of patients revealed that many diseases never previously attributed to radiation, such as infections like influenza or pneumonia, as well as chronic conditions (emphysema, heart diseases, kidney disorders, and paralysis), have now been linked to *very low doses of ionizing radiation.*

93

When the expert commission's work was nearing completion, it suddenly was discovered that the infamous 35-rem-over-70-years concept was not recognized by scientists even in this country. It was merely a hypothesis of one group of scholars. No more, no less. To become scientifically acknowledged, it had to be passed by a congress of the country's radiobiologists. But the congress rejected it! One can only guess at the reason for the unanimous support this concept of safe living in contaminated areas received from our government and the CPSU Central Committee—despite the fact that other scientists in Moscow, in Ukraine, and in Belorussia held different views. Finally, there was considerable foreign research experience.

But while Belorussian scientists resolutely rejected the 35-rem idea, having condemned it at two of their parliament's sessions, the Ukrainian program of elimination of the accident's consequences stubbornly clung to it. More than that, it turned out that their program carried no signatures. It was, in fact, anonymous. All the program had was data on cesium-137 contamination, but it did not say a word about radioactive plutonium or a dozen other radionuclides. Nor did it mention an assessed cost of decontamination work or its potential effectiveness. Some of the program sections were at variance with others. It also transpired that it had not been submitted to Ukraine's Supreme Soviet for hearing. Ukrainian people's deputies did not have the faintest idea what the program was about and what its underlying criteria were. There's a caring leadership for you!

Later I obtained, from the Ukrainian Supreme Soviet, a few documents pertaining to Chernobyl. One of the papers turned out to be the resolution by two Ukrainian Supreme Soviet commissions, for industry and for environment protection and rational use of natural resources. It was named "On the Proposal by Deputy K.M. Sitnik about Submitting for the Consideration of the Ukrainian Supreme Soviet the Issue of the Environmental Situation in the Republic and Urgent Measures to Improve It Radically." The people's deputy proposed examining, among other things, the consequences of the Chernobyl nuclear accident. The resolution was passed on September 22, 1989. The matter was even tentatively included on the agenda of a Supreme Soviet session scheduled for October 25–27, 1989. Chernobyl was item 4 on the agenda. Yu. G. Bakhtin and I. O. Teteruk, executive staff members, were instructed to "ensure timely preparation of a Council of Ministers report on the current state and measures to further speed up work on the elimination of the Chernobyl nuclear accident's consequences" and also "a draft to be submitted by the Ukrainian Council of Ministers to the Ukrainian Supreme Soviet." All of that was to be done by October 10–15, 1989. But on October 17, the Ukrainian Supreme Soviet Presidium, with Ms. Shevchenko at the head, struck the item off the session's plan, citing "other pressing matters" as the reason. What matters in Ukraine could have been so very pressing as to induce the leaders of the people's deputies to drop the issue that was the most vital one for the country's population? Still, it was agreed that the whole thing should be postponed till 1990. But at the 1990 session no mention was made of any special program of elimination of the disaster's consequences. The audience listened to a report, then to a supplementary report, and then several people's deputies took the floor. All this was mere going through the motions. A sham.

In almost four years since the nuclear disaster, that was the first hearing in Ukraine's parliament of the aftermath of the national tragedy on a global scale. And this points to an alarming tendency. We are all at risk, because we let such people govern us and because anything can be done to us "in the national interest." This argument is always used when governments face criticism from a large segment of the population. Wasn't there also a U.S. government cover-up after the Three Mile Island accident?

How else to explain what happened even after that Supreme Soviet session, four years too late, when nearly all the people's deputies had rejected the 35-rem-over-70-years concept, and even after Ukraine's government did not bother to alter in any way its anonymous program submitted to our expert commission. In that context, how should one take the assurances by K. I. Masik, deputy chairman of Ukrainian Council of Ministers, at the parliamentary hearings on the Chernobyl tragedy in Moscow, when the experts' work had already been done: ". . . the 35 rem concept, it is not recognized by the scientists of our Ukrainian republic, nor is it recognized by ourselves. It has not been approved by the country's government, but it was and still is used as a basis for the conception of safety for the population"?

As the state team of experts' work began to wind down, more curious things began to happen behind our backs. At one of the sessions we suddenly learned that. Academician S. T. Belyaev, deputy chairman of the expert commission, signed, without even letting us know, a document titled "The Main Target Goals and Criteria for Drawing Up a Program for the Union and the Republics on Eliminating Chernobyl Nuclear Accident's Consequences." That was a devious attempt to torpedo the experts' work and keep afloat the 35-rem concept at all cost, although, as academician Andrei Sakharov used to say, an idea can only be fought with a better idea. Among the signatories of the fake document were the old familiars: "for the USSR ministry of health, A.I. Kondrusev, L.A. Ilyin; for the state commission for food and procurements of the USSR Council of Ministers, N.V. Krasnoshchekov, A.P. Povalyaev; for the USSR State Committee for Hydrometeorology, Yu.S. Tsaturov." (Fifteen years after Chernobyl, Mr. Povalyaev was already boasting how brilliantly he had worked.)

They must have exhausted all scientific methods of defending their conception. So they used administrative, departmental pressure as their last-ditch argument. It was as if issuing a council of ministers decree on repealing Newton's law, say, would have instantly made it ineffective. In the explanatory note appended to the product of their intellectual endeavor, the above gentlemen used the same trusted mantra: "If the external and internal radiation exposure dosage over a person's lifetime is impossible to limit to 35 rem set by the USSR ministry of health, the residents must be resettled." In the *Main Goals and Criteria* they suggested "ensuring production of agricultural produce (including on personal subsidiary plots) whose radionuclide content did not exceed the established temporary permissible levels." True, the authors did not specify how many years or decades those temporary permissible levels would remain valid. They had already been in effect for nearly five years, and there was no sign that they might be dropped any time soon. So was that still temporary or already permanent? As international experience shows, temporary levels are allowed to stay in effect for a period of just twelve months, not more!

In practice, the situation with those temporary standards sometimes became positively ludicrous. Permissible levels for potatoes used as fodder were half of what was allowed for human consumption. On seventeen collective farms in the Narodichi District, for instance, only people were allowed to eat their own potatoes, whereas the same potatoes were considered too radioactive to be fed to animals. In the same recommendations, the learned gentlemen went even further. They invited farmers to plow, sow, and grow industrial crops at the radioactive cesium-137 contamination density of 40–80 Ci! That, moreover, when cows had been known to graze on meadows at 1 Ci and still give radioactive milk.

The expert commission had not yet finished its work, but the document, unbeknown to its members, including people's deputies, was already sent to the USSR government and even acquired executive force in the form of resolution 587 by the Government Commission for Eliminating the Consequences of the Chernobyl Nuclear Accident. The paper contained two points:

1. "Accept the Main Target Goals and Criteria for Drawing Up Programs for the Union and the Republics for Eliminating the Chernobyl Nuclear Accident's Consequences on the Territories of the RSFSR, the Ukrainian SSR, and the Belorussian SSR, and the Necessary Measures for Their Implementation, worked out by the coordinating council of the presidium, USSR Academy of Sciences."

2. The paper instructed the Soviet Union's state planning committee and constituent republics' councils of ministers to be guided by "The Main Target Goals and Criteria" when devising the program in question. The order was signed by V. Kh. Doguzhiev, chairman of the Government Commission for Eliminating the Consequences of the Chernobyl Nuclear Accident.

Those were the kinds of Byzantine games the Kremlin played behind our backs while we were busy working. It was extremely unscrupulous and unsavory. Having learned the particulars of those cloak-and-dagger tricks from academician Belyaev in person at one of the sessions, we sent a letter to Yu. D. Maslyukov, chairman of the state planning committee (Gosplan). In it we described how we felt about such methods of "scientific" infighting. Nearly a month later, when we had already finished work, I received a reply from Yu. K. Karsky, chairman of the Gosplan state expert commission. He informed me that "the letter rightly pointed out that Comrade S. T. Belyaev should not have signed the document concerned with one of the controversial points used for the programs before the experts' opinion had been given." But the horse had already bolted, as it were. We had been duped in a most shameless fashion.

Ilyin team's last argument in favor of their conception was an appeal to President Gorbachev by ninety-two specialists (among them were several persons who had nothing to do with radiobiology). What a disgrace! The president got the letter. He certainly read it. But the expected order to have the 35-rem conception introduced in science never came down. Later, there was one more attempt to influence public opinion. The journal *Meditsinskaya Radiobiologiya* ("Medical Radiology") and the newspaper *Tribuna NTR* ("Tribune of Scientific and Technological Revolution") also published a statement by a group of scientists specializing in radiation security and radiation medicine in connection with the post-Chernobyl situation.

Their main idea was that exposure to radiation within the 35-rem limit was perfectly safe. And until a person had absorbed a total of 35 rem, there was nothing to worry about. Human health was not in jeopardy.

But did not the following simple thing ever occur to any of them?

Supposing I, an adult, absorb a total of 35 rem in, say, ten years—gradually. This is one situation. But take a twelve-month-old baby or a two-year-old. Let's suppose they absorb the same dose, only not over ten years but within a year or two. Could the two situations be compared in terms of safety? Comparing adult exposures to a small child's is apples and oranges. It does not take a medical academician or a radiobiologist to see these simple facts. And these are not just my speculations. This is the reality that we encountered in our region. There are villages in which children absorbed over 20 rem in just the first two years, and in some cases, in one short period of hours or a few days. And some had actually "gulped down" 500 rem over the same one- or two-year period. To a fragile juvenile organism that level of radiation exposure endured in so short a time has a potent effect. You may also recall that, because of the government cover-up, their parents were unaware of the consequences. One can only imagine what a shattering blow the revelation became for the "people in the street," as Ilyin referred to them in one of his reports.

Expressly for Ilyin and his conceptualists I shall name the twelve villages in the Narodichi District where the residents, including children (not the staff employed at the Chernobyl Nuclear Power Plant), absorbed between 10 and 20.15 rem in just the first two years of official lies about Chernobyl. (And now all of twenty years have passed! Some are far distant; some are dead, as Pushkin wrote in *Eugene Onegin*.) These villages are Rudnya-Ososhnya (the first village where I managed to go in secret, fooling the authorities), Zvizdal, Lesser Minki, Shishalovka, Lesser and Greater Kleshchi, Peremoga, Polesskoe, Khristinovka, Old Sharneh, Nozdrishche, and Khriplya. Even five years after the accident, people were still living in those radioactive ghettos. The state proved to be utterly helpless. There was nowhere to move them, no accommodation, no building materials, no one to do the building, no manpower. No this, no that, no nothing . . .

Wasn't that the main "scientific" reason why a group of scientists doggedly clung to the 35-rem-over-70-years model with the Union government's active backing? The object was not to protect the lives of millions of people scorched by radiation but to use that model to give our government the comforting illusion that all was well and nothing threatened the people's health. Apparently, it is not only household items, such as an apartment, an armchair, a gas cooker, that can be comfortable, but also "scientific" calculations. And the people have to pay dearly for their government's comfort.

Here is what speakers said about the Ilyin concept at a parliamentary hearing in the USSR Supreme Soviet committees:

A.G. Nazarov, doctor of biology:

> One of the fundamental points everyone keeps talking about here is the so-called 35-rem conception. We have explored the issue from various angles, not only medical, but also social and psychological, sociological, environmental, and even in terms of landscape ecology, and so on. Well then, from those points of view, from the viewpoint of a comprehensive approach, the thing called the 35-rem conception does not meet the requirements of a [scientific] conception. Because the criterion itself—you can take 35 rem, of course, or 40 or 30—numerically it does not have much scientific justification; we have examined all the scientific materials submitted to us by the Academy of Medical Sciences and the Health Ministry and concluded that in its present form, the 35-rem model cannot be the guiding conception for decision-taking.

E. M. Borovetskaya, committee expert of the USSR Supreme Soviet:

> The figure 35 rem was obtained simply by multiplying by 70 years the annual dose of 0.5, the currently accepted maximum exposure dosage for Class B persons, that is, the ordinary public not employed at nuclear facilities. The question arises: why was it necessary to do so? For one purpose only—to disguise as a scientific approach the arbitrary raising of the allegedly safe dose for humans from 0.5 rem per year to 35 rem. Indeed, the permissible lifetime dosage conception seems to imply that a 35-rem dose is equally harmless whether absorbed over a few hours, months, or decades. Thus it actually means that the commonly recognized maximum dose of 0.5 rem per year has been replaced with one 70 times higher, which dose is allegedly the limit beyond which people are to be moved away from the contaminated area. But this kind of human tolerance dose substitution is utterly inadmissible. . . .The 35-rem lifetime conception ignores the distribution of the dose over time and, so, creates the impression that severe radiation exposure of 35 rem is the same as the same amount absorbed over 70 years. But this goes against the entire body of scientific data. In reality, when a

radiation dose is condensed in time, its harmful effects can be much more powerful. The 35-rem-over-lifetime model completely fails to take into account the different sensitivity in different age groups ... Children are far more radioactivity-sensitive than adults, to say nothing of the elderly, while some persons may be several times more sensitive to radioactivity than others of the same age. The 35-rem-over-lifetime model notes only such consequences as acute or chronic radiation sickness but overlooks such deficient-immunity-related effects as enhanced susceptibility to disease and heightened sensitivity to various harmful influences, including cancerogenic ones, all of which are well known to specialists but have not yet been adequately researched. The 35-rem dose is close to the radiation dose that doubles the incidence of gene mutations in humans. This means that if people have absorbed this dose before the end of their reproductive period, the chance of their having children with genetic disorders will increase.

The text read out by E. M. Borovetskaya was signed by four hundred scientists. That was a collective rebuke on behalf of the conference on "The Genetic Aspects of Radiation Effects on Populations and Ecosystems in Connection with the Chernobyl Nuclear Accident," prompted by the letter of a group of scientists espousing the 35-rem conception published in the *Meditsinskaya Radiobiologiya* ("Medical Radiology") journal and the *Tribuna NTR* ("Tribune of Scientific and Technological Revolution") newspaper.

V. S. Budko, people's deputy from Ukraine, chairman of the Narodichi District Executive Committee:

We take it this conception has more to do with the economy than with medicine. This is a betrayal of the people living in those areas. Why am I saying that? Because nothing has been taken into account of what happened there in April and May 1986.

E. P. Tikhonenko, people's deputy of the USSR, member of the Supreme Soviet Committee for the Environment and Rational Use of Natural Resources:

The basis of the policy that the central departments have been pursuing since the first days of the Chernobyl disaster, from 1987 on, has been the 35-rem-over-a-lifetime model. It was intended to do the following: calm down public opinion; relieve the party and state bodies and individuals of responsibility for the consequences of the accident; reduce as far as possible the amount of compensation for the damage caused to the victims and residents of affected areas; and also present as unfounded all anxiety over people's life and health. This conception is fundamentally inhumane, which is borne out by its resolute rejection everywhere. . . . It is downright cynical.

Indeed, the model insisted on by the USSR Ministry of Health (Minzdrav) proved a universal substantiation for such a policy.

Yu. N. Shcherbak, MD, people's deputy of the USSR:

Our science and our society in general have been harmed tremendously by the situation of monopoly. I suppose it was the same with the Chernobyl affair. I mean here the monopoly, in particular, of a group of medical experts headed by academician Ilyin—of this I am firmly convinced. This monopoly thrusts on us the 35-rem model. . . . This conception is being imposed on everyone and introduced under various pretexts in every official document. I returned from Switzerland five days ago, from a meeting with major specialists in radiation protection. They were baffled by this conception.

Dozens of speakers took the floor at the two-day parliamentary hearings. Almost every one of them dwelt on the 35-rem model in some way. And only one person defended it tooth and nail, cynically comparing the losses caused by the Chernobyl disaster with road accident casualties. Interestingly, in the course of the debate at the parliamentary hearings, V. Kh. Doguzhiev, chairman of the state commission for eliminating the consequences of natural accidents and disasters, changed his stand. It was he who had issued government order 586 in support of the infamous 35-rem model before the state expert commission could finish its work. But after the experts resolutely rejected it as totally groundless, V. Kh. Doguzhiev suddenly announced, without outside prompting,

Talking of the purely radiological side—a dosage and all that—it may be understandable. . . . But the comrades here have been rightly saying: how about this—we do not know what effect minor doses might have in the long run. Indeed, this is a question that probably has no answer as yet. So when someone says that this 35-rem conception, well . . . it hasn't been approved by the government, has it now?

So there, it hasn't been approved, he says! Then why did he not revoke his order when the debate was over?

Ilyin was also among the speakers at the hearings. He took the floor after swallowing quite a few bitter pills administered by the audience. Possibly it was the conclusive nature of reports by experts and scientists, the evidence of total health deterioration in the disaster area cited by the leadership of Russia, Ukraine, and Belorussia, by the people's deputies of the USSR and the constituent republics, that somehow affected the academician himself. He failed to produce any really serious arguments in defense of his conception. Knowing how assertive Ilyin tended to be, many of us were amazed at the unaccustomed tone of his speeches. He never once ventured to utter the word *radiophobia* in that hall. He thus explained his viewpoint:

> When that maximum level of the 35-rem-over-lifetime load was proposed, it was assumed that all limitations on people living in one or another area would be automatically removed. Since ionizing radiation is believed to have a no-threshold effect, the whole thing boils down to this: theoretically, any radiation dose, however small, may, with a corresponding probability, cause various pathological conditions. These pathologies can be of two types: malignant tumors and genetic damage. Well, to decide these matters, it is first of all necessary to settle on a maximum dose level that can be permitted. Pre-accident norms for the residents of areas surrounding the location of nuclear facilities amount to some 0.5 rem per year. It is legally wrong to view the people finding themselves in radioactive fallout areas as belonging to that category. It is not humane; it is wrong. I mean, the people are not responsible for the accident. They ought to live in normal conditions in terms of dose loads.

Bravo! Could this really be the same Ilyin speaking? But there was more to come:

> Now let us examine a different situation, if we take 7 rem over 35 years. This is easy to calculate; we have made similar calculations. I could simply show them to you. According to our estimates, given this exposure level, instead of 166,000 people now designated for resettlement, we would have to multiply the figure roughly by ten. Then the rehousing project would involve over 1.5 million people.

Of course. And if estimates were based on the 7-rem-over-70-years dosage, as in other civilized countries, where would we be then? Not 1.5 million, but dozens of millions would have to be rehoused. And wasn't that economic aspect of the issue the whole "medical" point of the Ilyin conception?

L. A. Ilyin):

> Now society should weigh all the risk and all the *profit* [italics mine] involved in such an act. I should think that these matters must be decided fundamentally, because the statistics I have cited to you earlier about how the decision is currently carried out, and the government, and doctors' recommendations to date, convince me that these figures, when it was about some fourteen or fifteen villages and the republics' councils of ministers failed to ensure it [resettlement] where it really had to be ensured . . . . So I repeat: the matter of adopting any figure requires comprehensive analysis. . . . We have a firm stand with regard to this conception, or rather not conception, but taking a decision on the 35 rem . . .

Someone in the audience asked him, rhetorically, "Your whole 35-rem conception and today's speech suggest that you have been speaking to us here not as a doctor but as an economist. Does it not go against medical ethics by any chance?"

Yes, indeed, that's what it must have been all about. A medical doctor, instead of discussing a safe human habitation model, talks of profit. He turns into an accountant, flicking abacus counters back and forth—a life goes this way; another goes that way—plus or minus, makes no difference! How was something like that possible at all?

And here's another question, since we are on economics now. What is more profitable—to resettle people in "clean" areas to live a normal life or to sink money in extra payments and construction in "dirty" ones? Belorussian writer Vasil Yakovenko told me that experts at the Mogilev regional executive committee had shown him some interesting calculations. If people were left to live in contaminated areas and supplied with everything they would need for twenty-eight years (the half-life period for cesium-137), that would cost the state two and a half times as much as resettling the same people in safe areas. This emphasizes once again how shaky the props are under the so-called 35-rem concept not only scientifically but even in terms of economics.

I. N. Smolyar, chairman of the commission for eliminating the Chernobyl nuclear accident's consequences under the Belorussian Supreme Soviet:

> We are talking of forces, of the cost, of economic benefits. But it is really about the greatest asset of all, human health. Here we are trying to compare costs—thirty billion, forty billion, and so on. . . .

I found very distressing the speech of the Gosplan representative, when he started wrangling with us like a shopkeeper, fearing that he might sell his goods at a loss and give us more than we need, thus making our life in the Gomel area too prosperous.

Such undisguised commerce in people's health by high-ranking civil servants was disgusting. It was no longer about a scientific conscience (a scientist may be sincerely in error) but about researcher ethics and moral principles. After all, the 35-rem model was proposed by the USSR Health Ministry as an alternative to the commonly accepted linear no-threshold theory, recognized by practically all experts in radiology and radiobiology both in this country and abroad. This concept rests precisely on the moral imperative of "victim inadmissibility," to quote Albert Schweitzer, the imperative of "venerating life." The financial accounting and economics principles of our Kremlin court medical establishment, on the other hand, determined the fates and certain death of people living in contaminated areas by postponing by several years their resettlement outside of the danger zones and lulling them by comforting myths.

The Soviet 35-rem threshold norm is the antipode, and deeply immoral antipode at that, of the no-threshold theory, based on rejecting the very possibility of sacrificing human lives. With its underlying idea of a collective safe radiation dose, its adherents are forced to admit a "statistically negligible" number of potential victims, setting aside admonition "to first, do no harm." Naturally, all of that was seen in light of the law of averages. While analyzing the so-called 35-rem belief, experts concluded that it should be designated as an "admissible losses concept." When justifying this theory, the national radiological protection commission of the health ministry assured us that at 35-rem-over-lifetime exposure doses they could guarantee absence of "a detectable increase in the incidence of cancer, genetic disorders and pathology in progeny caused by fetus exposure to radiation." Yet what is the risk of expected disease and related change in life quality? How many of those diseases may be expected to kill members of the current "Chernobyl generation" and those whose genes are passed on to future generations? What overall effect will it have on the nations subjected to an unprecedented penetrating radiation dose, above all on Ukrainians and Belorussians? Academicians who are confusing medicine with accounting have the same answer to all questions: "There is no danger to human health."

Guarantees of cancer incidence, that is, risk estimates in the Ilyin doctrine, were based, we were assured, on previously obtained data. But there exists a body of precise epidemiological and dosimetric data from the International Commission on Radiological Protection, suggesting that the risk of malignant growths is actually 2.4 times higher than formerly believed. The international commission intends to review the maximum permissible radiation doses and risk levels for the population. I doubt that the official ideologues of the "expected losses" prototype could be ignorant of that.

The final report by the State Expert Commission for the Consequences of the Chernobyl Nuclear Accident contains the following data:

> In terms of genetic risk, estimates based on materials by the UN scientific committee on the effects of atomic radiation predict 50 to 347 cases of serious hereditary anomalies at a 1-rem dose per million of newborn progeny of parents exposed to radiation. At a dose of 35 rem over a lifetime, the incidence is expected to reach 1,750 to 12,100 cases of serious hereditary anomalies. So in that eventuality one can expect actual genetic mutations in the progeny of radiation victims. Physicians who ignore this established research are guilty of medical malpractice. [That would be sacrilegious to ignore.] With chronic exposure to ionizing radiation, several successive generations later there may occur a roughly tenfold increase in the mutation level against the effect observed in the first generation. That makes between 450 and 3,400 cases of hereditary anomalies per one million newborns from the initial dose of just 1 rem.

The 1982 report by the same UN committee also used inferior-quality life indices (time spent in hospitals, etc.) and shortened life span to assess genetic damage. This scientific information is particularly interesting to us, a country where human life has never really been valued. Well then, assuming that the average life span is seventy years (70 million years per 1 million newborns), the cited estimates of genetic risks yield the following damage estimates: at the dose of 35 rem, genetic loss in the first generation per 1 million newborns will amount to 39,000–247,000 years of inferior-quality life and to 46,500–358,000 years off the life span, scientific data on damage sustained from the "pure" dose, which is not applicable to the post-Chernobyl situation. After all, the 35 rem should also include, as a matter of course, the exposure dose received in the first days after the accident. Does anyone know how much that was? The documents cited in the previous chapters show that doctors were forbidden to enter the first days' doses in the medical records both of residents and of liquidators (people recruited to clean up the accident site). So the reliability of that already-suspect criterion becomes even more suspect, and the consequences even more unpredictable. No, not in the aggregate mass of human lives. Flick the abacus counters—a life this way; a life that way. What does it matter—but in veneration for each, unique, full-blooded and inimitable human life? Every single one. And this is normal. Normal, that is, for a normal human society.

This is what the so-called 35-rem-over-70-years model would mean in practice. Oddly enough, I have never heard anything like that from its champions, whether in the press or in speeches addressed to people's deputies and residents of contaminated areas. Certainly not the risks forecast by scientists, all the prospective deaths, all the curtailed lives. Those were diagnosed as "radiophobia," as far as the man in the street was concerned.

Sci-fi writer John Wyndham has an excellent tale about mutants on a post–nuclear war Earth. A girl who had six toes on her left foot was to be killed in order to correct the "genetic failure" lest it should get transmitted into the future. This is frightening. Through a clash of opinions, a battle of ideas, through taking into account global experience and their own data, even if incomplete and not always reliable, the scientists on the state expert commission arrived at the conclusion that the 35-rem-over-70-years conception had no scientific basis.

From the state experts' report:

> The chief criterion used in the programs [of eliminating the consequences of the Chernobyl nuclear accident] is the density of nuclide contamination on territories and in food products based on the size of the permissible dose absorbed by the residents defined as 35 rem over 70 years. It does not take into account the condition of people's health as it was at the time of the accident and the presence of risk groups among them. Using the lifetime dose as the only criterion is also impossible because retrospective estimates of absorbed radiation doses from short-lived radionuclides were made with a major error in the magnitude that virtually cannot be assessed by means of physical dosimetry. Also absent is the prognosis of dosage dynamics as the potential migration of radionuclide contamination has not been taken into account.

It would have been just great if this had solved all the problems. But here is what came of it all. There were hundreds of us, people's deputies from the three biggest republics hit by the nuclear disaster. For two years we fought for all we were worth to ease the suffering of those unfortunate people, to get the Union government to cough up the money. After all, the faulty reactor was not Ukraine's property; it belonged to a Union-level department, the USSR Ministry for Atomic Energy. And it would be natural for the latter to make good the losses to the republics. But what did it mean, given our system, to make good the losses from the atomic energy ministry's kitty? Did it have one? After all, everything in this country was strictly centralized, with every screw tightened to the utmost. The ministry's kitty was also ours. One big kitty for all. What it got had been taken away from us. So we were demanding not something of theirs but our own that had been taken away.

And so we managed to get the money at long last. Somehow or other, the Union government (the "Center") released dozens of billions. We contrived to get the inhuman 35-rem-over-70-years model discarded. What happened next? People had to be resettled as a matter of urgency. But there was always some snag in the way of that. There was the money, but building materials were scarce. Or else the materials were available, but the builders were not. Every Union republic had its own woes and its own problems—the horrendous earthquake in Armenia's Spitak, the bloodletting in Tbilisi, Georgia, the standoff in Riga, Latvia.

At the very core of the Chernobyl tragedy is this central issue. The permissible dose could be altered to fit the fluctuating theories of the radiation "experts." But who are the experts with the skill to resettle whole villages, and where can the desperate families be moved? This is the awful truth, plain and unvarnished. So that is what the authorities should have told the people, however bitter the reality. They should have told us the truth about the state's helplessness in the face of the disaster, instead of masking its bankruptcy with the 35-rem dogma, accusations of wholesale radiophobia, assurances that the victims' health was not at risk, and the fabrication, "no cause for concern." The truth about how many people were really in jeopardy. So many unanswered questions. So many lies.

How much time has already been wasted! How much of the nation's health ruined! And how much more will yet be lost?

9

Dissident Experts

Meanwhile, despite the triumph of common sense at the parliamentary hearings and the Chernobyl state expert commission, where the "homegrown" 35-rem model was given a vote of no confidence, the struggle between the two ideas, the threshold and no-threshold radiation effect on Chernobyl victims' health, went on in Soviet science. At the time, translations of foreign literature on small radiation doses and their influence on human beings were virtually unavailable in the Soviet Union. And that was what the "Kremlin academicians" relied on in pushing through their inhumane doctrine, which had such a dire effect on the life of the "man in the street." In a similar way, academicians Alexandrov and Dollezhal had pushed through their RBMK (acronym for "high-power reactor of the channel type") reactor model that became infamous at the Chernobyl Nuclear Power Station.

But times were changing in the Soviet Union, and we were changing with them. The first timid challenges to previously taboo ideas about the no-threshold health effects of small radiation doses gradually forced their way through the concrete slabs of the Soviet official media. I first learned of that in the Narodichi District authorities' offices permeated with deadly rays, not in the Kremlin. There I was shown a letter by Moscow professor and radiobiologist Yelena Borisovna Burlakova addressed to the public group for radiation protection of the local population. In the post-Chernobyl years, dozens of various public organizations and local administrative bodies appealed for help to all kinds of organizations and never once were dignified with a reply. Yet here was a public group (at the time we still had no NGOs in the Western sense of the word) that had actually received a letter. It came straight from Moscow, from a professor and chairperson of the academic council for radiobiology at the USSR Academy of Sciences. It was dated July 1989, and it became quite an event for the small town.

Prof. Burlakova wrote that after a visit from a team of scientists, her academic council sent letters to the country's parliament and several other bodies, "requesting a settlement without delay of the issue of moving people out of contaminated areas. We are now trying to organize a trip to your locality so that a group of geneticists and ophthalmologists might work there monitoring the actual exposure dosages to the district residents. This has proved something of a problem; we are currently negotiating the matter with Academy of Sciences research centers and the eye microsurgery center." Frankly, I was surprised. Dozens of scientists came and went, but there was never any feedback; even if they did make analyses, they did not report the results as a rule.

In the summer of 1989, Prof. Burlakova and radiobiology academic council secretary V. I. Naidich, candidate of chemistry, sent letters to several addresses—to the Supreme Soviet committee for the environment, to Academy of Sciences president G. I. Marchuk, to the environment commission of the Academy of Sciences, and personally to USSR people's deputies Boris N. Yeltsin and Vasily I. Belov. The letter informed them that an extended session of the academic council bureau had discussed the results of the scientists' trip to the Narodichi District of the Zhitomir region. The conclusion was as follows: "The residents of the Narodichi District must be resettled in other, nonradioactive, areas." It does not take a lot of imagination to visualize the panicky reaction this must have caused at the top. It was a brilliant challenge to the Kremlin's court of radiobiologists.

The radiobiology academic council team sent a special letter to Alexei V. Yablokov, corresponding member of the USSR Academy of Sciences and deputy chairman of the Supreme Soviet committee for the environment. I shall quote it as written evidence of what scientists outside the official health establishment think about when faced with the haunting specter of my fellow compatriots and their children whose lives have been shattered by the invisible and death-dealing fallout. Am I being too dramatic when I ask the reader to feel these cries for help from those who have no reason to hope? And think of the courage of those who confront the bureaucracy as they pen this letter.

First, a few words about the emotional side. It is not only animal mutants that are horrifying—blind piglets, an eight-legged 'web-footed' foal, tailless calves with hare lips, cats and dogs with all sorts of deformities. More horrifying even is the scream of a woman: "I want to live, I'm still young!" The words "Our children are dying. Please help!" break one's heart. Even more frightening are the tears of a doctor telling us of four categories of children who absorbed between 50 R and 1000 R of radioiodine in their thyroid glands; they did not develop common appendicitis, yet their abdominal cavities are filled with pus.

We are still haunted by the memory of a woman screaming desperately: "I'm a tiller of land! Let me work! My hands are longing for the earth, my children are dying!" It is frightening when men cry. That land rings with crying and moaning. The people are unanimous in their demand: "We want the right to live. We demand resettlement!"

The leadership of Ukraine's ministry of health, the official medical establishment, and agricultural committee representatives has lost the people's trust. They are dismissed as scoundrels, criminals, individuals who deliberately report reduced radiation dosage. The situation is aggravated by the fact that most medical measures related to the treatment of residents in strict-monitoring zones (in particular, iodine therapy) exist on paper only.

We consider it our duty to call your attention to the following facts: (1) A sharp increase in the incidence of malformations in newborn animals, particularly involving limbs and organs of vision. (2) Increased incidence of ophthalmologic disorders in the local population, especially in children, as well as of pneumonia, pharyngitis, nasal bleeding, dizziness, easy fatigability, etc. Adults employed on sheep-breeding farms suffer from larynx tumors. (3) These areas were recommended for living on the basis of dosimetric data prognosticating the state of radioactive contamination. But the initial radiation shock was not, and still is not taken into account. Totally ignored was the contribution of strontium, plutonium, and cesium, which resulted in considerably reduced amounts of actually absorbed radiation. (4) The population receives virtually no uncontaminated foodstuffs: their rations include two cans of stewed beef a month per person and one orange per child per month. This is a mockery. People have to give their children locally produced milk and eat contaminated food. (5) To give a well-grounded forecast of radiobiological consequences in those areas, it is necessary to have specific dosimetric data on every kind of ionizing radiation in the contaminated areas of the Ukraine, Belorussia, and the Russian Federation. What data there are at present, are inaccessible not only to radiobiologists at the USSR Academy of Sciences, but even to most researchers at the health ministry and the Academy of Medical Sciences. (6) It is criminal to ban publication of statistical data on child and adult morbidity in those areas, particularly on ophthalmologic pathology, etc. (7) Urgently needed is a dosimetric analysis of the affected territories involving the full range of nuclides. (8) When defining permissible exposure doses, researchers must take into account, without fail, the initial radiation shock the population has already sustained, which is typically ignored by the medical personnel, and also various synergistic factors resulting in aggravated injury: stress, pesticides, nitrates, nitrites, vitamin deficiency, appalling hygienic conditions (two cakes of soap per person a month, etc.). (9) Urgent measures must be taken to resettle the residents in uncontaminated areas, while the affected areas should be turned into radio-ecological preserves where scientists of various disciplines could conduct comprehensive research into the aftereffects of the accident. Scientists from other countries could also be invited to take part in this work.

This will now be the future of our children, too, children who live a relatively long distance away from the lands affected by the Chernobyl nuclear disaster.

That was a proper civic stance taken by scholars from the radiobiology council of the USSR Academy of Sciences. They became serious and dangerous opponents of academician Ilyin and his team. They were dangerous for two reasons—they were intelligent, thinking scientists and they did not have to obey instructions from the top. They represented a species of dissent in radiobiology, unorthodox experts, so to speak.

I received a copy of that letter from the Narodichi Communist Party District Committee, which had also started to show defiance—that is, to speak the truth. By then, the article "Remote Health Effects of Small Ionizing Radiation Doses," by M. D. Brilliant, A. I. Vorobyev, and E. E. Gogin, had already been written and published in the theoretical and practical monthly *Terapevticheskiy Arkhiv* ("Therapeutic Archive"), vol. 59, no. 6 (1987). And doctor of biology V. A. Shevchenko, head of the ecological genetics laboratory at the General Genetics Institute of the USSR Academy of Sciences, also prepared an article for the monthly journal *Priroda* ("Nature") based on the data collected in the Narodichi District. That, too, looked into the effect of small radiation doses on animal organisms. The same subject attracted the attention of other scholars not involved with the ruling establishment. They all made trips to the contaminated areas and saw what was actually happening there, not the picture painted in reports by the Kremlin spin doctors and international nuclear lobbyists.

Thus Soviet radiobiology witnessed a fierce standoff. On the one hand, there were the fathers of the 35-rem life-and-death accountancy and their team. On the other hand, those who could not accept that approach and painstakingly looked for answers to the questions posed by real-life situations—those who did not hasten to modify their conclusions depending on the cost to the treasury of resettlement but who worried about the people's health and about keeping their reputations intact.

The scientists of the radiobiology council would over and over again go to the affected areas, write many more letters to civil servants, and demand access to classified results of medical examinations of people who had named themselves, with bitter irony, "guinea pigs," including those in Ilyin's Biophysics Institute of the USSR Ministry of Health. Largely, thanks to their efforts and research results, the Chernobyl state expert commission decided that the 35-rem-over-70-years model was mistaken and detrimental. A big group of scientists from Russia, Belorussia, and Ukraine spent several years trying to prove that the problems and estimates of the radiation risk posed by the long-term consequences of the Chernobyl disaster were a multiple thing. Their conclusions were incorporated in the government expert report. But what next? After all, having rejected what the official medical establishment was trying to push through, they had to propose something of their own. Moreover, they had to do it quickly and efficiently. The people in the contaminated areas just could not wait.

The expert commission's final report listed emergency measures to be taken over the next two years to eliminate the consequences of the Chernobyl nuclear disaster. The rest was a matter of scientific concepts and principles and of substantiated conclusions about the effect of small radiation doses, about consequences of protracted exposure over many years.

The scientists who had to do battle royal to put an end to the 35-rem invention in the state experts' report felt responsible for offering their own more accurate estimates of the consequences of the Chernobyl disaster. The research they had undertaken was not unlike the laborious work of an artist in ancient China—tracing out minute details with a tiny brush to depict the smallest detail, so that everything, the faintest penumbra, the finest vein, was distinctly visible on the tree of radiation-affected life. On September 1, 1990, the USSR Supreme Soviet presidium passed a resolution, "On Setting up a Commission for Examining the Causes of the Accident at the Chernobyl Nuclear Power Plant and Assessing the Actions by Officials in the Post-Accident Period."

Among the commission members were also scientists from the radiobiology council of the USSR Academy of Sciences who espoused the idea that every human life was unique and irreplaceable—the health risks from the no-threshold model, specifically, from small radiation doses. And that was perfectly logical. On January 23, 1991, that parliamentary commission met for one of its sessions. Prof. Burlakova delivered an extensive theoretical report. She talked about the human organism's response to small radiation doses. Her report was based on the work of a group of scientists on various data and medical examination results from heavily affected areas that involved local residents and the liquidators who risked their lives in the aftermath of the accident. What we heard then became the first glimmer of truth in nearly five years since the Chernobyl blast. With one stroke of her scientific pen, Burlakova had ripped off the shroud of secrecy and deception, a shining example to the Soviet bureaucrats and medical leaders around the world of scientific independence and raw courage.

The scientists had to find answers to numerous questions, and these answers could influence research results. Were the people evacuated in time? Was anything really done to reduce the iodine impact on the population, especially on children? What was the role of the 35-rem model relative to the people's health?

Ms. Burlakova pointed out,

> I would like to say at once that a poll of doctors we conducted in the Ukraine, Belorussia and the Russian Federation showed that iodine prophylaxis had either been omitted or had taken place on a very limited scale. Moreover, in those areas of the Russian Federation where it had started, it was subsequently called off. Some of the medical experts have plainly admitted that when they started iodine prophylaxis in the wake of the accident, they received phone calls from higher authorities and were ordered to stop because they "were spreading panic." No talks to explain the situation were given to the public, no one told the public how things ought to be done; as a result, not only was not thyroid damage prevented, but many people, unsure how iodine should be properly used, harmed themselves injuring their mucous membranes, while others conducted iodine prophylaxis three or four months after the accident [It is only effective within the first week because such is radioiodine's half-life.] Naturally, this situation is on the conscience of our official medical establishment.

A second matter the scientists were to settle was finding out whether there had ever been sufficient training of doctors to prepare them to treat large numbers of victims of an accident like the one at Chernobyl. After all, the party press wrote that what had happened in Chernobyl had never happened before. So naturally, everyone was at a loss as to how to respond or what to do with the inaccurate data on hand.

Ye. B. Burlakova:

> To find out if there were such grounds and relevant knowledge, we conducted a thorough medical examination of the people irradiated on the river Techa (after a series of accidents at the Mayak secret military complex in 1948–1951) because of radionuclides pumped into the river. Also, of the people who happened to be in the contamination zone after the Kyshtym disaster (in 1957), and of the people caught up in the so-called Eastern Urals radioactive plume. Analysis of those data revealed a lot of most interesting facts that no one had properly noted before.

It turned out that chronic radiation sickness was found in residents of the Techa villages six to eight years after radionuclides had been dumped in the river. Research showed how the symptoms had built up. It was conclusively stated that the people suffered from a chronic disorder. It had "blurred" features, as it were, and displayed patterns that had not been described in specialist literature. However, the combination of symptoms allowed it to be diagnosed as chronic radiation sickness. All publications on the subject agree that radiation sickness develops when the exposure dose reaches 100 R. But medical examination of the Techa population revealed that people got chronic radiation sickness after different doses. Many of them absorbed doses way below 100 R.

Ye. B. Burlakova:

> That alone has prompted the idea that speaking of the same threshold for *all* is wrong. And we had even then grounds to suppose that the Techa people, afflicted as they were by various diseases or tending to develop various disorders in the given environmental conditions, could find themselves in situations where chronic radiation sickness would develop at lower doses. Analysis of the Urals situation revealed another important point: in numerous cases, people contracted increasingly widespread diseases that had not been described in domestic radiobiological sources as radiogenic.
>
> What conclusions are doctors making? Possibly, in those cases when there is an added background of some disease, the effect of radiation may render the condition far more acute. Although in other cases, where the disease is not so common, you can fail to detect the tendency. This is another fact denied by official medicine.

115

Point three now. It was discovered that there was a complex relationship between changes in the state of people's health following exposure to radiation and the dose received. Occasionally, it was just an increased level, regardless of the actual dose; in other cases a certain moderate dose was singled out that caused the most damage. That was observed in many instances. And again the fact was overlooked—even though all of that had been duly recorded.

So the group of independent scientists concluded that if we compare the diseases observed after the dumping of radioactive waste in the Techa and after the Chernobyl reactor meltdown, we will see a very similar range of diseases. For instance, the data submitted to the commission (the state expert commission) from Ukraine showed that the incidence of cardiovascular disorders had increased 1.8 times and endocrine disorders, in particular diabetes, had doubled. A sharp increase in the incidence of a whole spectrum of other diseases occurred. Not one textbook makes a mention of this. No one has ever shown experimentally that irradiation may cause infarction. Yet analysis of the data obtained as the result of the Techa pollution suggests precisely that. Some groups of cardiovascular diseases decreased, while angina pectoris, say, became more common—both among the people irradiated on the Techa and those hit by Chernobyl. There was evidence of a sharp increase in the incidence of infectious diseases among the Techa villagers. A similar situation was recorded in Kiev and in other radioactively contaminated areas. It is now crystal clear that a wide range of diseases present, down to so-called blooming rickets, in which children are diagnosed with rickets even though their appearance does not seem to indicate any problem.

It appears that all the data obtained after the examination of the Techa locals and people caught up in the Eastern Urals radioactive plume allowed researchers to prognosticate the illnesses in which an upsurge was registered around Chernobyl. Anyway, independent radiobiologists believe so. Then why is the official pro-Kremlin medical establishment silent on the matter?

Ye. B. Burlakova:

> Of considerable interest are the data obtained during the study of neurological syndromes. Around the river Techa their incidence increased sharply, though the exposure dose was a mere seven centisieverts. The authors argue that this is simply the reaction by the body's regulatory systems to irradiation. Then why, when similar data were obtained in Chernobyl, was it alleged that the whole thing

was the fault of the media which had got the public all worked up? It was implied that the syndrome was due to fear.

Also very important is the requirement by official medicine that there should be linear or near-linear dose–effect dependence. When the dose is higher, the changes should be more pronounced. And when there was no evidence of this kind of dependence, it was taken as proper grounds for declaring that these changes in the people's condition had not been caused by radiation, that they must be attributed to some other factors.

Analyzing the Techa material, and the data from the Chernobyl records for the Bryansk region, we see that the range of diseases caused by irradiation is roughly the same, although our science does not link these diseases to radiation exposure. Then the question arises: what can the reason be and how is one to understand this? The answer to this question can have three different approaches. Possibly, our medical statistics are so inadequate that they do not allow certain statements to be made with any reliability. Thus, every time when an increased incidence of some diseases has been registered, we are told at once that these are statistically unreliable differences and therefore it is impossible to link them to the exposure dose and consider that radiation was the cause. Point two. It is quite possible that what we are dealing with is actually a very different kind of doses from those we are talking about. There are now data on comparisons between genetic modifications in lymph cells and in the teeth that correlate nicely with the dose absorbed. For instance, biodosimetric data on chromosome aberrations in lymphocytes and on the number of long-lived free radicals in the teeth are of this kind. At the same time, they differ from the doses officially "assigned" to the population. In some cases the difference is tenfold. Prof. Vorobyev found that circumstance extremely worrying: children arrived with a record of a certain dose received, while the current level of knowledge warranted the supposition that in reality they had absorbed a much greater dose.

The question arises: what is the reason for the divergence in the data (barring the possibility of ordinary deliberate lies, or of our population being the most scared in the world)? I would say that our people tend to display complete indifference to danger; they would think nothing of venturing into contaminated areas because "berry and mushroom picking is good there." So why did it happen that precisely in those areas which had been irradiated we observed a greater increase in illness incidence than in control areas? Why are we unable to explain this in terms of radiobiological factors, in terms of those risk values that international commissions propose?

In this context, it is interesting to look at experimental research a group of scientists conducted on animals. So what did they find?

"It was shown," continues Prof. Burlakova, that where there were minor doses, given irradiation intensity ten to one hundred times greater than the background, there was no direct dependence on the dose. This dependence may have a nonlinear, variable character. For instance, a dose below 50 µSv displays the usual linear dependence; then, as the dose increases, the effect diminishes, while at the next stage the effect increases again, along with the dose, and we get a loop, in radiobiological parlance. Not only the data obtained from experiments with animals, but also hematopoietic system damage in humans developing after accidents at nuclear power stations (Chernobyl included) suggest that, because the human population is not uniform, a person who has absorbed 8 R and one absorbing 175 R may develop an equally serious disease. Or say, people absorbing 15 R and 300 R.

The same kind of result was received in experiments on animals. There can be an identical effect after doses with a 20-fold difference!

Point three. Synergism (effect enhancing) is present precisely in the case of small doses. When animals were injected with a toxic agent causing certain reactions in the body, and were simultaneously irradiated, the overall reaction was greater than a simple sum. At higher exposure doses this was not observed.

So why can many health deterioration indices at 20 R or 1 R doses be so considerable? What is the matter here? We discovered that at small doses cell repair systems are not switched on. For instance, there are two systems of membrane repair: one, when you remove damaged molecules and replace them with new ones; the other, when you repair the damaged molecules within the membrane. It turned out that the first system becomes active at 300 R-plus doses. What happens below that? Under 300 R, changes are not repaired. And when the system fails to repair minor damages, these damages, in terms of effect, come up to those resulting from much higher doses. So the doses, say 50 R, at which 90 percent of the system gets repaired, i.e. practically one-tenth of the damage remains, and 5 R, when the systems have not been restored, their effects are roughly the same. That means that there are doses at which the repair system does not switch on.

Now, why hasn't our nature been taught to respond to prolonged influence of weak irritants? We live against a certain background, and transition from one background to another is a shattering experience. So the dogma previously preached, to wit that the effect of a 100 R dose absorbed at one go is far more powerful than that of 100 R acquired over 12 months, is correct. Ten roentgens at once is far harder than 10 R over a year. Equally correct. . . . But 1 R over 12 months and 1 R at once will reverse the situation.

That was the quintessence of the independent radiobiologists' new knowledge after the Chernobyl disaster. Those data, though, are fragmentary and as yet incomplete, according to the professor. They were obtained in the course of experiments on animals several years after Chernobyl. It was also discovered that such radiation doses were not lethal. But they changed the organism's adaptability. What follows from that fact? It is not smoking that enhances the effect of irradiation, but the other way round. And instead of pesticides enhancing the effect of irradiation, the reverse is the fact. Thus, when we are exposed to radiation, our immune system is weakened and is subjected to greater risk from other environmental exposures.

Therefore, it can be predicted that in the areas where certain diseases build up, irradiation will result in an increase. In areas where infarction-related mortality is above the average, its rate will climb, and in areas with low irradiation and cancer rates, incidence rates and noncancer effects will rise, as they have after Chernobyl.

So what do we have here? A new concept? Or possibly, the moment of truth? It wasn't just journalists who were kept in the dark. The Kremlin bosses were adept at hiding the facts from academicians who were cloistered away in their ivory towers, naive to the machinations of bureaucrats.

Through all those years, even before the nuclear disaster struck at Chernobyl in 1986, few people knew what the word "ecology" meant. As for radiobiology and radioecology (just like genetics and cybernetics in their time), they merely gave a toothache to the authorities. Even among narrow specialists, there was no consensus (still there isn't, coming to that) on whether that is a science in its own right or an interdisciplinary study area. In this country, even in the academic circles, few people went abroad to attend professional international symposia, and those who did had to be vetted by the KGB and were obligated to submit reports to that agency about what they had heard and seen. Only a few could read foreign science journals, and these were again delivered to the persons passed by the party authorities as loyal to the regime. And since few people were fluent in foreign languages, various secret research centers and design bureaus employed teams of translators equally bound to secrecy who handed Western knowledge on to the court scientists.

Personally, I did not see a live Western scientist until 1992 when I met Prof. John Gofman of the United States, a prominent scientist who had made several discoveries in the field of nuclear energy and later actively explored the health effects of small radiation doses. He arrived in Stockholm where we both received the international Right Livelihood Award. It is also called "the alternative Nobel." Gofman was among those who worked on the Manhattan Project, but after he concentrated on small radiation dose problems and published, jointly with Prof. Arthur Tamplin, information that the probability rate of radiation-related cancers is ten to twenty times higher than that was officially recognized, he was banished from all of the U.S. official research centers. Chairman of the Congressional Joint Committee Chet Holifield, who supervised the work of the Nuclear Regulatory Commission, told Gofman at one of the committee meetings:

> What do you think you are doing opposing the commission programs on nuclear energy? Others have tried it before you. We took care of them. And we will take care of you too.

The chairman was as good as his word.

The career of Prof. Gofman in science is in some ways reminiscent of Andrei Sakharov's, who was also out of favor with the authorities. Studying the effects of radiation on human beings, branded as disloyal researcher, thrown out of official research labs in the United States, Gofman established and headed the Committee for Nuclear Responsibility, an NGO that comprises many world-famous scholars and Nobel Prize winners. A fate similar to Gofman's befell another American, Dr. Rosalie Bertell, who likewise, having published the results of small dose research that displeased officials, had to emigrate to Canada. Regrettably, her comprehensive and thorough monograph *No Immediate Danger* has not been translated into either Russian or Belorussian or Ukrainian.

So right there, in Stockholm, in the Swedish parliament, at the award ceremony, as I listened to the speech by John Gofman, doctor of medicine and doctor of nuclear physical chemistry, I heard for the first time about the research results involving small radiation doses that were unknown in our closed society. Not just any old radiation, mind, but our very own Chernobyl variety. Actually, it was that research that had won Prof. Gofman the Alternative Nobel Prize. What he was saying was consonant with what independent Russian, Ukrainian, and Belorussian experts had said at parliamentary hearings. It suddenly dawned on me that in different countries, scientists were simultaneously inventing the same wheel, figuratively speaking. But that was precisely the case when the wheel should indeed be invented by various research groups, in order to compare the notes—the results—in the end.

Prof. Gofman in his hefty tome entitled *Chernobyl Accident: Radiation Consequences for This and Future Generations* (first published in Russian only in 1994, in Minsk) managed to formulate the methodology and describe the results of his three lines of research into the consequences of the Chernobyl nuclear accident. The first line was to do with estimates of early radiation consequences. The cohort studied comprised 116,000 persons evacuated from the accident zone at the time of the blast and also numerous residents in areas with an increased radioactive contamination level, plus 600,000 liquidators (it is now known that there were 800,000 of them), both military and civilian.

The second line of research was forecasting the long-term effects of penetrating radiation before any manifestations appeared. This is what Prof. Burlakova spoke about in her report from experience gained observing victims of previous nuclear accidents. And line number three covered estimates of latent radiation effects on millions of people residing in territories with minor radioactive contamination levels who were daily exposed to small radiation doses. These include Ukraine, Belarus, Russia, and also Continental Europe, Great Britain, and the Middle East. Prof. Gofman has proved that pre-Chernobyl research points to very large aggregate instances of disease among millions of people even when irradiation doses are extremely small. According to the professor's data, worldwide incidence of terminal cancer caused by Chernobyl radiation is to grow to 340,000–475,000 cases. And the number of cases of curable cancer will increase by the same amount (Dr. Bertell estimates as many as 1.4 million).

Prof. Gofman's chief conclusion about the small-dose effect, including Chernobyl, is that there is no safe dose and that any, even the smallest dose of radiation, carries the risk of a whole series of most dangerous illnesses. At small doses, John Gofman believes, the probability of cancer per unit of absorbed dose is higher than that with medium and high doses.

John Gofman's stand as a scientist is also attractive for its civic ardor. He says he would like to stress that he is opposed to any attempt to exaggerate the negative side of the effect of radiation on health. But he is also against attempts to belittle the role of radiation in the incidence of cancer, leukemia, and genetic disorders. If scientifically grounded data confirmed that radiation was less harmful than he imagined, concluded John Gofman, or caused no harm at all, he would be only too glad. But if there was some concealment or unscientific methodology used to understate radiation risk, he would be compelled to set the record straight.

Prof. Gofman knew full well, from the Western press, about the pall of secrecy over the Chernobyl disaster in the Soviet Union and about the unscrupulous quasi-scientific games played by pronuclear international bodies that acted in concert with the totalitarian Soviet Communist regime. It is thanks to John Gofman that the manipulation of radiation doses was finally exposed, as were the unscrupulous approach and research methods applied to Chernobyl radiation health effects used by the International Atomic Energy Agency (IAEA) and the World Health Organization (WHO). The IAEA, writes Gofman in his book on Chernobyl, simply discarded the exposure dose readings that exceeded the previously established levels to which those doses had to conform. In compliance with the WHO directions, only those diseases were studied in the course of the program implementation that were related to thyroid malfunction, changes in blood composition, and leukoses, that is, the traditionally expected radiation effects. These priorities, says Prof. Gofman, seem to reflect contempt for the whole of humanity, denying it the unique chance of learning something definite about early health consequences of nuclear accidents. Gofman also suggested creating a global institution of independent international experts to assess nuclear safety, the so-called watchdog authority.

John Gofman must have been looking in a crystal ball when he talked of some scientists' unscrupulousness. It transpired, after Chernobyl, that the Biophysics Institute of the Russian Ministry of Health had, at its disposal, all the facts about the consequences of the Techa accident. For years, no one could access those papers. Everything was strictly classified by the regime. But why didn't the Ilyin team use them to compare the findings with the results obtained after the Chernobyl blast in affected areas? Dog in the manger? This is precisely what Prof. Gofman was talking about—forecasts of long-term consequences of radiation before any symptoms appear, based on the studies of previous nuclear accidents. Or did they use the data after all, but the conclusions, as usual, were classified? There is still no answer to these questions for experts, for journalists, or for the public, even twenty years after Chernobyl. So much for scholarly honesty.

John Gofman's six hundred–page monograph on the consequences of the Chernobyl accident for this and future generations became the first uncensored book to be translated into Russian (already after the collapse of the Soviet Union) and to discuss, frankly and competently, the cardinal problem of the Chernobyl tragedy. Especially as far as the health of people exposed to treacherous small radiation doses over long periods of time was concerned. It became a veritable hit both with specialists and with journalists and residents in affected areas.

The Gofman breakthrough was followed up by *The Petkau Effect*, a book by Swiss nuclear energy expert Ralph Greyb, published in Moscow in translation. (Its publication was no merit of this country's official publishers; the book was translated by a nuclear research enthusiast, Vladimir Yakimets) It was the first publication to provide a complete picture of the path the world's scientists had traveled, from the first description of a case of x-ray-related skin cancer in 1902, followed by a gradual investigation into radiation until scientists hit upon the spectacular results revealing health effects of small radiation doses. A salient point there was the findings of Canadian scientist A. Petkau, who discovered in 1972 that the longer the time of exposure, the smaller the dose before the membrane gets perforated. (He experimented with artificial cell membranes in water suspension subjected to radiation.) It followed from his experiments that chronic exposure to low-dose radiation could have more dangerous effects than a large dose absorbed over a short period of time. That went against the previous ideas about the horrendous effects of radiation. It was nothing if not a revolution in science.

Later, American scientist Dr. Ernest Sternglass demonstrated the Petkau effect in biological systems. It was confirmed that small but chronic radiation doses resulting from nuclear power plants' emissions were one hundred to one thousand times more harmful than the doses absorbed by victims of nuclear bombing of Japan.

By 1980, radiation was already seen as one thousand times more dangerous than that in 1958.

All that became a shattering eye-opener to Soviet society closed against the rest of the world. But who in this country knew anything about these facts even after the Mayak accident in the Urals and after the Chernobyl disaster?

The pro-Kremlin medics certainly had all the facts. But even as they spoke in parliament before people's deputies, or at the sessions of the state expert commission for Chernobyl, they never once said a word that a totally different scientific life had been bubbling away beneath the surface of the iron curtain for nearly one hundred years, where scientists conducted research of paramount importance to nuclear power and made discoveries about man's coexistence with radiation, particularly its small doses that, in full view of the entire world, consumed millions of people in the Soviet Union (as it still does, in the now independent states).

But let us go back to our dissident scientists. In their search for the truth, a group of researchers from the radiobiology council of the Academy of Sciences not only visited the stricken areas, where they studied the local residents' health, but also turned their attention to the physical condition of the liquidators of the disaster consequences— of those poor wretches forsaken by God and Soviet medicine. Prof. Burlakova had to go to Yerevan, Armenia, for that was where local liquidators were monitored by the local radiology institute. Just think, Chernobyl and Yerevan, thousands of miles apart! People had gone from Armenia right into the radiation inferno, thinking little of the dangers. But the state, having used them, instantly forgot all about them. Alas, that is the way it has always been here.

Prof. Burlakova observed,

> Those young guys complain that they feel sick and weak, they have constant headaches, and even an easy walk makes them short-winded. But there is a carefully cultivated view of liquidators' complaints—they make it all up. Could hundreds, thousands of people make all these things up? People in Yerevan, Narodichi, Kiev, Belorussia? Making it up, moreover, in a curiously identical way.... Oh, what's the use! Even kids with thyroid disorders are not registered as accident-related cases in some of the affected areas.

All things in this world may be in a state of continual flux, but in this country nothing seems to change. The secrets of initially accumulated data on people's health in the Urals and in Chernobyl areas are securely buried deep within the vaults of the Biophysics Institute of the Russian Academy of Sciences. No researchers are allowed anywhere near the place—either Russian or Ukrainian, never mind the inquisitive Japanese. And the institute's director, making use of his privileged position, from time to time writes fiction in the form of diatribes against unaccommodating scientists, and also journalists who spread those lies about cancer, when our experts know it's just that disease in the head—"radiophobia."

10

"The Monster is Huge, Massive, and Barking!"

Yes, that popular quotation from *Telemakhida* by the eighteenth-century poet, Vasily Trediakovsky, just about sums up Chernobyl. "The monster is huge, massive, mean, hundred-jawed and barking." It was a global catastrophe. That was the conclusion first made four years after the accident by the state expert commission on Chernobyl. "Its long-term consequences make the accident at the Chernobyl nuclear power plant the greatest disaster of our time." What is the meaning of that? The life span of our blue-green planet is put at approximately ten or twelve billion years. The earth has already covered over a third of that. Well then, during this one-third of the earth's life, there has not been a more devastating man-made disaster in terms of its impact upon the health of millions of people worldwide. Admittedly, there have been other instances of hazardous events involving the "peaceful atom." The worst accident the United States has known, the one that is now described as a Chernobyl warning bell, occurred in Pennsylvania in 1979, at the Three Mile Island Nuclear Power Plant. Before and after it there have been a couple of dozen serious accidents at nuclear reactors, many of them unreported.

In the Soviet Union, there were three accidents that can be viewed as Chernobyl precursors, starting with the disaster in 1949 at the Mayak Nuclear Facility, a secret production operation on the river Techa in the Urals. "During the 11th five-year period, 1,042 emergency reactor stoppages happened, including 381 at nuclear power plants with the RBMK high-power channel reactors. The Chernobyl plant had 104 such cases, 35 of them the fault of its personnel. In September 1982, a nuclear accident occurred at the plant's unit 1 reactor, resulting in the destruction of the technological channel and ejection of the fuel assembly beyond the graphite wall," a quotation from the top secret minutes of the Politburo meeting dated July 3, 1986. Local radioactive contamination was registered after accidents at the Leningrad, Chernobyl (1982), and Kursk nuclear power plants. Yet the people knew absolutely nothing about any of this!

However, all that taken together is but a drop in the radioactive ocean that flooded the earth after the blast in Ukraine. The scale of the Chernobyl disaster, even as cited in the official report of the state expert commission, is mind-boggling. The Soviet report at the IAEA Vienna session in 1986 stated that an aggregate of 50 million curies in various radionuclides had been released into the environment. Special emphasis was made on the 1 million curies of radioactive cesium and 0.22 million curies of radioactive strontium. At the 1989 international conference on nuclear power plant safety in Dagomys, some scientists gave their own estimates: according to them, the released cesium radioactivity had been higher than that. Foreign specialists cited amounts that were 1½ or two times higher than the Soviet ones. For instance, if the Soviet Union, in its report to the IAEA, insisted that iodine-131 emissions amounted to 7.3 million curies, the US Lawrence Livermore National Laboratory's estimates were double than that—14.4 million curies. The same laboratory recorded more than twice the amount of released cesium-137 against the Soviet statistics, while, according to research done by several specialists at nuclear power engineering research centers, the aggregate emissions of cesium-137 equaled three hundred Hiroshimas.

For several weeks after that fateful day of April 26, 1986, the jet stream carried millions of radioactive curies around the world. Scientists were panic-stricken and rendered impotent, helpless in the face of unknown amounts of radionuclides burning in the reactor's destroyed fuel core, where temperatures reached 2500°C. In the dead of night, a silent blanket of sickness and death began to spread out over the Russian landscape and stealthily crossed neighboring borders, invading whole cities and farms of unsuspecting residents.

It seemed the entire periodic table had flown out of the reactor, plus something science was yet to recognize. Here is an assessment of the disaster by Dr. N. N. Vorontsov: "in one way or another, the entire globe is within the Chernobyl zone in a broad sense of the word; and in particular, the whole of the Soviet Union's population. We have a map of dispersal . . . one can see that one of the plumes stretches across the Soviet Union's European center and extends further to the Urals and Western Siberia."

An increase in the radiation background was registered not only by our immediate neighbors Poland, Romania, Norway, Finland, and Sweden, but also—would you believe it!—in Brazil, Japan, Austria, Italy, and other countries. This is what Soviet Hydrometeorology Committee chairman Yu. A. Izrael said.

> Contamination passed via Sweden to Poland, Bulgaria, Germany, Britain, and southern Germany. In those countries contamination levels are above 1 Ci/km². Though only marginally so, 1.2 to 1.5 curies . . . this map I got not only from our meteorologists, but also from their foreign colleagues, it shows very pronounced boundaries; it spread over Northern Italy at the time, and in Bavaria. And where it rained, the stuff (radionuclides) fell out, mostly cesium.

At a session of the parliamentary committee on the environment, Yu. A. Izrael showed us a booklet where wind direction was recorded. Using that booklet, one could trace the movement of radioactive clouds not just by the day, but literally by the hour. "Observe," Yu. A. Izrael pointed out, "here it says exactly—on the 26th, at 15:00 hrs; on the 27th, at three. Part of the Baltic shore within our territory has already been covered. But on the 27th at night, the cloud was here, over Copenhagen. It's the one that emerged at three o'clock in the morning on the 26th." That is to say, within twenty-four hours, radioactive "smoke" had reached the Danish coast.

The people's deputies literally had to squeeze the truth out of Yu. A. Izrael. Once he smelled bad trouble coming, he tried to save his skin. Now, here are the scenarios that the Politburo approved, with Yu. A. Izrael as a coauthor, contained in the appendix to the CPSU Central Committee's top secret resolution, "On the Plan of Propaganda Measures in Connection with the Chernobyl Nuclear Accident Anniversary" (minutes no. 46, April 10, 1987).

> "SECRET." List of publications in the press, radio and television broadcasts, and TASS materials on measures taken in the USSR to eliminate the consequences of the accident at the Chernobyl nuclear power plant. (3) What did the wind rose smell of in April? It is alleged in the West that during the accident a considerable amount of harmful substances was transported to the territories of certain European countries. Commentary by chairman of the USSR Goskomgidromet Yu. A. Izrael who refutes these allegations on the basis of various data. L. Kravchenko, first deputy chairman of the USSR committee on television and radio.

Another "refuter" if you please . . .

According to the data the weather committee chairman cited to the people's deputies, it was still assumed, even four years after the accident, that among the badly contaminated territories in the Soviet Union were just four Russian regions, five Ukrainian regions, and five Belorussian regions. We know that within the first few days after the accident, 116,000 people were evacuated. About 144,000 tracts of farmland liberally sprinkled with radionuclides have been "mothballed" for good. It is a dead zone. Just how many more contaminated lands are plowed and yield crops that are then harvested? To this day, according to official data alone, in the three republics most generously "pollinated" with radionuclides, cesium-rich farmland registering between one- and hundred-curie levels occupies almost 10 million hectares. Over 3 million of those are extremely fertile arable land.

Let us look in greater detail at the global environmental disaster in the aftermath of the Chernobyl blast in the three worst-hit republics.

Ukraine: This breadbasket of the country, as it used to be known in Soviet times, has 377,500 hectares of "dirty" soil with upward of 5 Ci/km^2. These symbols need to be spelled out according to the official data submitted to the State Expert Commission. On top of that, there are the 3,316,000 hectares registering under 5 Ci. The figures seemed dubious to me, so I sent an inquiry to the radiology department of Ukraine's state committee for agricultural industry. The reply surpassed expectations: "dirty" farmland in the Ukraine, I was informed, takes up 7,220,000 hectares. Contamination is especially bad in the Kiev and Zhitomir regions. As deputy chairman of the Kiev region's executive committee N. Stepanenko said, over 1,600,000 hectares of land in the Kiev region were radioactively contaminated. In the Zhitomir region, the total area of "dirty" lands reached 466,700 hectares.

Even today, twenty years on, it is still not known quite how much land is contaminated with radioactive strontium, plutonium, americium, and hot particles that, on getting into the human stomach, turn it into a sort of mini-reactor. Radioactive cesium contamination is averaged in official reports. Often these values are clearly underestimated. For instance, in the village of Ostapy, Luginy District, and Zhitomir region, they are almost double the markings on the official radiological map. When I hear experts talk of average radiation levels, I recall the old joke about the average temperature of hospital patients. (The country's hydrometeorology committee took three years after the accident to release a kind of "crash course" in average radioactive contamination levels of Ukraine's territories. You know, a sort of tranquilizer—with a print run of 425 copies for a country of 250 million inhabitants.)

Take this example. According to the Ukrgidromet (Ukrainian hydrometeorology committee) data, the township of Polesskoe, Kiev region had an average contamination level of 24.7 Ci/km². However, according to data obtained by the Kombinat production association, that level varied from 15 to 300 Ci, and more. On the territory of a Park of Rest (as pleasure grounds are known in this country), four years after the accident, the level was kept at 67 Ci. So whom should we believe? The Kombinat data were obtained on the basis of minute examination of the territory with seventeen hundred samples collected. As for the data of Ukrgidromet, they were based on a mere two hundred samples. This example is quite typical—not just of the Ukraine, either, but of Russia and Belorussia as well.

But even the Kombinat data could hardly be called entirely accurate. After all, they took into account only radioactive cesium. Polesskoe, however, was also contaminated by the fallout of strontium, plutonium, and other radionuclides. The plutonium contamination density there practically equals "temporarily permissible maximums."

Years after the accident, the number of cities and villages listed as contaminated territories has also risen. One such area is the whole of my native Zhitomir region. But even today, twenty years on, as the deputies in the Supreme Rada (Ukraine's parliament) admit, Ukraine still does not have a complete inventory of affected villages. The authorities benefit from this situation. A precise list is an extra headache, as all the victims will have to be provided with benefits.

Belorussia: The primary data submitted to the state expert commission for Chernobyl listed 7,000 km² of land as radioactive in 1989. One-fifth of the arable land was judged extra dangerous for human beings. But the latest data cited by a group of specialists at the Minsk Radiation Medicine and Radiological Research Institute in 2004 wrote off 43,500 km² as contaminated with long-lived isotopes of cesium and strontium. This is more than six times the area originally believed contaminated. Which means that millions of people lived on radioactive land for years, unsuspecting, inhaling and eating radiation! The heaviest burden in Belorussia fell on the long-suffering Mogilev and Gomel regions.

Russia: The program of elimination of the accident's consequences submitted to the expert commission by the republic's council of

129

ministers mentioned just one area, the Bryansk region. It was pointed out that there, in seven western districts, 1,000 km² of land had been affected. Unofficial sources mentioned a figure that was five times higher. The expert commission, meanwhile, established that there was also the Orel-Kaluga-Tula patch where contamination density for cesium-137 was about 5 Ci/km², and in the town of Plavsk, Tula region, it reached 15 Ci/km². The patch spread over more than 2,000 km².

In fact Russia's council of ministers ignored the instructions issued by the USSR government to work out a long-term program for eliminating the consequences of the disaster throughout the whole of the republic. Here is what deputy chairman of the state expert commission A. G. Nazarov, doctor of biology, said in his speech at the parliamentary hearings on April 12, 1990:

> We have just heard a somewhat strange speech by Comrade Tabeev (first deputy chairman of the Russian council of ministers, chairman of the commission for the elimination of the consequences of the accident) relative to the interpretation of the program for the republic.... We have examined, and are still examining, two republic-level programs—one for the Ukraine and one for Belorussia, and a regional program for the Bryansk region—which is presented as the government's program for the entire Russian Federation. There is no information, no mention even, of the huge patch marked on the Goskomgidromet map and covering the Tula, Kaluga, and Orel regions. Nowhere, not at any stage, was that examined, and there is still no comprehensive program for the Russian Federation.

No program for Russia—four years after the accident!

In fact, a whole six years after the blast, the population of sixteen regions in Russia instead of just four—around 2 million people—were daily exposed, unaware of the risks from small radiation doses, while getting not a red cent from the state to make up for health damage. No one has yet been called to account either by the public or by law for that criminal cover-up.

Radioactive contamination maps presented by Gosgidromet to the expert commission gave only a partial idea of the depth and scale of the accident's destructive consequences. Isometric lines marking concentrations of cesium-137 radionuclides are drawn on them with a +/− 30 percent error, or even 50 percent errors at times. Information about strontium-90 was highly misleading. And it was altogether absent when it came to plutonium-239, to say nothing of other types of fallout generously scattered all over the area.

The state expert commission's report points out that radioactive plumes also smeared Krasnodar Territory, an area in the vicinity of Sukhumi, Abkhazia, and another near the Baltic Sea. Krasnodar Territory includes the Black Sea coastal area of the Caucasus. There are hundreds of sanatoriums, holiday homes, and children's summer camps there. Every year, millions of people make a trip to the sea or to the mountains for rest, recreation, and recuperation. I also took my children to Krasnodar Territory, in May 1986, firmly convinced that no Chernobyl plume would reach us out there, for a few weeks at least. Unfortunately, we were mistaken.

To find out exactly what went on there, I sent an inquiry to weather committee chairman Yu. A. Izrael. I asked, "Which *places* precisely, which localities were covered by radioactive fallout patches in the Baltic republics, Krasnodar Territory, and Sukhumi, how badly contaminated the soil was, and what the gamma radiation background was?" The reply came from my acquaintance of long standing, in terms of official correspondence—deputy chairman Yu. S. Tsaturov. This is what he wrote, among other things.

"In the aftermath of the Chernobyl nuclear accident radioactivity levels of atmospheric precipitation and of the atmosphere increased throughout the country, including in Krasnodar Territory, the city of Sukhumi and the territory of the Baltic republics. Thus, on some sections of the USSR western border and in the west of Georgia, USSR Gosgidromet units registered a significant but transient rise on pre-accident atmospheric radioactivity values in late April and early May, 1986, which, however, never reached maximum permissible doses." Lower down, he cited background levels registered in late April and early May, 1986, in Vilnius, Riga, Sukhumi, Tskhaltubo, and Tbilisi.

Passing on to the issue of soil contamination, Tsaturov reported, "In 1986, on the Black Sea coast of the Caucasus, in the vicinity of Sukhumi and Batumi, the cesium-137 contamination density reached 0.2 to 1 Ci/km^2 against the 0.06 to 0.1 Ci/km^2 levels before the accident. In Krasnodar Territory and the Baltic republics the cesium-137 contamination density was considerably lower, under 0.3 Ci/km^2. In August and September 1989, a repeat aerial gammaspectrometric survey of the Baltic territory was carried out, which confirmed the 1986 values." Next Tsaturov remarked, however, that contamination densities had been obtained from surveys "with a spacing of several kilometers." And that means that in-between, local "dirty" patches still lurked undetected. "The 1986 on-site expedition examination

131

revealed minor patches in the vicinity of Batumi where cesium-137 contamination density reached 1 to 1.5 Ci/km^2." (Incidentally, in Sweden, people who sustained radiation exposure on territories with even 1 Ci/km^2 enjoy certain benefits.) "[I]n 1990, in Batumi's Young Pioneers Park," the letter goes on, "were registered increased radiation levels that peaked at 400 mR/hr in one place. The contaminated soil was promptly removed and taken to a burial ground."

And that was that, more or less. True, I did not quite gather from the reply how it was that Georgia's Batumi, Tskhaltubo, and Tbilisi had been part of Krasnodar Territory (which is in the Russian Federation). I asked specifically for information about the radiation situation in Krasnodar Territory, not in Georgia. Let me note that this manner of failing to hear what someone is asking, be it a people's deputy or a voter, has long since become the trademark style of many officials. I had to try again, insisting on more precise and accurate information about contamination levels in Krasnodar Territory, thousands of miles away from Chernobyl.

Here is what I got, this time from the chairman, in person.

> In early May 1986, following precipitation, radiation levels registered in Sochi, for instance, reached 120 mR/hr, with Anapa, Lazarevskoe, Kanevskaya registering 60 mR/hr, and Kushchevskaya and Gornaya, 35 mR/hr. Owing to the decay of short half-life radioisotopes, the contamination dosage rapidly decreased. For instance, in Sochi it did not exceed 35 mR/hr in 1987, dropped to 20 mR/hr in 1988, and is currently within the natural background level at 10 to 15 mR/hr. As for cesium-137 contamination, it averages 0.4 to 1.4 Ci/km^2 in Sochi, 0.34 Ci/km^2 in Tuapse, and 0.1 Ci/km^2 in Gelenjik, Novorossiysk, Anapa and Krasnodar. Similar and lower values have also been registered in other towns and villages in Krasnodar Territory, while gamma radiation dosage rates do not differ significantly from the natural radioactive background, i.e. they vary between 10 and 20 mR/hr.

The reply also warned that there could be local patches with contamination levels "somewhat higher than the cited values. A case in point—206 local anomalies of one to several dozen square meters, where the 1989 aerial gammaretrospective survey revealed gamma radiation emissions between 90 and 600 mR/hr. The biggest contaminated area was observed in the vicinity of Adler Airport (up to 250 mR/hr) and near the water inlet in Sochi (up to 160 mR/hr)."

Let me remind the reader that I sent these inquiries to the committee for hydrometeorology in the summer of 1990, four years after the accident! The replies came back—dripping with honey! There was trouble, granted, but it's all over now. And then, more than eighteen months later, the daily *Izvestia* published an article called "Chernobyl Traces in the Center of Sochi." It turned out that five years after the accident, nine hundred radioactive patches had been discovered there, smack dab in the center of the city, on top of the four hundred patches registered previously. The article said that the discoveries happened in the most unexpected places in residential areas, on streets, on Flower Boulevard, beside the Winter Theater, and on the lawns next to the city executive committee premises. Two hundred of the nine hundred patches had already been decontaminated. The "dirty" soil was being removed and buried on the burial site in the vicinity of the Mamai Pass.

Some thirteen hundred newly discovered radioactive patches (in just two years) in the center of an international health resort—isn't that a bit over the top? For nearly five years, people had been walking over those patches, vacationing there, and breathing in that stuff. How many people? Hundreds, thousands, millions? And where are they all now? In Leningrad? Dushanbe? Berlin?

And how many more years will our government need to conduct equally detailed examination of the entire territory not only in Krasnodar but in other regions as well, those that got polluted by radioactive fallout? True, if the government proved unequal to the job of resettling those who had already absorbed more than their fair share in hard radiation zones, what's the use talking about other villages and towns thousands of miles away from the center of "nuclear warfare" in Europe? That's what I said, the center of nuclear warfare. After all, the official data mentioned a total of 50 million Ci in radioactivity released in the wake of the reactor meltdown, while a typical A-bomb explosion in the atmosphere yields a "mere" 150,000 Ci. When I was writing these lines, I had not yet seen the top secret document by the Politburo that described a meeting on Chernobyl where the Politburo members referred to that disaster precisely as a "mini-nuclear war in the heart of Europe." What they were saying to the world at large painted a different picture.

After the Soviet Union disintegrated, each of the three republics worst hit by radioactive fallout has been trying to tackle its problems single-handed. By the time the Commonwealth of Independent States was set up at the end of 1991, the total area of cesium-137 contamination in the aftermath of the Chernobyl accident, with a density of upward of 1 Ci/km², was over 100,000 km² in the Russian Federation, the Ukraine, and Belorussia taken together!

The humanitarian consequences of the catastrophe are nothing if not global. Vast numbers of people found themselves in the radioactive catastrophe zone. Four years after the blast, the government officially registered 2,504,000 of them. This defies all logic. In Russia alone there are 2 million people living in the sixteen regions with contaminated territories! According to the UN, there are currently 9 million people residing in areas rendered radioactive by Chernobyl—including much of Europe!

The genes pool in Belorussia has been pushed to the brink of destruction. As the representative of the Belorussian Supreme Soviet Commission for Eliminating the Consequences of the Chernobyl Nuclear Accident said at pre-parliamentary hearings, "life has made sure that the tragic history of the Belorussian nation was re-enacted. Whereas in the Second World War we lost every fourth citizen, the Chernobyl accident is taking away every fifth."

For the reader to visualize the full depth of despair people in affected areas experience, I would like to cite the following fact. In twelve districts of the Gomel and Mogilev regions, five hundred villages are contaminated. Of those, 184 villages are within strict-monitoring zones. There, radiation levels reach 140 Ci/km². In one of the villages in the Krasnopolye District, the cobbles in the kindergarten courtyard register over 100 mR/hr. Next to the sandbox, it is over 200 mR; on the grass of the lawn, 450 mR. That, given that the human tolerance level is 20 mR. And just a stone's throw away, in someone's orchard, the dosage rate is almost 400 Ci/km². According to the latest data, 2.1 million Belorussians (i.e., 23 percent of the population) still live, twenty years after the explosion, in areas with radioactive cesium contamination levels exceeding 40 kBq/m². Some 135,000 have been resettled in "cleaner" places within the same republic. Why cleaner and not just clean? Because there aren't any clean areas!

In the Ukraine, according to the first official data made public (four years after the event), it was assumed that living in contaminated areas were 1,480,000 people. My inquiry as a people's deputy about resettling in safe localities the people who live in hazardous areas sent to Ukraine's Council of Ministers elicited this response from deputy chairman of the Ukrainian State Planning Committee V. P. Popov:

"In 1990–1991, 45,000 persons will have to be resettled." Over twenty thousand people were to be moved out of radioactive villages in the Zhitomir region and resettled in its southern parts—although even four years after the accident the affected area had 93,000 people living in 455 residential localities, among them almost 20,000 children. The numbers keep spewing out, but they can never describe the pain and suffering of so many hundreds of thousands of families who have been uprooted, their lives literally brought to a standstill.

Another problem was what to do with the people in new houses built in the Zhitomir region for evacuees in obviously radioactive areas. That was hundreds of millions of public money down the drain, to say nothing of the moral injury and irreparable damage to the health of thousands upon thousands of utterly innocent people. And what of future generations who will carry the mutational scars, the grim result of their scrambled DNA? Who gave his blessing to this enterprise? Who took responsibility for the decisions?

I tried in vain to find this out while I was still touring the radioactive villages in the wake of the accident. In the previous chapters, I described the behavior of various persons in authority who ignominiously tried to shift the blame onto one another as soon as they got my drift. Today I know all the addresses. I learned them from a reply to my inquiry as a member of parliament from chairman of the Zhitomir Regional Executive Committee, A. S. Malinovsky. After all, construction work in hard-radiation zones had been conducted "in accordance with the resolution by the Ukrainian Communist Party Central Committee and Council of Ministers." Some consolation!

In all, there had been six such incompetent and irresponsible resolutions by Ukrainian Communist Party and government. Besides, there were four relevant circular letters issued jointly by the Zhitomir Regional Party Committee and the Regional Executive Committee. According to official information, ninety-three families of evacuees had been moved out of their houses in dangerous zones and given newly built accommodation in equally "dirty" areas. If that is not a crime, I would like to know what is. Meanwhile, Comrade Malinovsky is now teaching students at the Zhitomir Ecology Academy (formerly the Soviet Agricultural Institute). I doubt that he has been telling them about his own "heroic" Chernobyl past in his capacity as regional executive committee chairman.

A similarly frightening situation emerged in the Kiev region. In more than seventy villages, contamination density reached upward of

135

5 Ci/km^2. Particularly badly hit was the Polesskoe District. The townships of Yasen and Shevchenko were not fully evacuated even in 1990. As academician L. A. Ilyin informed the people's deputies, the village of Yasen had not been included in the resettlement list till 1993. What did that mean for the villagers? Even according to official data, their dosage load by then would have grown to almost 35 rem. The Kiev Regional Executive Committee intended to resettle the inhabitants of thirteen villages, that is, nearly twenty thousand people. The reason why the authorities did not try to preserve the health of more people was easy to explain—lack of money. It also remained shockingly incomprehensible why a person willing to leave the contaminated area could not do it on his or her own. Why did they have to wait for the authorities to move their family? A woman speaking at a people's meeting in Narodichi said, in a fit of anger, aiming her words at the authorities, "I don't want anything from you, no money, not anything. Just let me leave this place. I don't want to stay on here. Help me go away so that someplace else, where it's clean, I could get a job and registration." What was that if not serfdom Soviet-style? Nearly five years after the accident, they started discussing resettlement for the inhabitants of six villages in the Rovno and Chernihiv regions, while the residents of Ivano-Frankovsk (i.e., Western Ukraine) learned about radioactive clouds that had fallen on them that fated spring.

Today, Russian experts argue, 2.4 million people are living in radioactive areas in Ukraine. Over five hundred thousand of them are children under age fourteen. That is a million (a whole million!) more than four years after the accident. So the farther away from Chernobyl, it seems, the deadlier its embrace. But the people who found themselves in the worst quandary in the first years after Chernobyl were Russians. Those living in Belarus and Ukraine had some knowledge of the accident, and there was at least some resettlement, however inadequate, but it took several years for the truth about the Kaluga-Orel-Tula plume to emerge. No one in the government had a clear idea of the numbers of people involved. The entire radiation situation in Russia was officially restricted to the Bryansk region. There the affected area contained over seven hundred villages. One-fifth of the region's population lived there, with nearly thirty thousand children in the strict-monitoring zone. By April 1990, a mere 20 percent of the residents had been evacuated from danger zones. In the villages of Zaborye, Tsukovets, Kobali, Porki, and Nikolaevna, where life itself had become a hazard, people were still living well after the Soviet

Union's collapse, although quite a few of the children had already absorbed dosage exceeding even Ilyin's norms.

The report by Russian specialists M. S. Malikov of the All-Russia Living Standards Center at the Russian Labor Ministry and State Duma expert O. Yu. Tsitser stated that currently there are 138 administrative districts, 16 towns, and over 7,700 residential localities in Russia affected by the Chernobyl fallout, comprising 2.7 million people. According to the same report, residential localities in affected territories have been decontaminated in the wake of the Chernobyl accident and radioactive soil has been removed from 630,000 m². Thirteen thousand people in contaminated areas in the Bryansk region have been resettled, and eighteen townships and villages have been evacuated. By 1993, some fifty thousand people had been rehoused or had voluntarily left the contaminated areas in the Russian Federation.

Lately, a fair number of theories have been voiced as to whether the radioactive material from Chernobyl could have taken a different tack. Belorusian writer Ales Adamovich published a letter in the national press to deputy chairman of the USSR Council of Ministers and chairman of the Fuel and Energy Complex Bureau, B. Ye. Shcherbina, and Nuclear Power Engineering minister, N. F. Lukonin. He asked if it was true that parts of the Mogilev region, a fair distance from Chernobyl, the Krasnopolye, Slavgorod, and Cherikov districts, in part the Kostyukovichi, Bykhov, Klimovichi, and several other districts (as well as some districts in the Bryansk region) had absorbed such a mammoth dose of radiation because the Chernobyl cloud had been "forced down" there. The cloud that was being blown toward Moscow was shelled to induce precipitation and forced down to earth.

Some scientists have also voiced similar conjectures. As for the residents of the Mogilev region, they do not doubt it at all.

But is this true? And if so, what shape could the radioactive plume have assumed if the wretched cloud had been allowed to speed on and on? Where would its most likely "landing site" have been in that case? This question inevitably arose also at the Environment Committee session, during the conversation between people's deputies and experts, on one hand, and Weather Committee chairman Yu. A. Izrael, on the other. His explanation is as follows:

> About the 10th of May Nikolai Ivanovich Ryzhkov (chairman of the country's Council of Ministers) phoned me and said, "Let us do everything humanly possible to prevent rain from falling in the Chernobyl area. Radioactive decay is under way. The 'hottest'

material will decay. To achieve that, it would be necessary to send aircraft to meet ordinary clouds moving toward Chernobyl (some days there weren't any, and sometimes there was quite an intensive cloud drifting), and also heap clouds, fairly powerful, so that the clouds would be induced to release moisture." We did that, starting from May 10. Later another problem arose. Ukrainians and Belorussians said, "Do you know if this can cause drought?" There was that fear, you know, and Nikolai Ryzhkov again told me, "Come on, leave those clouds alone, God knows what it may do, in the matter of drought." And I repeat that our aircraft flew strictly within that sector and only into clean clouds and induced rain where it was safe to do so. The first rainfall in the Chernobyl area occurred after June 15, when we had already finished the job.

Yu. A. Izrael rejected out of hand Adamovich's version that the cloud had been forcefully "precipitated":

> there are these totally absurd ideas that came from somewhere that the patch was precipitated on Belorussian territory. Incidentally, the radioactive plume formed there in the very first days. It did indeed rain heavily there on April 27 and 28. So that remote patch, the Tula, and the Mogilev, and the Gomel one, these resulted not only from rains but also from the fallout.

Then the cloud-shelling version was a myth? However, it is also certain that if the clouds had not shed the stuff they were carrying on Belorussian fields and on Bryansk forests, they would have sailed over as far as Moscow. That is something everyone seems to admit. As for heavy particles, they reached the capital all right. They were found even in flowerpots on balconies. It is perfectly possible that some drifted into Muscovites' homes through open windows.

Another post-Chernobyl disaster positively global in its consequences was the mindless plowing in the fields and meadows sprinkled with radioactive cesium, and harvesting and processing of crops that glowed with radiation. When, way back in the spring of 1989, people's deputies resolutely demanded that all radioactive farmland be put out of circulation before sowing started; chairman of the State Commission for Chernobyl, V. Kh. Doguzhiev, reassured us that the matter would be attended to. "No one was going to plow and sow there," he said. But that too was a lie as no decision had been taken. The fields were duly sown and harvested.

Here is a memo by chairman of the USSR State Committee for Agricultural Industry, V. S. Murakhovsky, attached to a top secret resolution by the CPSU Central Committee Politburo of May 8, 1986. It said, among other things: "In areas subjected to radioactive contamination (apart from the evacuation zone) agricultural work is being carried out according to plan, which is a means of reducing the intake of radioactive substances for plants and animals [Priceless, isn't it? This Party hypocrisy!]. By May 5, a total of 83 percent of the spring crops had been sown, including 84 percent in the Kiev region, and 88 percent in the Gomel region." These are precisely the two most contaminated regions.

The Belorusian Agriculture Committee made the following estimates five years after the accident: for the "dirty" produce from "dirty" fields to conform to at least the temporarily permissible increased levels, thus the republic would have to spend one billion rubles a year. How do you like that? Investing so much money (given our dire poverty!) in improving the produce that would certainly be heavily contaminated. What a stroke of genius!

Some time ago Belarus' "dear leader" Lukashenko gave orders to resume work on radioactive fields, to bring them again into agricultural circulation, and to forget about improvement.

This is the twentieth spring of radioactive sowing in what are now independent states. Work has started on the quiet on cesium lands in Russia, too. Here, it appears, special agrochemical research was done on radioactively contaminated territories to reduce the radionuclide content in agricultural produce. In some parts of the Bryansk, Orel, Tula, and Kaluga regions, the areas sown with forage crops have been expanded, while those sown with cereal crops have been cut down. Buckwheat and rapeseed are not sown at all. As some experts, like ex-chairman of Russia's State Committee for Chernobyl Nuclear Accident Consequences Elimination, V. Ya. Voznyak, allege that the measures taken allowed soil fertility to be increased and the rate of radionuclide absorption by plants to be reduced 1.5 to 4 times.

Personally I feel grave doubts about these figures, particularly when cited by V. Ya. Voznyak, with whom I had a talk back in 1989, when everything was still kept under wraps, not least thanks to his silence. Just as I doubt the fact that it is necessary to plow, sow, and harvest anything at all in obviously radioactive fields to produce food for humans or even for animals only. As this Moscow bureaucrat sits in his comfortable office, he decides what people need, those unfortunate souls who live in a zone of daily risk to their health. This is beyond my understanding, totally unacceptable. What hubris! Besides, wasn't the expanse of Russia vast enough to yield cleaner land for plowing? That taciturn ex-Party functionary, incidentally, got a D.Sc. degree for his thesis on Chernobyl, what else. Indeed, it's an ill wind that blows nobody any good.

Today, peasants continue to plow and sow and harvest radionuclide-contaminated fields; they graze cattle in cesium meadows; they rear pigs on farms. And all that ends up on out tables. Radioactive mushrooms, potatoes, and meat are delivered to all parts of the country, even to Black Sea Coast sanatoriums. Get well, dear comrades. Radiation is still traveling about uncontrolled, *dulcis fumus patriae.*

It used to be told in Ukraine as a joke that the Narodichi District, the worst contaminated of all, was named the winner of the All-Union socialist emulation in the first half of 1989 and awarded the Red Banner for the feat. But that was no joke, it was just the idiocy of Party bosses. The district produced a thousand tons of meat more for the state than the previous year. Potatoes, vegetables, eggs, and meat from that district were sent not only to Ukraine's regions, for example, to the Donetsk Basin miners, but also to the Moscow and Leningrad regions and to Central Asia.

For many years, the radiation "experts" have spoken in glowing terms of temporary tolerance levels (TTL) and maximum permissible levels (MPL). Temporary implied twelve months at the most, as a rule. But as the popular saying goes in these parts, there is nothing more permanent than temporary things. The MPL is the maximum permissible radionuclide level. The actual level, even four years after the accident, was eight to nine times than that in beef, and five times than that in pork and mutton. After Chernobyl, there appeared a new quasi-scientific term—"internal irradiation leveling." For instance, contaminated meat from the Gomel region is sent to Minsk. And today Minsk residents are getting radiation doses equal to that in the natives of one of the worst contaminated regions. Twenty years on, the levels have got so beautifully "leveled" that at present, according to Belorusian scientists, cancer incidence in the Minsk and Vitebsk regions is catching up with the Gomel and Mogilev figures.

In the first five years after the accident, Zhitomir's meat processing and packing factory every now and then returned "dirty" meat to collective farms, with radiation counts far exceeding even the raised MPLs. V. Puziychuk, chief livestock specialist with the Svitanok collective farm of the Narodichi District, wrote in his memo for the visiting inspectors from the regional authorities, "In 1988–1989 we delivered livestock produce. The livestock was accepted with high radioactive contamination levels at my request." And Prof. Burlakova described a high-ranking ex-Agroprom (Soviet super-ministry for agriculture) official telling radiobiologists, with pride, "Thanks to raised temporary tolerance levels, the state has saved 1.7 billion rubles!" What were they economizing on? The health of our people? Our own future?

It is still quite a problem that residents of stricken areas eat contaminated foodstuffs from their own plots—above all, milk and dairy products, as well as meat, wild fruit and berries, and mushrooms. Also, fish. If, during the first few years after the accident, there was at least some monitoring of locally produced foodstuffs. Now all attempts at control have been abandoned. Another problem yet to be solved is the delivery of clean food to the people living in contaminated areas. For instance, in 1995, Ukraine supplied barely 8–20 percent of "clean" milk, oil, butter, meat, vegetables, and sugar as compared to the 1991 level, and deliveries of vegetables, meat, oil, and cereals had been halved. Milk and sugar consignments have shrunk by more than two-thirds. The same is true of Russia and Belarus in many of the affected areas.

Here is what deputy prosecutor general of the USSR, V. I. Andreev, replied to my inquiry as a people's deputy.

> The USSR State Agricultural Industry Committee failed to ensure strict radioactivity monitoring of farm operations in radioactive contamination zones, as well as of produce disposal. As a result, in the period between 1986 and 1989, 47,500 tons of the meat produced in those zones, and two million tons of milk, had contamination levels exceeding tolerance dosages. The bulk of that produce went outside the contaminated areas in the Ukraine, Belorussia, and Russia. Belorussia alone sent 15,000 tons of contaminated meat to other parts of the country. These policies resulted in radioactive contamination of foodstuffs being sent throughout the country and may adversely affect public health.

In the wake of the accident, Belorussia produced 28,100 tons of radioactive meat. Some four thousand tons was buried. Five thousand tons was put to good use—processed for dry fodder—and fifteen thousand tons went to replenish the Union stocks, for the benefit of the brotherly republics' citizens. By official permission of the Russian Federation's Council of Ministers, "dirty" meat from the Bryansk, Mogilev, Kiev, and Zhitomir regions was sent to the Arkhangelsk, Kaliningrad, Gorky, Yaroslavl, Ivanovo, Vladimir, and other areas and also to the Chuvash Republic and the Komi Autonomous Republic.

The deputy prosecutor general of the Soviet Union pointed out that "the temporary tolerance levels of radioiodine in drinking water and foodstuffs, as well as permissible levels of radioactive substances in foodstuffs were worked out and approved by the USSR Ministry of Health in those weeks after the accident, causing extra irradiation of the population from consuming food contaminated with radionuclides." Just try and take in these words, this utter and complete bureaucratic gibberish. Because some wise guy in Moscow pronounced this apple fit for human consumption on account of permissible limits raised by this selfsame wise guy, it has not become less radioactive, has it now? It is every bit as contaminated as it was before. That is, no "extra irradiation," but extra deception. However, it is unlikely that Mr. Public Prosecutor understands the full meaning of what he signed.

The same applies to blanket decontamination. To perform it, 220,000 servicemen of chemical warfare units were pressed into service. Experts concluded that there were no scientific grounds for that. The expected effect was never achieved. The topsoil was sliced off and dumped into burial sites—Ukraine alone has eight hundred of them, but shortly afterwards, the fresh cuts were again filmed over with radioactive cesium. Right after the accident, this kind of decontamination cost a million rubles. Five years later, the cost shot up to one billion rubles. Such is the price of fraud and abuse. Speaking at the session of the Supreme Soviet Chernobyl Commission, G. S. Sakulin, coordinating expert and doctor of chemistry, described decontamination in areas with superhigh contamination levels as "ineffective," but the army simply obeyed someone's stupid order. Now, what currency, what unit would be adequate for computing the amount of health those young soldiers ruined while doing that work? Their collective irradiation dose added up to almost 1,000,000 rem, gift of Mr. Ilyin and company.

The global-scale catastrophe destroyed not only fertile land but also superb forests. Millions of hectares have been stricken. The whole world has heard of the "rusty forest." It is dead. In the end, the woods were disposed of as radioactive waste, and now there is new growth in their place. What is happening to wild nature in strict radiation-monitoring areas? Mammoth mutants have appeared—oak leaves, pine needles, acacia spikes, and other parts of plants. Birch trees grow unusual doubled catkins. Narodichi residents say that their vegetable plots produce enormous cucumbers and pumpkins with odd-looking stems. Certain deviations from the norm have also been detected in small mammals. Already within the first two years after the accident, the share of dead animal embryos rose to 34 percent. The normal rate is 6 percent. Our less fortunate brethren display bone marrow disorders and defective cellular structure of liver and spleen. Some of them have lost their hair.

In economic terms, the consequences of the global catastrophe at the Chernobyl Nuclear Power Plant cost the country over 10 billion rubles, according to official estimates (in 1986 prices). The Three Mile Island accident in the United States incurred $135 billion in losses for that country, but there is no comparison when it comes to the health consequences. And that makes one doubt the accuracy of Soviet statistics. After the U.S. accident, just a few people absorbed 0.35 rem each, according to the American authorities' official reports. In this country, several million people have been exposed to higher doses. The modest figure of Chernobyl losses cited by Soviet officialdom strongly suggests that there, too, ideological juggling must have been at work, implying that nothing much had happened. Thus, no need to worry. But today, Belarus alone spends a quarter of its budget on dealing with the ongoing effects. In monetary terms, according to President Lukashenko, this amounts to one billion dollars a year.

By some independent estimates, the country's losses from the Chernobyl accident until 2000 were 180 to 200 billion rubles (in 1986 prices). Does this figure take into account the losses from illnesses and deteriorating quality of life endured by thousands upon thousands of people? Hardly.

The collapse of the Soviet Union and the systemic economic crisis hitting the newly independent states merely exacerbates the global nuclear disaster, while the nuclear industry sits smugly on the sidelines, confident that their technology is safe. Are the weak economies of the newly independent states up to overcoming the Chernobyl catastrophe, a disaster on a global scale?

Even now, the reactor continues to leak its deadly poison. Is it possible that our scientific elites will be unable to contain this angry atomic genie? "The monster is huge, massive and barking!"

11

Reactor 'Round Our Neck

The villagers of Ladyzhino in the Vinnitsa region are hardly aware of having been spared by the grace of Lord only. This act of divine mercy happened on March 15, 1966. That was the day when the USSR Energy Ministry approved the village of Kopachi in the Kiev region as the site for the Central Ukrainian nuclear power plant—although the original option was Ladyzhino. The board of the Ukrainian Gosplan (state planning committee) chose the Kiev region, a neighborhood not far from the capital. That was the plant christened Chernobyl, after the nearest district center. The decision by Ukraine's Gosplan of February 2, 1967, was confirmed by a resolution of the CPSU Central Committee and the USSR Council of Ministers. That was the beginning. The end we know only too well.

As the years pass between today and the Chernobyl meltdown in 1986, the closer we seem to be moving to it—even as we sort out the mountain of lies. Anatoly Dyatlov, who had absorbed nearly 500 rem, spent three years in prison and was freed, but the release was not much better than parole for him. To be free from what had happened, from his endless painful thoughts, was beyond comprehension. Dyatlov would not have been released but for the public effort, the intercession by people's deputies of the USSR, and ultimately, the intervention by Mikhail Gorbachev. (Gorbachev was fully aware that the convicted men were mere scapegoats). Dyatlov died a short while ago, quietly, unnoticed by the country at large. The main protagonist and witness of the terrible man-made disaster has died, but the consequences of that disaster will leave its genetic imprint forever.

While rummaging through my Chernobyl archives, I came across one more curious document pertaining to that judicial farce. Its large capital letters caught my attention. "SECRET. CPSU CENTRAL COMMITTEE. On the court trial of the case connected with the Chernobyl nuclear power plant accident." In one corner it sported a stamp saying "14 April 1987, Sector Two 1301. To be returned to the general section of the CPSU Central Committee." In part, the paper read as follows:

> In accordance with instructions contained in the memorandum by chairman of the USSR Supreme Court Comrade Terebilov on the procedure of conducting the said trial and certain organizational matters involved in it. At present the anti-Soviet campaign abroad is gathering momentum in view of the approaching anniversary of the Chernobyl accident. Therefore it would be advisable to start the court proceedings later (in June or July 1987). Holding the trial in Kiev appears inexpedient. It can be held in one of Ukraine's towns, for instance in the town of Chernobyl or in the township of Zeleny Mys in the Kiev region. . . . Detailed coverage of the case is not recommended. . . . The local state and Party bodies, as well as the USSR atomic power ministry and the USSR medium engineering industry ministry, should be instructed to render all necessary assistance to the USSR Supreme Court in organizing the trial. We request approval. N. Savinkin, Yu. Sklyarov, I. Yastrebov, V. Petrovsky, G. Ageev.

These are the signatures of the authors of the secret decision. Their status and titles were omitted. All of them were heads of departments at various levels and in the CPSU Central Committee. Some regularly attended the task group's secret sessions. The consent they requested was duly given, at the highest level, on the same day! "Agreed. Ligachev, Lukyanov"—and a few more illegible signatures scrawled by hand, which I have not yet managed to identify.

Today, twenty years on, few people may remember that in the course of the court trial in the summer of 1987, a separate case was initiated. It was supposed to inquire into the reliability of the design of the RBMK reactor that was used not only in Chernobyl but also at nine more nuclear power plants. (It still is, for that matter.) Here is what deputy prosecutor general of the USSR V. I. Andreev told me concerning the proceedings late in 1989:

> The prosecutor general's office of the Soviet Union, for the purpose of clarifying the issue of design reliability of this reactor type, initiated an action and, while investigating the case, conducted an expert examination involving respected and acknowledged specialists in nuclear power engineering. The experts agreed that the technological devices of the reactor's control and protection systems ensured safe operation of the unit, provided the maintenance schedule was observed. In connection with the aforementioned experts' report, the case was dismissed, because the accident had occurred as a result

of numerous violations of reactor safety rules, including deactivation of several technical protection devices.

In short, everything was perfectly normal.

Or was it? To learn the particulars of the case, our parliamentary commission for examining the causes of the Chernobyl accident and assessing the actions of officials in the postaccident period had to exert considerable effort to obtain the case materials in the USSR Supreme Court. Several days later there was a phone call from the Supreme Court, and we were told insistently to return all the documents most urgently. But the commission leaders decided to keep the papers until we had examined them thoroughly. The USSR prosecutor general's office offered us the assistance of seven prosecutors as legal experts.

The heavy batch of folders "in the case of persons who failed to take timely measures to improve the design of the reactor units of the RBMK-1000 type" contained quite a few interesting revelations sprinkled with more than just radioactive dust.

These are a few of the question–answer exchanges between the court and the experts.

"Did the reactor design affect the course of the accident?" Answer: "Yes, it did."

The report by the government commission also indicated the following:

> The course of the accident that caused reactor disintegration was due to design defects in the reactor. . . . The immediate cause of the initial reactivity increase was the boiling of water in the fuel core. . . . That initial radioactivity growth revealed a fault in the reactor design: a positive steam effect caused by the active section structure.
> The initial reactivity growth was not suppressed at an early stage of regulating and safety rod movement after the reactor's emergency protection system was activated. That highlighted a second fault in the reactor design—the flawed design of the regulation and safety rods.

During the next several months, our commission received a fair amount of extremely interesting documents shedding light on the mystery of the second case, the one that was supposed to inquire into reactor design faults but never was taken up by the court. We found one Mr. A. A. Yadrikhinsky, a specialist at the Kursk Nuclear Power Plant, who, as it turned out, had sent a warning letter to the state committee for nuclear power engineering supervision a whole six months before the Chernobyl disaster. It indicated that RBMK-type reactors were unsafe, arguing for an independent expert examination. He also wrote that they had to be shut down so that the regulation and safety system could be redesigned. In reply, his conclusions were dismissed as groundless.

What was the reason for such a cavalier attitude? Excessive self-confidence? An honest mistake? Or sheer arrogance? Some dim-witted retired inspector-engineer for nuclear safety—what could he possibly know? Talk about a prophet not being heard in his own country! The horrendous prediction of Yadrikhinsky was fulfilled just six months later, with devastating results. After the Chernobyl accident, Yadrikhinsky was sent to the disaster site. He was permitted access to the documents and to the wheezing, dying reactor, and he calculated and quantified everything all over again. His painstaking work, a report entitled "The Nuclear Accident at the Unit 4 Reactor of the Chernobyl Nuclear Power Plant and Nuclear Safety of RBMK Reactors," has now assumed a near-legendary status. Many people have heard of it. Few have read it. Our commission had the original version of the report at its disposal.

At this point I would like to digress a little. On June 24, 1989, a session of the USSR Supreme Soviet Committee for the Environment and Rational Use of Resources was convened. The meeting discussed chairmanship nominations for a new committee, the USSR State Atomic Industry Monitoring Committee. You see, there used to be two of them—the state committee for technological supervision and the state committee for nuclear monitoring, but now there was just one—the state committee of the USSR for supervising safety in the industries and in nuclear power engineering. Was it good or bad? One thing was clear. In view of the international commitments this country had made, it had to have an independent committee for safety monitoring in nuclear power engineering.

This is how the contender for the post of the new joint committee chairman, V. M. Malyshev, explained the issue:

> The United States is the only country in the world to have a proper supervisory body looking after safety in nuclear power engineer-ing. It has a commission headed by a chairman appointed by the country's president. The commission of 3,400 employees has a $400-million budget. $120 million funds research that ensures relevant policies of safety on a centralized basis, that is, feasibility studies, research projects, et cetera. This is the only example of its

kind. In every other country these commissions or committees exist as part of various other committees. When I was offered this job, I refused it out of hand. When asked why, I said that in my view it was wrong.

People's deputies, too, voiced doubts as to the wisdom of the decision. But this country, as ever, opted for untrodden paths.

On February 27, 1990, on the orders of the newly formed committee, a commission was set up to look into the causes and circumstances of the accident at the Chernobyl Nuclear Power Plant's unit 4. Its report, signed by commission chairman Nikolai Steinberg, contains almost eighty pages of typescript. Just the list of research papers relative to the accident by domestic and foreign scientists, design data, service forms, and records takes up five pages. The amount of work that went into it was enormous. Isn't it odd? By the time the Steinberg report was written, five years had passed since the accident, dozens of seminars had been conducted, as had research and technology consultations and domestic and international symposia. Finally, reports had been sent to the IAEA. Still, feelings ran high in the scientific community over the Chernobyl-type reactor. Was it not because in the postaccident years not a single really comprehensive publication had appeared in specialist periodicals that could be regarded as definitive? Personally I, and many other members of our commission, saw the Steinberg report as such at the time.

What proved unexpected and tremendously interesting was the result of analyzing reports submitted by the Soviet Union to the IAEA expert conference held in August 25–29, 1986, in Vienna, and to the international conference on nuclear power engineering safety held in September 28–October 2, 1987, named "The Chernobyl Accident: A Year On." In both of those reports the official version of the causes given by our government cited "an extremely unlikely combination of operating conditions and breach of procedure by the unit personnel." And that was that. The curious thing is, though, that the Kurchatov Atomic Energy Institute's report, which was approved later than the IAEA report, states that the "primary cause of the accident was an extremely unlikely combination of operating conditions and breach of procedure by the unit personnel that *revealed the faulty design of the reactor as well as of regulating and safety rods.*" The words I have emphasized are absent from the report to the IAEA. Why this omission? The truth for domestic consumption vs. the truth for export?

Here is what the Steinberg commission writes in its report, among other things:

Deviations from the safety norms and regulations in nuclear power engineering present in the RBMK-1000 reactor design and its inherent faults were known as early as the end of May and the beginning of June, 1986. Information to that effect exists in various statements and reports submitted to the government commission. However, the revealed defects of the reactor design and its unsatisfactory physical characteristics had not been conveyed to the broad circles of specialists and the public. Nor are these facts present in the materials submitted to the IAEA. Much earlier, on December 28, 1984, the interdepartmental science and technology council for nuclear power engineering passed a resolution approving the proposals by expert commissions 4 and 5 set up by the council to work out measures for partly bringing the RBMK-1000 reactors now in operation up to the requirements of safety regulation documents. However, the council's expert commissions unfortunately overlooked certain features of the RBMK-1000 reactor that proved crucial in the triggering and further course of the 26 April, 1986 accident.

Back in 1967, the country's national economy had been offered three reactor types to choose from—RBMK-1000, RK-1000 (gas-cooled nuclear reactor), and VVER-1000 (water-cooled and water-moderated reactor). The first type had the worst technological and economic characteristics. But then it was at a much more advanced state of development and could offer better equipment delivery terms. So the original decision to use the gas-cooled and graphite-moderated reactor was reconsidered and another, fatal, decision was taken in favor of the RBMK-1000.

In its report the Steinberg commission cites dozens of instances of nuclear safety regulations at atomic power plants having been violated and general regulations of safety insurance during nuclear power plant design, construction, and operation ignored. Hence the sad conclusion:

The listed set of negative features in the reactor of the examined type must inevitably predetermine the prevalence of emergency situations rather than suggest their exceptional nature, given an extremely unlikely combination of operating conditions and breach of procedure by unit personnel.... The reactor designers must have been aware of the dangerous consequences entailed by its characteristics as well as of the ways to enhance the RBMK-1000 safety standards. This is borne out by the fact that within just six weeks of the accident the immediate technological measures to be taken to enhance the reactor safety were listed. . . . Clearly, the essence of these measures does not tally with the official version that the accident was caused exclusively by personnel errors.

So why did several personnel have to go to jail? How did it happen that the information sent to the IAEA was so one-sided? Had there been any scientists and experts who understood and pointed out the design faults of the RBMK-1000 type reactor? Apart from Yadrikhinsky, who became the forerunner of this approach, the interdepartmental commission under A. G. Meshkov, the newly appointed USSR deputy minister for medium engineering industry, pointed out just that on May 5, 1986, that is, after the accident.

A week earlier, on May 1, 1986, V. P. Volkov, head of the reliability and safety of nuclear power plants group, sent a letter to the director of the Kurchatov Institute For Atomic Energy, giving his own version of the accident, which "was caused not by the actions of the personnel, but by the reactor core design and a faulty understanding of the neutron physical processes inside it." On May 9, he sent an identical letter to the country's leadership as well. But who would have bothered to read those disturbing letters there? A group of experts from the USSR Energy Ministry also sent in addenda to the accident investigation report, discussing the reactor design faults. Even though the reactor design faults were duly demonstrated at two sessions of the interdepartmental science and technology council, on June 2 and 17, 1986 (weeks after the accident), chaired by academician A. P. Alexandrov, they were not taken into account. According to these experts, the accident was caused by mistakes of the reactor managers and engineers. And that became the official party line. The same view was conveyed to the IAEA on behalf of the Soviet Union. Indeed, could it have been otherwise? Alexandrov vs. Alexandrov? What a cruel joke!

On May 17, 1989, the *Literary Gazette* carried a most interesting "investigative dialogue" by political commentator Igor Belyaev, "The Right Direction—or Is It?" His interlocutor was V. A. Bobrov, acting head of the state invention examination laboratory at the Nuclear Information Research Center. He explained why the RBMK-1000 reactor had not been registered as an invention. The people who had filed the application for registration were academician A. P. Alexandrov, director of the Atomic Energy Institute, and other members of the Institute staff.

In 1967, I returned the first version of the application (a page and a half of typescript without the formula of the invention or any drawings) to the authors to be reformulated. What followed was positively incredible. The new version of the RBMK application, dated October 6, 1967, had not yet been examined, when, merely four weeks later, Academician Alexandrov, in the daily *Pravda*, announced, "Soviet scientists managed to solve the problem of improving the economic efficiency of nuclear power plants." One of the reasons why the design had not been recognized as an invention was the absence of any industrially useful method of reducing the cost of electric power through employing the RBMK reactor that had an antediluvian under-30 percent efficiency. It was that reason for refusal that the applicant contested after its forced introduction in nuclear power engineering in 1973—at the Leningrad nuclear power plant where, let me remind you, a number of accidents subsequently occurred, all of which were hushed up. Academician Alexandrov's allegation that the RBMK reactor was up to the "most advanced technological standards" proved groundless, because the state expert patent bureau had not recognized the reactor as an invention either.

Academician Alexandrov nevertheless contrived to force his pet creation on the country's economy on a grand scale. The next five-year plan for 1971–75 provided for two-thirds of the total nuclear power plant capacity to be covered by those dangerous reactors.

While sifting through my archives, I discovered a curious document pertaining to the time when the Chernobyl plant was being constructed. Already, at that stage, a lot of things went wrong, as was usually the case in the Soviet Union. As you see, this paper was hidden away from public view. Here it is:

> SECRET. To be returned to the general section of the CPSU Central Committee. The state security committee of the USSR. February 21, 1979. On the construction flaws at the Chernobyl nuclear power plant. According to information in the KGB possession, in certain sections of Unit 2, there are instances of deviation from design, as well as violations of engineering and installation techniques that may result in accidents and casualties. The engine room frame columns have been erected as much as 100 mm off the layout axes; in places horizontal stays between columns are lacking. The wall panels have been laid up to 150 mm off the axes. The laying of casing plates has been done with deviation from the supervising author's instructions. The vertical water proofing has been damaged in many places . . . [this] may result in subsoil waters getting into the plant building and in radioactive contamination of the environment. As the extra heavy concrete was being put in place, the process was interrupted

on several occasions, which resulted in the formation of cavities and the layering of the foundations.

The document had the signature of KGB Chairman Yuri Andropov.

Though the unit referred to here was number two, I do not doubt for a moment that the others were just as problem-ridden. In the almost fifteen years of working as an industry and capital construction section journalist with a regional paper, I gained a good deal of experience in the area and published a fair number of articles on Soviet Party whitewashing and slipshod workmanship. The topics I covered sometimes resulted in summons to the regional party committee for insults, reprimands, and even legal proceedings against me. In the case of the Chernobyl Nuclear Power Plant even the "iron-side" Andropov and the KGB proved helpless.

This is from the Steinberg report of the USSR State Atomic Industry Monitoring Committee, "On the Causes and Circumstances of the Accident at Unit 4 of the Chernobyl Nuclear Power Plant on April 26, 1986":

> The staff did indeed commit violations of maintenance regulations. Some of those violations did not affect the triggering and further course of the accident, while others proved conducive to bringing out the RBMK-1000 design faults. The violations committed were largely due to the unsatisfactory quality of operation documents and their controversial nature resulting from the unsatisfactory quality of RBMK-1000 design. The personnel were unaware of certain dangerous properties of the reactor and therefore did not realize what consequences their violations could entail. But this points precisely to the lack of safety culture not so much in the operating personnel as in the reactor designers and the operating organization.

The report cites an interesting fact about the [U.S.] designers' reaction to the Three Mile Island accident in the United States. They and government investigators, did not try to put the blame on the operating staff because engineers might need hours and even weeks to analyze the first minute of an incident if they were to comprehend the event or forecast the developments under altered conditions. An operator has to describe hundreds of ideas, decisions, and actions taken during the transition process. Edward R. Frederick, the American operator who made erroneous decisions late on April 28, 1979, was never publicly criticized. He later wrote, "How I would like to go back and change those decisions. But they cannot be undone and must never happen again; an operator must never find himself in a situation that engineers have not previously analyzed. Engineers should never have to analyze a situation without taking into account the operator's reaction to it."

The main reason, the Steinberg commission concluded, was not the personnel errors or their psychological or professional problems. Any other team could not have changed anything. The disaster had been programmed. "The faulty design of the RBMK-1000 reactor operated at Unit 4 in Chernobyl predetermined the serious consequences of the accident." Such was the final diagnosis of the state atomic industry monitoring commission. Even twenty years after the Chernobyl disaster, neither the Soviet prosecutor general's office (prior to the Soviet Union's disintegration) nor its counterparts in the now independent states of Belarus, Ukraine, and Russia have shaken the dust off the dismissed case of the RBMK-1000 reactor design reliability. Will justice ever be done? The Chernobyl blast put a huge black question mark over the future of nuclear power engineering. That event nurtured and strengthened antinuclear movements in the West. The Green Party campaigning for dismantling nuclear power plants broadened their support base.

Following a national referendum, Sweden became the first country to give up electricity obtained by such hazardous means. In the southern part of that country there are twelve nuclear reactors in use today. They provide half of Sweden's total power consumption. The Swedish government has decided to dismantle all the reactors by 2010. (I should note that these reactors are not the Chernobyl type.) In 1999, Sweden embarked on a lengthy process of closing down its nuclear power plants. The first Swedish reactor was shut down despite vehement protests by the Sydkraft Power Company. The issue of the government's right to make decisions on closing a privately owned nuclear power plant was examined by Sweden's court of appeal and also by the European Court. In the end Sydkraft dropped its suit and sensibly accepted compensation.

The Chernobyl accident also goaded the Swiss government into action. A group of experts were tasked with drafting a long-term program of power engineering development. By February 1988, the program was ready. "The experts' report was a bombshell," wrote the newspaper *Revue Économique Franco-Suisse*. The program provided that all the nuclear power plants are to be closed down by 2025—on condition that strict energy conservation measures were to be introduced and non-power-intensive industry branches developed.

Among those who plunged into battle against nuclear power plants were not only the Scandinavian public but also the Greens in France, where such plants account for over 70 percent of the country's electricity output.

In September 1990, the Greens in the French Parliament invited me to the international forum, "Turn Over the Page." It was held as an alternative to the Lyon international conference on further development of atomic power engineering. For the French activists, the main and most convincing argument "against" was Ukraine's Chernobyl. In Lyon I unexpectedly met the film director Georgy Shklyarevsky, the maker of a documentary on Chernobyl, the very same documentary that, in the atomic industry monitoring committee experts' opinion, could compromise the Soviet Union. We held two press conferences on the Chernobyl accident and its consequences—one for the media and the other for the antinuke activists. On both occasions the hall was packed. The audience displayed a keen interest in everything, especially the consequences of the disaster.

The French were also worried about the activities of Prof. P. Pellerin of France during his visits to the Soviet Union. They knew that on June 19–25, 1989, Prof. Pellerin, director of the radiation protection service at the French Health Ministry, in company with Dan Beninson, president of the Argentina Atomic Energy Commission, and also with Dr. Veith of Canada, head of the radiation protection group under the WHO secretariat, arrived in this country at the Soviet government's request as WHO experts. That was the Soviet government's response to criticism from USSR people's deputies at their first Congress. The esteemed guests were to dispel all doubts that had been sown by people's deputies and journalists. V. M. Kavun, then first secretary of the Zhitomir region's party committee, gleefully observed that once the international team arrived, it would voice the right kind of opinions. Small wonder—the group of experts was securely shielded from any outside influence by our old friends, Messrs. Ilyin, Kondrusev, Romanenko, and Ms. Guskova. However, that circle of associates was the foreign experts' own choice.

First Secretary Kavun was dead right. The WHO experts drew up a report that repeated almost verbatim Ilyin's homespun version of events. They agreed that 35 rem "constituted very little risk to human health compared with other lifetime health hazards." That reminded me, irresistibly, of a speech by one of the scientists at our parliamentary hearings when he had likened the nuclear disaster to a traffic accident. The foreign experts reassured us, saying that if they "were asked to establish lifetime tolerance dosages, they would settle for twice or even three times the 35-rem figure," as though they had been totally unaware of small radiation doses, their no-threshold effect on humans, or the initial radioactive shock that everyone, newborn infants included, had received. That was blatant nuclear industry public relations and scientific obfuscation—this time not Soviet deception, but by international experts. Of course, we were expected to take it on trust. Communist-controlled newspapers and television (which were the only kind at the time) reported all that with relish. See how tough they are in the West, they seemed to imply. So you'd better keep your mouths shut—or else.

Prof. Pellerin of France also visited Narodichi, in my own Zhitomir region. Here is how V. S. Budko, chairman of the Narodichi district executive committee and people's deputy of the Ukraine, described the event at a round table discussion organized by the *Moskovskiye novosti* weekly:

> Professor Pellerin came to Narodichi, and when I mentioned in my speech that our villages were of two kinds—'clean' and 'dirty,' that is, the first category was supplied with 'clean' foodstuffs, while the second was not, he was utterly dumbfounded and asked me three times through the interpreter if it was true that people living with radiation density of over 100 Ci/km^2 in some places were not fully provided with 'clean' food. He refused to believe it.

But the party press never said a word about that exchange between the French luminary and the Ukrainian people's deputy.

The foreign experts' tour of radioactive areas in Ukraine and Belorussia provoked a new stream of lies from the local press as well. The *Radyanska Zhitomirshchina* newspaper of August 7, 1989, carried a "topical interview" with Dr. V. G. Bebeshko, director of the Clinical Radiology Institute under the All-Union Radiation Medicine Research Center, Ukrainian Academy of Medical Sciences. It was named "Irradiation and Health" and had a telltale subtitle, "WHO experts draw conclusions that coincide with the view of Soviet scientists and doctors."

It does not take a mastermind, either, to guess why Bebeshko was the interviewer's choice for mouthing platitudes about "coinciding conclusions." His progovernment stand was only too well known. Even then, the "topical interview" made pretty revolting reading.

Given all that, who would not subscribe to the view of Prof. A. Mishchenko of Moscow University, voiced at the February 8, 1991, press conference called "Environmental Disasters: Facts, Causes, Consequences"? This is what he said: "The government turns to foreign scientists when Soviet ones disagree with the government's projects. Then the search starts for more amenable consultants— who are promptly found abroad." Lately, we find the words "nuclear mafia" and "nuclear lobby" being used in various contexts. Prof. Elena Burlakova is confident that "radiation medicine is a political science," and that "there exists a certain nuclear lobby. Radiation medicine is in the hands of that lobby, of atom-mongers, of nuclear engineers who have created it not to protect people but to promote nuclear power engineering."

Several years after the catastrophe, the newspaper *Nabat* ("Alarm Bell"), published by Belarusian writer Vasil Yakovenko and distributed in several republics, printed a curious item by Alexander Lyutsko, assistant professor at the Nuclear Physics Department, Belorussian State University. He writes about the practices prevailing in the IAEA. "The samples of soil and foodstuffs I brought there, which had been tested for radioactive contamination in Belorussia, were unexpectedly 'taken into custody.' After consultations at the IAEA HQ, laboratory director Roberto Danesi negotiated the matter with me. Much to his distress, the IAEA earnestly requested that I should drop my demand for obtaining radiometric results on these samples, as the agency would not like to be involved in their use for political purposes." There! Lies *can* be used for political purposes, but the truth can't. Alexander Lyutsko described this cloak of secrecy over the independent international examination of the consequences of the Chernobyl accident conducted at our government's request. Special orders on that secrecy were signed by Hans Blix, IAEA director general. "The text was pinned to every door of the IAEA Seibersdorf laboratory in a Vienna suburb," wrote Lyutsko.

It has long been clear why a pall of secrecy surrounded independent international experts. As members of the Ukrainian parliamentary commission for Chernobyl accident issues said, the international experts practically invalidated everything that had formed the basis of legislation on the status of radioactively contaminated areas and persons affected by the accident. The question arises—so, was it expert scientific evaluation or a lesson in criminal loyalty to the government that was immeasurably guilty vis-à-vis the victims? And what part did the "independent experts" play in all this? What or who were they independent from? From ordinary human conscience.

Here are some interesting statistics. Between March 1990 and January 1991, the Soviet Union welcomed almost fifty visiting teams of experts, some two hundred individuals in all. All those visits were IAEA-inspired. No prizes for guessing whose interests they represented. American Prof. John Gofman, an independent scientist investigating low-dose radiation, writes in his book, *Chernobyl Accident: Radiation Consequences for This and Future Generations,* that all nuclear power engineering and radiation effect research programs are controlled directly by governments. Lack of financial support makes independent expert examination of radiation health effects a rarity. Gofman gives a most revealing example. On May 21, 1991, the Associated Press Agency quoted Lynn R. Anspaugh, a researcher who supervised the medical side of the IAEA report, as saying that the worst evil was not radiation as such but fear of radiation (radiophobia). Yet the agency failed to inform its audience that Anspaugh was employed by the U.S. Department of Energy and worked at its Livermore National Laboratory. Moreover, that person was one of the authors of the so-called zero risk model for estimating disaster consequences at nuclear power engineering facilities. So what else could Anspaugh and Anspaugh's colleagues have said? It was people like these who were selected for trips to Chernobyl zones, both by the Soviet government and by the IAEA. The purpose was clear—to cover up the more shameful parts of Soviet nuclear power engineering by using the added authority of international "expert assessment" and to silence recalcitrant journalists and people's deputies such as me.

But let us get back to France. At that "Turn Over the Page" international forum, copies of a letter, including in Russian, by the Stop Nogent Committee, were circulated. Among the signatories were members of the Scientists Against Nuclear Energy movement, the staff of an independent French laboratory, the public of Nogent, a town 80 km from Paris, where a new nuclear power plant had been built, and the French Greens. Most of the letter is reproduced here, to give you the attitude of truly independent nuclear criticism.

Paris, 20 September, 1990

Dear friends,

As you must be aware, anti-nuclear activists in France are neither numerous nor powerful. The situation is highly alarming: the French atomic industry is second or third in the world. It can now be said that in the wake of the Chernobyl disaster even the Soviet nuclear program has slowed down. Not so in France. And, unfortunately, this is not the only problem: we have learned that several French citizens with responsibility in the French nuclear complex tried to talk Ilyin and the Soviet authorities into slowing down evacuation from areas contaminated by the Chernobyl accident. But the public in Belorussia, Russia, Ukraine, and elsewhere ought to know that France also has activists who will attempt to counter this monstrous activity.

This is a matter of solidarity, but not only that, because French nuclear power plants are dangerous, too. However, Professor Pellerin, should France experience a nuclear accident, would be the chief supervisor of official health decisions. You can read about this letter in the press, in the text issued by the conference that took place in Paris on March 5, 1990. Its subject was Professor Pellerin's activity in Belorussia, the Ukraine and France. The reason for the conference was the open letter to the health minister (Prof. Pellerin is practically dependent on that administrative organ).

In March and April this year the French media finally told the public of the consequences of the Chernobyl disaster in the Soviet Union. They said hardly anything about it previously, and they are again silent now. People in Eastern Europe often believe that our mass media are honest. This is entirely untrue, particularly in matters involving nuclear power. The public here realizes that the French atomic complex is dependent on an atrocious bureaucracy, but the people are at as loss what to do. All of that means that we find obtaining reliable information about the state of nuclear industry in the Soviet Union very difficult.

As you know, the French state continues underground testing of nuclear bombs in Polynesia, and people are falling ill over there. We are for a world without nuclear power.

The Stop Nogent Committee

Quite a few decidedly unusual things happened to this fearless letter and my part in that major international antinuke forum in Lyon, France.

159

Its leaders invited me to speak about Chernobyl at the European Parliament. In 1990, soon after some European parliamentarians learned of my as yet unpublished book, *Chernobyl Is with Us* (it existed in manuscript form only), they decided to have it translated and published in French. European Parliament counselor Jacqueline Trélon played a great role in that whole affair. Once the translation was completed, my Paris publishers suddenly confronted me with a request that sounded incredible and downright suspicious. They wanted me to remove from the French translation the pages pertaining to the conference, most particularly the bit on the Stop Nogent Committee letter. Frankly, I was flabbergasted. You see, we in Russia were firmly convinced that over in the West it's all democracy and freedom of speech. We were certainly naive!

It turned out that the publishers feared there would be repercussions and retaliation if they printed the criticism that was there in my book concerning France's nuclear industry and the part about the French scientists who propped up the myth of its safety. Was I to understand that France, one of the most democratic countries in Europe and the world, had no freedom of speech if that speech touched upon one of its most politically powerful industries—nuclear power engineering? In France, one was apparently welcome to criticize the Soviet government and Soviet reactors to one's heart content, but the French ones were strictly taboo! I had no alternative but to agree, for publishing my book in French on the big lie about Chernobyl was then my only chance of telling the West the truth about its catastrophic consequences. With a heavy heart, I accepted. That section was cut out from the French edition of my book, *Chernobyl: The Forbidden Truth*.

The report on the visit of the WHO Pellerin–Beninson–Veith group of international experts drawn up by the Soviet Health Ministry and published in the 1989 issue of *Information Bulletin* of the interdepartmental council for information and public relations in nuclear energy asserts, "The experts observe with satisfaction that they had access to complete information and that the data were likewise available to Soviet scientists." Which scientists and what kind of scientists are referred to are not specified. To dupe its own people, the official Soviet medical establishment had to appeal for aid to its foreign counterparts.

Incidentally, the entire collection under the heading *Information Bulletin* can be held up as a model of warped departmental glasnost.

Its compiler, Ye. V. Guliy, contrived to amass articles on the consequences of the Chernobyl accident that earned plaudits from the party faithful.

After the Lyon press conference, the local journalists told us that the police had dispersed protesters campaigning for the closure of the Nogent Nuclear Power Plant. The next day, over at the Paris headquarters of the Green Party, we were shown a newspaper with a piece on the event and a photo of a demonstrator sporting a bloody forehead. This is how the public in France fights against the "peaceful atom."

On one of the days during my sojourn in Lyon, Switzerland was holding a referendum on the future of its nuclear power engineering. Its outcome, a ten-year moratorium on nuclear power plant construction, was a welcome event for my new friends in France. Unfortunately, in 2003, Swiss ecologists suffered a reversal; the moratorium was not extended for another decade. The nuclear lobby (nuclear power plants there provide 40 percent of the energy) carried the day. Not unlike other significant events, the lessons of Chernobyl had apparently been consigned to the dustbin of history.

On learning that there were people from Ukraine among the delegates, the Ukrainian community in Lyon invited us to a meeting. They also wished to know what was happening after Chernobyl and how they could help their brothers back home. The meeting took place in an Orthodox church, with heavy rain pouring outside. The meeting organizer was Guenia Cousine, a French Ukrainian who was positively raving about her ancestors' country. Her mother had emigrated from Western Ukraine. Guenia herself was born in France, as was her son, yet they both spoke Ukrainian and read Ukrainian books. The family worshiped all things Ukrainian. Guenia absolutely adored traditional Ukrainian embroidery. Pride of place in her apartment was demonstrated by a portrait of Ukraine's greatest poet, Taras Shevchenko, draped with embroidered towels. That summer Guenia was going to Ukraine for the first time in her life. She was very excited. Looking at her, listening to her speak, I caught myself thinking that they were totally unaware of the realities of our people's life and our daily concerns. Away from our Ukraine, they invented one of their own. They believed in it. It was their religion, that delicious opium that must be so tempting to absorb if you could not get a return ticket to Kiev.

Some time after leaving Lyon, I received a letter from Guenia. She wished me Merry Christmas and said that their community had collected thirty thousand francs for the children of Chernobyl. To what

161

address could they send the money, she asked. I phoned the Green World Movement HQ in Kiev, and we decided that the best way would be to spend the money in France on medicine for a Kiev clinic that treated Chernobyl kids. We kept up our correspondence for a number of years, but eventually we lost touch. But I still keep in my library, where I am writing this book, the gift of an electronic clock from Guenia. The clock ticks away the days, months and years of our post-Chernobyl life, forgotten by God and the world.

The Chernobyl blast has also boomeranged on domestic power engineering. What is its condition? Will it continue to exist at all? And if it will, what should it be like? This is a major subject in its own right, which, unexpectedly to me, was revealed from a hitherto classified document some six years after the Chernobyl disaster. I intend to tell you about this amazing piece of journalistic luck in a separate chapter. For the present I will cite various opinions on the subject expressed by experts and people's deputies at preliminary parliamentary hearings and discussions of appointments. We did not know much at the time. Nuclear power engineering was still closed to us then, a mystery sealed with seven seals, the global character of the accident and the country's progress toward complete glasnost notwithstanding. Information had to be gathered bit by bit, slowly and laboriously. As an example, V. M. Malyshev, a contender for the chairmanship of the newly set up state atomic industry monitoring committee, said, as his nomination was being considered, that "checks revealed 24,500 violations in nuclear power engineering. Two thousand and four hundred persons have been prosecuted." What a staggering admission! The body in charge of civil reactors was the state committee for supervising nuclear power engineering, the one that had been disbanded. But apart from the civil reactors, there were also (and still are) research nuclear reactors, more than seventy of them. And just fourteen of these had been under the committee's surveillance. The rest were looked after by their respective departments. Moreover, even after the Chernobyl disaster, there were still fourteen Chernobyl-type reactors in operation. What was to be done?

Malyshev, now chairman of the USSR State Atomic Industry Monitoring Committee, observed the following:

> The nuclear power plants currently under construction are up to world standards, but on the whole, safety levels here [in this country] are lower than in advanced capitalist countries. Why is that? Quite

simply, nuclear power plants began to be built in this country in the absence of a suitable normative basis. Sixteen power-generating units have been built without a protective dome, although they have other [protective] devices. Unfortunately, this country's regulations did not specifically demand protective domes. Those units have other faults as well, all of which results in inadequate safety systems. What did we come up against? We came up against the conviction of research and design operating organizations that they could go on using those units for the period stipulated by their designers. Meanwhile, that period, as you know, is 30 years, and some of them were put into operation in 1980, so they will have to go on running till 2010. We demanded that all those units be decommissioned by the year 2000. But their withdrawal schedule will depend on the fact that in 1989 reconstruction designs are to be produced which will include safety feasibility assessments; the actual condition of the given unit must be examined, how it is being operated, how well it conforms to the new standards, how far it is from cities. I imagine we will have to be most resolute in the matter of decommissioning two power-generating units—numbers one and two in Leningrad, and numbers three and four in Voronezh. The issue will be settled depending on how comprehensive argumentation and feasibility studies will be, in short, depending on the safety of those units.

Those words of warning were uttered fifteen years ago. But nothing much has happened since. All the Chernobyl-type reactors (with the exception of the Chernobyl Nuclear Power Plant closed down in 2000) continue to work, even twenty years after the accident. Not one hazardous nuclear reactor has yet seen early decommissioning—either at the Leningrad Nuclear Power Plant or at the one in Voronezh. Moreover, even when the Leningrad plant had reached the end of its service life (and it was the first Soviet nuclear power plant equipped with RBMK-1000 reactors), its projected lifetime was simply extended for another decade.

In Germany, several years ago, a special law was passed to ban nuclear power plants. In 1998 the Green Party made the scrapping of nuclear power engineering the principal condition of its joining the coalition with the Social Democrats. The German authorities are planning to shut down nineteen nuclear power plants within the next twenty years, switching over completely to alternative energy sources. On November 14, 2003, the closing-down process started at Stade, one of Germany's oldest nuclear power plants. Two worlds—two ideologies? Wasn't that the phraseology of the late unlamented Soviet press that hinted at the capitalist bad guys?

Malyshev went on:

> I must say that we also feel concern about substandard designs and important critical remarks regarding design. As of January 1990, a quality program should be in force; as of 1991 [it] should have sections on decommissioning, because right now it lacks any such sections, also sections on waste burial, et cetera. We have had re-actor unit stoppages, but no trace of people responsible for them, no one to call to account. Apropos of Rovno. There was a fairly low level of operation activity there, a year ago at least. The numerous failures there were mostly due to the turbine section malfunction, but there was also evidence of considerable neglect during start-up and adjustment.
>
> Apropos of [plans for] underground nuclear power plants. I will only say that, given the current public mood, underground nuclear power plants are a lot safer. I will propose that design and feasibil-ity studies be prepared so that we might have something concrete to discuss.

And here is what people's deputy N. A. Usilina said:

> Local residents have signed a letter of protest against the building and commissioning of the Gorky Nuclear Power Plant. There is no full safety guarantee for three million people. If put into operation, the plant would jeopardize the people, dozens of enterprises might go out of service, and the Volga basin might be contaminated. In our Gorky region (currently, the Nizhny Novgorod region) we have the Semenov District where radioactive waste is buried; people there, especially children, are seriously ill most of the time. My voters wish to know when this is going to stop.

And Deputy E. P. Tikhonenkov: "At the Crimea Nuclear Power Plant 20 percent of cavities have been discovered in the unit's 'jacket.'"

And Yu. A. Izrael, chairman of the USSR State Committee for Hydrometeorology:

> At present a new set of general safety regulations is being considered for nuclear power plant construction. It states very clearly the mini-mum distance [from residential areas] at which any work is allowed. And another thing. It is necessary to examine each specific situation. I for one believe that nuclear power plant operation must now be made as safe as possible. At whatever cost to the state. Let me state the main idea here. The thing is that the worst accident on earth was not Chernobyl but the Three Mile Island, USA. It was under a protective dome, and whatever the reactor released stayed under the dome. The dome cracked, but very little radioactivity escaped.

But the reactor itself released more stuff than did the Chernobyl unit. So we should build protective domes and sink nuclear power plants underground.

To conclude this chapter of my book, I shall quote academician Sakharov:

Alternative, clean energy sources cannot currently compete with "dirty" ones, nor even with hydroelectric stations. The status quo will apparently remain unchanged for a long time to come. Although here, too, things are constantly changing, of course. Nuclear power engineering is now more expensive than electricity obtained from the old sources, but oil and gas will eventually run out, coal is very bad environmentally, and all thermoelectric plants contribute to the greenhouse effect. Presumably, in the long run it will still be nuclear power engineering that will be increasingly important—at least to the extent covered by our technical forecasts. Obviously, it must be made safe. There are various ways of achieving that. First of all, nuclear reactors must be improved. There are now water-cooled and water-moderated reactors with nothing to burn; gas-cooled reactors where the explosive blend, firedamp, is not formed; reactors that reduce reactivity at the slightest malfunction. All of that is basically feasible. And yet these things can never be 100 percent safe. For instance, as long as we continue to live in the world as it now is, there will always be the danger of terrorism, missile bombardment, and air bombardment with conventional explosives. In short, my conclusion is this: a really radical solution to the safety issue is placing reactors underground.

Sakharov's idea regarding placing nuclear reactors underground provoked a tidal wave of just criticism on the part of ecologists and the public. Reactors may develop leaks, and then all the subterranean waters connected to the world's oceans will be threatened with contamination. One thing is certain, as night follows day. Only one thing is clear: now the humankind surviving after Chernobyl will always wage the life and reactor.

12

Did Chernobyl Babies Smoke?

On the face of it, there was nothing unusual in the International Sakharov Congress, dedicated to the seventieth birthday of the Soviet H-bomb's father, who became the first Soviet ban-the-nuke activist. The organizers chose to focus on the global consequences of the Chernobyl nuclear disaster and the future of nuclear power engineering. The Congress was held in Moscow during May 21–25, 1991. That was a special day—nearly eighteen months since the sudden death of Andrei Sakharov, the world famous Soviet dissident and academician. I well remember that last evening with Sakharov, when we, members of the Interregional Group of Deputies, the first opposition faction in the Soviet parliament, discussed late into the night the documents we planned for the next session in the Kremlin. He looked weary and at times seemed to doze off, but that appearance was deceptive. As soon as he heard someone say things he disagreed with, he actively joined in the discussion.

In fact, he had been ill for a few days. Without making any fuss about it, and no matter how hard we tried to persuade him to go home, he would not hear of it. The day before, during the session of the Soviet parliament, I took him to a vacant back bench in the session hall and handed him a pile of letters of support from my constituency. He was grateful for that as the radical Communist press was still baiting him at every opportunity. When Sakharov got up after our talk, he looked around in a confused way to locate his seat in the hall, headed in the wrong direction, and needed my help to find his bearings. At the time, I thought he was under the weather, and I timidly suggested that he should go home and have a little rest, but he refused and stayed on for the evening session of the Interregional Group. He personally introduced amendments to the document we were drawing up for introduction the next day. We dispersed very late, but, on waking we learned the heartbreaking news. Sakharov was dead!

So that Congress was special, a Sakharov Congress without Sakharov. And it was so very important that it should retain the Sakharov spirit. Among its participants were the flowers of Soviet and foreign humanitarian philosophy and science, colleagues and friends of the late academician: Physics Institute director, Leonid Keldysh, chairman of Czechoslovakia's National Assembly, Alexander Dubcek, Dr. Sydney Drell of Stanford University, president of Portugal, Mario Soares, Italian writer, Vittorio Strada, and others. The special guests at the Congress were Sakharov's dissident comrades-in-arms, the human rights activists, including the onetime political prisoner, once Soviet and now US citizen, first chairman of the Moscow Helsinki Group, Yuri Orlov, human rights campaigners, Sergei Kovalev, Lydia Chukovskaya, and Cornelia Gerstenmeier.

The Congress organizing committee was headed by the academician's widow, Yelena Bonner.

The topic of Chernobyl was the theme of Congress discussions, certainly of great interest to specialists and even more so to millions of people living in the affected areas. So many people were waiting with hope in their hearts for the outcome of the debate that centered upon the uncompromising integrity of academician Sakharov. It was then five years after the explosion, and the truth was still hidden behind "curtains of fog and iron" (Churchill's apt phraseology). We still did not know the whole truth about Chernobyl. It seemed a bit strange that only three Soviet scientists had been officially invited as experts on the subject. Thirteen others came from other countries. But it was presumed that this eccentricity (for who could know more of the Chernobyl issues than we did?) would be complemented by the competence of Western experts, a truly Sakharovian approach to the problem. This was all the more important because Vienna was just then hosting a UN session where IAEA experts reported on the results of their work in the Chernobyl accident zones—and every conclusion voiced there was far from acceptable to people in Russia, the Ukraine, and Belorussia.

At the very first plenary meeting of the Chernobyl Congress, all those who had even a modicum of information about Chernobyl were shocked to hear the report by Professor Richard Wilson of Harvard University. He began by saying that they had not received information from the Ukraine until four months after the explosion, that "Legasov had withheld information," that he "had not told lies but had not told the whole truth either." Then Richard Wilson announced that scientists in the West, on learning the details of the Chernobyl accident as late as 1988, had got a big shock, that full information had not been made public even in 1990, that the veil of secrecy caused distrust. Having said all that, though, Professor Wilson proceeded to "wittily" compare the aftermath of the Chernobyl disaster with smoking effects (20 rem is roughly equivalent to smoking 20,000 cigarettes, he said). Then he stated, reassuringly, that the fires in Kuwait had done more harm than had the Chernobyl accident and also compared the radiation disaster with the floods in Bangladesh. In conclusion, he advised us all to take more fresh air.

At one point, the professor held up a Geiger counter to show the audience, observing in passing that he had taken it to the Chernobyl plant and the counter was still ticking from residual radiation, which came as a nasty shock to those present. (True, after the break, Richard Wilson again took the floor for a brief comment, explaining that there was really no radiation in the counter or in the hall—it had all been simply the interpreter's mistake.) Western speakers repeatedly complained from the podium that they did not have all the facts, that their reports were based not on their own conclusions but on the opinions of other, including Soviet, scientists, and that information about Chernobyl was still shrouded in secrecy. Meanwhile, sitting in the hall and listening to those admissions of helplessness were other scientists—the Soviet parliamentary experts who for several years had been focusing exclusively on the Chernobyl issues and who possessed the fullest information in the country and in the world about the various aspects of the consequences of the Chernobyl disaster. But none of them were invited to speak, nor was there any intention to let them speak. The situation was paradoxical, to say the least.

Was it not because academician Sakharov's widow, Yelena Bonner, as if to program just such a turn of events, had quoted the IAEA report in her speech at the Congress plenary meeting to the effect that it was stress and uncertainty in the political future that was causing disease? And it was she whom Richard Wilson echoed in his report when he said that the risk of irradiation was not very great; the stress- and secrecy-related risk was much greater, according to him.

Human rights campaigner Bonner seemed to have shouldered the burden of a nuclear lobbyist that did not suit her at all—the opposite would have been more logical to expect. Many people wondered why she wanted to do it and what was going on at the Congress anyway.

Professor Wilson's shockingly irresponsible speech was emotionally discussed in the lobbies during the intervals between Congress sessions. Neither academician Yuri Ryzhov nor writer Ales Adamovich, both of them people's deputies, or Professor Anatoly Nazarov, had a clue as to why none of the people in possession of sufficiently full and reliable information about the disaster's consequences were allowed anywhere near the Sakharov Congress podium. Someone let drop bitterly: "It's Satan ruling again." Someone else suggested walking out of the session as a sign of protest, but the majority rejected the idea. We had to go and work in groups and find a means of proving to the visiting Western experts how wrong they were about paradise on post-Chernobyl territories. If that failed, then we would make a special statement for the press.

During a break, I shared my fears with Ms. Bonner. If the final recommendations were based on the Western scientists' pontifications about the consequences of Chernobyl, Sakharov's name would be compromised, for Richard Wilson had been saying almost verbatim what we had been hearing here for the last five years from the official medical establishment, from academician Ilyin and his team. Although after five years, the weight of indisputable facts had compelled even the academician himself to admit at the environment committee parliamentary hearings that 1,600,000 children daily exposed to small radiation doses "are currently in a state causing alarm." But Yelena Bonner said (hesitantly, it seemed to me): "Well, you've got to believe someone." You have indeed. People and doctors in the affected areas believe their own eyes, first of all, as well as the results of their own research, not the tales about comparing the accident's global consequences to smoking (could those 1,600,000 children also be lighting up now and then?), even if those tales came from overseas.

No, I do not object to Western scientists sharing their views with us; on the contrary, I am all for it. But I would also like to see us Russians finally develop some self-respect. Why, in a country as huge as ours, the Congress organizers, being well aware of what was really happening in contaminated areas, had failed to find an independent Soviet scientist who could report on his/her own investigation, without reference to "official" documents (I had spoken earlier about Chernobyl to the wife of ex-President Jimmy Carter, Rosalyn, at her request, in

Yelena Bonner's apartment and with her participation). Mercifully, there are people like that, and their names are well-known—Doctors of Biology A. G. Nazarov, V. A. Shevchenko, Ye. B. Burlakova, Belorussian and Ukrainian academicians Ye. F. Konoplya and D. M. Grodzinsky, and lots of other worthy scientists.

What happened to the assessment of Chernobyl in general does not surprise me at all. The pro-nuclear lobby's warfare against Chernobyl victims had been going on for a long time, both in this country and abroad. It was something else that seemed unusual. An equally shameless attempt was made at the Sakharov Congress! That was what was least expected and most painful.

Pursuing their own ends, the Congress organizers did not hesitate to announce at the plenary meeting that no one must attend working groups' sessions unless especially invited! I have never witnessed, before or since, such humiliating treatment of participants or such brassy impudence! At our own risk, a group of concerned people's deputies and experts ventured to attend a Chernobyl section meeting at the Congress. To be fair, I must say that Elena Burlakova did get an official invitation to the meeting. The room of just twenty square meters was crammed with forty-five people!

At the section meeting, in that narrow circle, the parliamentary experts banned by Ms. Bonner from speaking from the Sakharov Congress main podium got some of their own back. Then it was the turn of foreign scholars to be amazed. For the first time in years, they heard information by academician Ilyin, a representative of the official medical establishment, exposed as false. "The allegations that immediately after the accident 5.4 million people in the Soviet Union were subjected to iodine preventive treatment are totally untrue," said Alexander Lyutsko, assistant professor at the Nuclear Physics Department of the Belorussian University. "In Belorussia, there was virtually no timely iodine treatment. And where anything at all was done, it was done five to seven days after the accident. Thus, the whole thing was not only quite useless, it was actually harmful." He gave the disgraceful particulars of the Western experts' trip to the Chernobyl area. "Pellerin and Beninson did not take any measurements in Belorussia," said Lyutsko, "yet they did make reassuring statements."

Another eye-opener for the Western professors was the truth about the scale of the disaster, the number of people exposed to radiation, and the health effects of small radiation doses.

The papers issued to the servicemen mention doses of 3, 5, or 7 rem. That was the amount "prescribed" by their senior officers. But the data got into the national register. This is a crime not only against the public, but also against science. Everything has been falsified ... the statistics ignore the servicemen and tens of thousands of prison and labor camp inmates.

The foreign experts also heard other Soviet assessments of their IAEA colleagues' work.

The commission report is largely based on official Soviet data. It worked for just eight weeks. Meanwhile, there are mounds of material accumulated over the five years. In Belorussia, the commission visited only two towns, while nearly 80 percent of the republic's territory had been contaminated.

In that heated discussion, I was most surprised by the words of a Greek pediatrician, an IAEA expert and, let me note, a young woman, who discoursed, with great confidence, on permissible casualties among children. She endorsed Wilson's smoking-and-radiation "theory," remarking that "risk perception depends on the way this risk is presented by the mass media." Words straight from Ilyin's mouth, almost! And, in conclusion, the lady declared that the disaster "had a positive effect, even though people sacrificed their lives. But there was also a display of solidarity and humanism, and we all felt bonded with one another." Some solidarity that! Perhaps she wouldn't mind a couple of more blasts to see even more intoxicating feelings of solidarity and humanism? It is difficult to understand this kind of logic when you discover that the author of these statements is on the IAEA payroll. Venality has no ethnic features.

Professor Richard Wilson opened the section meeting by apologizing to Professor Burlakova for not having contacted her until the previous evening. According to the session program, his speech at the plenary session (where he had so unfortunately demonstrated the Geiger counter) should have been a review of her research, too. We discovered, though, that the esteemed professor had found time, all right, to meet and exchange opinions on Chernobyl with Oleg Pavlovsky, a close associate of academician Ilyin, whose department created the "veil of secrecy" that the American professor had so passionately deplored in his public speech. Odd, isn't it? Pavlovsky is the laboratory head at the Biophysics Institute of the country's health ministry and falsehood incarnate of the Soviet medical establishment. He attended and spoke at the experts' session of the Sakharov Congress despite the fact that the USSR prosecutor general's office had already initiated a legal action against him on the grounds of information concealment. To all intents and purposes, that fact did nothing to discourage those who inspired and organized the pro-nuclear congress. I suppose Andrei Sakharov was turning over in his grave as he watched this outrage committed in his name. Apparently, Pavlovsky, just like his boss, relished the opportunity to involve Western experts in the whitewash and criminal concealment of information about the disaster's consequences at the precise time of the Sakharov Congress, quite a shock to ordinary folk who were used to associating this name with truth and decency.

The dramatic position of independent experts and people's deputies at the Congress notwithstanding, we still managed to break through the "cordon sanitaire" erected by the organizers. We finally succeeded in convincing our Western colleagues that when infants in hard-radiation zones fell ill, it was not because they were in the habit of lighting up from the cradle, that the floods in Bangladesh were not quite the same as the blast in Chernobyl, and neither were the fires in Kuwait. At the close of the discussion, stunned by the spate of facts hitherto unknown to him but absolutely shocked by their sheer volume and accuracy, the reserved Dr. Toshiyuki Kumatori of Japan could not help crying out, "I never expected to hear this kind of discussion, and I am not ready."

The official medical establishment used to feed to foreign experts only those facts that were beneficial to it (and it is still doing so). How else could this enterprise justify itself before future generations for their criminal deception? Just pile one lie upon another until the deck of cards collapses! Whenever foreign scientists come to this country, they are securely shielded against any glimpse of reality by our old friends—Ilyin, Guskova, Povalyaev, Romanenko, Bebeshko . . . Their names are legion in our triune fatherland of Russia, Ukraine, and Belarus.

Much to our surprise and astonishment, another set of circumstances began to unfold (something similar was to have happened at the Sakharov Congress too). Even as the official team was brainwashing Western audiences in Vienna, for the first time on record, the well-oiled wheels of the system began to fall off. The Congress approved the recommendations on the Chernobyl theme without the usual semi-official versions. They were recommendations by uninvited and unwelcome experts. From their humble origins, the reports by Assistant Professor Lyutsko and Professor Burlakova traveled to various countries. The world received the information so long and so carefully guarded in the Soviet Union against outsiders. Even the human rights section's recommendations said in black and white, "There is risk of substituting the myth of 'radiophobia' for the actual situation in Chernobyl"—the pet myth, let me note, of academician Ilyin and our government.

Thinking back on that unfortunate incident connected with Chernobyl at the first international congress in memory of Andrei Sakharov, I realize that a political response from the international community was far more important for its organizers than the Congress itself. It was meant to arouse a lot of interest in the West. The event was important because it raised the nuclear issue worldwide, but it should never have been done at the expense of Chernobyl's children. Nor was it permissible to neglect the sick children and a scandalous misuse of Sakharov's name to cover up crimes against the masses who were still suffering in radioactive zones.

At present, Yelena Bonner lives in the United States with her family and occasionally lectures the people of Russia on how they should order their lives. We are very grateful for these lectures, of course. She would also do well to apologize to experts and peoples' deputies at the Congress who, fifteen years after the event, preserved her spouse's good name, and she should remember that there are nine million Chernobyl victims still suffering in contaminated areas, fighting for their right to live. I often wonder if she even cares.

13

Korosten, Luginy, and All the Rest

Years after Chernobyl, I decided to make another tour of the radioactive villages in my region. If immediately after the accident there were dozens of them, at this time there were several hundred. Most of them were unknown to the general public. These were chiefly remote villages in Polesye (forest country), surrounded by woods on every side. Sometimes it looked as if they had not been touched by civilization at all. So what had changed since the accident?

It was almost three years after the disaster, on June 1, 1989, that the village of Voronevo in the Korosten District learned that it was sitting smack in the hard-radiation zone and was therefore entitled to the 25 percent extra pay in "coffin money." Accompanied by a member of the local administration, I measured the gamma-ray level on the ground in the center of the village by the village's only shop. The meter said 0.112 mR/hr. The air a yard above ground registered 0.046 mR. The natural background there was 0.015—0.017 mR. The locals and the village children were beginning to flock toward us. We talked about life in general and about their health.

Valentina Petrovna Bekh, a cleaner at the village school:

> My son, Vova, is seven. He is sick. He has been registered as an invalid. He has heart murmurs. A while ago, he had bronchitis. My daughter, Tanya, is ten. After the Chernobyl explosion, she has been having nosebleeds all the time. And she suffers from constant headaches.

It turns out that the village does not even have a registered nurse. There is no pharmacy and no kind of communication with the district center. The vegetables grown locally are "dirty," milk from the villagers' cows, ditto. And the shop has nothing at all to offer.

They've had some pork twice. The children's rations are just one can of condensed milk [per month]. Also, they are supposed to get canned stew. Only, there isn't any. Fruit juice in three-liter jars. No baby food.

We heard similar stories from the locals at another village in the strict monitoring zone, Obikhody. True, it had been listed as such way back in 1986. Right on May Day. It had the same empty shelves in the village shop. The same tearful mothers said, "Visiting commissions say, 'Wash twice a day. Then you'll stay alive.'" The villagers were also advised to "boil potatoes twice." There were no extra payments of "coffin money." I asked the villagers if there was a hospital there. They pointed it out to me. We approached a ramshackle shed, which the leadership described in precisely those terms. The local bosses complained of lack of money for new construction. But just across the street, there was a brand-new building of the village Soviet. The authorities remembered to look after themselves all right. Incidentally, this is not only the pride of these local authorities. It's also the policy of their bosses at the regional level. The now ex-chairman of the regional executive committee, V. M. Yamchinsky, once showed me an album with color photographs of splendid buildings that housed village Soviets in various localities. It was a showpiece, packaged as a great achievement of Soviet power. In the Brezhnev years, even a national newspaper wrote about this practice in the Zhitomir region. They would have done better to build hospitals for people.

In the village hospital, old men and women lay in beds in shabby "wards." They had the advantage, of course, of admiring the view of the new village council from the windows. One of them said bitterly: "Here, cowsheds are better kept than the hospital. There are tiles in them cowsheds." The district executive committee chairman showed me a list of "facilities to be built (or refurbished) to meet the social and cultural development needs of the village of Obikhody, Korosten District." Some heading, that. So what had Obikhody lacked all the while to promote its "social and cultural development"? "Clubhouse seating 300, hospital for 25 beds, bridge over the River Oleshnya, water pipeline 47 km long, paved road 45 km long, public bathhouse, tractor facility, installation of gas service for 450 houses, reconstruction of the farm, boiler house, renovation of thatched roofs on 103 houses." And so on. Fourteen items in all. Then, was the Chernobyl blast a blessing in disguise?

We went down the streets to measure radiation levels. The locals advised us to start with the yard of Natalya Gritsenko, a mother of two. The meter readings said 0.150 mR/hr. Next to the house of the village Soviet chairman the level was 0.117 mR. On average, soil contamination levels in Obikhody were around 22.6 Ci/km^2. It was late August. The air was hot. The country roads had been churned up by vehicles. There were children playing in the sand. Obikhody counted 130 of them. It was announced that the Obikhody villagers were to be resettled—four years after the Chernobyl accident . . .

M. F. Ignatenko, chairman of the Korosten District Executive Committee:

> We don't even have the instruments for measuring radiation levels. There is not one such device in the whole district. Here are the two we have borrowed from Narodichi. Five commissions have come here to check the gamma radiation background. In thirty-two localities, the milk is "dirty." . . . In twelve, the level exceeds 15 Ci/km^2. But only two villages, Voronevo and Obikhody, are getting supplies of "clean" milk and meat from special reserves. And even so, there is far too little. Say, in the third quarter, Voronevo needed 660 kg of meat, but they only got 209 kg. They needed 870 kg of chicken meat, but they got just 80 kg. Milk comes from Kiev. There is a daily shortage of 100 tons.

Mikhail Ignatenko was leafing through a sheaf of documents, addressed to these party stalwarts: head of the regional trade directorate, P. I. Verbilo; G. K. Streblyanko, deputy trade minister of the Ukrainian Soviet Socialist Republic; S. V. Litvinenko, board chairman of Ukraine's cooperators union; V. M. Yamchinsky, chairman of the Zhitomir Regional Executive Committee; V. Ye. Kachalovsky, member of the Ukrainian Communist Party Central Committee Politburo, first deputy chairman of Ukraine's council of ministers; V. S. Masol, chairman of Ukraine's council of ministers; V. S. Shevchenko, chairperson of presidium, Ukrainian Supreme Soviet; once again to Masol; M. S. Gorbachev, chairman of the USSR Supreme Soviet; V. Ya. Ben, first secretary of the Korosten District Committee, Ukrainian Communist Party; USSR people's deputy V. P. Krishevich . . . Good grief! . . . And always with the same request, the same entreaty—"to include in the strict monitoring list the following localities . . . to allocate 'clean' foodstuffs," including milk, sour cream, curds, sugar, butter, fish, meat, vegetables . . . gas . . . hospital . . . radiometer. In short, everything—as if they had not lived before and had not needed all those things. Or maybe they really hadn't lived?

P. F. Ivanenko, chairman of the Korosten District consumers' union:

> We are given only what we manage to obtain by fighting and shouting. We have a meat processing and packing factory here, but no meat.

A. P. Gutevich, deputy head physician of the central district hospital:

> Ours is a unique situation. The polyclinic is in the district center. The hospital is in Ushomir. That's twenty-five kilometers from here. The neurology ward is in the village of Bekhi. The building in Ushomir is a pre-revolutionary affair, built in 1902.

As the locals told me, during World War II, the building in Ushomir had doubled as the stables. There were eight to ten patients to a ward. Because of the condition of the building, the maternity, trauma, and surgical units had to be closed down.

Meanwhile, eight kilometers from the tumbledown hospital, a new "construction project of the century" had been launched in the village of Grozino—one more imposing edifice for the administration, one more comfortable home for the bureaucrats—for the management of the Ukrainian Non-blackened Earth Zone Research Center . . . Could their need be greater than that of the patients, of the people deceived by the powers that be?

In all the villages of the districts hit by radiation that I visited in the period after the accident, people demanded extra pay, "clean" foodstuffs, and compensation for resettlement. (This is understandable. To them, this means life.)

But in one village, I heard a new demand. In the village of Bekhi, Korosten District, I was met by a crowd several hundred strong. They did not talk about meat or money. They beseeched the authorities to give them back the church that had been taken away from them before the war. That was truly remarkable.

I will dwell in more detail on this case of believers fighting for their souls' salvation in a radioactive village in a separate chapter. That was a fight to have the church restored not only to the village but to the people's hearts.

Here is a touching letter I received from semi-literate old peasants:

> We beg of you, help us return our holy site, our church. It was built in 1904 by the old graveyard. Its iconostasis alone cost 11,000 rubles then. Buried in the old graveyard are our fathers, brothers, and sisters. In 1934, they took our church away and turned it into a clubhouse. Under Nazi occupation, the church resumed services and continued to hold services until 1949. But then, they again took the church away from the believers. Everything inside was smashed up, a layer of bricks was added on the outside, inside the walls were paneled and mirrors hung up, and that was called a clubhouse. We appealed to the executive committee in Korosten and in Zhitomir—to the person in charge of religious matters. We were told that there were no grounds for having the church returned. What grounds should there be? It is the property of the believers.
>
> Now churches are being restored to believers everywhere. And we want to have our own church back. Most of the people in the village are old. We cannot travel long distances to churches in other villages. Buses pass through our village packed, and we have to walk to the nearest church. We worked all our life on the collective farm, and now there are more old age pensioners than youngsters here. But our chairman wrote that the village had 110 young people. He simply included in the list young villagers from Voronevo and Sokoriki. Those villages have clubhouses of their own. So why don't our youngsters go there? We want our church back. We demand a fair decision.

This letter was signed by "War and labor veterans of the village of Bekhi—Vasil Petrovich Bekh, Feodor Yefimovich Bekh, Victor Sergeevich Bekh, Maria Arsenyevna Bekh" and contained the signatures of over five hundred people.

I sent a request for help to the council for religions at the USSR Council of Ministers and also to His Eminence Pitirim, the Metropolitan of Volokolamsk and Yuryev. All I got from the metropolitan's office was a useless, waffling letter.

In April, I received a letter from the council for religious affairs at Ukraine's council of ministers signed by its first deputy chairman, P. D. Pilipenko. The reply was more than weird. I had asked for the requisitioned church to be restored to the parishioners, but the letter informed me that "the believers of the village of Bekhi applied to the executive committee of the Korosten District Soviet of people's deputies requesting registration of a religious community of the Ukrainian Orthodox Church and construction of a prayer house, which is being considered under the established procedure." Curiously, a few lines earlier, the man had written that "the religious situation in the village of Bekhi was examined on site by the staff of the council for religious affairs."

Apparently, the local authorities contrived to dupe not only the village believers in Bekhi but also the inspector from Kiev. The village bosses must have been really hard-pressed to hastily throw together yet another alternative "community"—so long as the believers were prevented from recovering their church. And this "community" (which, according to believers, consisted of the village activists), demanded registration and "construction of a prayer house." In their haste, they had even listed a dead person among the "community" members. The trick worked. It had been devised by the Bekhi village Soviet, the Korosten District Executive Committee, and the Zhitomir Regional Executive Committee. The lie got as far as the council for religious affairs in Moscow. And from there, from the very top, I got a reply to my inquiry. "Responding to the application from the Zhitomir regional Soviet of people's deputies and to the proposal of the council for religious affairs at the Ukrainian council of ministers, the USSR Council for Religious Affairs has registered the Orthodox Christian community of the village of Bekhi, Korosten District, Zhitomir region, and authorized it to construct a building for the purpose of praying, as the believers themselves desired."

To make sure once more what it was that the "believers themselves" desired, I went to Bekhi. How eagerly they had been waiting for me, those elderly, old, and truly ancient men and women! We entered the church-cum-clubhouse. It was packed. At my request, one of the collective farmers went to the village Soviet to invite its chairman. The chairman refused, citing urgent business. In the full view of the villagers, he got into a car and left. We stayed in the desecrated church for several hours. Toward the end of my talk with the believers, the village Soviet chairman turned up after all. Mikhail Ulyanovich Bekh failed to tell us anything intelligible about the "new" community that wished to get registered and build a new church. He declared that this was the first time he heard about it.

After the meeting, where it was unanimously decided to return the church to the believers, we went outside. I became part of an unusual cross-bearing procession, with the old ladies leading me around the building. One of the women pointed to what had once been a sacred burial site.

This used to be an ancient cemetery. They leveled it out with a tractor. These are the only two graves that are still intact. The rest have all been smashed up.

A mother dropped down over one of them. Embracing the stone, she screamed that her daughter was lying underneath. Here and there, gravestones still lay about. The graveyard periwinkle lavishly wound around the "clubhouse." Old women poked their fingers at the ground. Here lies my mother, and over there—my dad . . .

Right there on two graves, a latrine was put up for the convenience of nighttime merrymakers. "The toilet stands on the chests of Pa Alexander and Ma Galina," I was told. Their relatives were still living.

At the entrance to the courtyard of the clubhouse, a fresh patch of asphalt had been laid for summer dancing, should it get too stuffy inside. The asphalt had been laid just before my arrival. I was also shown the extension tacked on to what used to be a church building. It was added right on top of a communal grave. When I was saying goodbye, one of the old men stopped me, and several people broke into the *Mnogaya leta* ("Many years to come") plainsong. Then someone handed me a letter saying that it had been written by a woman so old that she could hardly walk. She asked them to give this to me. I read the letter, written in an unsteady scrawl, on the way to Zhitomir.

> I am a permanent resident of Bekhi. I saw the church being built, but I know how it was destroyed. The cupola and the crosses were thrown away and the graves bulldozed flat with a tractor . . . I beseech you, help our hearts to regain peace, to get our church back. I only went to the elementary school and cannot write well. We are searching for justice to have our church opened again.

I was going home late at night thinking that if Chernobyl had been sent to us in punishment for anything, it must have been for this too, for the Bekhi church, for the destroyed village graveyard, and for the latrine on top of the graves. Lord, forgive us!

After my trip to the believers, I again applied to the regional executive committee, this time firmly demanding that those people get back what they had been deprived of. And I received two replies, one from the deputy chairman of the Korosten District Executive Committee to the effect that the committee session had decided not to return the church, and the other was from the regional executive committee, saying that there were several options. I marveled at the authorities' recalcitrance. For them, it was not enough to take away the church and defile the graves. It was not enough that the village was in the area of radioactive contamination and that the elderly villagers had for the last few years been effectively abandoned to live out their days in misery. They must now be prevented from having a decent burial with a church service. The village rebelled, including hundreds of old age pensioners who had spent all their lives toiling away on the collective farm, who had never been to any place other than their village. And the more the local people's deputies and communist activists resisted, the more determined became the Orthodox worshippers.

A while later, I was accompanied by Ukrainian People's Deputy Yakov Zaiko. We went to meet the believers at their request. For a change, our twosome was reinforced by a third party, R. R. Petrongovsky, the head of the regional executive committee culture section. It was Sunday. Summer was drawing to a close. The asters had just come into bloom. We had been detained in Zhitomir and were late in arriving, but the people were standing there waiting for us. Hundreds of them had gathered by the church/clubhouse. We were given a red-carpet welcome, with the traditional bread-and-salt, bouquets of marigolds, and embroidered towels. As before, we went to the building to hold the meeting there. But—the "clubhouse" door was locked. Several village Soviet members stood there undecided, plus there were some district Soviet deputies who had come to attend the meeting. Finally, we had with us Roman Rafailovich Petrongovsky, who represented the regional authorities. The club manager announced that he did not have the key. He just didn't, and that was that.

And so we all stood about in the yard, on the ancient church's steps, talking to the people.

Now I feel certain that if there are indeed any specimens of that proverbial species, *homo sovieticus*, they must be the Bekhi Communist bosses. You should have seen the venom with which they pounced on the old men and women, almost coming to blows—the old people, mind, who were more dead than alive, having stood for hours by the locked "clubhouse" door. Some of the "activists" were schoolteachers. And the mentors were backed up by their youthful charges. They had poured out of the building's side door as soon as we opened the meeting. Like their mentors, they screamed abuse at their parents and grandparents. One of the lady activists yelled into my face that I was scheming to force her children into churchgoing. As if a child of hers could get worse from going to church than from dancing on the bones of his ancestors or relieving himself into an open grave! Such was the moral code of these builders of Communism. This time, too, the meeting ruled that the church must be returned to the believers—even the youngsters seemed to have seen the light toward the end.

Several days later, the daily *Radyanska Zhitomirshchina* carried an interview that regional executive committee culture section head, R. R. Petrongovsky, had given to Irina Verova-Golovanova, the newspaper's ideology section chief. The two assured the readers that people's deputies Yaroshinskaya and Zaiko had tried to seize the clubhouse, clamoring for the keys. . . . My friends asked me sarcastically if, by any chance, I had not approached the church in an armored personnel carrier. By the end of September, all that bureaucratic and ideological hullabaloo had ended. And shortly before Christmas, I got an invitation to come to Bekhi. The church was to be consecrated, and the graveyard was being restored. Later I received a sad letter from Maria Feodorovna Bekh, the main thorn in the side of the local authorities. She was telling me that radiation was making her life hell and that building materials for church restoration were in short supply.

Years after the accident, I discovered all was not well in the district center of Korosten either. Suddenly, there appeared patches in the streets and in the courtyards where radiation levels were extremely high, up to 100 and even 200 Ci/km^2. The title of an article on the situation in the area, written by deputy chief editor of *Radyanska Zhitomirshchina*, Stanislav Tkach, looked to me like a mockery—"The Special Attention Zone." What "attention" could one talk of if Korosten residents had for years been kept in the dark about the real scale of the calamity in their city and district? The paper's Communist Party cell secretary changed the special deception zone into one of "special attention." My further trips to radiation-affected villages, this time in the Luginy District, were equally disheartening. Of the forty-nine villages and settlements there, twelve were listed as strict monitoring areas. Besides, two villages were included in the list almost eighteen months after the Chernobyl accident, and the rest, four years later—an inadmissible delay in terms of people's health.

We entered the shop in the middle of the village of Moshchanitsa, hit by hard radiation. We started talking to people—and heard an endless litany of complaints . . .

183

Raisa Ivanovna Demchuk, head clerk at the shop:

> Everyone's saying they feel ill. The authorities are going to build roads and things here. But it would be cheaper to resettle us, if you ask me. All the younger people here are all for it, but the old folk are against it. And there are lots of kids in the village, of ten or eleven. They had a checkup at school. But we haven't been given any recommendations. We don't have a clue.

The villagers told us to measure radiation by the Kobylinskys' house. There's a strip of freshly laid asphalt nearby. It had just rained. We approached a spacious solid-looking house. A gate. A path leading to the porch. On either side—tall hollyhocks, white, pink, and red. The owners of the house came out, and we explained who we were and what we meant to do.

Vasily Feodorovich Kobylinsky, old age pensioner:

> We have children, and grandchildren, too. But they do not often come to visit us these days. Don't want to. Because of fear. So far, we have had enough money to get by. It's our health that is a problem. I have difficulty breathing in the morning, can't talk, there's something wrong with my throat. They did the tests on our stuff. And the soil here was also tested. The beets and potatoes and onions—we brought all of those for testing. But they won't tell us a thing—is it safe to eat this or that, or not. Still, we eat it. There's nothing else. We eat what we grow.
>
> They issued us with accumulation counters. We carried them about all the time. They came and took the things away. Nobody knows what was in them. We haven't been told. They did decontamination by our cowshed. Took off some ten to twenty centimeters of top soil. But in a little while, the level here went up again.

Kobylinsky took us to his vegetable plot. The counter registered 0.175 mR/hr on the ground. One corner of the plot had not been plowed. It was overgrown with birches and grass. A small lawn. A haystack from last year. It registered 0.705 mR. The wheat on the homestead showed 0.110.

As we left, we measured the gamma radiation background a meter above the soil—0.075. That's five times the natural level. And there were people living there. Life goes on. If you can call it life, of course.

On leaving Moshchanitsa, we entered a fragrant forest. It smelled of pine needles and decaying leaves. It was warm. Birds were singing. Everything seemed to be the way it always was, on the face of it, at any rate. But we placed our dosimeter on the ground under a tree.

Forty seconds, and the needle pointed to 0.106. We took two more measurements. The same. The forest was a health hazard. A district executive committee representative said that previously timber was exported. Now it will not be accepted just like that; buyers demanded certificates because of radiation. "The district has three thousand hectares of woodland, but we cannot take so much as a twig."

The next village on our way was Malakhovka. At the approach to the village, there was a monument—a granite slab with a young lad's face and a legend reading: "Field named after A. Martynchuk, who died while performing his internationalist duty in Afghanistan." The dosimeter registered 0.110 mR/hr on the grass next to the monument and 0.050 mR/hr in the air. Opposite the field and the monument, there was a beautiful orchard.

It seemed to be the pattern. We were again talking to the people by the shop in the middle of the village. Tamara Alexeevna Gerasimchuk, school cook, told us:

> Children are more susceptible to radiation. I have three. My youngest, a four-year-old, had 0.64 Ci of cesium, the eldest has 1 Ci. He has been sent to Odessa, to the Young Guard sanatorium. The kids have been tested for various things, but no one tells us what the results are. Two hundred children are examined every day. But if we try to ask something, we get no answer.

Lydia Afanasyevna Glevchuk, librarian:

> Myself, I come from Lipniki, but I work here. My little boy is eleven. He has Grade 2 thyroid enlargement and a liver condition. Kids sometimes get seizures in school. They faint during the morning parade.

Yekaterina Ivanovna Svidenyuk, field workers' team leader:

> I have three kids. Their health is poor. The youngest boy is four. He is on the medical register in Zhitomir. His lymph nodes are enlarged. They don't pay us the 30 rubles for "clean" food in the village. If you work here, you get 25 percent extra. If you go to work a couple of kilometers farther away, there's nothing for you.

Galina Ivanovna Ryabchuk, collective farmer:

> There is no work here in winter. The earnings come up to some 20 or 30 rubles a month. And we work seven days a week. There are twenty-eight women like that.

185

We were told:

> If a person lives in Malakhovka but goes to work in Lipniki, he or she is not entitled to the 25 percent extra pay. Sometimes people are members of the same team but work on different fields. And though the fields are next to one another, one may be listed as "clean" while its neighbor is "dirty." Who established that, and how, is a mystery. A person works in the village office and gets a 25 percent allowance. But next door, there is a schoolchild, or an old age pensioner. They get nothing. What's the logic of this? No one knows. So people keep complaining. They write endless letters. But it's ever so difficult to get anything done.

Grigory Grigoryevich Vlasyuk, director of the Lipniki State Farm:

> Our state farm comprises four villages, two under the strict monitoring regime, two "normal." The strict monitoring villages are Moshchanitsa and Malakhovka. Osny and Lipniki are not on the strict monitoring list. Malakhovka is two kilometers from Osny. There's a field across the road with a ditch going through it. On this side, people get the allowance, but on the other side, they don't. Meanwhile, the dust does not ask if this place is on some list or not. It flies where it pleases. In Moshchanitsa, all milk is "dirty." The slaughterhouse stopped accepting bullocks from there. The people have lost interest in life. They fall ill, complain of pain in the joints. Moshchanitsa has eighty-one homesteads. We believe it should be evacuated. It has higher radiation levels than the 30-km zone. The cesium there is at 30 Ci/km^2.

We then went to Lipniki, the state farm's main village. It was well kept, and there was a riot of flowers everywhere. The streets were neatly paved. The local café could be the envy of any town. A canteen. Foodstuffs were locally produced, so everything was cheap. In short, the farm workers had no complaints about their living conditions. But they looked very worried when talking of radiation. They told us that several days after the head physician of the Lipniki hospital, I. Ye. Nevmerzhitsky, had spoken at a session of the Luginy District Soviet of people's deputies, a commission arrived from the regional health department to inquire into the quality of his work. So what had Ivan Nevmerzhitsky done wrong? He had told the truth about the health of his patients. He expressed his lack of confidence in the official medical establishment. He had ironically suggested "building a children's summer camp near the village of Moshchanitsa or Chervonna Voloka." He had asked awkward questions of gentlemen from Ukraine's Health

Ministry: "Is it possible to live in Moshchanitsa where the radioactive background fluctuates between 340 and 1500 mR/hr? Is it right when responsible or rather irresponsible persons are ready to raise human tolerance dosages almost daily? Why is a person dying of wounds in Hiroshima or Nagasaki declared a victim of the American attack, but someone dying of radiation-induced cancer in our zone is denied victim status?" The head physician and his patients are still waiting to hear answers to these questions.

On the way from Lipniki to Luginy, we were intercepted by Nina Ivanovna Danilyuk, director of the Ostapovsky state farm. And although we were pressed for time and there were still visits to be made to the district executive committee and a variety of other district bodies, we did not dare refuse these people.

Danilyuk poured out another sad tale.

Ours is an immaculately clean area, and everyone is telling us that we are the picture of health. But if so, why did thirty-seven children out of the fifty examined turn out to suffer from Grade 2 thyroid hyperplasia? Thirteen of our kids are in Kiev, in the republic's radiation center. Would healthy children be hospitalized there? They came to check us for cesium in the tissues. The examination went on in two rooms. Well, so first I took my daughter, Galina, to one room for the check—0.9 micro Ci of cesium. Then I took her to the other one next door, and there they told me it was 0.1. And a third time, it was 0.57. What sort of checks are these?

We have "dirty" milk here. And there isn't a kindergarten. Children go into the fields together with the adults. Here is a report on farmland examination. It says: grazing dairy cattle in areas where the content of radioactive cesium in the raw weight of grass and the ground part of the grass exceeds a certain level must be prohibited. And the report specifies that level. We have a total of 139 hectares of pastureland. If these recommendations were to be observed, we could graze cows on a mere twenty-five hectares. The rest are unfit for that. But we graze cattle on all of them. What else can we do? The radiation level is thirty-six times the norm in the Staritsa meadow, and in Krugloe, it's eight times the norm.

They have made the people of the whole district give a written undertaking to abstain from drinking homemade milk. Ditto in Ostapy. An undertaking that we would not drink it ourselves or give it to our children. Each family head signed those papers. They have done it twice all over the district. But no one delivers clean foodstuffs to us! Neither meat nor milk. We have to use firewood for heating. But the forest is "dirty." They should install gas and water supply systems, because the dust here is something terrible. We get

187

the riddlings from the Zherevtsy quarry, and Zherevtsy is a "strict monitoring" village. We need "clean" food, especially for children; and other benefits—paid leave, allowances. They are building a school here, but there is no bathhouse, no soap or washing powder. How are machine-operators and hop-growers to wash? And what about families with many children?

Valentina Ivanovna Primenko, chairperson of the Ostapy village Soviet, added a personal note:

We have been told for several years that things are okay here and that the levels are low. So why have I been issued a warrant for treatment at the cancer clinic? Why is my eight-year-old in and out of hospitals all the time? Why does he have lymph nodes enlarged by five centimeters? He has lost 70 percent of his eyesight. Who will answer for that?

After our tour of radiation-affected villages, we returned to Luginy. At the district executive committee, I was told that until June 15, 1989, there had been no radioactive contamination map of the district. Of course, the state farms had been working their cesium fields all the time. Agriculture experts insisted that if their recommendations were followed to the letter, it is possible to obtain "clean" produce on "dirty" land. Maybe it is—though this is hard to believe. But—will somebody please tell me how the suggested farming techniques can be applied in the absence of a contamination map? Do you need another example of state secrecy? Take the word of Nadezhda Pavlovna Kovaleva, director of the Luginy veterinary laboratory.

On the orders of the regional agriculture and industry committee, I regularly take samples for radiological tests there. They never tell me the results. Loshchilov, director of the Kiev Agricultural Radiology Institute, has been here twice. He took samples of milk, soil, and fodder in Ostapy. What was found in them we still do not know. I was told in Kiev that there were different temporarily permissible levels for selling milk in different localities. The "cleanest" goes to Moscow, Kiev gets a "dirtier" variety, and Zhitomir "dirtier" still.

According to research done by the Luginy sanitary and epidemiological station, a considerable proportion of wild berry samples, nearly half of the medicinal herbs, more than half of fish and dried mushrooms, and two thirds of honey exceed human tolerance levels. I was also shown the results of checks by the Luginy veterinary lab, including test samples of water, silage, green fodder, and privately produced milk. Virtually all of them exceeded even the temporary permissible levels. Studying those mind-boggling papers, I recalled a story one of the despairing mothers told tearfully at a government commission's meeting with the residents of the region's northern areas. "When I surprised my five-year-old son by the milk jug, he begged me in fear—'Mommy, please, do not scold me. I did not drink the milk. I only dipped my little finger in it.'"

For years, the visiting medics were in no hurry to acquaint the public with their findings. Sometimes a year passed before the analytic results could be wrung out of the offices in Kiev. And anyway, the point of most examinations was to soothe rather than to heal. On occasion, two hundred children were "examined" in a single day. What standards can there be here? Incidentally, there is one hospital for five thousand inhabitants of "strict monitoring" villages, and even that is in a ramshackle building that was not originally constructed as a hospital. Three years after the blast, medical examination results paralyzed public consciousness. Thyroid problems had increased by one third, blood circulation disorders had doubled, and so on. This emergency situation notwithstanding, the district had been issued orders to produce 260 liters of donor blood a year! Who will donate this blood? And who will get the transfusion? Thoughtless, crazy, and cruel—without medical justification!

V. K. Chumak, head of the Ukrainian Academy of Sciences center for environmental problems of nuclear power engineering, and senior research officer N. P. Belousova drew these conclusions concerning the radiation situation in the district.

> The possible maximum exposure doses absorbed by the residents [of the Luginy district] who consume locally produced foodstuffs may reach 10 rem a year. The dose that the population gets from external irradiation . . . may reach 0.8 rem a year. Given the seven-to-ten-year period of effective semi-decontamination of soil typical of the Luginy District, it would be wrong to expect noticeable improvements in the radiation situation in the near future.

In the years since the Chernobyl accident, more than three hundred letters, telegrams, complaints, and applications have been sent from the district to various authorities. The citizens' pressure group sent an urgent letter to V. S. Shevchenko, chairperson of the presidium of Ukraine's Supreme Soviet, and to V. A. Masol, chairman of Ukraine's council of ministers, to inform them of the dramatic situation in the district. The letter was delivered by special messenger. A month later, head of the RM10 general section, S. K. Vasilyuk, told me, "We had a visit from, would you believe it, a KGB officer, who came to check the radiation situation and the people's mood."

Three years after the Chernobyl accident, I received a letter from A. A. Pokreshchuk, a lecturer at the Higher Party School of the Ukrainian Communist Party Central Committee, with an academic degree in law. Here is what he wrote, among other things.

> On June 21, I attended a session of the Luginy District Soviet. The next day, I was urgently summoned to my place of work. The school president told me that they had had a call from the first secretary of the Zhitomir region's Communist Party committee who complained that I was fomenting unrest among people in the district. (The first secretary had not been present at the session.) I was advised to retire. And my actions were judged provocative. I refused. Then the school president suggested that I write an explanatory memo, a copy, of which I enclose . . .

The explanatory memo by the lecturer at the Department for the Development of the Soviets and Law, addressed to the president of the Higher Party School, I. P. Grushchenko, contained no words of repentance or apology. The author wrote that he had been officially invited to Luginy and that he "took part in editing the session's draft resolution." Also, he "proposed that the *My Land* program crew from Ukrainian TV make a report on the session."

I contacted the president of the Higher Party School, Prof. I. P. Grushchenko. "Indeed," the president confirmed,

> I had a call from V. M. Kavun, regional party committee's first secretary, who said that Pokreshchuk had created panic at the session and instead of helping, just whipped up hysteria. I asked the regional committee for an objective testimony in writing about his behavior there. I have got it already. The party cell will discuss his behavior at the session.

In the letter addressed to the Higher Party School president, second secretary of the regional party committee, V. A. Kobylyansky, thus describes Pokreshchuk's behavior: "In his speech, he failed to clarify the issue, but tried to put a negative spin on the work of party and Soviet authorities, expressing unfounded criticism of the republic's leaders and proposed sending the tape to the Second Congress of the USSR People's Deputies." The letter ended with the following conclusion: "All that has not helped normalize the situation in the district . . . and is causing dissatisfaction among its people." It appears that the cover-up of radiation information had not seemed reason enough for the party regional committee to write letters of protest and make emotional phone calls, presumably because such concealment caused satisfaction while making that information public "caused dissatisfaction."

There were others, besides Pokreshchuk, who incurred the wrath of the party bosses. The district authorities, too, fell in disgrace. It was unheard of for anyone to hold a session without authorization from the top. Moreover, the session dared discuss a matter painstakingly concealed from the public—the consequences of the Chernobyl accident. As if that were not enough, they invited a consultant from Kiev, people from television, and representatives of four equally contaminated neighboring districts! Several days before the session was about to be held without the regional authorities' blessing, a stern phone call came from the regional executive committee promising all manner of punishment if they did not desist. After the session, the unruly district executive committee chairman was summoned to the regional executive committee for a dressing down. There were also calls from the regional party committee. What did that man Pokreshchuk think he was doing? Obviously, just following orders. No, it was not radiation levels nor the people's health that was the party functionaries' concern. Not one member of the regional leadership deigned to "bother" to attend the event that was top priority to the district's inhabitants. It was something else that made them jittery—that the truth might come out! Troublemakers and malcontents must be punished.

The unauthorized session of the Luginy District Soviet of people's deputies was broadcast outside the building. People stood in the street—listening. The four-hundred-seat hall was packed to capacity, though just seventy-five people's deputies were expected to attend. After several years of Chernobyl silence, for the first time in this country, Luginy deputies started acting the way they should have acted from the start. The session witnessed by thousands of people, in the hall and outside, discussed the dramatic situation in the district and wrote letters demanding that the USSR Atomic Energy Ministry be called to account. The letters were sent to the USSR prosecutor general and the chief state arbitrator. The losses incurred by the district following the accident were computed, and a damages bill was drawn

191

up totaling 314,630 rubles. Small wonder that this did not go down well with those who were hiding the truth from their own people about the Chernobyl aftereffects, with behavior that can only be described as a kind of sadistic fervor.

This is where the editor of the regional daily *Radyanska Zhitomirshchina*, Dmitry Panchuk, should have displayed his honesty and adherence to high principles. Yet not a word of truth was set in print about what had happened at the rebel session, when people tried to defend themselves and fell in disfavor with the authorities.

Finally, a bit of honesty from S. I. Rashevsky, first secretary of the Luginy District party committee and people's deputy:

> One third of the district has already been classified as a hard radiation area. But in other districts and villages, things are not much better. Even in Luginy, there are places where the gamma radiation background reaches 0.32 mR. "Practically not a single village or town," I am quoting the report by experts at the Nuclear Testing Institute of Ukraine's Academy of Sciences, "has cesium levels in milk below the temporarily permissible levels, whether in the private or in the public sector, while in some areas the temporarily permissible levels have been exceeded ten and more times." . . . Children in the village of Rudnya Povch absorbed far higher radiation doses than children in the Ovruch District. The commission that came over tried to prove to us that here in our district we were perfectly all right, living as we did in virtually health-resort conditions. Ukraine's health minister, Comrade Romanenko, likewise took a stand we find difficult to comprehend. We have repeatedly raised the issue of public health in the district in our appeals to him. But he keeps pretending that he is unaware of the actual state of affairs and that there is no threat to people's health. Nor do our republic's leaders, Masol and Shevchenko, show much concern about the life and health of our people in this difficult situation.

The authorities in the Luginy District were making the same mistakes as their counterparts had done in the Narodichi District. That, too, was frankly discussed at the session. The people of Luginy were allocated millions of rubles to cope with the accident's consequences. In Malakhovka, a strict monitoring village, money was earmarked for building a medical station and a bathhouse as well as paved roads. In Moshchanitsa, with just eighty-one households, a water supply system was being constructed, and new fences were being put up. Whatever for? Why bury good money in cesium-saturated earth?

S. V. Kobylinskaya, schoolteacher in the village of Moshchanitsa:

> Why do we need this road, and the bathhouse, the water and gas pipelines, when several years from now, or maybe in a year already, there will be no one here to use them? This money could be spent on resettling people—because all the villagers complain of increasingly poor health. It is impossible to live here. We have seen lots of various commissions. The Kiev commission said that radiation levels in our village were higher than in the 30-km zone. And right next to the clubhouse, it's 2.1 mR/hr.

P. M. Kravchuk, tractor driver on the Ukraine collective farm, district Soviet deputy spoke of other problems,

> None of the republic's leaders at the First Congress of People's Deputies so much as remembered Chernobyl problems. Our deputies worried about all sorts of things—what badges the Baltic deputies wore on their lapels, how the hospital building was progressing in Yakutia, the rumors about gunmen squads possibly being organized in Georgia, the note pushed under someone's door that asked for support for Gdlyan and Ivanov (dissenting public prosecutors who used to investigate links between corruption in Soviet Central Asian republics and senior officials in Moscow). Ours was the only republic that had no problems worthy of their attention. We were the most problem-free republic at the Congress.

This is true. None of the republic's leaders so much as mentioned Chernobyl at the First Congress.

The head physician of the Chernovolotsk Hospital, P. G. Kozel, had these strong words:

> Our health authorities assured us that there was no cause for concern about our future, that it was now easier to breathe. Then we were branded panic-mongers and radiophobes. But what do we see now? We see that we have been duped. Now we see that 70 percent of our children have thyroid pathology against the regional average of six cases per one thousand . . . I learned only a short while ago that there was an emergency commission under the regional executive committee. If it did its work properly, we would know, you and me, that in these parts, people mustn't pick berries, gather herbs, or burn firewood from our forest. And why didn't commission members come to us at least once in those three years? Why did the commission conceal from us information about the real radiation levels in our district, and still does, for that matter?

Although there were representatives of the regional health department and Ukraine's hydrometeorological committee, none of them gave intelligible answers to the deputies' questions. As for Deputy Health Minister Yu. P. Spizhenko, he declared brazenly: " I cannot say anything about the environmental situation in the district because I have not specifically prepared to talk on the subject."

Three years after the catastrophe, Spizhenko—who, incidentally, had been head of the Zhitomir regional public health department in 1986—proposed to the session that they "form an objective-minded commission that would include doctors, representatives of the local authorities, and journalists who would cover the work of the commission and assess the degree of objectivity in the commission's data." Now, isn't this odd? Who, pray, was to form that commission? A tractor driver from the Mayak collective farm, maybe? Or the district Soviet chairman? Comrade deputy minister was indeed completely unprepared to deal with the situation. Then why bother to come and meet the people at all? Someone in the audience said to him, "The impression is that you are not ready to respond to today's proposals, nor do you have any suggestions for improving the environmental situation. And the arrival of the republic's deputy health minister in the district is just pro forma." With an air of injured pride, Yuri Spizhenko snapped, "That is not for you to judge." Shortly afterward, Deputy Health Minister Yu. P. Spizhenko was promoted to minister. And in this new capacity, he replied, on instructions from the government, to my inquiry and the enclosed collective letter from the village of Ostapy, Luginy District: "At present, all the materials arguing for the need to introduce extra benefits for the population, including the inhabitants of the villages of Malakhovka, Moshchanitsa, and Ostapy in the Luginy District of the Zhitomir region, are being considered by the republic's government."

An amazing answer. Had the minister even read my letter? Had he really heard what people discussed at the Luginy District Soviet session? What extra benefits for Moshchanitsa and Malakhovka were he talking about if they already had all those benefits to which they were entitled? Both the "coffin money" and the 25 percent extra pay. The message of our letter was different. Why bury more millions of rubles in the radioactive land of those villages? The people demanded to be resettled in safe areas! Or was the minister's reply to the deputy just pro forma, once again? So what is more terrible—radiation or our own bureaucrats' heavy artillery that destroys the human soul?

Things were hardly any better after all these years in the long-suffering and now notorious Narodichi District. Of the eighty "clean" villages in the district, sixty-nine had become "dirty." It used to be thought that in eleven of the "clean" villages, the local milk was safe to drink and fruit and vegetables in the villagers' gardens could be eaten without mishap. Although, in reality, milk from Bolotnitsa, for instance, was thirty-six times more radioactive than the maximum permissible level, and milk from Chervonnoe, Rubezhovka, Slavkovtsy, and Old Kuzhel was fifty times more radioactive while in Vyazovka, the figure was one hundred times. Radiometric monitoring of water in the wells there was not conducive to optimism either. In Singai, the radioactivity level was fifty-two times the norm! In Rubezhovka, it exceeded the norm almost fifteen times, and in Slavkovtsy, nearly seventeen times. The Zhitomir meatpacking and processing factory refused to accept meat from the village of Vyazovka—its radioactive contamination level proved monstrously high.

Those eleven villages had nearly three thousand inhabitants. About six hundred were children. Whereas in "dirty" villages, every youngster got at least the prescribed can of condensed milk and an orange a month, here kids were denied even those measly handouts. Who or what rubber stamp in which office condemned the children to drinking radioactive solution in place of milk? According to the data of the Narodichi Central Hospital, in those "fortunate" villages, the number of cancer patients was growing apace, and in just one village attractively named Laski ("Caresses"), within the first three years after the accident, more than fifty children had been diagnosed as having Grade 1 or 2 thyroid hyperplasia. Prior to the Chernobyl blast, there had been only fourteen such children there. Call these villages "clean"?

It is sadness all round. I always return from radiation-affected villages with a heavy heart. . . .

Podgatye, Ovruch District, a village of just seven houses. There were seven old people living there. That place was uninhabitable, but how can they abandon it?

Rudnya-Radovelskaya, Ovruch District. The village split into two camps. One half wanted to leave. The other wondered where they could go. Yet leave they must, apparently. For some reason, people do not plant trees in the newly built villages.

To give up the lot, to leave everything behind is scary. Hearts bleed. They flutter like birds in a radioactive cage. In Narodichi, Moshchanitsa, Polesskoye—and all the rest of them—the tragedy resembles a death spiral.

195

14

"I Only Dipped My Finger in the Milk!"

That was how a frightened little boy tried to explain to his mother what he'd done. He had been strictly forbidden to drink fresh milk from the family cow. Letters from the radiation zone are soul-searing human documents: confessions, collective and personal ones—from ordinary people who live there, from pressure groups, from working collectives, from public organizations, and even from local authorities. Sometimes, people driven to despair send poignant poetry or their diaries. Far from becoming less urgent with time, these letters will yet come into their own, and "their time will come like that of good old wine" (as the poet Marina Tsvetaeva wrote about her immortal poems). I am printing them here, warts and all, without any editing. These are *genuine documents*, not specially constructed pieces, amended and reinterpreted to suit a commercial goal or the reporter's ambition, when it is difficult to make out whether it is still the author of the original document talking (writing) or the reporter himself or herself adding frills to the rough coat.

I am not yet 32, but I find myself in a hospital bed several times a year. And all of my four children (under 12) are also ill most of the time (they feel weak and listless, they have joint pains in arms and legs, their hemoglobin is below normal, they have enlarged thyroid and lymph nodes, headaches, stomach pains, constant colds). And it is the same in every family.

We want to live. We want our kids to live and grow up healthy, and to have a future. But through the heartlessness, callousness and cruelty of those on whom our lives and the lives of our children depend, we are condemned to the worst possible fate, and we are only too well aware of that. It is only bureaucrats in comfortable chairs who do not or will not see that.

In the Narodichi district at least several of the villages have received promises that they will be resettled, but as far as our district is concerned, it is silence all round. We have had to eat, drink and breathe radiation for years, waiting for our last day. And this is happening in the Soviet state, too, where it has always and everywhere (on the radio, in the press, at school) been said that the human being is in the center of attention.

That is just not true! No one gives a damn about the likes of us. Who can we turn to? If I knew the address, I would write to the UN, because our local agencies, and the press too, are just as helpless as we are.

We ask and beseech you: please help us in our need, help us save our children!

Valentina Nikolaevna Okhremchuk, mother of four little boys, and all the mothers of Olevshchina.

Writing to you are the villagers of Norintsy, Klochki, Maryanovka, Savchenki, Nivochki, Latashi, Old Dorogin, Snityshcha, and the collective farmers of the Maxim Gorky collective farm in the Narodichi district, Zhitomir region.

We have tried applying to every level of authority, but all were indifferent to our grief, to the fate of our children. Three years have passed, but the reverberations of the Chernobyl tragedy are increasingly affecting our children's health. We all of us live 60 kilometers from Chernobyl. A mother's heart bleeds to look at the children. Lately the children's health has deteriorated sharply. The children feel weak, sick and often headachy, their eyesight is failing, there are cases of fainting, and bone fractures have become more frequent. They are doing markedly worse at school. Class registers show great numbers of absentees. Cheerfulness is gone. And this is just after three years. What will happen later, in five or ten years' time? What will those not yet born be in for?

Twice a year our children were examined (if you can call it that), but we were left in the dark about the results. Though even the little information we have is alarming. Of the 132 children at the Norintsy secondary school, and 65 children at the Latashi secondary school, only 42 have been given a checkup. Thirty-nine have been found to have pathological conditions. They have been told to go to the republic's radiological clinic for a more thorough examination. This is causing concern. We are afraid to let them go to the river or the forest, and these things are so important to a person's childhood. Only a bureaucrat can divide areas into the "clean" and the "unclean." It worries us when we are told that things are normal, that a person will absorb 35 rem during a lifetime, that is, during 70 years. But we can see that someone just wants to use us as guinea pigs. Consider: in just one of the checked villages here, people have accumulated 1.087 rem in their systems within a year. Who will be responsible for our health, may one ask? What will become of our children? Nearly all the children have enlarged thyroids, many have an abnormally big liver, and there is an increased incidence of cardiovascular disorders.

In adults the incidence of cancers has increased. At present there are 40 people registered as cancer patients at the clinic. In just two years, 1987 and 1988, 14 cases of cancer on our collective farm were registered. When a whole team of doctors came to our district from Kiev, in March this year, to conduct a checkup, they did not manage to fit into their schedule a checkup on our children—although we know that the number of sick children in the villages of our collective farm is no smaller than in the "strict monitoring" villages. We have repeatedly applied to the USSR ministry of public health, to the council of ministers, to the television program "Perestroika Searchlight," to the Ukrainian council of ministers, personally to Comrade Kachalovsky (our delegation was granted an audience with him), but we have not received a single direct reply from any of those people.

After the Chernobyl accident occurred, we hoped that we would meet with understanding, both in the region and in the republic. But the reverse happened: for a third year now we are being completely ignored. People from the regional services that visited us merely tried to reassure us and closed their eyes to everything else. No one wants to try to see our side of it. We have been abandoned, and we cope with our woes all on our own. Therefore we request your attention and intervention as a people's deputy in the settling of the following issues: resolve the matter of extra pay and pay of 30 rubles per family member for clean food; delivery of clean foodstuffs.

Please try to see our plight as a mother. What shall we tell out children five or ten years hence, let alone our grandchildren? It may happen that our children and we, too, have no future. We enclose the signatures of our collective farm villagers.

The letter was signed by almost six hundred people.

We, the villagers of Maryanovka of the Narodichi district, Zhitomir region, are appealing to you for help. We have been left alone to face our sorry plight. We will never forget April 1986. Although three years have passed, we feel increasingly concerned about the accident at the Chernobyl nuclear power plant. It is increasingly affecting our children's health. With tears in our eyes we are watching them, unable to help. It is already obvious that our children are not what they were. Where's their vigor, joy, laughter? They are often ill. And these are not isolated cases. Also, we have to cook the food for our children and ourselves from what we grow on our plots—even though we know we shouldn't. But it can't be helped. On our entire collective farm milk contamination is high, several times the permissible level. The village shop never gets supplies of fruit and vegetables. Milk is delivered only rarely. As for sausages and meat, that is delivered only when there is a surplus in the villages entitled to supplies of "clean" foodstuffs. Those villages are just three or four kilometers from ours.

Our village is small. Living here are almost exclusively collective farmers. There is no farm work now, so the earnings are low too—on average, 60 to 70 rubles a month. Some families have three or four children.

The letter was signed by thirteen collective farmers of the village of Maryanovka.

Quite a few of the villagers in Mezhileska have changed residence. But most of us have stayed on. We trust that our state will not allow any harm to come to its working people. There is just one thing that made us write this letter to you: not far from our village, in Bazar, Golubievichi, Greater Minki and others, people are getting 25 percent extra pay, and 30 rubles per capita on top of that. We do not know what the difference is in the conditions here and in their villages. Because a radiology lab came to our farm and we gathered from a talk with its assistants that test results here were the same as over there.

Not to make unsubstantiated statements, here is a corroborating fact: sheep have already been removed from our farm to other areas. Because, owing to certain radiological statistics, wool produced on our farm was unfit for general use either last year or this. They have also measured radiation on cows, and it's very high; even the fattened beasts cannot be sent to the meat factory.

Seventy percent children of school and pre-school age display changes tending toward thyroid anomalies. The children were prescribed a six-month treatment and advised not to drink home milk, and generally cook food from clean products brought from the outside.

There is a primary school in our village. For some reason, soldiers came and took off and away the topsoil around it, and covered the ground with crushed stone. When people asked them what for, they were told that radiation was high.

And that made us appeal for a fair settlement of the issue. After all we work conscientiously on the farm and in the fields, and will go on working so, though we feel great anxiety about our children. But we are told that in due course things will be back to normal. We request to be paid extras here, like in the neighboring villages. Then we could buy "clean" food for our children.

Working people of the villages of Mezhileska and Osoka.

The letter had ten signatures.

Writing to you are the villagers of Rokitno of the Ovruch district, Zhitomir region, who live in the radiation-affected zone.

The experts who have more than once tested the soil, water and locally produced foodstuffs tell us that radiation exceeds natural background indices several times. We have been told that we are entitled to extra pay of 25 percent of our wages, and another 30 rubles, like in villages with increased radioactivity.

We have repeatedly appealed to Moscow, but you must know that all the letters are returned to the region, and the regional branch of the agricultural industry committee is presided over by Comrade Bystritsky, and he replies to our letters that radiation is within the norm.

The sanitation and epidemiological station and representatives from Kiev come and say that we are entitled to allowances and "clean" foodstuffs deliveries. Foodstuffs are delivered once in a while. We turned to the district executive committee to find out about pay for high radioactivity; they told us that the money was being allocated, but three years have passed, and the matter has not been resolved.

The people in our village suffered in the war. The village was burnt down and its people executed, like in Khatyn in Belarus.

On behalf of the residents of Rokitno, Anatoly Ivanovich Baranovsky.

Writing to you are the villagers of Priluki, Zhitomir region, Ovruch district, and the staff of the 2nd Zhitomir regional psychiatric hospital located in the same village.

Following the accident at the Chernobyl nuclear power plant, the radiation background in the village of Priluki was higher than normal, and foodstuffs and water were contaminated. From June 1986 to February 1987, 25 percent extra payments were made. Then the payments stopped, on account the situation had normalized. At the same time on two occasions (in June and October 1988) decontamination work was done in the village and in the hospital compound by chemical warfare defense units. The medical examination of children (90 children in all) found 43 percent to have pathological conditions: five of the children examined were sent to Kiev for a more thorough checkup and treatment. The results of blood tests are kept secret. The children of the villagers and hospital staff resident in the village of Priluki are taken to school by bus, to the township of Pervomaisky, as it is the nearest. The children are at school from 07:40 till 16:00 hrs. This happens in a contaminated locality whose inhabitants are getting compensation money for high-caloric diet and 25 percent extras added to their wages. As for us, we get no extra pay, though we live and work in a similar area; we cannot provide "clean" food for our children.

The villages nearest to ours (Berezhest, Rudnya Mechnaya, Pekhotskie, Duminskie, Vystupovichi, at a distance of 4 to 9 km) are supplied with "clean" foodstuffs, and get 25 percent extras plus 30 rubles per family member. Going through our village is the Minsk-Izmail highway. All the vehicles from hard-radiation-affected villages go along it.

In April 1989, at the insistent demands of Priluki villagers, the Ovruch district sanitation and epidemiological station took test samples of food here. Radiometric examination revealed that milk, mushrooms and berries were unfit for human consumption.

We tried appealing to the district executive committee, the regional executive committee, the regional health department, to the chairman of Ukraine's hydrometeorology service, to request a study of the environmental situation in the area and take measures to minimize its adverse effect on human health. But we have had no response so far.

Staff of the 2nd Zhitomir regional psychiatric hospital and residents of the village of Priluki.

Our 400-bed sanatorium New Racha, which is in the Narodichi district, still accepts patients. The head of the regional tuberculosis clinic came over, assembled the staff and announced that our sanatorium was to be closed down, the pulmonary department was to be transferred to the TB clinic in Belokorovichi, the bone department would go to the village of Sadki of the Zhitomir district. (. . .) Since our district had suffered radioactive contamination, we believe that the sanatorium is being liquidated because of the radioactive contamination. If so, and background radiation does not allow a sanatorium to be kept here, liquidate away. But the people should be honestly told as much, and they should be evacuated, just as people from radioactively contaminated areas are evacuated.

This is the time of democratization of society, the time for straightforward, honest talk. So why don't you act honest? The press writes that we have the lowest level of radioactive contamination here.

In August 1989, at a meeting in Narodichi, one of the women who spoke there handed me her diary—a school exercise book with lined pages. This confession is a festering wound. How often do rural dwellers keep diaries? What had to happen to a person, to this person's soul, to induce her to take up a pen and write to herself? Here is just one day's entry from the diary:

June 17, 1989. The worst thing that can happen to one is loss of faith—faith in the truth, however bitter. I have a heavy heart, I feel pain, I could cry—I feel so offended by the people, the scientists, the leaders in charge of the laws; I am hurt by their cunning and lies.

We are said to be sick. All the people in the district have the same disease. The disease is called radiophobia. Why have we all, to a man, so different in terms of age, physical development and disposition, succumbed to this one disease? No, dear Comrades Romanenko and Spizhenko, we do not suffer from radiophobia, we have contracted Chernobyl disaster. While you and your ilk, who for three years have been concealing from us everything the Chernobyl disaster did to us, have lost the people's trust. And what is a person worth who has lost that trust?

I am a mother; I have four children of my own, and four grandchildren. I worked at school for 23 years, and every child there, from Grade One to Grade Ten, knows me—even though I am not a teacher. But as a mother and a woman I am used to paying attention to children. So what do I see? Over the last few years children have changed beyond recognition. They have grown indifferent; you can't surprise or delight them anymore. They yawn; they are sleepy, tired and irritable. They have no appetite, their complexion is different, and they look pale, sallow, gray. The children's eyes have gone dull; they lost that roguish light. Our children faint during morning parades after standing for 15 or 20 minutes.

Everyone, children and adults alike, complains of discomfort and stabbing pain in the eyes, dryness in the mouth, burning sensation and tickling in the throat, their heads swim, they have aching pains in the joints of the arms and especially of the legs. Is that radiophobia?

And why won't you and your ilk admit that we have been absorbing strontium for three years, and also cesium from fresh vegetables? After all, for three and a half years our children and we have lived on the land that glows, we have breathed the air that is ablaze, and we have been eating things we grow on our land that irradiates. We don't even have clean water, for God's sake! Go on, test our water—it's a proper chemical agent.

I am a lab assistant of the Chemistry Room at the Narodichi secondary school. At one lesson I was to make a copper-sulfate solution. When I poured copper vitriol into the test tube and added water, instead of a blue solution the children saw a green-colored one. I had to go to the pharmacy for distilled water. Our systems absorb poison from water, soil and air. Besides, there is the stress on the psyche from lies and bureaucracy.

Previously, when we got together for an idle chat, the subjects were usually the ordinary: who had planted, mowed, harvested or canned how much of what. It has been a long time since I last heard this kind of talk. Whenever two or three women get together, they talk of nothing but their children's illnesses.

Our district has 26,000 inhabitants. Some 65 million rubles has already been spent on new construction. And another 37 million has been earmarked for the current year. Simple arithmetic suggests that this money would be enough to build 90 five-story houses, three sections each, which could accommodate all of us. Where do they invest this money, if the problem is still to have people resettled away from this land? Who profits by throwing millions down the drain? Who profits by hiding the truth about the radioactivity situation in the district? Why not use this money to build housing in clean areas and re-house the people there? Surely, the state would benefit more from saving our lives than from having us die a slow death? Why go to the trouble of delivering "clean" food here if we could grow everything ourselves on clean land?

They have laid in water pipes, and are doing the same with the gas pipeline; the roads are being paved, and houses and kindergartens are being built on our lands glowing with cesium. We find none of this a matter for rejoicing. The river, the forest, the meadows are out of bounds for our children. Can one live like that?

When visiting teams of doctors left, we had to dispose of countless bottles with protective solutions; they had washed hands with mineral water. They had eaten preserves out of tin cans. Let Ukraine's health minister Romanenko and his entire ministry come over and live here like we do. That would be useful for science. Only this week we have sent a truck to Lyubar for potatoes—it returned empty. Another truck was sent to Kherson for tomatoes—same result. So much for "clean" foodstuffs.

On my plot pumpkins used to grow poorly, but in 1986 one grew so huge that I could not haul it to the yard. Corn leaves changed color, becoming striped. The cow calved producing a freak; our bitch had a litter of tailless puppies; the cat had a hairless kitten, which died, and the cat died soon afterwards.

More radiophobia, is it? This time in animals? Are dumb beasts too under stress?

What have we done to the state to make it ignore us so utterly? They know we exist, they must know it. If they did not, who would be giving us a 30-ruble allowance? If they did not, who would be paying the 25 percent extra? They know, too, of the 12 villages that should be evacuated without delay.

For three and a half years we have been living in Zone Three—an exclusion zone. By the district party committee premises alone soil contamination is at 1.5 mR/hr; around the district consumers union's building—more than one; on Sverdlov Street, where the health center is, and in the homestead of Nina Karas—close on two. And air contamination is between 0.2 and 0.5 mR/hr.

The letters we have written to various power bodies over these years! Dear me, there must have been hundreds. The commissions we have seen! Dozens of them. So how many more will it take for them to understand us, to see that we are not the nagging sort, we don't ask for anything, we do not want "benefits" and handouts. None of this is our fault. We just want to live a normal life.

A woman from Narodichi sent me a poem. It is well short of literary perfection, but it is a wail of despair that should be heeded:

What awaits our children, we do not know. A string of paper cranes in hand? To everything, the medics incoherently give explanations in gobbledygook. I am a mother and a wife; my purpose is to bear children, then raise and love them. Now one thing only is gnawing at my brain: What will become of us, how are we to live on? Bear more children? No, I'd rather have a termination. And the cry from the heart—why live at all? Oh God, have mercy! How can a woman not be a mother?

A worker at one of the factories in Smila, Cherkassy region, on receiving a letter from his aunt in Narodichi, also wrote bitter lines under the heading "Do not come over, my own loved ones!"

Do not come over, loved ones! Letters fly to and fro. . . . This is the Narodichi people trying to send out messages. I can hear Auntie's voice. Not a voice, a cry from the heart. Do not come over, little ones. And you, my grandson, bide your time!

We will not discuss the merits of these lines as poetry. This poem was not written with a pen; it was written with the heart. And the heartbeat in it was not always rhythmic. So much pain!

Every day spent in the "dirty" zone serves to confirm how cruelly they deceived us hiding the truth about Chernobyl. For a fifth year running high-ranking officials at Union and republic ministries and departments, covering up their inactivity and indifference, have been trying to convince us, irresponsibly and criminally, that it is perfectly possible to live in contaminated areas, and they keep delaying resettlement in ecologically clean places. Meanwhile, we are the ones to pay for their actions with our health, and possibly life itself.

The Chernobyl calamity has entered every home, missing none, whether adults, children or the elderly; it affects every family, every working collective. Having canceled out the future of thousands of people, it has brought pain and sorrow into their lives, becoming a hopeless tragedy. Our patience is running out. We are at the end of our tether.

We expect specific problems, those most painful problems to be addressed urgently: evacuation from "dirty" areas; full publicity as regards the state and republic programs for dealing with the consequences of the accident, and earlier government resolutions on the issues; a complete set of measures to provide recuperation for all victims of the accident, especially children; supplying everyone with ecologically clean foodstuffs in adequate amounts; drawing up and passing (at the current session) a law on the status of the Chernobyl accident's victims that would guarantee high-quality medical assistance and regular thorough checkups by specialists, provide for the right to free medication as prescribed by doctors, guarantee the right to early retirement—at 50 for women and at 55 for men, if they have lived and worked in contaminated areas for five and six years, respectively, not for 12 years as the recently approved "benefits" resolution requires. With this kind of "benefits" there will be no one left to draw the pension. Don't the authors of the resolution know that our health, and that of our children and parents, has been seriously damaged? Because of radioactive irradiation our peers at the band-weaving factory and other industrial enterprises are not up to working an eight-hour day. Can machine operators gulp down radioactive dust for 12 years and live to get a "special" pension? Can drivers, tractor drivers, cattle-breeding farm workers?

What of our children, our future, who faint in class and cannot cope with the studies? The "benefits" resolution obligates them, too, to live for a minimum of 12 years in the zone. And what are people to do who are nearing retirement age and have lost energy and health, and are now being slowly killed by ruthless small radiation doses? Must they also wait for 12 years? Or die without waiting for the "benefits"?

We regard as an unpardonable crime the actions by high officials and agencies which, by issuing resolutions like that, force people who have taken the first and worst blow from radiation to live and work for many years in a nuclear hell.

Given the current conditions, we consider it fair if it were decreed that each year of working in the strict-monitoring zone be counted as two years of job seniority.

Health protection is impossible without carefully considered regulatory documents approved at the very top. Precisely for that reason we demand that each person who has fallen victim to Chernobyl be issued a sanitary passport-and-guarantee authenticated by the government and signed by the relevant officials. A document like that would ensure decent housing and everyday conditions for them, and would provide for a guaranteed future.

Without that we feel like nuclear hostages abandoned to deal on our own with our fears and misfortunes. We are into the fifth year of an unprecedented national tragedy, but neither V. V. Shcherbitsky (now deceased) nor V. S. Shevchenko, ex-chair of the Ukrainian Supreme Soviet presidium, nor yet V. A. Masol (we appealed to him four times) or V. A. Ivashko has found his way to Narodichi.

So our sufferings, the lives of our children and parents do not count for anything with them. We feel increasingly convinced that the only way out left to us is to turn for help to the UNO, or else perish on our native land ravaged by the atom. Yours respectfully . . .

This levelheaded but heartrending letter has twenty-five signatures of Young Communist League secretaries at collective farms, enterprises, hospitals, a health center, an executive committee culture section, the district consumers union, a school, and other establishments in the Narodichi District. If Young Communist League secretaries, who have always been the trusted assistants of the Communist regime, wrote a letter like that, that could only mean that they, too, had lost faith in their party and their power.

A telegram sent on September 30 to M. S. Gorbachev, N. I. Ryzhkov, V. S. Ivashko, V. Kh. Doguzhiev, and me read thus:

> The *Pravda* publication of the 29th inst. [September 1989] about dealing with the consequences of the Chernobyl accident suggests that the envisaged measures of dealing with the problems in our and similar districts will overlook the main thing—the right of families with children to leave.
>
> The people's last hope for the safety of the life and health of their children has been thwarted. The departments responsible for our situation, particularly the health ministry, have taken a stand bordering on the criminal.
>
> The situation in the district may become unpredictable. We request an urgent consideration and settlement of our problems that brook no delay. On behalf of the Narodichi district committee bureau of the Communist Party of Ukraine, Zhitomir region, district committee secretary V. Budko.

"We the teachers of the Narodichi district . . ."

"On behalf of the residents of Narodichi, the members of a public action group for radiation protection of the population are appealing to you . . ."

"Appeal from the district trade unions council, the women's council of the Narodichi district, Zhitomir region. The residents of most villages in our district continue to live in exceedingly harsh environmental conditions . . ."

"This is an appeal from the public committee for the radiation protection of the population . . ."

"We the workers of the band-weaving factory in the town of Narodichi . . ."

The stream of letters from the Narodichi District is endless.

> The residents of the Ovruch district in the Zhitomir region. We are asking you to consider our proposals at the session of the Ukrainian Supreme Soviet (plenary session of the Ukrainian Communist Party Central Committee). We are not indifferent to the health and future of our children and our population. We hope that the citizens of the Ukrainian republic will show an understanding for our proposals and our district will receive help, the district

being one of the worst hit and located in the immediate vicinity of the Chernobyl nuclear power plant, in the following matters:

1. Delivery of "clean" foodstuffs from the republic's districts and regions unaffected by radioactive contamination (first and foremost their distribution among the kindergartens and schools in the town and the district);
2. Annual three-month recuperation holiday for pre-school and schoolchildren, from May 25 till August 25, with medical examinations and health monitoring, together with one of the parents;
3. Establishment of territorial sanatoriums with mandatory recuperation and monitoring for every resident of the town and the district at the given round-the-year sanatorium;
4. Extra pay for living in contaminated areas;
5. Early retirement;
6. Providing personal dosimeters for all;
7. Speeding up the gas service installation in the town and the district, as forest firewood is contaminated;
8. Lift restrictions on delivery of detergents for our district.

Enclosed are 15 pages with signatures of residents in our district.

The letter was signed by more than five hundred people and had the following postscript: "Consider these demands as signed by all the 80,000 residents of our district."

Here is another telegram:

The conclusions by the commission that examined the radiation situation in the Luginy district are not objective and contradict earlier data; they are aimed at minimizing compensation payments. I request the use of materials previously obtained in the district when addressing the issue.

Luginy, Zhitomir region.
Vladimir Maximovich Goncharenko.

I live in the city of Mogilev, but I am writing to you. We live like so many nuclear hostages. There are no dosimeters in the families, and we cannot check the [radiation] data. Nor is there any hope of acquiring any, even though it has been reported here and there that their production has started. As for official tests, they were taken two per square kilometer. Meanwhile, it should have properly been at the interval of 10 to 15 meters (as when looking for radiation sources). So I suppose we are in for a good many surprises.

Did you watch the *Vzglyad* ("View") television program about our hematology clinic in Moscow where it is so crowded that even the dying cannot be removed from general wards for lack of room?

Let alone the absence of disposable syringes. There is a constantly rising incidence of cancer, mucous membrane problems, bronchitis, thyroid disorders, etc. We are not sure we eat clean food, whether state-produced or bought in the market, given the constant lies we are fed. So why do we have to prove that our environmental situation is unfavorable (putting it mildly)? We already have a therylene factory, and they are planning to expand the production of chemicals to boot, and of sausage casing, though we don't get any sausage here. Any expansion of chemical production in this area must be vetoed. As for our chemical plant, it is a source of carbon disulphide and hydrogen sulfide pollution in the city.

Everyone is writing of how unreliable and explosion-prone is the reactor type used in this country and in Chernobyl. So what more are we to wait for? For when the next unit explodes? We have already got our share of radioactivity, I suppose. And are adding more to it every day. As for the "shortage of electricity" in the country if nuclear power plants were to be closed down, this is not true. We export electricity abroad (under international contracts), while our people here are dying. Isn't the price of that export a bit too high?

We don't buy mushrooms and berries, nor beef either, we do not go to the forest, and try to spend as little time in the sun as possible . . .

Dr. Zinaida Filippovna Ozheskaya. Mogilev.

Lately, the nature of letters from radiation-affected areas has changed somewhat. People keep writing about resettlement foul-ups, the dishonesty (unscrupulousness) of certain officials who, taking advantage of their official status, occupy the best apartments, and get rehoused before ordinary mortals.

We the villagers of Lesser Kleshchi and Old Sharneh in the Narodichi district are to be resettled. We were told to leave our old houses as far back as July 20, 1989. But we have not been given any accommodation—although regional executive committee representatives promised to purchase houses for us. We applied for help to the Narodichi district executive committee; we heard promises from the Baranov district executive committee. Gotovchits and Malinovsky [members of the Zhitomir regional executive committee; Gotovchits has died since] promised us everything in Narodichi, but when we came and found housing for ourselves, these comrades refused to help us. Comrade Gotovchits slammed down the receiver and would not talk to us. Where can we go? Where shall we take our children? Where will they attend school? They have no opportunity for that. Please help us soon, because we have nowhere to live.

The letter was signed by twelve evacuees.

They came to me at night, from work. I was on duty supervising the printing of the paper's issue at the printing office. Young women cried. The men were saying that if their families were not given accommodation, they would put up tents the next day in the square before the regional party committee premises. So bitter was the start of a "new life" after evacuation for these families.

I earnestly request that you look into the matter of unfair distribution of apartments for people rehoused from Narodichi.

I, Natalya Yevgenyevna Nitsovich, have lived in Narodichi since 1975. I arrived here to work upon graduating from a music school. I got married. By this marriage I have two sons, aged 10 and 13. Since 1984 I have been a widow. At the time of the Chernobyl accident my children and I were living in Narodichi. After two years in the high-radiation area my children started falling ill, and following the doctor's advice I had to take them away. I sent my younger son to my parents in Zhitomir. The elder one I took to my mother-in-law in the Ivano-Frankovsk region. My family has thus disintegrated. And it has been two years now that I have not been able to live with my own children. My children have lost their father. And now they are also denied maternal love and warmth. In 1989 there appeared some hope of resettlement and of a roof over our heads, of living together. Alas. The members of the apartment distribution commission dashed my hopes, citing as the reason my alleged crime of taking the children out of Narodichi at the cost of separation.

I was not included in the first group of people re-housed in Zhitomir (37 apartments). Then Kiev allocated 200 apartments for us. I had my name entered in that list, but was refused again, and was put on the second Zhitomir list. But Zhitomir has not yet provided any more apartments, and some are promised only for 1991.

Of the 37 families given accommodation, three have refused. And those apartments were taken by the district executive committee members who have adult children over 18—Lukyanenko, deputy chairman of the district executive committee for construction, and Shulyarenko, deputy chairman of the district executive committee. So where's justice?

Chairman of the apartment distribution commission Comrade Kovalchuk was registered in four regions, but finally opted for Kiev. Comrade Ivanchenko works at the district executive committee planning department, and has already got authorization to an apartment in Khmelnitsky, and a week later also in Kiev. Comrade Shelyuk, head of the registry office, was on the Zhitomir list. But not yet having her name removed from that list, she obtained authorization to a Kiev apartment. So it works out this way then: if you are on the staff of the executive committee or someone in their "retinue," you can change apartments to your heart's content. While people like me are blatantly ignored—though the families to be re-housed before all others are those with children under 14. I could go on with this litany of injustices. For this reason, I am turning to you. I tried applying to the district public prosecutor's office as well. The deputy prosecutor reprimanded the commission members, but there was no response. I am asking you to look into the matter and help me live together with my children and get an apartment in the city of Zhitomir.

N. Nitsovich.

I took this letter to the Zhitomir regional executive committee. From there I received a reply saying that "citizen Nitsovich has been given warrant No. 4/2 of June 5, 1990, for moving into an apartment at 85, Shevchenko St. in Zhitomir. The apartment block is to be completed in the first half of 1991." Not a word about abuse of power by officials. I had to send a copy of Nitsovich's letter to the prosecutor's office. This letter is far from the only one of its kind in my mail. What are we coming to, I wonder, if even here, amid this nationwide misfortune, there are people doing their damnedest to grab bigger chunks for themselves?

Forgive me for taking the liberty of writing to you. I do not know if my letter will reach you. Wherever I have tried sending letters, I have got no help anywhere. I wrote to the session of the Ukrainian Supreme Soviet, and to other addresses. I have been resettled from the village of Greater Kleshchi of the Narodichi district to the village of Galchin in the Berdichev district of our region. The ordinary folk here gave us a warm welcome. We are grateful to them for this. When I was moving out, I got all kinds of promises. We did not want to take contaminated things with us. I had three grandchildren with me—my son's daughter, 10, and my daughter's little boys, 3 and 11. All of them just kids. My son lives beyond Ovruch, in Pervomaisk; it's a strict-monitoring zone over there. And my daughter is in Narodichi; a month ago she moved to Brusilov, but the new cottage there is very damp, and our youngest grandson is with us all the time.

Well, so I have been making rounds of the Berdichev trading organizations begging to be sold a carpet or a rug, or a runner five or so meters long. The children have to sit on a bare floor. And I asked for a bedroom suite or something like that; I get ten people coming over for weekends, there's nowhere to put them up for the night. I keep going to all those places, but it's no use. It is now an embarrassment entering the offices where the bosses laugh at me.

We are all sick, and worst of all my wife and the children. My wife has twice come back from the dead. We are old, we have worked for

80 years between us. Calling the ambulance is a problem; we have to go to the neighbors for that. It's not too bad if it is in the daytime. But if something happens at night, we have to wake the neighbors. They are fed up with us already. For a whole year I have been asking the head of the Berdichev district communications board to put us on the phone line, even if it is the kind that only works after six in the afternoon. Well, he simply shouted me out of his office, and I am an old man. It is not a whim of mine, the telephone. The district communications department boss just has no shame, he is young enough to be my son.

They have laid gas pipes in Galchin. I was promised gas too. So I bought pipes off some profiteers. The three of us, my son, my son-in-law and me, dug a hole in the middle of the yard. And that hole has stood there open until my three-year-old grandson fell in and dislocated his arm. We cabled my daughter. No matter where I went about that gas, they wouldn't help. So we go on burning the firewood we brought with us from Kleshchi—poisoning ourselves and the rest of Galchin. And all it takes is welding a 30-meter length of pipes and moving the boiler.

God preserve those bosses and their grandchildren and children from our kind of sorrow. If we had known how it would be, we would never have moved. After all, Kleshchi was our home, our native land; we were born there.

I have been working since I was 14. And so has my wife. Is it our fault that we have moved? Foreigners are helping, and here are our own kind doing nothing. . . . It hurts. And how about our children and grandchildren? How can I look them in the eye? For a year I have been going everywhere begging: please let me have this and that, let me buy it. If they had met with disaster, I'd have given them whatever I had to give.

You know, I have lived a long life, and I never thought that that's the way things were going to be in this country. Goodbye. And accept my apologies.

Alexander Feodorovich Zaichenko and his family. Galchin.

Such was a letter full of hurt from an old man who had got lost in the maze of bureaucratic offices at all levels whose doors he was haunting. I had to intercede for the old people. The reply to my inquiry came from the regional executive committee:

Citizen Zaichenko A. F. received 5 (five) m³ of firewood from the Chernaya Loza forestry, and two suckling piglets from the Progress collective farm, the village of Nikonovka. In February work was completed on the construction of an external gas pipeline as far as his house, and the layout inside, in the kitchen. Connection to the outside pipeline will be performed after the gas distribution substation has been completed. The applicant's house has been put on the telephone.

Well, couldn't they have helped the unfortunate old people without interference from a deputy in the Kremlin?

These letters can be quoted endlessly. They are born out of unbearable pain and incredible suffering. They have not remained unanswered. After a series of my articles on the problems of Chernobyl victims, other letters piled up on my desk next to these—with offers of help. Letters from all over the country. They too were like a high-concentration clot, this time of kindness and of mercy. They counterbalanced, as it were, the first dose of pain on the balance wheel of life. If they did not exist, it would be hard, unimaginably hard, to live. But they do exist, thank God.

Here is what Olga Dmitrievna Guseva writes from Ivanovo:

> A short while ago my father and I went to his native village of Korino, in the Teikovo district. There are very many empty houses there. They are still in good condition. So I thought, why don't people from the contaminated areas in the Zhitomir region come to live here? Naturally, those poor people who suffered so much from radiation have the right to demand new housing, official aid, and all the rest of it from the government. But will it not come too late, if they wait for that? Would it not be better if the public joined in? If my help is required, I am ever at your service.

With her letter, Guseva, that kind lady, enclosed an article from the local newspaper, *Rabochi krai* ("Workers' Land"), with a list of collective and state farms in the Ivanovo region that invited settlers and instantly provided housing for them.

N. I. Samoilenko, a disabled person living in Berdichev, writes that in the villages of New Alexandrovka, Nizgurtsy, Singaevka, and Sadki, Berdichev region, quite a few houses stand empty as well. She does not doubt that "people ought to be offered this option, too, at once, while there are no new apartments. In this way children will be saved!" During my reception hours as people's deputy, I saw an elderly person who had this request: "I am living at my children's place in town, but I still own a house back in the village. I would like you to give it to a settler family."

The Ukrainian Society in Lithuania, jointly with the Sajudis popular movement, sent a whole heavy truck of clean food to Narodichi for the local children. The international charity

Médecins Sans Frontières, whose representative telephoned me from Paris, offered free medical assistance, checkups, and dosimeters. I contacted the chairman of the district executive committee, V. S. Budko, and asked if the district needs this kind of help. "It does indeed," Mr. Budko replied emphatically. The same organization had been known to render assistance on other occasions as well—in Armenia, after the devastating earthquake there, and in Tbilisi. Jerusalem offered to accept Narodichi children for recuperation and treatment. Armenian kids also went there on holiday, after the earthquake . . .

If only words of mercy could deliver us from radiation! If only they could!

15

Warning Signs from the Urals

If you need further evidence of radiation secrecy, consider when it was that Soviet citizens first learned of nuclear accidents that had occurred forty years prior to Chernobyl. Yet it took another three years after the accident for information to trickle out, not only about this major blast but three nuclear power plant disasters in the Urals beginning in 1949. Of course, the rest of the world knew about those disasters while we were shielded by the Iron Curtain, completely ignorant of these events. That must have been the bureaucratic tactic of protecting our peace of mind. Surprisingly, on July 18, 1989, the USSR Supreme Soviet Committee for the Environment and Rational Use of Natural Resources organized the first ever hearings on the 1957 disaster in Kyshtym. Radiobiologist Zhores Medvedev, the Soviet emigrant in Britain who was invited to the hearings, said that Soviet scientists, when asked back at that time at an international forum why radioactivity in the area had suddenly gone up, replied that the reason was an experiment—"artificial pollination with radioactive particles." Unfortunately, we must look back into the dustbin of history to discover the source of the lies about radioactivity in this country (the same is true in the U.S.).

Today, as we read the records of the session, I can see that even then representatives of the official medical establishment invited to the parliamentary hearings and members of the so-called "medium engineering industry ministry," who were in charge of all nuclear facilities, were not telling the whole truth.

They were in complete possession of the relevant information yet never said a word about the first accident in that part of the country that had taken place at the Mayak Production Association facility in 1949. Nor about the 1967 accident and the vast pools of stagnant radioactive water in that terrible lake called Karachai that continued to hang over all of us like the sword of Damocles. There was not a word about radiation-affected townships that are all but household names today, thirty or forty years on. None of that was mentioned, as if none existed, even though glasnost was already the order of the day. On the contrary, they tried hard to show to us, the people's deputies, that it was nothing much to worry about, that all the people had been evacuated in time and that those who had been exposed to radiation were feeling splendid. Instead of using the experience gained in dealing with those accidents, they used the experience of blanket deception, following the same pattern in the wake of the Chernobyl explosion.

Here is what deputy director of the biophysics institute, L. A. Buldakov, was saying, for instance, at the parliamentary hearings on July 18, 1989:

> Over three years, we constantly monitored the condition of people's health. Fortunately, we did not register a single case of radiation sickness. We have concluded that there is little difference in the state of health of persons who lived within the radioactive plume and those outside it. Therefore, there is no difference between the plume area and the regions. The impact levels in the aftermath of the disaster were such that we managed to avoid disease in people at an early, and thus most sensitive, age.

The daily *Pravda* of August 25, 1989 echoed his views in this piece by Professor V. A. Knizhnikov: "We did not observe any exposure—child mortality relationship, radiation-induced anomalies in the offspring, or a rise in the incidence of malignant growths . . . ." As I was listening to this pack of lies, I seethed with indignation.

Meanwhile, this is what surfaced at the next parliamentary hearings a year later (pity that neither of the learned gentlemen were present). I am quoting from the record of those hearings:

> Irradiation affecting the population in the upper reaches of the River Techa (the site of the Mayak production association, where the nuclear accidents had occurred) resulted in chronic radiation sickness being diagnosed in 935 persons, according to medical documents made at the time. The majority of the cases were identified in the years 1956, 1957, 1958, and later. Of those 935 cases, 217 patients have died by now. All the cases of chronic radiation sickness are connected with the dumping of radioactive substances in the River Techa. Of the 935 patients, 106 have not been covered by monitoring. They just went away somewhere and could not be traced. They are not in the register, and their fate is unknown. Apart

from chronic radiation sickness, the villagers living along the Techa banks and in nearby areas were found to have radiation reactions. The overall mortality rates among upper Techa villagers were 17 to 23.6 percent higher than among their counterparts in the same administrative areas who had not been exposed to radiation.

The final report by the parliamentary group of experts had this to say:

> Irradiation affecting the population in the upper reaches of the Techa is causing chronic radiation sickness (especially in the village of Metlino where in the year 1956, 64.7 percent of the adults and 63.15 percent of the children examined were found to suffer from CRS). According to medical documents, a total of 935 persons were diagnosed with chronic radiation sickness. Besides, not all the people who had been exposed to radiation had medical checkups. For instance, in the village of Asanovo, that is, in the immediate vicinity of Metlino, not a single case of radiation sickness was registered, apparently because its residents had not been covered by regular medical examination. Chronic radiation sickness could affect 3 to 5 percent of the population in the villages around the upper Techa.

At the first parliamentary hearings, academician V. A. Buldakov alleged,

> We are doing all we can, sending out booklets with instructions, giving public talks. This is not very effective, because people tend to disbelieve us. People say they do not believe Soviet scientists since it's their job. To dissuade them is impossible. It will take time.

That was about Chernobyl.

But here is what he said in *Pravda* dated August 25, 1989: "We honestly described the situation to the people, and they treated the whole thing with understanding . . . ." That was about Kyshtym. So honest had they been that only thirty years later were the facts about the accident finally made public. As *Pravda* reported in the same issue, thirty years after the accident, "first deputy minister (of the medium engineering industry ministry) Nikipelov, academician Buldakov, and Professor Knizhnikov toured the districts of the Chelyabinsk region, met with the local inhabitants, and told them about the accident and its consequences." (As though that had been the only accident in those parts!) Accusing people of ignorance and radiophobia, and effectively justifying the culprits responsible for the ecologically criminal situation in the Urals, *Pravda*'s own Chernobyl correspondent, Vladimir Gubarev, mentioned only in passing, "the lake contaminated with radionuclides since the 1950s." He was fuming at the public protests against the construction of the South Urals Nuclear Power Plant there. "Could it be," the author exclaimed rhetorically, "that fear and ignorance prevailed over common sense?" I would like to ask him, "Could it be that the cushy job of a party reporter prevails over common human decency?"

Here is how former Central Committee apparatchik A. P. Povalyaev talked about one of the accidents in the Southern Urals at a seminar in the Institute of Nuclear Power Development Safety of the Russian Academy of Sciences. (He had been an active participant in the secret operations around the accident and its victims.)

> We learned of the tragic occurrence quite by chance. It was rumored in the Urals that fallout had occurred of some noxious stuff somewhere. And then a local vet from the village of Greater Allahi telephoned his superiors in Moscow. He asked for a specialist who would come and help him sort out the situation with animals afflicted by some strange disease. The person dispatched there was one Sereda, a fairly competent radiologist from the All-Union Institute of Experimental Veterinary. He brought over a slow atom indicator and detected contamination. And the dairymaids complained to him that the bull was ignoring the cows completely. He would just amble over to them and turn away. Sereda, who was not exactly au fait with veterinary practice, inferred from this that the bull had developed radiation sickness and gone impotent. When the word impotence was uttered, men started to worry, particularly the bosses. "If the bull has become impotent, what will happen to us?" The matter was referred to the regional public health department and on to the republic's health ministry and agriculture ministry.

The deputy health minister at the time was G. M. Nikolaeva. So Comrade Nikolaeva phoned Burnazyan, the head physician of the Mayak combine. "Avetik Ignatyevich, what's gone wrong in your parts?" His reply, "Nothing at all, Galina Mikhailovna, no need to worry."

These are the witnesses and accomplices in the crime against humanity. Even today, they describe those tragic events in a flippant manner and with some pride, forces that will go on affecting them for a long time to come. These people cite those examples to teach the new generation. But what beneficial lessons are being transmitted?

It was fortunate that the vet in the village of Greater Allahi proved a genuine professional. It was fortunate that the bull made him suspect that something was amiss. Otherwise, how would Deputy Health Minister Nikolaeva have learned what was happening not only to the bulls but also to people at and around Mayak in the Urals? Unfortunately, the person nominated for the state award for "work on eliminating the consequences of the accident at Mayak" was not the vigilant vet, as the reader has undoubtedly guessed already, but the man, Povalyaev, who had once worked on a farm providing foodstuffs for the Communist Party Central Committee—a high distinction indeed.

So what was it that happened in the Urals more than forty years ago? In 1949, the country's first industrial complex for plutonium production was put in operation in the Chalyabinsk region. Later it was renamed the Production Association Mayak. There, in deepest secrecy, the first Soviet A-bomb was being made. Over a number of years, from 1949 to 1951, radioactive waste was dumped into the River Techa. The Techa took that stuff to the Iset, the Iset to the Tobol—in all, some 3 million curies of deadly waste. Naturally, the people living nearby knew nothing about it. That dumping was the cause of the first emergency. The 124,000 people who lived along the Techa banks had been exposed to radiation. The worst hit was the village of Metlino, where the inhabitants got 170 rem per person.

The year was 1957. A second accident at Mayak. It was that accident that the authorities, thirty-two years later, had to declassify for the people's deputies, and then the first parliamentary hearings were held. A tank holding radioactive waste blew up. A total of 18 million curies were deposited around the storage site. A radioactive cloud of 2 million curies formed in the area that later became known as the East Urals Radioactive Trace. It covered 217 villages and 272,000 people. In the wake of the accident, over 10,000 people were gradually resettled. The people in three villages absorbed an average of 52 rem each, within a week of living in the contaminated zone. The year was 1967. There was one more radioactive plume caused by the wind blowing up aerosols from Lake Karachai during a drought. That time, over five hundred thousand curies became airborne.

The net result of forty years of work by this military–industrial complex facility is this: about 5.5 million curies of radioactivity spilled in plumes over the Urals, leaving some 27,000 km² of ground contaminated. Eighteen thousand people have been resettled in other

219

areas. All of that started under the watchful eye of the Stalin arch-executioner, Beria (one of the streets was even named after him). The whole thing was top secret. If it had not been for the Gorbachev liberalization, a travesty of freedom of speech though it was, this information would still be classified. But exactly who classified it? And what orders were given on the matter? If the answers to these questions in Chernobyl were obtained after a struggle, the facts about the disasters in the Urals are still unknown to the public. Not even the two parliamentary hearings managed to clarify the issue.

V. I. Kiryushkin, MD, member of the coordinating council at the Chelyabinsk Regional Executive Committee observed:

> The thing is that at the time when, you know, the secrecy situation bound everyone hand and foot, we were instructed to enter a coded diagnosis of radiation sickness in patients' medical records that went into the general network. The diagnosis was the so-called neuralgic syndrome. And this was indeed done, and those in the know knew that it implied radiation sickness.

This is what is known from the final report of the parliamentary expert group:

> The urgent need to create nuclear weapons, the imperfect technologies, absence of experience, and lack of information about the health effects of ionizing radiation resulted in most of the staff at the plutonium production and fission processing facility absorbing high radiation doses in the first years of work. Ten thousand staff over the forty years of the operation of that facility, chiefly in the early period, developed occupational diseases while four thousand died of acute radiation sickness. The residents of villages around the facility, owing to the secrecy regulations, for years remained in ignorance of the danger. Those people were largely left to their own devices, because in the first years after the biggest radionuclide discharge in the Techa basin, there were few medical checkups for the population. The first checkups started two years after Mayak began dumping radionuclides into the Techa, and they involved the inhabitants of just one village in the upper reaches of the river—Metlino.

At present, Mayak is the planet's "worst radioactive hazard." The popular definition of the situation, though, was different: the Chelyabinsk region has been turned into a global nuclear waste dump. And there are legitimate reasons for this pessimism. In 1956, the Techa was dammed. In 1963, another dam was erected. The resulting pools of water are known as facilities nos. 10 and 11.

Together with three others, they are brimming with liquid radioactive waste of some 2 million curies. Below the dam of facility no. 11 lie the Asanovo marshes. They cover some 30 km². There is radioactive waste in them as well. From there, the waste gets back into the River Techa. Another 2 million curies of radioactivity is in the Old Marsh. But by far, the most contaminated is Lake Karachai: it has absorbed 120 million curies! Roughly two more million curies are in the waste buried on Mayak's own territory. On top of that, almost 1,000 million curies are in liquid form in storage tanks. Some 150 million curies are in radioactive sediment deposited from liquid waste and stored in special depots.

Within the lifetime of the military–industrial facility, the environment has received about 25 million curies' worth of radioactivity. It has dusted over 626,000 km² of land, covering the Chelyabinsk, Sverdlovsk, and Kurgan regions.

Overall, radioactivity of more than a billion curies has accumulated in the lakes, trenches, storage sheds, and burial grounds. This is fraught with a new disaster. Especially dangerous are trench burials with a clay cutoff that contain 150,000 tons of low-activity waste. They are not equipped with any monitoring and measuring instruments, and some of the burials are still to be located. The Zlatoust city Soviet of the Chelyabinsk region sent the following resolution to the Kremlin:

> We, the people's deputies of the Zlatoust city Soviet, express extreme concern and anxiety about the fact that for many years radioactive waste from all of the country's nuclear power plants and nuclear ships has been brought to the territory of the Chelyabinsk region, thus reducing the region to the position of the nation's radioactive dump. At present, there are nearly one billion curies' worth of radioactive waste already concentrated on Mayak's territory, some of it dumped straight into the River Techa, within whose basin are located the villages of Muslyumovo, Kunashak, and Metlino, for decades exposed to radiation. External irradiation on the river bank is 700 micro R/hr, whereas the normal level being 20 micro R. Given the above, we are appealing to the people of the Chelyabinsk region for support of our demand that the USSR Supreme Soviet: (1) make public the radioactivity effects in the Chelyabinsk regions; (2) discontinue the practice of bringing radioactive waste to the Chelyabinsk region; (3) instruct the main directorate of the USSR Health Ministry to examine without delay all the residents in the region directly or indirectly involved with radioactive waste and pass on the information to the main health directorate of the Chelyabinsk region executive committee.

On October 5, 1990, the issue of the Chelyabinsk region effectively being turned into a nuclear dump was raised at the second parliamentary hearings on the environmental situation in the area. A representative of one of the departments announced that "processing of waste brought over from all the COMECON (Council for Mutual Economic Assistance) countries to our country is commercially profitable." That elicited vehement protests from the people's deputies and the region's representatives. The speaker tried to soothe them by saying that for these services, the ex-COMECON countries would pay in "freely convertible currency." What "freely convertible currency" means and why they need it is hardly something that the ordinary villagers in affected areas could define.

From the final report of the parliamentary expert group:

> Things are out of control now, and, with regard to the catching basins, have become completely unmanageable. The strategy of environmental rehabilitation of the territory has no alternative. Procrastination may result in a tragedy infinitely worse in terms of consequences than the Chernobyl disaster.

Those who live on the banks of the Techa are well aware of the health deficit caused by the huge amount of radiation to which they have been exposed. It was also pointed out at the parliamentary hearings that "the early effects of irradiation could have gone unregistered," that "there has been a complete failure in this respect," and that "we have not yet found reliable medical data based on observation of the population exposed to radiation in the wake of the dumping." In three emergency situations, 437,000 people have been exposed to increased radiation levels. However, no records were made on these situations until 1968, nearly twenty years after the first instances of radioactive waste dumping in the river. This means lost time and experience for the health-care system. And it also means loss of health and of quality of life for the people. It is now virtually impossible to assess irradiation's long-term effects on the population.

Thousands of people are still living in conditions of constant irradiation, more than half a century after the first lot of radioactive waste was dumped in the River Techa in the Urals. The village of Muslyumovo still has not been evacuated(!), and it is just thirty kilometers from the Mayak facility. In 1949, it had four thousand inhabitants; now there are barely two thousand. The concentration of cesium 137 in the Techa silt near Muslyumovo is such that it is virtually radioactive waste.

From the final report of the parliamentary group of experts: "In terms of exposure dosage levels, the village of Muslyumovo remains critical, with an average effective equivalent dose of 28 rem. The effective equivalent dosage in the village children exceeds 0.5–1 rem a year." The village of Muslyumovo has recently welcomed more than one commission from the federal authorities. But nothing much has been done for these people.

Contaminated food is as much of a problem as in Chernobyl, yet few people take any notice of that. In Urals villages, like in their Polesye counterparts, people eat homegrown contaminated potatoes and drink "dirty" milk from family cows. For these villagers, the inevitable prospect is years of internal irradiation. From this viewpoint, several more villages should be included in the critical list—Tatar Karabolka, Bagaryak, and Red Partisan. However, this does not seem to bother officials in any way. The people have been left to survive as best they can.

Information in the press after the parliamentary hearings came as a shock to the Urals villagers, who realized that they had been living for forty years in horrendous environmental conditions in total ignorance of the fact. The shock was all the more telling because they also learned that the people affected by the Chernobyl disaster, who had lived in similar conditions for a "mere" five years, were receiving at least a measly allowance from the government. Special laws and decrees were adopted for the benefit of the Chernobyl population, albeit after a long delay. As for the people in the Urals, they seem to have been ruining their health for nothing. (I am not talking here of professionals who consciously sacrificed their lives to the "country's nuclear shield." I am talking about ordinary folk, the rural population.)

It was not until 1993, nearly forty years after the first radiation leaks into the River Techa and after the Soviet Union had already collapsed, that the federal law on social protection for persons exposed to radiation in the aftermath of the 1957 accident at the Production Association Mayak and discharge of radioactive waste in the river was finally approved. In August 1995, I went to the Chelyabinsk region to visit the contaminated villages along the Techa. There, I met the residents and the authorities of the Kunashak District in the Chelyabinsk region. This trip is worth a more detailed account. What had given me the idea was a request by several Austrian journalists for a holiday in the Urals that they sent to the Russian Journalists Union (for almost a decade, I was the Union secretary). They had long been eager to see for themselves what the hinterland of Russia was like. The journalists' union leadership arranged the affair with one of the holiday homes in the Chelyabinsk region, and that was where the Austrians went. A week later, Union Secretary General Gennady Maltsev and I also flew to the Urals to meet our Austrian colleagues. By then, my second book on the Chernobyl disaster, *Chernobyl. Top Secret*, had come out in Berlin in German. During an informal meeting, I gave a copy to the Austrians.

I must say that the place where the guests were vacationing was absolutely fabulous. The holiday home is hidden away in a primeval coniferous forest. The sun spikes toy cones on fir branches, birds are singing nonstop, and nearby is an amazing forest lake with crystal clear water. What more could one desire? As we gathered together for breakfast, I sensed something was setting our guests on edge. They were clearly jittery. I could not understand it. Finally, one of them told me, "We were reading your book all evening yesterday . . ." Then the light dawned. They must have also read the chapter on radiation disasters here in the Chelyabinsk region! But how was I to know that they had not even suspected anything like that? I assumed that since they were journalists, they had wished not only to spend a vacation in the Russian outback but also wanted to gather material on those tragedies. And now the story of the effects of that radioactive accident in my book, which they had read at bedtime, became a little personal tragedy of their own. They started worrying about their own health.

I had to do my best to try and convince them that this brief visit posed no threat whatsoever. Why should I place myself in danger? Once a journalist, always a journalist, though. My explanation eased their minds. After a short conversation among themselves, they asked us to arrange trips to the radiation-affected villages along the River Techa. Frankly, there was not much organizing to do because, prior to leaving Moscow, I had telephoned the Kunashak District, asking for an interview with its leadership. So in any case, with or without the Austrians, I was going to visit the affected territories in the vicinity of Mayak.

The foreigners were absolutely shaken at what they heard and saw at the meeting with G. A. Gabitov, the Kunashak local administration head. In their presence, Gabitov asked me for help (at the time I was a member of Boris Yeltsin's Presidential Council). It turned out that the law on social protection for persons exposed to radiation in the aftermath of the 1957 accident at the Production Association Mayak and discharge of radioactive waste in the River Techa was not enforced.

The amount of compensation allocated for the population was more than ten billion rubles a year, but the money actually trickling down to the people's accounts was barely one tenth of that. In a letter that caught up with me after I left, administration head G. A. Gabitov wrote this:

> When visiting the Kunashak District in 1991 and meeting with the inhabitants of the village of Muslyumovo, the president of the Russian Federation, B. N. Yeltsin, treated the issues of environmental safety for the district residents with a lot of understanding. The documents on social protection for the population he signed later are evidence of that, but unfortunately, the president's decrees and resolutions relative to the rehabilitation program funding are not properly implemented, the money does not arrive on time, and then only through a multi-channel system and in reduced amounts.

Enclosed with the letter was a hefty pile of documents—correspondence between the district administration head and various officials, from his counterpart in the Chelyabinsk region administration to S. K. Shoigu, the minister for civil defense, emergencies, and elimination of the consequences of natural disasters.

The law adopted in 1993 to protect people living in affected areas was largely ineffectual. Patients afflicted with radiation sickness, evacuees, liquidators who had left the contaminated zone of their own accord were not entitled to interest-free loans that were specified by the law. Russia's Savings Bank replied that no money had been allocated for the program. More than four thousand people in the village of Muslyumovo and at the railway station of the same name were not given partially paid leave to look after children under three, with double the allowance paid during that period, as the law required. Pregnant women registering with the antenatal clinic at an early stage (before the twelfth week) did not receive a lump-sum grant in the amount of 50 percent of minimum monthly pay, as specified by the law.

The situation around resettlement of the residents of the area was likewise unworkable. If you left the contaminated zone of your own accord, without waiting to be resettled by the authorities, neither you nor your family members would get the lump-sum grant for settling in a new locality. Nor would the authorities provide new accommodations free or make up for the loss of your old home on radioactive territory. "You could wait for ages for our dear state to resettle us with all the compensations and privileges entailed," Techa villagers complained bitterly when they talked to us. "It's much less trouble to die." And I believed them. I knew what our state was like and what it had been doing to its people for a good seventy years.

The matter of people returning to the village and railway station of Muslyumovo was just as complicated. The law, it appeared, did not provide for paying compensation to those persons who returned to their native parts after it had been passed, even though the average annual effective equivalent irradiation dose there exceeds 1 mSv a year. People returning to their old homes did so out of despair. That much was obvious. Having failed to find a job at the new place (the district has a bad unemployment problem, and this is also something the administration head tried to alert his superiors to), they hoped in this way to get at least something from the state, which had for decades poisoned them with radiation at no cost to itself. Well, they hoped in vain! "Owing to discrepancies between some provisions of the law and the actual state of affairs on the contaminated territory at the time of radioactive waste dumping into the Techa," writes Kunashak District administration head, G. A. Gabitov, to the emergency situations minister, S. K. Shoigu, "the problems of people living in the district are not being addressed." Even though the rehabilitation of the contaminated areas along the Techa was actually carried out from 1949 to 1961, people did not receive compensations and benefits because the law says that rehabilitation measures ended in 1956. But there are archival documents to disprove that, and the people who took part in the work are still living!

When I toured the contaminated villages within the Chernobyl plume in the Zhitomir region, where new housing had been built for the resettled villagers, I could not even begin to think that a similar crime by the state against its people had been committed before. But it had—here, in the village of Muslyumovo, almost half a century ago, following the nuclear accidents at Mayak in 1949 and 1957. Imagine, my patient reader, that then, in 1957, here in Muslyumovo, in secrecy from the country and the world, the authorities pulled down the houses of those who lived right next to the River Techa and rehoused them—in the same village of Muslyumovo, at the other end of it, calling it "resettlement"—though the land there was obviously just as badly contaminated. So this is the kind of cynical lessons in falsehood the authorities learned from the South Urals nuclear accident, which they cynically used again after the Chernobyl disaster: as I have related in detail in the previous chapters, people evacuated from "dirty" areas were also resettled there in places just as "dirty."

I found unexpected confirmation of the Urals exercise in falsehood in a recent report by ex-Central Committee "farm manager" and ex-agriculture ministry official, A. P. Povalyaev, delivered to an audience of young scientists. He had been dispatched to sort out the nuclear accidents at Mayak and later in Chernobyl. This matter (Chernobyl), Povalyaev informed his listeners, "was even considered at one of the IAEA sessions, where our actions received high praise. True, they did not know about our previous Urals experience. We wrote a book about it way back in 1971, only then it was classified." Who did they write the book for then? Brezhnev? The Central Committee? Other people might be ashamed to admit that this boast was another cog in the party cover-up. They lied to us, they lied to the IAEA, and they have the nerve to brag about their lying.

So the law and the authorities refused to recognize those sufferers on the River Techa (just eighty-five left of them, in all) as victims of the disaster. But even the little provided for by the law—free medication, free school meals, free nurseries, and kindergartens—did not materialize for years, and still doesn't.

What kind of law is it that the Russian people's deputies approved for the people living around the nuclear monster of Mayak, people who had been deceived for decades? It seems the Muslyumovo villagers were right—it is easier to die than to live under that law, to say nothing of words of repentance from the government, which they have been waiting for this last half-century (maybe they are not anymore). A lot of them died never hearing those words.

Meanwhile, there are just under twenty thousand people living in twenty-eight localities in the Kunashak District who have been affected by radiation and require urgent measures, medical and social rehabilitation, and legally stipulated financial support.

Curiously, even before the Russian parliament passed that social law that is not quite a law, the authorities tried to tackle the environmental problem in the Urals area of radiation disaster in a most ingenious manner. The nuclear lobby intended to deal with a possible emergency—overflowing of the reservoirs containing radioactive waste—by building a South Urals nuclear power plant next to Mayak. This is really mind-boggling! The people behind this idea cited environmental considerations as their chief argument for building a nuclear power plant there.

From the final report by the parliamentary group of experts: "The construction project for the South Urals nuclear power plant, submitted for expert examination in November 1990, completely ignores, in terms of safety for the environment, the lessons of the 1986 accident at the Chernobyl NPP and its tragic consequences for vast territories in Russia, the Ukraine, and Belorusssia."

Consider this parallel: The town of Chernobyl was 16 km from the nuclear power plant, while its South Urals analog was to be built just 12 km from a city with one hundred thousand inhabitants. The report went on to say, "In its present form, the construction project should certainly be rejected as failing to conform to the most elementary environmental requirements for the choice of location for a nuclear power plant and its construction in the given critical environmental situation that is to be thoroughly studied and analyzed . . . ."

A reader, particularly one in the West, will probably find it difficult to imagine that the expert assessment of the South Urals Nuclear Power Plant project was carried out seven years after it was approved by the authorities and five years after construction began, when over 200 million rubles had already been sunk into it! And then, eight years after the nuclear power plant project had been completed and even after its construction had progressed, it became possible, at long last (thanks to perestroika!), to hold a referendum on whether or not the nuclear power plant should be built there. The referendum was initiated by independent nongovernmental organizations (NGOs) in the teeth of fierce opposition from the nuclear lobby and the authorities. The majority of the residents said "no" to the plant. And judging by the situation there, that was only to be expected. The River Techa situation worked as a strong warning . . .

While the people of Chernobyl were not in a position to profit from the Urals lessons (which were unknown to them), the people in the Urals, thank God, had learned the Chernobyl lesson all right. But now, more than fifty years after the Urals warning, and twenty years after the man-made Chernobyl disaster, the Russian government is again considering grand designs—resuscitation of the mothballed South Urals Nuclear Power Plant project, and it is taking vigorous steps to that end. The wheel has come full circle.

16

Secret Records of the Kremlin

Finally, five years after the nuclear disaster, the USSR Supreme Soviet grudgingly passed a decision to form a special parliamentary commission to investigate high officials and their Chernobyl-related activities. Although I had also applied for commission membership, the Soviet parliament's bosses made sure that I was not included, for my name to them was like a red flag waved at a Spanish bull. Actually, it was just a formality. Any people's deputy had the lawful right to take part in the work of any parliamentary committee or commission. So the Herculean attempts by Supreme Soviet Chairman Anatoly Lukyanov to keep this troublesome interloper out of the proceedings were all in vain. Running out of steam, he just "failed to notice" my attendance.

The commission's status entitled it to ask for and obtain any documents. In the end, nearly every department coughed up, with a lot of delays, the classified information we asked for—the health ministry, the ministry of defense, the state hydrometeorology committee, and others. And only the Politburo of the CPSU Central Committee kept ignoring all official inquiries. I am certain that we would have never received any documents if it had not been for the defeat of the August 1991 Communist coup. After Boris Yeltsin's decree banning the Communist Party in the wake of the coup, party archives began to be sorted out and we received, at long last, the secret minutes of the Politburo task group sessions chaired by Premier Nikolai Ryzhkov on matters related to the elimination of the consequences of the Chernobyl accident. Yet, no matter how long and passionately our experts, doctors of science, pleaded for at least one working copy of the minutes to be made for them by the parliament photocopier, they were refused.

One fine day in December 1991, when the Soviet Union had literally days to live, I drove up to the building on New Arbat Street that housed

Supreme Soviet commissions and committees, and I saw deputies' archives being briskly loaded into a vehicle to be taken away, destination unknown. It suddenly dawned on me that the secret minutes of the Politburo task group on Chernobyl might also be removed, never to be seen by anyone again. Besides, the commission members had not yet had the chance to read through those highly important papers. I then decided that, come what may, I had to make copies of those minutes. I entered the office where our Chernobyl commission usually sat, opened the safe, and took out a weighty pile of documents. I had not seen them before. Thumbing through them hurriedly, I realized that this was a priceless treasure marked "SECRET," complete with Politburo stamps and authentic signatures of the Soviet government chairman, Ryzhkov, and other comrades at the helm of the state. I quickly jotted down an application to the copying bureau and took forty secret protocols there, almost six hundred pages in all. I was promised the copies by the next morning. It has to be explained that in the Soviet Union, there were practically no photocopiers. Access for an ordinary mortal to the few that were there was altogether out of the question. In the Soviet parliament, there was just one copying bureau for the deputies. Every scrap of paper copied there was to be entered in a special accounting book over the people's deputy's personal signature.

I left the bureau confident that I would get the copies of those vital documents the next day. The USSR was already going through the process of self-liquidation, and parliament had just a few more months left in which it would continue to function. As a people's deputy, I had a lawful right to have any documents copied (or so I naively thought). But things did not work out that way. In the morning, the somewhat shamefaced bureau people told me that they had not been allowed to copy the Chernobyl papers! The person who had vetoed the job, it turned out, was one V. Pronin, who had introduced himself as a consultant with the Second Secret Sector of the USSR Supreme Soviet. That was a rude awakening indeed! So the deputies within the walls of the Supreme Soviet were closely watched by the secret services! I went to A. Burko, the special unit head of the Supreme Soviet secretariat, and told him indignantly that I was still a people's deputy with the obligation to perform my duties. He, in his turn, explained to me, unperturbed, that he had no right to permit the copying of those papers marked "SECRET" and "TOP SECRET," even for parliamentary commissions. To obtain permission, one had to turn to the very organization that had classified the documents, requesting their declassification. Then one could . . . Let me remind the reader that the whole thing was happening after the August 1991 Communist putsch. President Boris Yeltsin of Russia had already banned the Communist Party, and several of its Politburo members, the putschists, were pondering over their lives in prison. But the secrets of that organization were loyally guarded by its henchmen in the country's expiring parliament.

Seeing that I was being stonewalled, I collected the documents, returned to the commission's session room, and used the special line telephone to dial the phone number of Vadim Bakatin, the new KGB chief Mikhail Gorbachev had appointed to replace Vladimir Kryuch-kov, who was implicated in the failed coup. Having outlined the situation to him, I asked Bakatin to order his subordinates in the Kremlin to let me photocopy the secret documents of the Communist Party. Bakatin's reply came as a shock. "I am powerless to help you," he said. "Those are not our people. They won't take orders from me." Thus, I learned, by accident as it were, that in the depths of the USSR Supreme Soviet, there lurked some organization keeping tabs on the people's deputies, an enterprise that, according to Bakatin, was accountable directly to the chairman of the Supreme Soviet. And the chairman, putschist Anatoly Lukyanov, was likewise languishing in prison.

In short, I realized that I couldn't expect help from any quarter. Also, I realized that I could not simply replace the documents in the safe and wash my hands of the whole affair. So determined not to give up, I stuffed the papers in a plastic bag and went out. What to do now? There was positively nowhere else to have them copied—as I have said, at the time, photocopiers, in ample supply now, were virtually nonexistent. I decided to call the *Izvestia* editorial office, the newspaper that often printed my articles. It proved to be the right idea. There, I discovered a coveted photocopier (I was assisted in my quest by Lyudmila Savelyeva, a wonderful *Izvestia* journalist) and returned to the Chernobyl commission's session room with two bagfuls of papers—the originals and the copies.

Having locked the originals in the safe, I paused to think of the uncertain future. What if the Communists were back in power tomorrow? What would then happen to me and my precious family after I published those documents? They would just say I had made it up, and I would find myself where the putschists were—locked behind bars, no two ways about it. I opened the safe once more, removed the first set of minutes, the original, and substituted a copy for it. In this way, I tried to secure my family and myself, at least to some extent, against potential trouble in the future.

When the same daily, *Izvestia*, published my sensational article on the secret Chernobyl records, which was subsequently translated and published in Europe, America, and Japan, I received a call from the director of the Russian National Archives. He wondered where I had found those materials, since the National Archives did not have them! Thank God, I thought, that I had managed to have the secret minutes copied. Otherwise, the world would never have learned about the crimes against humanity committed by the totalitarian regime in the Chernobyl zone. As I reread these unique documents, I invariably think that the main and most terrible isotope escaping from the reactor was not in the periodic table. That isotope was Lie-86. The lie was as global as the disaster itself.

Lie no. 1 was about the harmful effects of radiation. The first session of the Politburo task group took place on April 29, 1986. Until mid-May, it met on a daily basis. Party leaders had always maintained there was a lack of information. (Only recently, Ryzhkov, when interviewed by Russian television, all but swore that at the time "they knew precious little.") Starting from May 4, the group had a steady stream of reports about the hospitalization of residents of the Chernobyl zone.

"SECRET." Minutes no. 5. May 4, 1986, session attended by: members of the CPSU Central Committee Politburo Comrades N. I. Ryzhkov, Ye. K. Ligachev, V. I. Vorotnikov, V. M. Chebrikov, alternate members of the CPSU Central Committee Politburo Comrades V. I. Dolgikh, S. L. Sokolov, Secretary of the CPSU Central Committee A. N. Yakovlev, Minister of the Interior, Comrade A. V. Vlasov. Report by Comrade Shchepin (first deputy health minister of the Soviet Union) about hospitalization and treatment of the population affected by radiation exposure. Fact to be taken into consideration: by May 4, a total of 1,882 persons had been hospitalized. In all, 38,000 persons have been examined. Examination revealed 204 persons suffering from various degrees of radiation sickness, 64 of them children. 18 patients are in a grave condition. The clinics and hospitals of the Ukrainian Soviet Socialist Republic have reserved 1,900 beds for the victims. The USSR Health Ministry, jointly with the Central Trade Union Council, has provided a specialized sanatorium in the Mikhailovskoe Moscow suburb for mild cases, and also sanatoriums in the cities of Odessa and Evpatoria, with a total of 1200 beds. In the vicinity of Kiev, 6,000 places have been reserved in sanatoriums, and 1,300 places in children's summer camps.

Secret report of May 5, 1986: . . . the total number of those hospitalized has reached 2,757 persons, 569 of them children. Of those patients, 914 display symptoms of radiation sickness, and 18 persons are in a very serious condition.

"SECRET." Minutes no. 7. May 6, 1986, session attended by: members of the CPSU Central Committee Politburo Comrades Ye. K. Ligachev, V. M. Chebrikov, candidate-member of the CPSU Central Committee Politburo Comrade V. I. Dolgikh, Secretary of the CPSU Central Committee A. N. Yakovlev. Report by Comrade Shchepin about the number of hospitalized people reaching 3,454 by 09:00 hrs, May 6. Report duly taken cognizance of.

Of those mentioned above, 2,609 persons, including 471 children, are receiving treatment at various institutions. According to the revised data, the number of radiation sickness patients is 367, including 19 children. Of these, 34 persons are in a grave condition. Hospital No. 6 in Moscow is treating 179 persons, 2 of them children.

What is truly shocking about all this is the cynicism of the authorities reflected in the secret document: "To be accepted: the proposal of the USSR Health Ministry regarding the expediency of making public information about the number and condition of patients receiving treatment in Moscow's Hospital No. 6, given that there are American specialists working there." What would have happened if Americans had not been working in that hospital?

"SECRET." Minutes no. 8. May 7, 1986. Taking part in the session of the task group was CPSU Secretary General Comrade M. S. Gorbachev. Session attended by: members of the CPSU Central Committee Politburo Comrades N. I. Ryzhkov, Ye. K. Ligachev, V. I. Vorotnikov, V. M. Chebrikov, alternate member of the CPSU Central Committee Politburo Comrade V. I. Dolgikh, USSR Minister of the Interior Comrade A. V. Vlasov. In the last 24 hours 1,821 more persons have been hospitalized. As of 10:00 hrs, May 7, the number of persons receiving treatment in hospitals is 4,301, including 1,351 children. Of these, 520 persons, including USSR Interior Ministry officers, have been diagnosed with radiation sickness. 34 persons are in a grave condition.

Secret report of May 8, 1986: . . . within 24 hours, the number of hospitalized persons has increased by 2,245, including 730 children. As of 10:00 hrs, May 8, the number of persons receiving hospital treatment is 5,415, including 1,928 children. Radiation sickness has been diagnosed in 315 cases.

Another secret report of May 10, 1986: . . . within the last two days, 4,019 persons have been hospitalized, 2,630 of them children. . . . In all, 8,695 persons are in hospital, including 238 radiation sickness cases, 26 of whom are children. Over the last 24 hours, two persons have died; 33 patients are in a grave condition.

Secret report of May 11, 1986: . . . within the last 24 hours, 495 persons have been hospitalized. . . . Altogether 8,137 persons are being treated and examined in hospitals, including 264 persons diagnosed with acute radiation sickness. 37 persons are in a grave condition. Within the last 24 hours two persons have died.

"SECRET." Minutes no. 12. May 12, 1986: Within the last 24 hours another 2,703 persons have been hospitalized, mainly from Belorussia. Receiving hospital treatment and examination are 10,198 persons, of whom 345 display symptoms of radiation sickness. 35 of them are children.

How does the flow of these secret reports at the task group sessions compare with the media's stubborn silence about thousands of sick people? The truth for the patricians versus the truth for slaves? Minutes no. 21 of June 4, 1986, the "instructions for participants in the next press conference for Soviet and foreign journalists" had this mendacious passage:

The proper indices have been approved for hospitalizing people. Over the previous period, all persons who applied to medical institutions have been examined. Diagnosed with acute radiation sickness are 187 casualties (all of them members of the nuclear power plant staff); of those, 24 persons have died (two died at the moment of the accident). Radiation sickness diagnosis in hospitalized members of the public, including children, has not been confirmed.

Starting from May 13, 1986, the reports by the USSR health minister mysteriously gave increasingly small numbers of hospitalized people, while the numbers of patients who had been exposed to radiation and were discharged from hospital grew by leaps and bounds. Secret report, dated May 13, 1986: It is to be noted that within the last 24 hours, 443 persons have been hospitalized, and 908 persons have been discharged. Under hospital treatment and examination are 9,733 persons, including 4,200 children. Diagnosed with radiation sickness are 299 persons, including 37 children.

Secret report dated May 14, 1986: Taken into cognizance: information by Comrade Shchepin that as of May 16, 1986, the number of people hospitalized is 7,858, including 3,410 children. Radiation sickness diagnosis has been confirmed in 201 cases. Total number of dead is 15, of these, 2 persons died on May 15.

But even these data, as the documents suggest, were not accurate or reliable. A session of the CPSU Central Committee task group decided to "charge Comrade Shchepin with verifying the data concerning the number of those hospitalized and afflicted with radiation sickness in hospitals in Moscow and other cities of the RSFSR, the Ukraine and Belorussia, including USSR Interior Ministry and army servicemen." The obvious question is: Where did the numbers of patients quoted in secret reports come from?

Secret report of May 20, 1986: . . . the number of people hospitalized in the last four days has risen by 716. Radiation sickness has been confirmed in 211 cases, including 7 children. The total number of fatalities so far is 17; and 28 persons are in a grave condition." From May 26, 1986, information about the people hospitalized in the aftermath of the Chernobyl disaster appeared in Politburo secret documents only occasionally, with some sessions getting none.

Secret report dated May 28, 1986: . . . there are 5,172 persons under hospital treatment and observation, including 182 persons diagnosed with radiation sickness. The total number of dead by May 28 has been 22 persons (plus two who died at the beginning of the accident). Another report, dated June 2, 1986: . . . there are 3,669 persons receiving hospital treatment, including 171 persons confirmed as radiation sickness cases. The number of dead by June 2, 1986 has been 24 persons (besides, two people perished at the beginning of the accident). 23 persons are in a grave condition. This was the last mention of the flow of hospitalized people in connection with the Chernobyl nuclear power plant disaster made in the secret minutes of the CPSU Central Committee Politburo task group, although the group itself continued in existence till January 6, 1988.

One cannot help wondering why patients started being discharged so precipitously after the number of hospitalized people from affected areas had risen beyond 10,000 on May 1, 1986. It would seem that the wider radiation spread over the country, the healthier Soviet people became. Ukrainian Health Minister A. Romanenko, even years after the accident, was still making soothing noises in the mercenary press and at Communist Party plenary sessions: "I can report with full responsibility that, apart from those taken ill, of whom there are 209 persons, there are no people today whose diseases could or should be related to radiation effects." The answer to the riddle was hidden in the documents of the task group. This is how thousands of people stricken by radiation made a miraculous "recovery" overnight.

"SECRET." Minutes no. 9. May 8, 1986: The USSR Ministry of Health has approved new permissible irradiation levels for the population affected with radioactive irradiation, which exceed the old ones 10 times (appended). In special cases, these norms may be raised 50 times against the previous levels.

Let me explain. This is five times higher than even the permissible levels of occupational exposure for servicing staff in nuclear power plants' machine rooms. Lower down in the appendix to the minutes: "Thus safety is guaranteed for public health in all age groups, even if a similar radiation situation prevails for 2.5 years." The norms were intended to cover even pregnant women and children. The secret medical-hygienic report based on state hydrometeorology committee materials was signed by first deputy USSR health minister O. Shchepin and first deputy state hydrometeorology committee chairman Yu. Sedunov. And so, without treatment and medication, thousands of our compatriots were instantly "healed" on May 8, 1986. (The effectiveness, simplicity, and profoundly "scientific" nature of the method prompts further innovations: Why don't we, given the state's current problems with free medication, hospital equipment, and beds for old age pensioners, pass a decree under which, for instance, as of May 1 this year, 38°C shall be considered normal temperature instead of the former 36.6°C? In special cases it could even be 39°C! Then the present "social" minister Zurabov could confidently report to the president that everything in the country was just fine. Then no one would want to block highways or go on strike in protest. There would be no more sick people in Russia.)

Obviously, the Soviet party leadership pushed up ten to fifty times the permissible radiation doses precisely in order to conceal the actual scale of radiation sickness. And their "ideological" trick largely came off. Kremlin residents stopped at nothing to achieve that goal. Not three months after people had been resettled outside the "black" zone, as the thirty-kilometer evacuation area was referred to in the secret letters by the first secretary of Ukraine's Communist Party Central Committee, V. V. Shcherbitsky, the authorities made a hurried U-turn: re-evacuation was now the order of the day.

"SECRET." To be returned to the Special Section of the USSR Council of Ministers Administration. Minutes no. 29. June 23, 1986: On the possibility and time of the population re-evacuation into areas that have undergone radioactive contamination. . . . Recommendations appended. Decision on the possibility of returning children and pregnant women to areas where radiation levels were within 2 to 5 mR/hr. (1) Permit re-evacuation (return) of children and pregnant women to all populated areas where the overall estimated dose will not exceed 10 rem over the first year (a total of 237 populated localities), [while in areas where] estimated exposure doses (with unrestricted consumption of contaminated foodstuffs) will exceed 10 rem—this is to be postponed until October 1, 1986 . . . (174 populated localities). Signed: Izrael, Burenkov, Alexandrov.Another signatory was Marshal Akhromeev who joined the threesome in other similar secret documents. A month earlier (minutes no. 10 of May 10, 1986), Izrael reported in a secret memo to the Politburo task group: "The areas with radiation levels over 5 mR/hr . . . have been judged dangerous for human habitation. . . . Areas with radiation levels under 5 mR/hr require introduction of strict radioactivity monitoring for foodstuffs, especially milk." It would be interesting to compare this with one more secret paper, "Report by Chemical Warfare Units Head V. Pikalov, the USSR Ministry of Defense, at the CPSU Central Committee conference on June 15, 1987." The report points out, among other things, that ". . . in the 'rusty forest', tree cutting and conservation (by sand covering) has brought down radiation levels from 5 R/hr to 7.5 mR/hr, which exceeds tolerance levels 15 times." That is to say, pregnant women and children were effectively re-evacuated to a species of "rusty forest"!

> "SECRET. P. 10 TOP SECRET." Minutes no. 35. October 17, 1986, Copy no. 1: "Conclusion as to the possibility of re-evacuating the population of 47 villages in the Kiev and Gomel regions within the previously defined 30-km zone . . . ." And an appendix listing 26 villages where "the radiation situation conforms to the criteria approved for population re-evacuation (cesium-137 contamination density below 15 Ci/km^2; strontium-90, below 3 Ci/km^2; plutonium-239 and -240, under 0. 1 Ci/km^2; and the total exposure dose for the population over the first year on re-evacuation below 10 rem)."

And not one of them shrank from forcing back, with a single stroke of the pen, pregnant women and children back into the nuclear ghetto, into the "black" zone! To them, people were no better than cattle that would take anything lying down.

Nearly twenty years after the disaster, while sorting out my Chernobyl archives that now contained vast quantities of diverse material, I came across a document that was nothing short of sensational. It bore immediate relation to the secret Kremlin reports, yet again confirming the massive scope of the authorities' lying and crimes. Over the post-Chernobyl years, I unearthed, read, and published dozens of kilograms of classified official documents, but I had not yet seen anything to match this. For the first time, the figures cited referred to specific, actual exposure doses absorbed by people in the first months after the accident.

On May 26, 1987, Ukrainian health minister A. Ye. Romanenko wrote a letter to his Soviet Union counterpart, Yevgeny Chazov, entitled "On the Progress in Executing USSR Health Ministry Order No. 527 (for official use only) of April 13, 1987," registered as no. 428s, marked "SECRET" and bearing the CPSU CC stamp "NOT TO BE PUBLISHED." The letter read:

> The areas with increased radiation levels in the Kiev, Zhitomir, and Chernigov regions have a population of 215,000 people, including 74,600 children. We identified 39,600 sick persons not registered previously. The people found to suffer from various somatic diseases have been placed under dynamic observation; they are receiving hospital and outpatient treatment. In all, 20,200 persons have been hospitalized over 12 months, about 6,000 of them children.

Here is a profoundly disturbing fact. "In the first months after the Chernobyl nuclear power plant accident, all the children have been subjected to dosimetric examination of the thyroid gland. 2,600 children (3. 4%) were found to have iodine radionuclide content exceeding 500 rem." It should be noted that this revealing letter is dated April 13, 1987. So the new doses from the Politburo task group's secret minutes increased ten to fifty times had been in effect for nearly a year. In real terms, this implies horrendous things. First, there are many more such children, ten to fifty times more. Second, that the doses accumulated by those covered by the letter are also actually ten to fifty times higher. Even the most hard-core medical conformists admit that cancer sets in after 100 rem. So what do we have here?

Was the Kremlin team headed by academician Ilyin unaware of these diagnoses—murderous ones, both figuratively and literally? With what degree of certainty in radiation dose estimates and prognoses regarding its effects can we discuss the issue? The question naturally arises: How many children in the Ukraine and in other republics were found to have thyroid glands with less than 500 rem? Alas, there are still no accessible accurate data on that.

Here is another document from my archives. As a follow-up to his secret correspondence, USSR health minister Ye. I. Chazov sent a memo to the CPSU Central Committee on November 16, 1987, no. 3634s marked "SECRET" and stamped "NOT TO BE PUBLISHED," which said: "As of September 30, 1987, 620,016 persons are covered by preliminary observation. 5,213 persons have been hospitalized for the purpose of thorough examination and a more precise diagnosis of diseases discovered during preliminary examination but not radiation-related." So it appears Ukraine's health minister Romanenko informed him that within just one year, more than 2,500 children had accumulated 500 rem of radioiodine in their thyroids (for which read certain cancer), and Chazov sent a secret report to the Central Committee to tell them that "no diseases have been discovered that could be related to the radiation factor!" How does one explain why those positively enormous radioiodine doses, even for adults, never mind children, are not "radiation-related"? I would like to know what is radiation-related! A substantial amount. Or was this kind of "truth" more pleasing to the Central Committee ears? Was that it?

And now, here's the draft resolution "On Fulfilling the 28th CPSU Congress's Resolution 'On Political Assessment of the Catastrophe at the Chernobyl Nuclear Power Plant and the Work on Eliminating Its Consequences'" of December 28, 1990, which the CPSU CC Secretariat sent to newly elected Secretary General V. A. Ivashko, who had been brought to Moscow from Ukraine. This secret document points out:

> The consequences of the accident continue to impact on the birthrates and life expectancy. Thus, in the Belorussian Soviet Socialist Republic over the last four years, the birthrate has dropped by 10 percent, whereas, cancer-related fatality rates have increased. In the Mogilev and Gomel regions, death rates have gone up more than 19 percent in the last five years.

These secret discussions at the CPSU Central Committee in no way correlate with those clearly cynical official dose estimates.

The real doses and their estimates were made secret and distorted as indicated in an article by Professor A. I. Vorobyev, full member of the USSR Academy of Medical Sciences and director of the Russian Hematology Research Center. Under the title, "Why Soviet Radiation Is the Most Harmless" (*Moskovskie novosti*, no. 33, August 18, 1991), the author writes that

> 40 percent of the examined residents of the Chernobyl area have been found to suffer from no exposure doses whatever. 50 percent

have absorbed under 50 rad; over 5 percent, 50 to 80 rad. The latter can be expected to display a distinctly increased tumor rates. Two percent of the residents of the contaminated area . . .have absorbed radiation doses of over 100 rad. The proportion of such persons among liquidators is even higher.

Vorobyev also notes that "some residents of Gomel and the Bryansk region have been found to have the kind of alteration in individual cells that point to exposure to extremely powerful radiation! There is a discrepancy here: the body on the whole has absorbed a dose of 30 to 50 rad, while some of its cells have accumulated almost 1,000 rad and more." The reader will see that this simply confirms the inferences we made after reading the secret letter by Ukraine's health minister Romanenko to his Moscow boss Chazov, namely that owing to the raising of dose levels as recorded in the secret minutes, people had actually absorbed upward of 1,000 rem. Those criminal facts the professor reported to the USSR Health Ministry and the Academy of Medical Sciences. The public is unaware of a reply, if any, to these scientific arguments. I suppose the professor ought to be grateful for keeping his director's job.

In 1989, the *Moskovskie novosti* weekly invited several people's deputies (myself included) for a round table discussion of the consequences of the Chernobyl disaster. Ales Adamovich, a prominent writer and a people's deputy from Belorussia, said that "when autopsy was performed on people who had allegedly died of other diseases, say, ischemia, they were found to have in their lungs—this is recorded by Prof. Ye. Petryaev—vast amounts of so-called 'hot particles.' Up to fifteen thousand of them! Two thousand such particles spell certain cancer!"

As Soviet nuclear physicist Sergei Titkin points out in his manuscript sent to me from Israel, this kind of solid particle buildup—tobacco smoke, coal dust, silica (which, absorbed in large amounts, will cause silicosis)—has been known for a long time. But in this case, the lung tissue incorporated motes of partly used reactor fuel lodged fast in the lungs.

I found confirmation of these terrible suspicions in the report by the USSR State Committee for Atomic Energy prepared for the IAEA conference of experts in Vienna on August 25–29, 1986, under the heading "The Accident at the Chernobyl Nuclear Power Plant and Its Consequences." The report cites shocking facts about the gamma-spectroscopic analysis of radiation emitted by the victims' bodies: "virtually all the patients, apparently regardless of the presence and

240

gravity of ARS [acute radiation sickness], were found to have absorbed a complex mixture of nuclides, primarily isotopes of iodine, cesium, zirconium, niobium, and ruthenium. There is also mention of radionuclide incorporation."

Observe the date when the document was drawn up—barely four months after the disaster! I am not in the least upset by the diffident wording the report authors have chosen—that all that nastiness was incorporated into the bodies of the Chernobyl victims "apparently regardless of the presence or gravity of ARS." It is clear to me that, first, ARS had already reached a stage where it was impossible to conceal from the specialists (the general public was another matter—we will leave the issue of decency alone for now). Second, if, translated from officialese into ordinary speech, the Chernobyl victims themselves were already emitting radiation and had been diagnosed with ARS, then only hopelessly blind people could fail to trace it to the unfortunate victims' meal of radionuclides. The more so since the same report intimates so very diffidently that several persons killed by acute radiation sickness had an assortment of radionuclides in their lungs.

After this, even the following conclusions do not come as a surprise: "... at the present stage, when estimating dosage loads, the inhalation intake of radionuclides during residence within the formed radioactive plume may be overlooked"—even though "extra mortality related to the accidental discharge by the Chernobyl Nuclear Power Plant will add less than 2 percent to the natural deaths from cancer among the radiation-affected population." (Meaning, not to worry—well, so some measly 2 percent will peg out from cancer. So what?) No need to fret over the "inhalation intake of radionuclides." All as recommended and passed down along the democratic centralism chain (whoever thought of that rubbish!) by the senior comrades in their secret minutes.

My own observations and interviews with hundreds of people in afflicted areas just after the accident and several months later showed clearly that the danger of incorporated nuclear fuel dust was simply horrendous. Literally all my interlocutors talked of radioactive dust, a tickling sensation (that was how they felt it) in the throat because of it; of tractors letting in dust (and in the fall of 1986 many farms harvested radiation); of their children playing in the sand where, as they put it, "radiation had nose-dived," too, and so on.

Obviously, no one took into account this feature, the so-called hot particles, dust from nuclear fuel, that got into the human system, at times bringing with it lethal radiation doses.

Nuclear physicist Igor Gerashchenko, once a Kiev resident now living in the West, sent me his handwritten article "The Missed Lessons of Chernobyl." (I do not know if it has ever been published.) The article cites fairly interesting facts—interesting in terms of remarkable coincidences. I cite this passage:

> So what radiation doses did people get in the disaster area? No one knows for sure. At first there were hardly any instruments capable of measuring radioactivity levels. A policeman I knew, an interior ministry captain, spent a week after the explosion as part of the cordon thrown around the accident site. He had not been issued with a personnel dosimeter and had no idea what exposure dose he might have absorbed. Drivers of vehicles used for evacuating the locals did not have dosimeters either. Was it accidental? Not on your life. That way it was easier to lie to the people and the gullible world public.
>
> According to unverified data, in the town of Pripyat (a township nearest to the nuclear power plant) radiation levels were between 1 and 10 R/hr. [According to the data verified by myself, the radiation level in Narodichi of the Zhitomir region kept at 3 R/hr during the first days, though Narodichi is 80 km from the Chernobyl nuclear power plant]. The correlation between radioactivity levels and the distance to the explosion site is very complex (it matters which way the wind was blowing, and whether or not it rained from the radioactive cloud, and lots of other things), but speaking in terms of the statistical mean, radiation levels are inversely proportional to the distance squared, i.e. twice as far from the explosion site, radioactivity is four times lower, and so on.
>
> The maximum radiation level I myself recorded in Kiev in late May [1986] was 0. 0018 R/hr. I did the measuring with a standard army instrument borrowed from the civil defense room at my place of work. According to measurements taken by some people I knew, radiation levels in Kiev in early May reached 0. 003 R/hr. The distance between Kiev and the blown-up reactor is about 130 km, while the town of Pripyat is less than 5 km away.
>
> It follows, in terms of the statistical mean, that the radiation level in Pripyat should have been . . . about 2 R/hr. Well, the figures 1 to 10 R/hr look perfectly plausible for Pripyat.
>
> Evacuation did not start till 36 hours after the explosion. So the Pripyat residents absorbed between 36 and 360 R. And on April 26, 1986, there were 45,000 of those residents. How many of them are still living? I do not know. [The manuscript of Gerashchenko's article is dated May 1987]. I only know that of those who were furtively brought to Kiev hospitals at night, about 15,000 died within the first six months.
>
> . . . I will say this: I have not been gathering panicky rumors. All the information I cite in this article came to me directly from those

involved in the elimination of the consequences of the disaster—truck drivers, hospital staff, servicemen in cordon lines, and others.

Doctors did not even attempt to treat the people brought to Kiev, nor did they have the means to do so. Where could they get enough blood for transfusion and bone marrow for transplants for tens of thousands of patients? Besides, those patients had to be put not only in radiology departments but just about everywhere—some in wards, some in corridors, and some even in hospital basements. One of the hospitals had even provided a portion of their morgue for the purpose. Those fifteen thousand people died of acute radiation sickness.

It is simply amazing the coincidence between various sources. According to the Politburo task group's secret minutes I have quoted above, the number of people hospitalized in the first week after the explosion was precisely fifteen thousand or thereabouts. Academician A. I. Vorobyev in his *Moskovskie novosti* article also reports, incidentally, that fifteen thousand were hospitalized. But he explains that once the medics had been told what acute radiation sickness was, the patients were discharged. Physicist I. Gerashchenko, an eyewitness then living in Kiev, also names the same figure. But with one awful addition—all those people died.

It is most revealing to analyze academician Vorobyev's remark about the fifteen thousand persons hospitalized and discharged following some "explanation given to the medics." For a start, what sort of medics were they if they did not know the first thing about acute radiation sickness (even high school students know that). Also, the "explanations" seemed to come after the maximum permissible radiation levels had been urgently raised at one of the Kremlin group's secret meetings. It was after that event that all the hospitalized patients, of which there must have been about fifteen thousand indeed, were pronounced healthy and discharged.

Judging by his publications, Professor Vorobyev could hardly have been let into the Chernobyl secrets of the Kremlin. His confession to me is yet another indirect proof of the fact that about fifteen thousand people got acute radiation sickness in the first weeks after the accident, and only special ARS diagnostics instructions introduced by the Politburo, thanks to their court medicos, helped the Soviet government conceal the fact, and moreover, deny hospitalization to other accident victims whose doses were below the newly raised maximum. They effectively did not exist. They had vanished—evaporated.

243

Here are the thoughts of physicist Gerashchenko:

> An attentive reader may indeed marvel at this figure. Hiroshima left almost seventy thousand people dead (only several thousand of them died directly from the explosion, while most succumbed to the consequences of radioactive contamination), but here we have just fifteen thousand with an explosion thousands of times greater. If you are thinking that the victims are far more numerous, you are quite right. First, I am only talking about those covered by the information at my disposal. Second, radiation effects take a long time to make themselves felt. Dozens or even hundreds more will yet die of cancer caused by radiation, but it will happen later; the incubation period may last years.

Gerashchenko made his statement about the fifteen thousand dead Chernobyl victims in an interview with the *New York City Tribune* and at the US Congress hearings on the consequences of the accident. He said also that the casualties were diagnosed with vegetovascular dystonia, vascular dystonia, and such instead of acute radiation sickness. And this is now an absolutely proven fact. In the medical records of the dead, doctors wrote: "received a course of treatment," "does not need further treatment."

Several years after the accident, speaking at a parliamentary hearing, even academician L. A. Ilyin, that originator of the infamous 35-rem-over-70-years concept, had to admit that "1,600,000 children have received radiation dosages that are causing concern. We must decide what to do next."

The secret minutes make it abundantly clear that radiation dosage was computed on the basis of the latest "prescriptions" from official science stamped with the "SECRET" mark of the Central Committee. And if one tries to look on these children from the accepted moral imperative of the inadmissibility of any victims, which all civilized countries adhere to, what should the figure be multiplied by?

Lie no. 2, about "clean" produce from radiation-affected farms. The secret prescription by the CPSU Central Committee task group for using radioactive meat and milk is another public health flimflam put out by the Kremlin spinmeisters.

> "SECRET." Minutes no. 32. August 22, 1986: Item 4—To be taken into cognizance: report by Comrade V. S. Murakhovsky (attached) about the recommendations and measures elaborated for agro-industrial production on territories with varying density degrees of long-lived

isotope contamination. The production process will be carried out in the usual way, with random radiometric control of the soil and agricultural produce, on territory with cesium-137 contamination density of under 15 Ci/km², covering 1.6 million hectares of farmland. On territory with contamination density of 15 to 40 Ci/km² (760,000 hectares of farmland) agro-industrial activity will proceed under constant radiometric monitoring in accordance with a complex of organizational, agro-technical, and zoo–veterinary measures ensuring a reduction in the radioactive contamination of the yield and production of good-quality foodstuffs.

The Kremlin elders whose decisions were recorded in those minutes could not fail to know that cows yielded radioactive milk after grazing on pastures fertilized with as little as 1 Ci/km² of cesium-137. A few examples.

Ibidem, Item 10: "To regard as expedient the stocking in state reserves of meat with an increased content of radioactive substances now in storage, and also to be purchased in the current year."

> "TOP SECRET." Resolution by the Politburo of the CPSU Central Committee dated May 8, 1986: Memorandum by Comrade V. S. Murakhovsky.... CPSU CC Secretary General M. S. Gorbachev.... On the state and possible measures of eliminating the consequences in agriculture within the plume from the accidental discharge at the Chernobyl Nuclear Power Plant.... It has been established that during the slaughter of cattle and pigs, hosing down the animals, and removing lymph nodes results in obtaining meat fit for consumption. Signed: V. Murakhovsky.

What did they do with the "removed lymph nodes," I wonder? Surely, those, too, could have been put to good use? Say, to stuff pies for undergraduates?

> "SECRET." Appendix to Item 10 of minutes no. 32: When processing cattle from areas located within the plume of the Chernobyl Nuclear Power Plant discharge, some of the meat produced contains radioactive substances (RS) in amounts exceeding tolerance levels. Currently in cold storage in several regions of the Belorussian Soviet Socialist Republic, the Ukrainian Soviet Socialist Republic, and the Russian Federation, there is about 10,000 metric tons of meat with RS contamination levels from $1.1*10^{-7}$ Ci/kg to $1.0*10^{-6}$ Ci/kg, and 30,000 more metric tons of similar meat is expected to arrive from manufacturers in August–December this year.
>
> To avoid considerable overall accumulation of RS in the human body from eating contaminated foodstuffs, the USSR Ministry of

Public Health recommends *maximum dispersal of the RS contaminated meat about the country* [emphasis mine] to be used in manufacturing sausage, canned food, and semifinished meat products mixed with normal meat at a ratio of 1:10 . . . To use the said meat as food and to ensure production in accordance with USSR Health Ministry standards, given its tenfold dilution with uncontaminated meat, it is necessary to organize its processing at meat factories in most regions of the Russian Federation (except the city of Moscow), Moldavia, the Transcaucasus republics, the Baltic republics, Kazakhstan, and Central Asia.

Chairman of the State Committee for Agricultural Industry V. S. Murakhovsky

In real life, though, things were not done as prescribed. In 2002, Issue 3 of the newsletter *Spasenie* (Rescue), a supplement to the RF natural resources ministry newspaper *Natural Resources Bulletin*, printed an account of the seminar "Radiation Protection: the Way It Was" that had been held at the Institute for Safe Development of Nuclear Power Engineering, Russian Academy of Sciences. There, A. P. Povalyaev, former worker at a CPSU CC subsidiary farm turned major advisor on radiobiology after the Mayak accident and later the Chernobyl accident and an active party to the criminal collusion, boasted to the young scientists:

The meat of animals slaughtered in Chernobyl was unfit for human consumption. It contained four to five times more cesium 137 than was assumed normal at the time. We put it in cold storage and later started supplying portions of that meat to meatpacking and processing factories with instructions to add 20 percent (of contaminated meat) to clean meat. This is a commonly accepted dilution principle: "Dirty" stuff is mixed with clean stuff until an acceptable concentration is obtained.

So in practical life, these Povalyaevs were deceiving the Politburo itself. The former Central Committee farm manager forgot to tell his young listeners one important detail, however: the Politburo decreed that this kind of choice meat be fed to the rest of the country barring Moscow and Leningrad. Just think of those people's moral fiber. They tried to make sure that there was enough meat from radioactive Chernobyl bullocks to go round—at enormous sacrifice to themselves!

One more appendix to secret minutes no. 32, Item 11 "On the Use of Milk in Some Regions of the Belarusian SSR and the RSFSR in Connection with Toughened Standards for RS Content":

As of August 1, the permissible radioactive substances content in milk standard in force throughout the territory of the USSR is $1*10^{-8}$ Ci/l ("clean" milk to the power of -12). However, in some districts of some regions in the Belorussian Soviet Socialist Republic, a proportion of the milk output still contains radioactive substances at the level of $1*10^{-7}$ Ci/l and would not stabilize at the level of the newly introduced norm, which hampers steady supply of milk to the population of these areas.

Considering the above, I authorize postponing the enforcement of the said norm until November 1, 1986. The produce of the regions in question shall not be used for export. P. N. Burgasov.

It is positively touching, is it not, this particular care taken to keep up a "steady supply of milk to the population." But for export—nix! Radioactive waste is strictly for domestic consumption. After all, everything in the secret papers tallies up; everything is within the norms, doses, and limits that suit the party, the government, and the West.

Here is how Povalyaev bragged about that at the seminar:

Milk remained a fairly serious source of irradiation for quite a long time. But we did what we could. During the first year, we saved something in the region of 8 million rubles: we did not discard milk but used it to make butter and curds. Keep curds for four months and you get a radioactivity-free product, and butter is practically clean.

When I described this recipe of Povalyaev's in one of the radiation-affected villages, a mother of sick Chernobyl children said bitterly, "May he gorge on such curds all his life!" Unkind, granted, but fair, I think. The professional competence of that "radiobiologist" stands out clearly in a story of one of his "scientific" recommendations. When the Communist Party dispatched him to the Mayak association in the Urals to cover up the nuclear accident ("I had Grade A access because I had worked at one time on a farm supplying the Central Committee with foodstuffs," Povalyaev explained proudly), he and his team could not think of anything better than to order two young staff members to draw up an executive committee resolution for cutting down 150 hectares of first-rate Urals timber. Thank God, there happened to be people of slightly higher intellectual caliber who stopped that "scientific" stupidity. Nor could the party do without Povalyayev after Chernobyl, either. It stands to reason—he was a ready-made professional! Many of the secret documents that cost a lot of people their health and life (which the USSR prosecutor general's office eventually admitted) bear his signature. One small problem. He forgot to tell that to his audience at that seminar.

Lie no. 3, about information for the press or how the Politburo taught the press to prevaricate. Nearly twenty years after the disaster, I came in possession of a paper marked "TOP SECRET (Working records.) SINGLE COPY." It is a record of the Politburo session of April 29, 1986. It must have been the first session, or one of the first, to discuss the Chernobyl issue. It took place on the third day after the explosion and was chaired by Mikhail Gorbachev. The meeting was attended by all the Politburo members. For the first time, they tried to figure out how much to tell their own people and the world about the accident. After Politburo member V. I. Dolgikh informed the assembly of "the glowing crater" in the ravaged reactor, of "dropping sacks from helicopters" ("for which purpose 360 persons were mobilized, plus 160 volunteers, but there were cases of refusals as well"), of "three plumes from the cloud—the western, the northern, and the southern ones," they started discussing how "information should be released."

Gorbachev: "The more honestly we behave the better." Bravo, Mikhail Sergeevich! But in the next paragraph, we read, "When we give information, it should be specified that the plant was under scheduled repair so as not to cast a shadow on our equipment." What price perestroika and "new thinking," Comrade Gorbachev? They did not apply to the Chernobyl accident, apparently. The working records of the top-secret minutes show with perfect clarity the Politburo members' confusion. They are discussing how best to pull the wool over the eyes of their own people and the world. The impression one gets is of a theater performance or a movie. But that was reality.

A. A. GROMYKO: It is necessary to give more information to the fraternal countries and some information to Washington and London. I'd advise giving the relevant explanations to Soviet ambassadors as well.

VOROTNIKOV: But how about Moscow?

GORBACHEV: It can wait. Let Comrade B. N. Yeltsin keep an eye on the situation.

H. A. ALIEV: Perhaps we should provide some information for our own people?

Ye. K. LIGACHEV: A press conference may not be a good proposition.

Gorbachev: I suppose it might be a good idea to make a statement about progress in dealing with the accident.

A. N. YAKOVLEV: Foreign correspondents will look for rumors.

RYZHKOV: It would be advisable to give out three communiqués—one for our own people, another for the socialist countries, and a third for Europe, the US, and Canada. As for Poland, we might send someone there. (In a 1992 interview with popular television journalist Andrei Karaulov, Ryzhkov would say, "We did not know anything!")

M. V. ZIMYANIN: It is essential to emphasize in the statement that there was no explosion, just a radiation leak in the wake of an accident.

V. I. VOROTNIKOV: We could say that the accident damaged the hermetic shell.

A. F. DOBRYNIN: That's right. I bet Reagan already has photographs on his desk.

GORBACHEV: Are we all agreed on the proposed measures?

POLITBURO MEMBERS: We are.

GORBACHEV: Resolution passed.

This working record in typescript is signed by hand: "A. Lukyanov." Anatoly Ivanovich Lukyanov is a friend of Gorbachev (they had been at university together). Three years later, Gorbachev would have him appointed chairman of the USSR Supreme Soviet, and another two years later, Lukyanov would betray him, joining the GKChP putschists and ending up in the Matrosskaya tishina (Sailors' Quiet) prison. But not for long. Judging by the Politburo task group's secret minutes, the mood and wishes of that first session were major guidelines for the Politburo's further activity. The press, needless to say, was not allowed to be present at its sessions. Only once, on May 26, 1986 (minutes no. 18), chief editors of national newspapers were invited and told expressly, "The focus should be on the measures taken by the CPSU Central Committee and the government to ensure normal working and daily-life conditions for the evacuated population, elimination of the consequences of the accident, and on covering extensively the working masses' active participation in carrying out these measures."

Almost every session considered some statement or other for the press, for television, or for a press conference. Every text was approved after a vote was taken, and the exact date of publication was stipulated.

> "SECRET." Minutes no. 9. May 8, 1986: (4) On the television appearance of Comrades A. I. Vorobyev and Ye. Ye. Gogin. Given the improved situation at the Chernobyl Nuclear Power Plant, it is best to abstain from the said appearance. (6) On the TASS report about several European countries imposing restrictions on imports from

the USSR. The text of the said address approved; to be published in the press on May 9, 1986. (9) On the next statement by the government. The text of the statement approved. Publication in the press suspended, pending special orders.

"SECRET." Minutes no. 5. May 4, 1986: The text of the TASS appeal approved. Publication of the next statement by the USSR Council of Ministers to be postponed until May 5.

Interestingly, the minutes contain neither the texts themselves nor their authors' names. And this is hardly accidental. In this they were wary of leaving fingerprints.

"SECRET." Minutes no. 1. April 29, 1986: (10) On government statements. The text of the governmental statement for the press approved. The text of the information bulletin about the accident at the Chernobyl Nuclear Power Plant and the measures taken to eliminate its consequences intended for the leaderships of certain Western countries—approved. The text of the bulletin for the leaderships of several socialist countries about the state of affairs in eliminating the consequences of the accident at the Chernobyl Nuclear Power Plant—approved.

On the same day, the same issue was also discussed at the session of the Politburo of the CPSU Central Committee. Its resolution says: "(4) To be prepared: information bulletins on progress in eliminating the accident at the Chernobyl Nuclear Power Plant for the population of our country, for the leadership of fraternal parties in socialist countries, and also for heads of state and government in other European states, the USA, and Canada (the texts attached)."

One of the appendices, likewise marked "TOP SECRET," is more specific: "Sofia, Budapest, Berlin, Warsaw, Bucharest, Prague, Havana, Belgrade—to Soviet ambassadors. Pay urgent visits to Comrade Zhivkov (Kadar, Honecker, Jaruzelski, Ceausescu, Husak, Castro, Zarkovic), or their deputy and, having explained that they are carrying out instructions [from the Politburo], tell them the following. . . . Explain that similar information will be forwarded to the leadership of the USA and a number of European countries. Add that, if the necessity arises, we will pass on additional information to our friends."

Note that enclosed were "texts," not "a text." One kind of information, or rather misinformation, was for domestic consumption, another for our brethren in Socialism, and a third for the "damn capitalists." Note also that additional information would be given to none but friends—"if the necessity arises." Is this a political diagnosis—or melancholy paranoia?

"SECRET." Minutes no. 7. May 6, 1986: The Goskomgidromet proposal about the expediency of regular reports to the IAEA on radioactive radiation levels in the vicinity of the Chernobyl Nuclear Power Plant—accepted. Information prepared for sending to the IAEA to be previously examined at the task group's sessions.. . . Proposal by the USSR Health Ministry about the expediency of publishing the data on the numbers and condition of patients receiving treatment in Hospital No. 6 in Moscow—accepted, *given the fact that there are Americans working at this hospital.* [my emphasis]

Many thanks to Americans. They helped us no end, forcing our lying party bosses to disclose at least something.

"SECRET." Minutes no. 3. May 1, 1986: A group of Soviet correspondents to be sent to areas adjacent to the Chernobyl Nuclear Power Plant location zone for the purpose of preparing materials for the press and television that would provide evidence of normal life in those areas. *Izvestia*'s own correspondent in Belorussia, N. Matukovsky, tried to draw the Politburo's attention to the situation there, but failed.

"SECRET." Appendix to minutes no. 28. Teletypists: This telegram is not to be shown to anyone but the chief editor. Copy to be destroyed.. . . Information. I am hereby bringing to your notice that the radiation situation in Belorussia has worsened considerably. In many districts of the Mogilev region, radioactive contamination has been detected whose levels far exceed those in the areas we have written about. By every medical standard, human habitation in these districts is fraught with tremendous risk to life. I have the impression that our comrades are at a loss what to do, particularly since the relevant Moscow officials will not believe the truth.. . . I am telexing this to you because all telephone conversations on the subject are strictly forbidden. June 8, 1986. Signed: N. Matukovsky.

The correspondent's alarming telegram was passed on to the Politburo task group. After it was read out, the group decided to "charge Goskomgidromet (Comrade Izrael), the USSR Health Ministry (Comrade Burenkov), and the USSR Academy of Sciences (Comrade Alexandrov), in cooperation with the Council of Ministers of the Belorussian Soviet Socialist Republic (Comrade Kovalev), with checking the radiation situation in the districts mentioned in the said report (enclosed), and reporting the results to the task group by July 20 this year." And, wonder of wonders, shortly afterwards, they recommended "considering evacuation of residents from 16 localities in the Mogilev region (a total of 4,109 persons)." Luckily, *Izvestia* chief editor Ivan Laptev managed to deliver the telegram to the addressee. Hopefully, those 4,109 persons were saved in what the party faithful referred to as the "red" evacuation zone.

Here is the way they primed themselves for press conferences with Soviet and foreign journalists:

> "SECRET." Appendix to minutes no. 21: Instructions for presenting at the press conference the main issues connected with the causes and progress in the elimination of the consequences of the accident at unit 4 of the Chernobyl Nuclear Power Plant. (2) While reporting the progress in eliminating the consequences of the Chernobyl accident: show successful implementation of major technical and organizational measures aimed at eliminating the consequences of the accident and preventing potential radiation damage without precedent in the world practice; emphasize the high degree of mass heroism in performing the said tasks. Highlight large-scale measures taken to ensure population safety, remarking specifically on care for the people finding themselves on contaminated territory. (4) Dismiss as groundless the claims and estimates, both by individual officials and the press in some Western countries, alleging that there has been considerable environmental and material damage done by small quantities of radioactive substances spreading with the air masses from the Chernobyl Nuclear Power Plant area.

Steps had to be taken—who could have doubted that!—to "intensify propaganda measures aimed at unmasking false allegations by bourgeois information outlets and secret services about the events at the Chernobyl Nuclear Power Plant." The instructions were part of a top-secret resolution by the CPSU Central Committee dated May 22, 1986, and signed by the secretary general. They were subsequently included in resolution after resolution with only slight alterations. Of course, they had to fight radiation in some way or other! And here is Ukraine's first secretary, V. V. Shcherbitsky, reporting on the same subject to the Central Committee in a top-secret message which is carefully filed along with a similar secret resolution by the Politburo of the CPSU Central Committee dated May 29, 1986: "Public opinion is being closely studied. Party activists and the population are informed on a regular basis (you see, the party activists are not part of the population somehow, a sort of superior caste). Fabrications by bourgeois propaganda are being exposed as are various rumors." Did anyone who wrote and signed these documents feel a sense of shame or guilt? Or have they become desensitized to the pain and suffering of their fellow countrymen? One who may have internalized the atrocity was Mikhail Gorbachev's adviser and former deputy defense minister, Marshal S. F. Ahhromeev, who, after the 1991 Communist putsch, committed suicide in his Kremlin office. How did his death fulfill *perestroika*, the new social ethic?

Lie no. 4: Situating a new residential area for power engineers from Slavutich smack dab on a cesium hot spot! Despite the increased contamination levels around Zeleny Mys (Green Cape), the place where the authorities intended to build the new town for Chernobyl power engineers, Akhromeev, in concert with the country's health minister S. P. Burenkov and state hydrometeorology committee chairman Yu. A. Izrael, wrote to USSR Council of Ministers chairman N. I. Ryzhkov, and I quote from secret minutes no. 31, dated August 13, 1986: "SECRET." Copy no. 1. On the basis of analysis of the radiation situation and radioactive contamination of the environment around Zeleny Mys (town of Strakholesye), it is tentatively concluded that a township for power engineers can be built in this area. This—despite the fact that, as they wrote in the same letter, "cesium-137 contamination density (from thirteen test samples) is between 0.28 and 3.12 Ci/km^2. The strontium-90 contamination density (from six test samples) is between 0.1 and 2.5 Ci/km^2, while for plutonium-239 it is 0.027 Ci/km^2."

What got into them I cannot know. Pangs of conscience seem extremely unlikely, but already, at the next session of the task group, the threesome wrote another letter to Ryzhkov that was the opposite of the first one. "Regarding Item 2 of minutes no. 33. SECRET. Copy no. 1. The data cited suggest that the site is unfit for the construction of a residential area for nuclear power plant staff and their families." Meanwhile, nothing had changed! And still the new town for Chernobyl nuclear power engineers *was* built on a "dirty" spot.

Reading these secret letters and the minutes, I remembered a forestry ministry representative fuming at our parliamentary hearings.

> When it was being decided where to build the town, we were against having Slavutich built where it is now. We had some data then. But no one would listen, and the town was built. The decision was made personally by Comrade Shcherbina, who headed the commission. And what do we have now? The forests around the town—you can't gather mushrooms and berries there. That's a fact. And instead of addressing the issue now so that the people might know the truth, they hold it against the foresters—"Take away the warning signs. Don't scare the public," they tell us. And this is the whole truth there is.

Even higher levels of contamination were confirmed two years later at the last session of the task group on January 6, 1988.

Regarding Item 4 of minutes no. 40. SECRET. Copy no. 1. Additional detailed examination of the radiation situation has been conducted in the town of Slavutich and surrounding area . . . cesium-137 contamination density within the town limits is between under 1 and 6 Ci/km². The worst contaminated sections of territory are in the wooded tracts 2 to 3 km west and east of the town. Maximum values of cesium-137 contamination density in some points within these tracts are between 0.7 and 13.0 Ci/km². Strontium-90 contamination levels of 0.1 to 1.0 Ci/km² and plutonium-239 and -240 contamination of 0.001 to 0.02 Ci/km² have been recorded within the town itself.

As for the actual radiation intensity of the spot where the authorities had the town built, as estimated by independent experts, it is between 0.1 and 10 Ci/km². Next door to the town in the forests, there are cesium spots of 19 Ci/km². Yet the minutes conclude triumphantly: "Even without extra measures, they (the doses) will be substantially lower than the maximum . . . established in the USSR and recommended by international organizations for the population (including children and pregnant women) resident in areas adjoining nuclear power plants." And after that, in parentheses: "(in an accident-free situation). Chairman of the USSR State Committee for Hydrometeorology Yu. A. Izrael; Minister of Public Health Ye. I. Chazov."

And to stop the wise guys among the locals making trouble, right there at the session it was decided to "charge the heads of the USSR Atomic Energy Ministry, the USSR Goskomgidromet, and the USSR Health Ministry with organizing, within a week, explanatory work with conclusive argumentation among the plant personnel, on the spot, with the participation of the Combine production association and Chernobyl Nuclear Power Plant management and their party and trade union committees (certainly, these are essential if people are to be lied to!), showing that life in the new town is not a health hazard." Naturally, all of this was carried out to the letter. Another plot; another crime.

Reading such stuff in almost every paragraph of the secret documents, I sometimes thought—what is it? Chekhov's *Ward no. 6*, or what?

Five years after the accident, a draft resolution by the secretariat of the CPSU Central Committee, dated February 13, 1991, was sent to CPSU Secretary General V. A. Ivashko. Its title, "On Implementing the Resolution by the 28th Congress of the CPSU-On Political Assessment of the Disaster at the Chernobyl Nuclear Power Plant and the Course of Work to Eliminate Its Consequences" stated:

> The situation at the Chernobyl Nuclear Power Plant itself remains difficult. The moral and psychological climate there is bordering on the critical. It is exacerbated by the fact that construction work in the town of Slavutich is not complete, besides the town, as the new data suggest (what utter cynicism!), happens to be located in an area of considerable radioactive contamination. The plant personnel, previously assured that the conditions there were perfectly safe for life and long-term work, had effectively been misled. That naturally provoked protests, which was graphically demonstrated by people giving up their Communist Party membership. Suffice it to say that of the 760 party members in the Communist Party local at the Chernobyl Nuclear Power Plant, there is barely one third left.

You see? Even five years after the disaster, it was not the health of the duped Chernobyl power engineers and their children that worried the Communist gang, but its thinning ranks!

The townspeople of Slavutich, the new residential area for Chernobyl nuclear power engineers, have for two decades now been doomed to daily exposure, thus becoming human guinea pigs for radiobiologists. Their lot all these years has been to write letters—to politicians and any who would listen, hoping, always hoping—doesn't it *spring eternal?* Here is a typical quote from a letter by the Pripyat Society members sent to every official address that mattered:

> Our families went through the accident and evacuation, and after untold hardships, voluntarily giving up our apartments in Kiev, came to settle in Slavutich. Some people among us have had radiation sickness. There are also those in need of medical examination and proper treatment. There are weak and sick children. At present, we would like to get comprehensive answers to the following questions: (1) What will happen to the former Pripyat residents when the Chernobyl Nuclear Power Plant is closed down? (2) How and at whose expense (of the health ministry? the atomic energy ministry?) will the real exposure doses be computed that we received at the time of the accident and afterward? (3) If Slavutich has been built on a "dirty" spot, what chance do our families have of returning to Kiev, where most of us vacated apartments that we had previously received? The condition of our children requires wholesome food, treatment, and recuperation opportunities.

I could go on endlessly about the authorities' lies—the Kremlin monsters described them in minute detail in the forty sets of secret minutes, convinced that no one would ever learn a thing about *this*, on and on, some six hundred pages of typescript, with maps, tables, charts, and technical specifications of the flawed reactor. Lie no. 5: Concerning army units taking part in the cleanup. Lie no. 6: Concerning personnel recruitment and "political and educational work" at the Chernobyl power plant in the wake of the accident. The torrent of lies flowed like a tidal wave, washing over the dead and dying. But thankfully, this flood could not eradicate all the fingerprints.

These secret papers confirm the old truth: on every occasion, to preserve itself, the totalitarian system had to do evil and cover its tracks. Starting with the clandestine execution, in the Ipatyev House basement, of the children whose only fault was that they had been born into the imperial family, they went on shooting us by the millions, out of court, packing us off to prison camps and loony bins. The system killed us at the Novocherkassk demonstration; it disposed of us in Afghanistan; it poisoned us with nerve gases in Tbilisi; it threw us under tank tracks in Baku and Vilnius . . . and then, Chernobyl—the slow dying amidst radioactive fumes. The Chernobyl atrocity ranks right up there with the other atrocities committed by the system and its inbred bureaucrats against its own people who it had been methodically exterminating for decades, like some mythical Medusa.

The only way to conquer the Gorgon is to chop off its head.

17

The Enemy Uses Poison-Tipped Needles

Before the Gorbachev parliament was elected, none but Communist public associations and organizations had the right to exist in the Soviet Union. Yet even they were not allowed to practice charity for the benefit of the Chernobyl victims—because charity was incompatible with an impenetrable wall of secrecy then in existence. Therefore, in the wake of the Chernobyl disaster, the first official public action, an act of goodwill by the Soviet government and a sort of safety valve for letting off steam was opening charity account no. 904 in aid for the disaster victims. The Soviet public was apprised of that fact by officials in the upper echelons of party and Soviet power. The account number and the bank's particulars were broadcast by every radio station and all the television channels and were printed in every party, Soviet, trade union, and departmental newspaper. The authorities approved these manifestations of public charity. Soviet citizens were invited to remit money for Chernobyl victims to that account.

At the time, it could not have been done any other way. No one besides the authorities had the right to open a bank account of any kind, including for Chernobyl. Soviet citizens did not have bank accounts, except in the state savings bank. Banks, in the accepted sense of the term, simply did not exist apart from the Central Bank and one or two others not intended for the general public. Destitute Soviet old age pensioners transferred a ruble or two to that state account. Those who were better off would remit their week's or month's wages.

In the spring of 1990, the country witnessed a globally televised "Chernobyl Marathon," which added over 76 million rubles to the account. Foreign-made equipment was also sent over. The display panel at the Rossiya Concert Hall in Moscow, where the TV marathon was held, flashed the figure $4,691,310. To Soviet people, that was a colossal sum. And how did the authorities use this money? Granted, a certain portion of it may have gone to pay for patients' treatment, medication, and equipment. We can't be sure as we have not seen any accounts. But we do have a different kind of information. Here is Order 684-p dated April 30, 1990, signed by chairman of the USSR Council of Ministers, N. I. Ryzhkov: (4) "Allocate 1.5 million rubles from the account at the USSR Zhilsotsbank, of the Foundation for Assisting the Elimination of the Consequences of the Chernobyl Accident to the USSR Atomic Energy Industry Ministry (we love long titles), specifically for the purpose of covering the costs of travel, accommodation, sojourn, catering, transport, and other services for foreign scientists and specialists according to UN standards and to meet the expenses of the working group set up in compliance with this order." Can you make out what that was for and who it aided? Wasn't it the duty of the atomic energy ministry to withdraw from its own account and transfer to charity account no. 904 a sum that would cover losses the republics and individuals in radiation-affected areas had incurred through its fault, plus huge compensation for pain and suffering?

The "order" must have been referring to the group of so-called "independent" experts headed by the Japanese scholar, Dr. Shigematsu. His commission concluded that the Chernobyl accident constituted no health hazard, and the international experts detected no changes in the people's condition. This judgment is totally without scientific foundation and is an indictment of our leading radiation experts and demonstrates their shocking lack of concern for the plight of our citizens. Poison needles! People the world over contributed what they could to help out the dispossessed in a desperate plight, only to find the money was spent on yet another duplicitous concoction by the party bosses.

In 1992, when I went to Japan for the first time as head of an official delegation from Russia's press and information ministry, where I worked at the time, by a quirk of fate, I unexpectedly encountered Dr. Shigematsu—in his laboratory. In the presence of others, I asked him if he did not feel shame for his "independent" expert opinion, for supporting the ignominious official 35 rem concept in which he saw nothing harmful even for babies' health. Not expecting either a question like that or such familiarity with the problem, he looked distinctly embarrassed and in the end had to admit publicly that things in and around Chernobyl were not quite as sunny as the international team of experts had made out in its report. So why were they paid and with money from the Chernobyl charity account, at that? It looked rather like the Russian folk tale where a badly pummeled character was duped into giving a piggyback ride to a healthy one. So our rulers made fools of us, using our own money and money donated by kind-hearted people in other countries of the world to satisfy their own misguided position. Such was the malevolent nature of the first official charity action for the victims of the Chernobyl nuclear accident.

After Mikhail Gorbachev came to power in 1985 and proclaimed the beginning of perestroika and "new thinking," illegitimate organizations started mushrooming all over the country—clubs for promotion of perestroika and people's fronts. Despite the ruthless struggle the party authorities waged against them at local and union republic levels, the very spirit of soon-to-come freedom made tough repressive measures impossible. The approach then dominant throughout the country and backed by Communist Party leader Mikhail Gorbachev was epitomized in the formula "what is not banned by law, is permitted" (as late as 1987, dissenters were still arrested and sent to prison camps).

In 1985, the editor of the *Zhitomirshchina News* journalistic agency, Yakov Zaiko, and I organized, in Zhitomir, an unauthorized political club named For Perestroika. Later, it grew into a mass regional movement, the Civil Front for Promoting Perestroika, providing enough work for the local KGB, their stooges, and also their subservient newspaper, *Radyanska Zhitomirshchina* (a subject for another book). One of the club's tasks was to spread the truth by every available means about life in affected areas. Since any such information was strictly taboo in the official Communist press, we had to resort to Samizdat techniques, using type texts and surreptitious handouts to the public. I typed at least one hundred copies of my first Chernobyl article, stuffing eight rice-paper sheets at a time into my typewriter that was not registered with the KGB, an absolute requirement to protect my independence. That typewriter was a GDR-made Erika my husband and I had bought in Zhitomir's central stores for 300 rubles—double my monthly salary. The venerable machine still languishes in a closet. It was that typewriter I used to type my first Chernobyl book in 1989.

In 1988, we also launched the Samizdat newsletter, *Stenogramma* ("Shorthand Record") under the For Perestroika club auspices. The publication was illegal. The paper was printed on specially adapted equipment with a print run of one hundred copies (that's right, one hundred—not one hundred thousand). Compared to the two hundred thousand print run of the official full-size regional party daily,

Radyanska Zhitomirshchina, it was a spectacular success. People longed for a breath of fresh air. The newsletter printed fiercely critical material, both on political subjects and on the situation in radiation-stricken northern parts of the Zhitomir region. Glasnost was the order of the day. People who were left to live in contaminated areas found themselves under an impregnable information blockade. No one in the country or in the world knew of them, of their suffering, illnesses, and deaths; therefore, no one could help them. That paper was the only one to print letters from the inmates of the Chernobyl Gulag in the years of oppressive Chernobyl lies. Its every issue was passed from hand to hand, read into tatters and smudges until reduced to total disintegration.

Those one hundred priceless copies of the self-made underground *Stenogramma* were printed in strict secrecy at one of Zhitomir's plants. Its chief editor, proofreader, editor in charge, and compositor, all rolled into one, was journalist, Yakov Zaiko, the authorities' thorn in the side. He would come to that plant in the evening after working hours. He would open the door with the key a friendly engineer had given him, lock himself in, and print the newsletter single-handedly on special equipment. In the morning, the lawful occupant of the room would give a prearranged series of knocks on the door. Yakov would let him in and then take the one hundred neatly pleated copies out past the plant entrance checkpoint (the maximum number he managed to print in one night). As for me, I looked after the journalistic and technological side of that clandestine enterprise. The "infernal machine" that Yakov used to print the politically inflammatory paper, worked on—used typewriter ribbons! Every issue required at least twenty of them. Typewriter ribbons were an item in perennial shortage in Zhitomir and Kiev, so I had to make endless trips to Moscow to get them—eighteen hours on the train's economy class carriage, a quick dash to the stationery shop on Dorogomilovskaya Street, conveniently located next door to the Kiev railroad station. Then, there was the long ride home. I am still not sure that it would be a good idea to disclose the name of the plant and the person who, at his peril, left the key and his "infernal machine" for the night so that the underground *Stenogramma*, that did its best to undermine the party, could be printed. Years later, a German student of the Samizdat perestroika press asked me to let her institute have at least one copy of that unique paper. Yakov Zaiko had similar requests from the US Library of Congress.

Thanks to the Chernobyl information breakthrough in the late 1980s alongside the pro-Party societies for environment conservation and people's patrol squads that never uttered a word about the Chernobyl events, the first independent environmental organizations started to emerge. In 1987, according to some data, the country of 250 million had a mere thirty-eight public environmentalist organizations, all of them under Communist Party control. In 1991, their numbers soared more than fivefold. Those were associations refreshingly free from Communist ideology, but they acted under the radar since the Communist Party, though in its death throes, still ran the country.

The first legal public charity foundations and NGOs genuinely anxious to help Chernobyl victims appeared in 1991, after the people's deputies convened by Gorbachev had struck down the USSR Constitution's Article 6 (on the Communist Party monopoly), and new legal standards had been enforced on party pluralism and public associations along with the law on public organizations and movements. The first such organizations were set up in Kiev, Minsk, and Moscow. After dozens of foreign journalists were allowed to visit contaminated areas in 1989 and articles on the plight of the victims started appearing in the press, hundreds of similar organizations also emerged in the West and in Japan, to help the people of Chernobyl. Our domestic NGOs joined them, thus acquiring international status.

In 1992, I received the Right Livelihood Award (the Alternative Nobel), and I established the country's first private ecological charity fund for aiding child victims of Chernobyl. Over the years, we helped 150 orphans in two orphanages on contaminated territory in the town of Klintsy, Bryansk region. On every New Year's Eve, the children wrote letters to the fund's "Father Frost" to list the presents they would like to get. We bought and delivered breast milk, baby food, and various juices to abandoned babies (orphanages take charge of children from birth to twelve years of age), and also medicines, syringes, footwear, books, toys, color televisions, and lots of other goodies. The touching and affectionate thank-you letters from both orphanage managers and schoolchildren are in my archives, the very best reward a person could receive.

I have always been troubled by the fact that the children lived in contaminated areas for years. I could not understand why they were not moved to some radiation-free place. We wrote a letter to Moscow's mayor, Yuri Luzhkov, requesting his help in the construction of a new orphanage on "clean" territory so that the orphans could be sent there instead of "dirty" Klintsy. The site was chosen along with all the engineering data, including the design of the building, but, alas, the work was suspended because of the second war in Chechnya (it's our Iraq). So the children are still living in that unwholesome area. As some leave the orphanage, their places are taken by newcomers. Presidents and governments come and go, new members of parliament are elected, but this matter is of no concern to any of them. They knit documents filled with poison-tipped needles!

As far as we could, and to the extent allowed by customs barriers, we also helped a children's hospital, old and disabled people, and families with many children in the city of Zhitomir and the village of Bazar in the Narodichi District of the Zhitomir region, Ukraine, funding open-heart surgery for children in poor and needy families resident in "dirty" areas. Recently, I received a letter from one such child of the fund, Anya Dmitrieva of Zhitomir. Today she is a high school student. Anya tells me about her life, her problems, and wishes. And this is most heartwarming, of course. We are also proud to have had several scholarship holders. We paid for the education of several undergraduates from needy families in Zhitomir.

Apart from that, the fund was used for publishing and distributing free ecological and anti-nuclear literature. I organized an international group of scholars, and we put together and issued the world's first *Nuclear Encyclopedia*, a fundamental academic work. It earned praise from UNESCO Director General Federico Mayor, who sent the fund a letter to that effect, and it also earned from scientists and the general public. Several chapters from it have been translated and published in Japanese (the English-language version still awaits a sponsor). The fund had friends in the West and in Japan. Especially close ties existed between the fund and the Japanese Chernobyl organization headed by Akiko Wada of Tokyo and Ikuo Kusaka of Hokkaido. Wada, together with her colleagues, had ties with the fund and acquainted herself with its work. Her organization also helped children in the orphanages through our fund, under our tutelage. Kusaka, a teacher from the Japanese island of Hokkaido, even went to Klintsy with some members of the fund staff to take baby food and shoes for toddlers there. I remember his reaction to some facts of our life. Having learned that nurses and teachers in the orphanages had not been paid wages for two years, he could not understand how they could be going to work for free. He said anything like that was altogether impossible in Japan. No one would tolerate it.

We also actively cooperated in research programs with Japanese scientists of the Kyoto University Research Reactor Institute (KURRI), Imanaka, Koide, and Kobayashi (incidentally, they are also among the contributors to the *Nuclear Encyclopedia*). Unfortunately, the severe financial meltdown in Russia in 1998 brought the fund to a virtual standstill.

The Chernobyl movement in this country and abroad was at its most active in 1989–94. With the Soviet Union's collapse, the movement of mercy and aid for victims of the "peaceful atom" went downhill. And twenty years on, it is barely alive, although the festering sore has not disappeared. It has just been driven deep inside by the authorities and society itself. At present, Russia has over fifty antinuclear nongovernmental organizations (NGOs) that directly or indirectly help those hit by Chernobyl. Also working here are several international NGOs in cooperation with their Russian counterparts. There are at present several dozen Chernobyl NGOs in the Russian Federation. Typically, they engage in various forms of assistance to victims of the Chernobyl disaster from lobbying for the necessary laws in parliament to research projects on the consequences of the accident to humanitarian aid, including medical assistance to individual organizations, primarily institutions intended for children, orphanages, hospitals, families, and private persons.

Among the Chernobyl NGOs, a particularly important role is played by those with Chernobyl victims in their membership who live in contaminated areas and struggle for survival and also organizations of disabled liquidators. In recent years, these heroic workers have been battling with the authorities for their rights as well as their own survival. One Chernobyl NGO I would like to single out is the Research Association of Chernobyl Disabled Persons at Moscow State University. Its activities have received scant media coverage, but they help many people find meaning in life after their personal Chernobyl adversity. The research association organizes charity events to render social, psychological, legal, medical, and material assistance to Chernobyl victims and persons affected by radiation elsewhere. The association also works with the families and homeless children who survived the accident, giving them psychological help. They have conducted research on more than twenty problems directly or indirectly bearing on the consequences of the accident, including "Radionuclide Content in Forestry Produce in Conditions of Radioactive Contamination," "New Medical and Biological Criteria of Life Quality Impact on

Human Health in Radioactively Contaminated Areas," "Developing Immunological Monitoring Methodology for Examination of Pilot Liquidators," "Developing Methods of Forming Immunity to Stress-generating Factors."

The Moscow State University Research Association of Chernobyl Disabled Persons also took part in the comprehensive program of social aid to invalids under the auspices of the Moscow City government. One of the most recent projects worked out by the research association of Chernobyl is coaching radiation-affected Muscovites' children who experience learning problems while preparing for further education. It is planning to render additional educational aid to five hundred children of Chernobyl victims.

But admirable though they are, the numerous efforts by domestic NGOs to help Chernobyl victims have been marred by a few flies in the ointment. After the glasnost breakthrough, organizations that had hampered the publication of factual information and had published lies after the Chernobyl accident quickly established charities to help Chernobyl victims, posturing as their best friends.

One such cynical episode happened in Zhitomir, involving the activities of a colleague of mine writing for the same paper. Back home from a trip to Japan, my fellow people's deputies involved with ecological problems brought me information about the Japanese experience of environmental protection and plans for joint projects along with a most welcome present. It was an issue of the English-language newspaper, *Japan Times,* with an item about the heroic battle for the health of children in the Chernobyl zone waged by a hitherto unknown journalist, editor of the *Zhitomirsky Visnik* weekly, Valery Nechiporenko. The Japanese paper painted the portrait of a new patron who had established an endowment for resettling people from affected areas.

Those who had never heard the name and did not know who it was would most probably experience a feeling of gratitude and admiration on reading the newspaper item. As for me, I felt nothing but loathing and bitterness. I know that name only too well. I used to work with the man on the *Radyanska Zhitomirshchina* paper. Only, unlike me, he was a disloyal journalist banned by the editor from going to pro-hibited, radiation-affected zones. I had to go to those areas in secret because I might be turned in by the likes of Nechiporenko. He was at that time currying favor with the boss. Like all the others, he kept silent when at a party meeting it emerged that "she [meaning me] has been seen in the Narodichi District," and the party faithful wondered, indignantly, "Who had given her permission and what was she doing there?" It was at Nechiporenko's tacit consent, too, that another, trusted correspondent was urgently dispatched there, and his article was printed without delay. In it, the author accused the resettled collective farmers of ingratitude because they had the temerity to complain about the poor quality of the houses built for them. The article completely omitted the fact that those houses had been put up on orders of the authorities in an area known to be contaminated, an area where it was impossible to live but where one could die from high radiation exposure.

On June 1, 1986, a few weeks after the accident, an article appeared in the columns of *Radyanska Zhitomirshchina*. Here is what we read in that issue:

> The people's mood and their state of health in Chernobyl are constantly in the focus of attention. Rule number one, "to take care of the people," has not been forgotten, nor will be. Either by generals, whose first questions were about the firemen or by officers and dosimeter operators. "Are the servicemen well fed? Are they feeling well?" That care was also revealed in halving the exposure doses the doctors and civil defense experts had permitted.

That was some care, cutting the dose in half, as if they had control over these exposures! The manufacturer of this idyllic picture, as the reader will have guessed, was Nechiporenko, and the quote comes from his report entitled "Where Volunteers Are Working." I could cite many more similarly beautiful passages from a whole series of Chernobyl articles commissioned by the party and written by Nechiporenko. The message was invariably praiseworthy exclamations for the authorities and their very solicitous concern about the liquidators' health and even their frame of mind! His articles contained—poison-tipped needles!

I have tried to document the regime's truly criminal "care" for the Chernobyl victims. Against this backdrop, the real worth of journalistic waffling by the Zhitomir traveler to Japan is especially repugnant. I would like to add to it one more piece of evidence by the president of the Chernobyl Union Executive Committee, L. M. Petrov (quoting from parliamentary records):

> I have the minutes of a scientific conference in Kiev, at the radiation medicine center, held by representatives of the health ministry.

This is what is written there. "The quality of available information about the dosage the liquidators received is poor. Some of the doses have been deliberately reduced, some increased, some lost. There are grounds for revising and restoring the data. It is proposed to create a special center for reviewing the doses actually received by the liquidators." This is important.

Indeed, one does not know whether to cry or to laugh at Nechiporenko's revelation that on someone's orders the (permissible) dose had been halved. What dose exactly? The author should have probed a little deeper to get at the truth of the matter since he had been given such a rare assignment. But the truth about Chernobyl was apparently the last thing the newspaper wanted. It had orders to prop up the official lies about the accident so the person dispatched to the zone was, quite naturally, one of the trusted loyalists. Some time after the laudatory articles about the care, work, and life of Chernobyl liquidators, the editor of the *Radyanska Zhitomirshchina* daily, D. Panchuk (doubling as chairman of the regional Journalists Union), promoted Nechiporenko to the position of editor of the *Zhitomirsky Visnik* weekly. And the next thing the two of them did, without a shadow of doubt about their moral right to do so—was to open a Chernobyl endowment attached to the Journalists Union and publish a charity account for Chernobyl victims! Such hubris! All this without a word of repentance, without a word of apology to the hundreds of thousands of people they had deceived. As though nothing untoward had happened! As though it was not the *Radyanska Zhitomirshchina* newspaper that for three years had been shouting from the rooftops what fine new housing was constructed in radiation-affected areas. As though it was not Panchuk and company who did their damnedest to keep my articles from the readers—and reports about the criminal resettling of people from "dirty" places to equally "dirty" other places within the same district and occasionally within the same village. As though truth and glasnost had not triumphed in the face of their rabid resistance!

It was very noble of them to launch that endowment. I do not suppose any amount of money collected at factories and elsewhere could be enough to pay off the signature of "Editor D. Panchuk," that for three years graced the masthead of the paper that covered up criminal conduct after the accident that affected the entire nation. This was the paper that extolled the virtues of Communist builders of virtual tombs in "dirty" villages with hard radiation. Those lies have branded

Mr. Panchuk for life. He was the editor of a perfectly mediocre paper where I had to work for nearly fifteen years. A pity that there were no newspapers except the party kind in the country until perestroika began and the people elected me and other independent thinkers to parliament, crusading against all odds for a variety of causes. They fought me because my critical anti-party articles in the national press also cast a shadow over the editor and regional party bosses. They fought the Civic Front for Promoting Perestroika, and they railed against the Ukrainian popular Rukh movement and my comrades-in-arms—the Ukrainian people's deputies such as journalist Yakov Zaiko and economists Vitaly Melnichuk and Alexander Sugonyako. They demonstrated great courage in sealing up (and thus closing down) the regional party committee after Gorbachev's incarceration in Foros and the August 1991 Communist putsch in Moscow.

Over the years of Ukraine's independence, against which this evil force fought with such blockheaded fervor, it has been shrinking inexorably, but it still tries to take a swipe at me—spiteful and mean-spirited, using the columns of their shoddy small-town rags, now dressed up in the white robes of democracy. But their efforts are futile. No one is interested any more in that deceitful Soviet laxative long past its shelf life, issued in small numbers for its own consumption.

Such is the real background and image of Nechiporenko, the "hero" and "savior" of the Chernobyl souls, as portrayed in the *Japan Times*. I bet he forgot to share with the Japanese journalists those trifling particulars. Murphy's Law lives on. So the Japanese Chernobyl-Tyubu NGO, genuinely anxious to help the unfortunate people, also fell for the artful bait cast by men without morals. The very persons who had connived at hushing up the Chernobyl tragedy traveled to Japan on the invitation of Chernobyl-Tyubu to tell the public and Japanese newspapers how valiantly they had been writing the truth about Chernobyl. Away from their own country, in Japan, where no one knew them, they built up a false image of tireless fighters for the rights of Chernobyl victims. This is the pinnacle of cynicism.

Vladimir Kirichansky, the head of that endowment, describing with relish the trip to Japan ("it was not easy," he says), tells us over and over again how very scrupulous the Japanese are and how they fear loss of face. Unfortunately, the author fails to see that, getting involved with such dubious characters as Nechiporenko and Panchuk, they (and he too, incidentally) have already lost face in the eyes of all those who are familiar with this immoral story. That story is known to and remembered by the entire Ukrainian, Russian, and Belarussian citizenry affected by Chernobyl. (I have had to publish explanations on that score on two occasions already.) As for the Japanese from Chernobyl-Tyubu, no one apprised them of the facts. They just did not know (still don't, for that matter) what sort of people they were dealing with. And this ignorance is the only thing that redeems them. The Japanese merit tremendous gratitude for what they have done and are doing for the sick people in the contaminated areas of the Zhitomir region. The principal beneficiaries of their mercy are the victims—even if their Zhitomir partners take pains to hide their true colors, drawing their iniquitous dividends from cooperation with the scrupulous Japanese.

That Zhitomir story is far from the only one. There are lots of other instances of Chernobyl truth persecutors turned into its defenders, people who have set up NGOs and even occupied top posts in the governments of now independent states in the wake of the Soviet Union's disintegration. There is a Russian saying that goes something like this: "It's war to some, but a loving mother to others. It is the Chernobyl disaster to some, but a good excuse for unscrupulous business to others. Dishonest people make use of radiation as reason to fight for unearned benefits, demanding most-favored-person status under the guise of suffering."

For instance, years after the accident, a group of latter-day "entrepreneurs," headed by the now ex-chairman of the Zhitomir City Executive Committee, V. S. Sadovenko, went as high as the USSR Council of Ministers, pestering that body to grant such a status to their commercial activities for the benefit of the victims. On paper, their motives were of the noblest kind. And this is what Moscow replied: "Given the emergency situation in the city caused by the consequences of the Chernobyl nuclear power plant accident, the USSR Ministry for External Economic Relations considers it expedient to endorse the request of the Zhitomir city Soviet executive committee for purchasing food commodities, including baby food, on barter terms, against exporting goods manufactured by city enterprises, including the quotable kinds outside quotas." USSR Foreign Trade Minister K. Sh. Katushev solicitously sent this document to deputy chairman of the USSR Council of Ministers, Leonid I. Abalkin. Knowing from within the rottenness of these potentates, I will never believe that this document could have seen the light of day without thorough greasing of palms.

In real life, things took a somewhat different turn from what they were on paper. Instead of baby food for Chernobyl victims, the non-existent enterprise, Interauto, received from Germany twenty or so Western-made limos instantly impounded by the customs. Their duty-free importation, as officially recorded by the customs report, had been blessed by deputy chairman of the USSR Council of Ministers S. Sitaryan. But what does that have to do with the Chernobyl zone, you may ask, and with the emergency situation referred to in the letters by high officials? Did they drop so much as a red cent from their car sales profits into the collection box of some Chernobyl institution? Not on your life. Chernobyl was no more than a convenient front for these shady entrepreneurs. I am all for business development—as long as it has a decent face. In this country, it is often difficult to distinguish between business and swindlers and con games.

In short, I had to intervene posthaste and discuss the matter with the ministers who, knowingly or not, had got into this shady business mess. I spoke at a session of the Zhitomir city Soviet to report my findings and suggested that the deputies dismiss V. S. Sadovenko, the executive committee chairman who doubled as a businessman. My motion was supported. It is wrong to cash in on the suffering of people, especially children. The session's decision to remove the chairman/businessman was greeted with a storm of applause from the backbenchers. That was a graphic lesson of direct democracy in action.

Unfortunately, that was not the last case of similar Chernobyl-related fraud.

Since the Zhitomir region is on the list of accident victims, the company, Zhitomirtourist, had a brainstorm. Why not try to tempt radiation victims with a Mediterranean cruise as a means of recuperation? Not a bad idea, on the face of it. The central council for tourism allocated 16,000 forex rubles for services abroad. Great! Only, who was basking on the decks of the dazzling white *Feodor Chaliapin* ocean liner all the ten days of the cruise? It took some effort to ferret out this closely guarded secret. After repeated reminders, letters, and phone calls, both to the central council for tourism and to the chairman of Zhitomirtourist, V. M. Mazur, I finally got the list of nearly 120 lucky passengers. Only twelve of them hailed from the region's radiation-affected areas! And even those twelve were, without exception, heads of various organizations, trade union committee chairmen, and useful contacts in trade. The rest had absolutely nothing to do with

Chernobyl and its victims. Nikolai Rubanov, chairman of the trade union committee at the Zhitomir Avtozapchast plant, complained that of the seventeen sanatorium vouchers for their liquidators, not one had reached the plant. Only after his intervention were the people thrown a miserable crumb—three vouchers. But there must have been those who availed themselves of the other vouchers, going on the pleasure voyage instead of the people who had earned it at the cost of their health lost by the crumbling nuclear reactor.

And so it is that some are driven by despair to protests, strikes, and hunger strikes, picketing administration buildings, campaigning for their rights and justice for the sufferers from radiation deception by the government, collecting money for them, while others, under cover of the Chernobyl tragedy, go on with their dodgy business on the quiet, making not only legal but also perfectly tangible capital out of it, and when the fighting is over, the battlefield is always taken over by scavengers. Still, I am confident that there are more decent and merciful people in this world. The exceptions I described in this chapter merely serve to prove the rule—that in every silver lining, there are interwoven a few poison-tipped needles!

18

Mikhail Gorbachev: "You are Wrong!"

Only recently, it seemed that there was nothing more to learn about the Chernobyl disaster. The extent of contamination had been verified not only in the former Soviet republics but also on neighbors' territories. The scapegoats, judged responsible for the blast by court ruling, had served their jail sentences. Those who had hushed up the scale and consequences of the explosion had not only already been awarded Orders of Lenin but also received international awards, as had ex-chairman of the Soviet Hydrometeorology Committee, Yuri Izrael, whose recommendations, among others, had been used to return pregnant women and children to the "black" radiation-affected zones.

The truth about the army's contribution had also come out, and we knew that some one hundred thousand officers and recruits had been exposed to radiation within just six months in 1986. It seemed that all the lies piled up around Chernobyl had already been exposed. After all, it's been years since the event! But here are some new top secret documents pertaining to Politburo sessions, marked "SINGLE COPY." One of the minutes, dated July 3, 1986, sheds light on something that has been concealed not only from the media and the public but also from uninitiated scientists. It pertains to the holiest of holies—the safety of Soviet nuclear reactors, not just the infamous RBMK-1000 contraptions (the Chernobyl type) but also all the others that are still in operation in Russia, as well as in the other states risen from the Soviet Union's ashes and in the one-time "fraternal" people's democracies.

I got hold of this document in a fairly unusual set of circumstances. I ordered some documents on the Afghan war from the Russian state archives and saw the Chernobyl paper sandwiched in between them. A stroke of luck or divine Providence? Chernobyl is the war of the government against its own people. It is also "minor mass destruction warfare" in the center of Europe, a term used by the Central Committee plutocrats in referring to the nuclear blast at their top secret Politburo sessions.

In my Chernobyl file I discovered a question by people's deputies that I, and others, had addressed to the USSR prosecutor general Alexander Sukharev, demanding to initiate criminal proceedings against officials who concealed information about facts that were hazardous to people's health. His answer was the usual claptrap that named only the smallest fry as the scapegoats—the management of the Chernobyl Nuclear Power Plant that had already been punished. The letter also said that the criminal case on the design quality of the RBMK reactor singled out for special investigation had been "dismissed as the accident was found to have resulted from numerous violations of safety rules in the operation of the reactor," meaning that the accident was blamed exclusively on the reactor operators. The court judged the reactor "above suspicion," ignoring several important documents related to its design, available to the court before and after the accident.

The document cited herein demonstrates the utter callousness of the regime and total disregard for the health of our citizens. "Reactor safety ought to be ensured by physics, not by organizational and technical measures." These are the words of Ye. Kulov, head of the USSR State Atomic Industry Monitoring Committee, in the heat of his argument with academician Alexandrov, the designer of the Chernobyl-type reactor.

> TOP SECRET. Single copy. (Working records.) Session of the Politburo of the CPSU Central Committee, July 3, 1986. Comrade M. S. Gorbachev in the chair. Session attended by Comrades H. A. Aliev, A. A. Gromyko, Ye. K. Ligachev, N. I. Ryzhkov, V. V. Shcherbitsky, M. S. Solomentsev, V. I. Vorotnikov, L. N. Zaikov, P. N. Demichev, V. I. Dolgikh, N. N. Slyunkov, S. L. Sokolov, A. P. Biryukova, A. F. Dobrynin, V. P. Nikonov, I. V. Kapitonov.
>
> 1. Report by the governmental commission for investigating the causes of the accident at the Chernobyl nuclear power plant on April 26, 1986.
>
> GORBACHEV: Comrade Shcherbina has the floor.
>
> SHCHERBINA, deputy chairman of the USSR Council of Ministers: The accident was the result of severe violations of the maintenance schedule by the operating staff, and also of serious design flaws in

the reactor. But these causes are not on the same scale. The commission believes that the thing that triggered off the accident was mistakes by the operating personnel.

The same old story, although by then the governmental commission certainly knew about the experts' sharply negative assessments of the design reliability.

Contradicting himself, the speaker says the following:

> Assessing the operational safety of the RBMK reactor, the group of specialists working on the commission's instructions concluded that its characteristics were not up to modern safety standards. Their report says that if subjected to an international-level examination, the reactor would be "ostracized." The RBMK reactors are potentially hazardous. Apparently everyone was under the spell of persistently publicized allegedly excellent safety standards of nuclear power plants. We should take the difficult decision to discontinue building new atomic power plants equipped with RBMK reactors. The board of the ministry (for energy and electrification) has not discussed issues related to nuclear power plant safety since 1983—not once. During the eleventh Five-Year Plan period, 1,042 emergency stoppages of power units have been allowed to happen, 381 of them at RBMK-reactor-equipped nuclear power plants. The Chernobyl Nuclear Power Plant had 104 such stoppages, 35 of them the fault of the staff. A nuclear accident occurred at unit 1 of the plant in September 1982, with the technological channel destroyed (a meltdown in the core) and fragments of fuel elements ejected into the carbon.

The commission chairman's report was followed by the Central Committee discussion of reactor safety. And it was then that some little-known secrets of the Soviet reactor saw the light of day. The transcript continues to unravel its secrets:

GORBACHEV: Did the commission find out why a half-baked reactor had been handed over for industrial production? The U.S. rejected this reactor type. Didn't it, Comrade Legasov?

LEGASOV: These reactors were never designed or used in U.S. power engineering.

GORBACHEV: The reactor was handed over for industrial production, and theoretical research was not continued . . .

SHCHERBINA: In 1956 a decision was taken that determined the fate of these reactors in power engineering. The safety of industrial reactors had been extrapolated to the power-engineering device.

GORBACHEV: Still, why wasn't theoretical research continued? Isn't it a case of some self-willed individuals drawing the country into a hazardous venture? Who suggested building nuclear power plants close to cities? Whose recommendation was that? Incidentally, Americans, after their 1979 accident, did not build any new nuclear power plants.

SHCHERBINA: It was assumed that the safety issue had been settled. A paper issued by the Kurchatov Institute says so; Legasov here was one of the authors of that paper.

GORBACHEV: How many accidents have been recorded?

BRYUKHANOV (director of the Chernobyl Nuclear Power Plant): On average, there were one or two accidents a year. We did not know that something similar happened at the Leningrad Nuclear Power Plant in 1975.

GORBACHEV: There have been 104 accidents. Who is responsible for that?

MESHKOV (first deputy minister for medium engineering industry): That plant is not ours; it belongs to the energy ministry.

GORBACHEV: What can you say about the RBMK reactor?

MESHKOV: A well-tried model, that. Except that it lacks a dome [this is a vital detail]. If all operating regulations are minutely observed, it is safe!

GORBACHEV: Then why did you sign the document saying that its production must be stopped? You amaze me. Everyone is saying that the reactor is not properly developed, its operation is fraught with danger, and you here are trying to protect the honor of your corporation.

MESHKOV: I am protecting the honor of nuclear power engineering.

GORBACHEV: You go on saying what you have been saying these thirty years, and this is an echo of the fact that the medium engineering industry ministry has been outside scientific, state, and party control. And while the governmental commission was working, Comrade Meshkov, I was told that you behaved in a very cavalier manner, trying to slur over obvious facts.

LIGACHEV: There is the world's nuclear power engineering. Why is it opting for a different reactor type?

GORBACHEV: It [the reactor] is the least explored thing [research technology]. Am I right, Comrade Legasov?

LEGASOV: That is so.

GORBACHEV: V. A. Sidorenko (a member of the USSR State Committee for Supervision over Nuclear Power Engineering) writes that the RBMK reactor will not be up to modern international standards even after reconstruction.

G. A. SHASHARIN (deputy minister for energy and electrification): The physics of the reactor determined the scale of the accident. People did not know that the reactor could get out of control in that situation. It is not at all certain that improvements will render it completely safe. There could be a dozen situations in which a Chernobyl repeat would happen. This is particularly true of the number one units at the Leningrad, Kursk, and Chernobyl nuclear power plants. The Ignalina Nuclear Power Plant cannot be operated at its present capacity. They lack an emergency cooling system. They should be stopped before any others. Building any more RBMK reactors should be ruled out, of that I am certain. As for their improvement, it will never pay off. The philosophy of extending nuclear power plant service life is not always justified.

GORBACHEV: Can these reactors be upgraded to international standards?

ALEXANDROV: All countries with developed nuclear power engineering use a different reactor type from ours.

There you have it! This time, at the Politburo session, the designer of the deficient RBMK-1000 nuclear reactor, academician Alexandrov, who had falsely informed all the international organizations that the plant staff was solely responsible for the accident, testified against himself. Meanwhile, way back in December 1984, the interdepartmental science and technology council for nuclear power engineering had approved proposals by experts' commissions to bring the operating RBMK-1000 units up to safety requirements, as specified. Nothing had been done. It was two years before the nuclear accident.

MAYORETS (member of the governmental commission): As far as the RBMK reactor goes, there are no two ways about it. No one in the world has opted for this reactor type. I insist that even after improvements this reactor will still fall short of all our current rules.

RYZHKOV: That accident was inevitable. If it had not happened now, it could have happened any other time, given the situation we have. At that plant, too, there have been two previous attempts to blow it up, but it came off only the third time round. It has transpired that not one year there passed without some emergency or other. The design faults of the RBMK reactor were also known, but neither the ministries nor the Academy of Sciences drew the proper conclusions. The task group believes that the RBMK nuclear power plants where most of the construction work has been done should be completed, and that's that—no more plants with this reactor to be built.

Such was the unequivocal judgment of experts, participants in the top secret session of the Politburo session on RBMK reactor safety.

Dozens of commissions, scientists, and academicians submitted proof of its dangerous nature, and conclusions were duly drawn—only they were the very opposite of what you would expect. Within a year of the Chernobyl disaster, two more power units with RBMK reactors were put into operation. To quote the offhanded quip of Chernomyrdin's, "They meant well, but it worked out as usual." Judging by the Politburo session minutes, Mikhail Gorbachev, a lawyer by training and secretary general of the Central Committee, proved the most exacting expert on all our reactors. For the first time in all the years of my Chernobyl investigation, I got hold of a document that revealed the inner workings of all of our reactor types, including the "good" VVER reactor. We would never have learned a thing about this but for the August 1991 events. Indeed, even the most elderly members of the Politburo, Gromyko and Solomentsev, announced indignantly at the session that they had never before heard this kind of revelation about Soviet reactor building.

GORBACHEV: How many times did you at the atomic energy supervision committee take up the issue of that reactor [RBMK]?

KULOV: In the three years of my work there the matter was never discussed from this angle. We mostly concentrated on the VVER-1000 type. Their units are less manageable. Not a year passed but some accident happened at a VVER unit [That's a confession to beat all confessions! And it comes from a nuclear supervisor, to boot. Never before or since have I heard anything like that from a person of that caliber].

GORBACHEV: What do you say to Sidorenko's allegations that the world has no experience of using RBMK-type reactors, that our VVER and RBMK reactors are not up to international standards, and that if we are to allow international inspection, it will be better to settle for the VVER than the RBMK type?

KULOV: The VVER reactor does have certain advantages, but its operation is not risk-free.

GORBACHEV: So you are telling me that the VVER units, too, ought to be shut down? Why didn't you report that VVER reactors should not be built?

KULOV: The VVER reactors are better than the RBMK kind, but the VVER-1000 series is inferior to those installed at the first units.

LIGACHEV: And why is that?

KULOV: The designs are wrong.

DOLGIKH: Was the VVER-1000 designed in accordance with modern standards?

KULOV: Yes, but the VVER-1000 units under construction are worse than the old ones. [If the VVER-1000 reactors under construction are "worse than the old ones," why build them at all?]

MAYORETS: The VVER-1000 is a new reactor. It is up to the latest security standards, but it is unreliable in operation because the measuring devices tend to fail. Which reactor would you prefer?

The man who asked that question was Politburo member Nikolai Slyunkov, and he was addressing deputy minister for energy and electrification, G. Shasharin. Shasharin meekly replied, "VVER."

Even today, years after the Chernobyl disaster, precious little has changed in the nuclear power engineering of the newly independent states that used to be the Soviet Union's republics. They still use the same old RBMK and VVER reactors. The Ignalina Nuclear Power Plant is again in operation, complete with RBMK units, just a few years after the Baltic patriots got the hated Moscow regime to shut it down. Armenia's president, Ter-Petrosyan, asked Russian nuclear scientists to help put in operation, as soon as possible, the nuclear power plant, mothballed in the wake of the devastating Spitak earthquake, even though the plant is sitting right on top of a seismic fault line. Power shortages soon made Armenians forget that. So the power plant was back in operation. In late 1992, units 1 and 2 were again brought into service. In 2000, the plant was finally closed down for good—under Western pressure. But there were new reactors put into operation at other nuclear power plants. Ex-chairman of the Belorussian Supreme Soviet, Stanislav Shushkevich, talked about the need to build two nuclear power plants in Belarus. Kazakhstan, too, is thinking of building a nuclear power plant. Almost twenty years after the Chernobyl disaster, Ukraine is planning the construction of eleven nuclear power units by 2030. The reason is, people in Ukraine's "Orange" cabinet explain, that the old units will have reached the end of their service life by 2011. Ukraine does not rule out that the old VVER-440 and VVER-1000 reactors will have to go on working even after that deadline—the very same reactors whose closure Politburo members and experts discussed at the secret session after the Chernobyl disaster. Construction of the first two units is planned at the Khmelnitsky Nuclear Power Plant.

The nuclear phoenix is slowly but surely rising from the Chernobyl ashes. Yegor Gaidar, then head of government, issued an order to renew construction of nuclear power plants in the country way back on March 26, 1992, without independent estimates of their potential problems and without explaining to the public the need for this decision. This, despite the fact that the National Academy of Sciences had recommended the closure of most of Russia's nuclear power plants on the eve of Boris Yeltsin's trip to the United States. Of course, the officials knew these plants failed to comply with international safety standards. Among the blacklisted plants were the Leningrad, Bilibino, Kursk, Beloyarsk, and Smolensk nuclear power plants, plus two units each at the Kola and the New Voronezh plants. Scientists recommended those dangerous reactors to be taken out of service within ten years. Scientists of the Russian Academy concluded that only two out of Russia's nine nuclear power plants were up to security requirements.

Gaidar's orders were the first step in the nuclear lobby redoubling its efforts to resuscitate the industry that had effectively blown up in the radioactive Chernobyl dust storm. On December 28, 1991, the Russian government issued a decree on nuclear power plant construction in the Russian Federation. It planned to put thirty-three new units in operation at nuclear power plants and district heating nuclear plants. Nineteen of them were to be located in the central, northwestern, and black-earth parts of the country. These are densely populated areas with gas and oil pipelines going to the Commonwealth of Independent States and Baltic and European countries. Among the reactors proposed for the new units are the good old RBMKs.

The paper on the concept of nuclear power engineering development in the Russian Federation, approved by the RF Atomic Energy Ministry board on July 14, 1992, gives a good deal of space to nuclear power plant safety that should be "improved to the extent where the possibility of a serious accident involving release of fission products into the environment would be ruled out." The reference is both to the existing plants and to their new generations. But is it at all possible to achieve maximum security levels with these reactor types? Many people still remember the tragic death of academician Valery Legasov, who was in charge of the clean-up operation at the Chernobyl Nuclear Power Plant and then took his life on the second anniversary of the accident.

At that secret session of the Politburo, Legasov told Gorbachev the following:

> The RBMK reactor is not up to international and domestic standards in several respects. It has no protection system, no dosimetric

system, and no external dome. It is our fault, of course. We should have been keeping an eye on the reactor. Both of the leading scientists in this section, those who dealt with that reactor's physics, have died. As a result the physics issues were somewhat neglected. We were aware of the section's inadequacy. This is partly my fault. This refers to the first VVER units as well. Fourteen of them are not up to the modern international and domestic security standards either.

This confession by a serious scholar, internationally respected and appreciated, is worth a great deal. Two years later, shortly before his death, Legasov was even more explicit in an interview for the documentary, *The Star Wormwood*. Here is what he stated:

> Since I have mentioned the reactor, I might as well make a clean breast of it. Very few of us have been frank and accurate when discussing the matter. Any approach to nuclear safety provision is threefold: first, make the item itself, say, the nuclear reactor in our case, as safe as is humanly possible; second, provide that item's operation with cast-iron reliability, but since 100 percent reliability is impossible, the safety philosophy requires introduction of the third component, which assumes that an accident will happen, sooner or later, and radioactive or some chemical substances will escape beyond the apparatus limits. So in view of this contingency the dangerous item has to be placed within a casing, the so-called containment dome. Well, in Soviet power engineering, to my mind, the third component was criminally neglected. If there had been a philosophy that treated the containment as a necessary element for any nuclear reactor, the RBMK could never have appeared as an apparatus [a working technology], if only because of its geometry. The fact that it did, in terms of international and just simply normal safety standards, was illicit; moreover, there were three major design flaws in its inner structure. But the main problem is violation of the basic safety insurance principle for such apparatuses (technologies)—they must be placed within the kind of capsule that would greatly reduce the chance of radioactivity spreading beyond the plant limits, beyond the apparatus itself.

At this point it seems appropriate to recall that, as Legasov, Izrael, and other scientists said, the world's greatest accident was not the Chernobyl blast. The world's biggest nuclear accident had happened before Chernobyl, in 1979, at the Three Mile Island Nuclear Power Plant in the United States. But over there the reactor was inside the protective dome. The shell cracked, but very little radiation escaped outside. Since then not a single new nuclear power plant has been built in the United States, with or without a secure dome. True, in recent years the nuclear lobby even in that country has been making headway in its attempts to convince the government that new plants are vital to the country. But since all U.S. nuclear power plants are privately owned, and return on investment is always a big problem, those private corporations are trying to force the government to fork over additional funding. (They prefer not to risk their own money!) So far the public has successfully resisted the prospect of this extra burden. After all, this is taxpayers' money, and over there that is an extremely sensitive issue. The Gaidar-inspired report of nuclear power engineering in the Russian Federation points out that by July 1, 1992, immediately after the collapse of the Soviet Union, Russia had in operation "28 industrial power units at nine nuclear power plants, including 12 units with VVER shell-type water-cooled and water-moderated reactors, 15 units with carbon-uranium channel reactors (11 RBMK-1000 units and four EGP units), plus one unit with a fast neutron reactor." It was this report, then, that Legasov referred to when he said, "We must think about some special measures to ensure accident localization with those 28 apparatuses (reactors), as it is economically and technically impossible to build domes over them." That is to say, no matter what scientists might do, whatever safety measures they might take (and quite a lot has indeed been done to render the RBMK reactor safer in the wake of the Chernobyl accident), the root cause of danger at currently working nuclear power units in Russia cannot be eliminated. This is the tragedy of nuclear power engineering in this country—from the start Soviet academicians imposed the wrong course of future development on it (which the frightened academician, Alexandrov, admitted at the secret Politburo powwow). This is a problem that "Soviet society above all should start considering, because this is our problem," Legasov said shortly before his death. He had admitted, at the top secret Politburo session in the summer of 1986, that "the RBMK weak points have been known for 15 years."

But there are people who have a different opinion on the matter. At the same Politburo session academician Alexandrov let drop, "The dome would have merely exacerbated the accident." Other scientists believe that "no one can be sure of that." So, on the one hand, a protective dome over the RBMK reactor is a technical impossibility, but on the other, even if it had been installed, it would have merely exacerbated the accident. Yet one five-year period after another, it was those dangerous power units that were persistently forced on our economy by academicians who were close to the country's rulers. Here we are, years after the demise of the Politburo and the Communist Party Central Committee. There are conclusive reports by dozens of competent commissions and expert groups on the causes of the Chernobyl explosion. There are built-in features of the reactor itself that caused the accident.

We have the reliable diagnosis made in 1990 by the Gospromatomnadzor Commission headed by prominent scientist N. Steinberg: "The faulty design of the RBMK-1000 reactor that was in operation at unit 4 of the Chernobyl nuclear power plant predetermined the grave consequences of the accident." Yet there is no evidence of any change in the approach to the matter, although people's lives are at stake. Indeed, where would it come from if the "Politburo" has not even moved to different premises? Their names and faces are known to all, and not just in Russia, either. First they lied to us about the causes and effects of the Chernobyl accident and took decisions about housing construction for evacuees in contaminated areas; then, with the full knowledge of the real causes of the accident, they shifted the blame onto the plant's personnel; and now they are again at the helm. Availing themselves of the fact that the general public is largely uninformed, they devise irresponsible plans of "nuclearizing" poor Russia with inherently dangerous reactors that cannot be rendered safe.

Following President Yeltsin's order no. 952 of June 17, 1997, the government of Sergei Kirienko (the one who declared the country a defaulter in August 1998), by its resolution no. 815 of July 21, 1998, approves the program for nuclear energy development in the Russian Federation for 1998–2000 and until 2010. Has anything changed? There is nothing new, apart from an aggressively bold plan by the nuke advocates and lobbyists who have now perked up, roused from their post-Chernobyl state of suspended animation. "By the end of 1997," the program remarks, "the Russian Federation had 29 power units in operation at nine nuclear power plants. Among them 13 units with VVER-type reactors (six units with VVER-440 reactors, and seven units with VVER-1000 reactors), 11 power units with RBMK reactors (. . .)." Yes, that's right. The same fundamentally flawed reactors that the Kremlin elders were thinking of shutting down after Chernobyl.

Now comes something new. "Analysis of the state of the power units' primary equipment, including the reactor sets, shows that it is possible in principle to extend their service life by at least 5 to 10 years." What is this all about? What about our old friends, the RBMK reactors, the world's worst botch job, as even their creators had to

281

admit. The service life has already been extended for the Leningrad Nuclear Power Plant. Four decrepit reactors of the Chernobyl type have been working there since 1973. The same is true of the Kursk Nuclear Power Plant. Their operating life is already over, or will soon be, but instead of finally discarding that nuclear junk, they spruce it up and slip papers about service life extension to President Putin for signing. That's the old new program for you. The nuke mobsters also intend to "complete the de-mothballed construction of power unit 3 at the Kalinin nuclear power plant, power unit 5 at the Kursk nuclear power plant, power units 1 and 2 at the Rostov plant and Voronezh heating nuclear plant, as well as continue the construction of the South Urals nuclear power plant with the BN-800 reactor." They are becoming greedier and greedier. Already they are planning "to complete the second phase construction at the Kalinin nuclear power plant, and the third phase of construction at the Kursk and the Rostov plants." Also in the pipeline is "the construction of new-generation nuclear power plants" modeled on old patterns: the New Voronezh and the Kola nuclear power plant-2, the main power unit in the town of Sosnovy Bor (near St. Petersburg). Everywhere you see the same Soviet VVER reactors of varying capacity, so fiercely attacked by experts at the highest level.

In Soviet times the Politburo worked out a plan for preventive counterpropaganda actions every year on the eve of the Chernobyl anniversary. The first time it was Comrade Falin who offered his services with particular zeal—the man who, in 1987, headed the KGB-dominated Novosti Press Agency; he feared "possible attempts by imperialist subversion centers at using the Chernobyl accident anniversary to mount yet another large-scale anti-Soviet campaign" (appendix to the Central Committee secretariat top secret minutes no. 42, dated February 26, 1987). At present, Falin has taken refuge in one such "subversion center" in Germany and modestly passes himself off as an historian. The "plan" was amended by Yegor Ligachev, the most odious character on the Politburo.

The planned pack of lies was passed unanimously, as usual, on April 10, 1987, at the Central Committee secretariat.

Top secret minutes no. 46: "Vote taken—Comrades Gorbachev, in favor; Aliev, in favor; Vorotnikov, in favor; Gromyko, in favor; Ligachev, in favor; Ryzhkov, in favor; Solomentsev, in favor; Chebrikov, in favor; Shevardnadze, in favor; Shcherbitsky, in favor." The ayes always had it without any opposition—proof that the well-oiled party machinery still turned the wheel, no matter that at their secret gatherings they frankly referred to the Chernobyl meltdown consequences as "minor-war effects" (A. Gromyko), comparable to "the use of weapons of mass destruction" (M. Gorbachev, S. Sokolov). But that knowledge was strictly for the high priests. As for the hoi polloi, they were assured that "there is no threat to the people's health," and they "re-evacuated pregnant women and children" to "black" radiation-affected areas, those heavily contaminated regions the "experts" had already identified.

Does a nuclear power development program of the Russian Federation for 1998–2010 and later look like a kind of "preemptive counter-propaganda plan shares"? And if so, then life on earth with a reactor is only possible when there is a "dome" on each person.

If this is living.

It isn't just Russian scientists, though, that are the culprits. Eminent biochemist Erwin Chargaff (Chargaff's rules) places the issue in a more expansive perspective in a May 21, 1987, commentary in *Nature:*

> Science was the never-ending search for truth about nature, a quest that would help us understand the workings of the world. That era ended with the splitting of the atomic nucleus, with the ability to modify the hereditary apparatus. A new era has begun: science is now the craft of manipulation, modification, substitution and deflection of the forces of nature. . . . What I see coming is a gigantic slaughterhouse, a molecular Auschwitz [genetic engineering] in which valuable enzymes will be extracted instead of gold teeth.

The corporate juggernaut rolls on—worldwide.

19

Guilt Established—But
No Trials

From time to time we, the people's deputies, acted as the proverbial pike that was in the lake, expressly to keep the carp awake. Both
individually and in groups, we doggedly wrote countless letters to the
prosecutor general's office to demand that they launch proceedings
against officials who had concealed information about the Chernobyl
disaster and its effects for the people left in danger zones. In this connection, it would be interesting to follow the changes in what might
tentatively be called the consciousness of the gentlemen at the top of
that supreme oversight agency.

In December 1989, I received yet another reply from V. I. Andreev,
deputy USSR prosecutor general. It was the same old pro forma
response, the same veneer of decency intended to conceal massive
deception at the state level. Not a word about government resolutions
ordering secrecy, not a word about other similar departmental instructions, or not a word about millions of people exposed to excessive
radiation doses as a result. Total silence about uncontrolled circulation
of radioactive foodstuffs all over the country—as though nothing of
that sort had ever happened. I read the public prosecutor's reply with
a feeling of bitterness and despair. Could that big wall of lies ever be
breached? (That reminded me of a maxim by Stanislaw Jerzy Lec: "If
you breach a wall, you may get into the next cell.")

As if in apology, Andreev wrote this in a paragraph of his letter.
"The USSR Constitution (Article 164) does not authorize the USSR
Prosecutor General's Office to oversee the lawfulness of the actions
of the USSR Council of Ministers and commissions instituted by it."
(Incidentally, Ukraine's public prosecutor, M. A. Potebenko, told me
exactly the same thing, albeit in connection with a different matter,
citing, instead of the Soviet Constitution, the USSR Law on the Public
Prosecutor's Office.) Refusing to believe my eyes, I looked through

both these laws. Correct. It is exactly as the prosecutors had written. This meant that the government could do as it pleased, issuing unlawful orders, acts, and resolutions, while the prosecutor's office, strictly in accordance with the law, wouldn't dare interfere. How smart is that? Positively brilliant!

When N. S. Trubin's appointment as the new prosecutor general was discussed at the Fourth Congress of the USSR People's Deputies, I publicly confronted him with a question about this. Trubin also said that things were indeed as stated here. But the republic's Supreme Soviet, or else the republic's committee for constitutional adjudication, he went on, could overturn a decision of council of ministers. It had the right to declare a decision of council of ministers unconstitutional. It was a trifle embarrassing to remind the experienced jurist aspiring to the post of the country's prosecutor general that the republics had never had any committees for constitutional adjudication and that there weren't any even at the Union level. How many times had the USSR Supreme Soviet or the supreme soviets of the fifteen republics overturned unlawful decisions and decrees by their governments on the grounds that those decrees went against the law? Nothing of the sort was remotely possible in a totalitarian state, nor could be. Or was this contender for the prosecutor's gown unaware of that?

Besides, overturning a decision is one thing. But did the USSR Supreme Soviet or its republic-level counterparts have the right to go further? For instance, could they initiate criminal proceeding with regard to a fact like that? Certainly not. Nor did the USSR committee for constitutional adjudication, a body formed for the first time under the pressure of the Gorbachev-era people's deputies, have that prerogative. In short, it was extremely convenient for someone that the USSR public prosecutor general's office could neither launch certain proceedings nor cancel them. And it was doubly convenient that this situation was enshrined in the country's constitution rather than some regulations or legislation. Wasn't that why the USSR public prosecutor general's office, for nearly five years after the accident, did not have the guts to make the mildest of protests against the Chernobyl hush-up by the USSR government and Communist Party Politburo?

In his classic brush-off of a reply, deputy prosecutor general V. I. Andreev told the people's deputies about the small-fry scapegoats. Something we had known, read, and heard, ad infinitum. Official propaganda had done a sterling job there.

The consequences were exacerbated by the fact that in the first hours after the accident its actual scale and nature were not disclosed. Nuclear power plant director Bryukhanov deliberately concealed the resulting high radiation levels and failed to put into effect the planned measures to protect the personnel and the public. The persons held criminally liable in this case were director of the Chernobyl nuclear power plant V. P. Bryukhanov, chief engineer N. M. Fomin, deputy chief engineer for the nuclear power plant 2nd phase operation A.S. Dyatlov, reactor room head A.P. Kovalenko, power plant shift manager B.V. Rogozhin, and Gosatomenergonadzor state inspector S. A. Laushkin. The Supreme Court sentenced all of them to various terms of imprisonment, and Bryukhanov, Fomin and Dyatlov—to maximum penalty for the said crime, 10 years in prison each.

And at the very bottom of the page, a modest few lines on the proper subject matter of our inquiry, in which deputy prosecutor general V. I. Andreev mentioned merely "instances of irresponsibility, mismanagement and dereliction of duty on the part of some officials in Soviet, economic and supervisory agencies, and medical institutions." While on the whole, one must assume, things were shipshape. Not a word concerning reactor design.

That was three and a half years after Chernobyl.

Within the next eighteen months, the prosecutor's confident style underwent a dramatic change. The scratchy record had developed cracks. The selfsame Andreev reported (this time to the parliamentary commission for investigating the causes of the Chernobyl accident and assessing the actions of officials in the postaccident period) that "as instructed by the 28th CPSU Congress, and in connection with discussions at the USSR, Belorussian, Ukrainian and Russian Federation Supreme Soviet sessions, the USSR prosecutor general's office organized an additional check of the observance of laws in eliminating the consequences of the Chernobyl accident." It was heartwarming, of course, that at least five years too late, "an additional check" was organized, and therefore an additional "conclusion was made"—"taking into account the social tensions." This speech plainly shows what great awe the deputy prosecutor general felt for the party-governing body. His supervisory work is guided first and foremost by "instructions from the Twenty-eighth CPSU Congress," while the highest legislative organs, the parliaments of the country and its three largest republics, rank distinctly second. One has to conclude that the party was way above the legislative authority in the eyes of the deputy prosecutor general. As long as prosecutors, both general and rank-and-file, were included in the party *nomenklatura* set, a law-governed state remained a pipe dream. That was absolutely clear.

Despite its ritual kowtowing to the Communist Party's Twenty-eighth Congress, the public prosecutor general had obviously made considerable headway in revising the Chernobyl situation. In fact, it was a proper guilty verdict both for the individuals involved and for the system as a whole.

> The USSR ministry for atomic power industry, owing to its failure to carry out appropriate measures under the standard plan of actions for protecting the staff and the public in the event of accidents at nuclear power plants, from the very start of the emergency did not conduct adequate radiation surveying and control at the plant and in the surrounding areas, did not forecast a potential radioactivity situation, and did not work out proposals for taking measures to protect the nuclear power plant personnel and the population of the town of Pripyat and other areas. As a result, the population of the areas around the nuclear power plant was not protected against exposure. The evacuation of the people in the towns of Pripyat and Chernobyl was not carried out in time, resulting in unjustified health injury from radiation. From the first days of the accident, and subsequently, the population of contaminated areas was not informed about the actual radiation situation. Resolution No. 423 of September 24, 1987, adopted by the governmental commission that ordered classifying information about various aspects of the nuclear accident and the elimination of its consequences that was banned from publication in the media, was not conducive to organizing all the necessary work on ensuring radiation protection for the public, and robbed people of the chance to take their own measures against ionizing radiation. These circumstances entailed considerable over-exposure of the population in certain areas in the Ukrainian Soviet Socialist Republic, the Belorussian Soviet Socialist Republic, and the Russian Soviet Federal Socialist Republic in the period from 1986 to 1989. Despite the considerably increased gamma radiation background, the USSR council of ministers, and those of the Ukraine and Belorussia ignored information about the radiation situation and failed to call off numerous May Day civil parades on May 1, 1986 (in the city of Kiev and other cities and localities in the Ukraine and Belorussia).

It's worth quoting the concluding section of the verdict:

> Measures were not taken on time to resettle the inhabitants of towns and villages where the radiation situation presented a health hazard.

Thus, the USSR council of ministers delayed till May 24, 1989 ordering resettlement in 1989–1993 of people from certain localities in the Bryansk, Kiev, Zhitomir, Mogilev and Gomel regions with a population total of about 20,000, so that the people were exposed to dangerous radiation levels over a long period of time. The RSFSR council of ministers, almost four years after the event, as late as January 26, 1990, passed a resolution on partially restricted consumption of milk and, if necessary, other locally produced foodstuffs in more than 500 inhabited localities of the Bryansk and Kaluga regions. The USSR council of ministers and its counterparts in the Ukraine and Belorussia took decisions to build housing on contaminated territories in towns and villages rendered unfit for human habitation by high radiation levels. Owing to these actions, the state incurred losses of about 600 million rubles.

All these circumstances put about 75 million people [remember this terrible figure!] in hazardous living conditions (in the Ukraine, Belorussia and central parts of the Russian Federation), and created conditions for increased rates of mortality, cancers, malformations, hereditary and bodily diseases, and changes in the people's capacity for work. The USSR ministry of health, in contravention of the Instructions for the use of stable iodine to protect the human thyroid gland against radioactive iodine isotopes, delayed preventively administering iodine to the population in areas adjoining the nuclear power plant and other territories of the country contaminated with radioactive iodine, which resulted in over-exposure to iodine-131. The 1.5 million people (including 160,000 children under seven years of age) resident in the areas with the highest level of iodine-131 contamination at the time of the accident, received thyroid irradiation doses of 30 rem (87 percent of adults, 48 percent of children), between 30 and 100 rem (11 and 35 percent, respectively), and over 100 rem (2 percent of adults, 17 percent of children).

This was a no-nonsense warning to V. A. Kavun, first secretary of the Zhitomir Communist Party Central Committee, and to other party bosses in Kiev and Moscow. His verdict confirmed what I had written but could not get published for almost three years. And it was this cover-up that was the reason why party officials had relentlessly hounded me. Such was the public prosecutor's response to the cynical seventy-page report by the "collective Ilyin" (signed by a group of people whom I cannot bring myself to call scientists) that was issued on the eve of the accident's third anniversary, assuring us it was the timely iodine prophylaxis that had saved many people's lives. The letter by the deputy prosecutor general also pointed out the blunders committed by the USSR committee for agriculture and the civil defense committee and their complicity in the overexposure and "migration" of radionuclides all over the country. Finally, into the fifth year since the accident, the USSR prosecutor general's office initiated criminal proceedings "in connection with new facts calling for investigation that emerged in the course of inspection."

The list of "facts" contains a great many names of organizations and departments responsible for the tragedy. Only two were conspicuous by their absence—the politburo of the Communist Party Central Committee, whose Chernobyl task group had been in session every other day, and the supervisory agency—the prosecutor general's office itself and its subsidiaries down the administrative line, the ones who were supposed to look after and protect the people's rights. Could anything like that happen anywhere else in the world? Three great Slav nations slowly exterminated over five years, in secrecy, with the knowledge and connivance of the government, while public prosecutors' offices, one on the Union level, three republic-level ones, and their countless subordinates just kept mum! All of these public prosecutors were members of central, regional, and district Communist Party committee bureaus that preached the so-called moral code of the builder of communism—while clinging onto their cushy jobs and that ID of the privileged Soviet caste, the party membership card.

Having received so encouraging a reply from the prosecutor general's office, I instantly sent a people's deputy's inquiry to our local prosecutor, A. G. Dzyuba. For who could be better informed of the goings-on in his domain? I requested to know whether "the regional prosecutor's office had started criminal proceedings in connection with the region's leadership in concealing from the public the consequences of the 1986 Chernobyl explosion." The reply came from his deputy, A. F. Batursky. It literally knocked the wind out of me. His response was "The prosecutor's office cannot launch proceedings in connection with a crime entailing liability for concealment or distortion of information about the environmental situation or population morbidity as a result of the Chernobyl nuclear power plant explosion because there is no such article. Article 227-1 of the Penal Code of the Ukraine that provides for this kind of liability was enforced by the Ukrainian Supreme Soviet decree dated January 19, 1990."

In short, Chernobyl was, is, and will be with us for hundreds of thousands of years to come because some radionuclides have such long half-life periods, but there is no proper article in the penal code. There will be no trial. Note that this reply, if that is the word, came after the USSR public prosecutor's office managed to discover a suitable article in the country's penal code after all and initiated criminal proceedings in connection with the post-Chernobyl spate of lies by those responsible for the death of thousands and the health deficit of millions of people. The provincial cynicism of our public prosecutors is truly boundless!

I refused to give up. I had almost three hundred thousand voters to back me. So I wrote another letter to regional prosecutor A. G. Dzyuba, enclosing his subordinate's reply. I had to inform him that "criminal proceedings on those issues (responsibility for concealing and distorting information about the consequences of the Chernobyl explosion) had been initiated by the USSR prosecutor general's office and regional prosecutor's offices in some contaminated areas in other republics." Therefore, I asked to be told why the relevant articles were found by those offices while you still cannot think of one. "What is the reason for that? Can it be that USSR laws do not apply to former leaders of the region who, armed with both maps and data [on contamination levels and diseases], deceived the public?" In short, I cornered the man. Dzyuba sent me a letter that read, "Comrade A. V. Slivinsky, senior prosecutor of the Zhitomir region public prosecutor's office, is a member of the investigative team of the USSR prosecutor general's office conducting an inquiry into the consequences of the Chernobyl accident. He has instructions to investigate the consequences of the accident on the territory of our region. Based on the investigation results, a decision will be taken in accordance with the law." Well, I am so glad to have helped the local prosecutors find the right article in their own handbook, the penal code.

To consolidate my victory, I also sent a people's deputy's inquiry to Ukraine's public prosecutor, M. A. Potebenko. In the summer of 1991, he wrote thus:

> It has been established that the USSR health ministry, the state hydrometeorology committee, and the state atomic industry monitoring committee exercised monopoly control over information about the radiation situation, and in some cases the information was not objective, which caused grave consequences. Thus, despite the sharp increase in the radiation level in Kiev and some districts of the Kiev region, May Day civil parades and festivities went ahead as usual. At the aforementioned departments' suggestion new housing and community facilities were built in the localities of the Polesskoe district of the Kiev region and in the Narodichi district of the Zhitomir region, whose inhabitants were liable for mandatory resettlement. The losses amount to 53 million rubles. Also built on land contaminated with

radionuclides were the towns of Slavutich and Zeleny Mys, with 23,000 inhabitants. The decision to construct these facilities had been taken by the USSR governmental commission.

Given that investigation has found officials in Union ministries and departments responsible for these and other wrongdoings, the republic's public prosecutor's office suggested to the USSR prosecutor general that proceedings be initiated in connection with abuse and dereliction of duty committed in the course of elimination of the consequences of the accident. The relevant action has been launched, and the USSR public prosecutor general's office is conducting an inquiry into the case.

Note how deftly Ukraine's prosecutor, M. A. Potebenko, shifts the blame onto Moscow officials, whitewashing his own. Not a word about any of the Ukrainian republic's authorities, including the health ministry, withholding vital information! Certainly not a word about the responsibility of the Politburo of the Communist Party Central Committee. So it was only to be expected that the regional prosecutor and his deputy should try to weasel out of giving a proper reply to my inquiries. One feels nothing but outrage and revulsion at the tactics of those legal beagles.

Today, twenty years after the Chernobyl disaster, ex-prosecutor of the republic, Potebenko, Mr. Fixit for the Shcherbitsky Communist regime in Ukraine, has become useful again, in the newly independent state of Ukraine. He is now a member of parliament, that is to say, a lawmaker, and he has the power to choose whom to bring to book and whom to spare under those laws. In the fall of 1991, our commission for investigating officials' activities after the Chernobyl nuclear power plant accident, after a year of hard work, was planning to start hearing in parliament the evidence of every official involved in Chernobyl-related crimes. The list of names filled several pages of typescript. Among others, it contained Ukraine's top bosses—V. V. Shcherbitsky, Ukrainian Central Committee first secretary; V. S. Shevchenko, chairperson of Ukraine's Supreme Soviet; health minister A. Ye. Romanenko; and heads of other departments and organizations. The Zhitomir region was represented by Vasily Kavun, first secretary of the Communist Party regional committee; V. M. Yamchinsky, chairman of the regional executive committee; chairman of the regional emergency commission A. G. Gotovchits; and member of the Party regional Committee bureau and editor of the *Radyanska Zhitomirshchina* newspaper D. A. Panchuk. The newspaper was the chief tool of misinformation and criminal cover-up to prevent the truth about Chernobyl from spreading to radiation-affected areas. Neither the republic's public prosecutor, Potebenko, nor his regional counterpart, Dzyuba, was of help in the end.

Parliamentary evidentiary hearings drafted conclusions that were to be sent to the prosecutor general's office and on to court. That was a highly novel and unorthodox democratic act hitherto unknown in the land of Soviets. Five years after the Chernobyl disaster, proper punishment was finally about to catch up with the shameless party and Soviet bosses, avenging the sorrows and suffering of seventy-five million people trapped under Chernobyl's radioactive pall. Deputy prosecutor general, V. I. Andreev, informed the people's deputies of the fact.

But at that very moment, a dramatic event threw a clinker into the works. The August 1991 coup literally saved those evildoers and other, even more highly placed persons, from inevitable punishment. The Soviet Union collapsed, and the subject of officials' criminal liability for Chernobyl melted away with it. The fledgling independent states apparently had other things to worry about. Now they were on their own, without instructions from the Kremlin. Besides, we already knew the views of Ukraine's prosecutor Potebenko. He preferred to lay the blame exclusively on the Union departments based in Moscow, not on the local authorities. And yet Chernobyl triumphed over Ukraine's prosecutor general's office in the end.

It took seven years to finally identify those guilty of concealing the truth about the consequences of the Chernobyl accident, as related to Ukraine. For that to happen, Ukraine had to proclaim itself as an independent state and ban the Communist Party that had left its own people to die a slow death in radiation-affected areas. Otherwise, I am sure we would never have heard high-ranking Communist bosses officially accused of hushing up the truth about Chernobyl—Vladimir Shcherbitsky, former member of the Politburo of the Communist Party Central Committee and first secretary of the Ukrainian Communist Party (found guilty posthumously); Valentina Shevchenko, ex-Ukrainian Politburo member and chairperson of the Ukrainian Supreme Soviet presidium; Alexander Lyashko, ex-chairman of the Ukrainian Council of Ministers, the republic's civil defense commander, head of the Ukrainian Politburo task group for eliminating the consequences of the accident, and Politburo member; and also Ukrainian health minister Anatoly Romanenko. However, this truth came as an eye-opener seven years after the nuclear disaster to no one except perhaps the Ukrainian prosecutor general's office itself. The ordinary folks had long since known the names of the liars-in-chief.

On the desk in front of me are the conclusions by public prosecutor general's office of Ukraine based on the materials of "Chernobyl case" no. 49-441. These are the things the ex-leaders of the republic covered up for seven years, and here is the chronicle of their criminal lying. Early in the morning of April 26, 1986, Shcherbitsky, Shevchenko, and Lyashko received reliable information about what had really happened at the Chernobyl nuclear power plant from a variety of sources, including the nuclear power plant management, the Kiev regional party committee, the regional executive committee, civil defense operations centers, Ukrainian Communist Party Central Committee, the Council of Ministers, the health ministry, and Ukraine's hydrometeorology committee. Yet their concern was not about people's safety. The same day, Lyashko informed the USSR Council of Ministers that radiation levels were going down, and the situation was calm at the plant and in the town of Pripyat. This shows how much they cared about the people or, better yet, how they panicked at the prospect of being deprived of access to the money bin.

On April 28, 1986, the Ukrainian hydrometeorology committee's report on the radioactive contamination in Ukraine hit the desks of Shcherbitsky, Shevchenko, and Lyashko. It said that the Chernobyl and Polesskoe districts of the Kiev region registered radiation backgrounds between 80–120 and 800–1,200 μR/h; in the Ovruch District of the Zhitomir region, it was 1,000–2,000 μR/h; in the villages of Semenovka and Shchors of the Chernigov region, it was about 1,000 μR/h. And in the vicinity of the Chernobyl nuclear power plant, all of 500,000 μR/h. But even these horrendous figures did nothing to alter the policy of the criminal Communist Party trio. They didn't do a thing to save the people, or at least the children and pregnant women.

On April 30, 1986, Ukrainian deputy health minister, A. Kasyanenko, reported to the republic's council of ministers that in Kiev the gamma radiation background had shot up to 1,100–3,000 μR/h—in the Dneprovsky and Podolsky districts, and in the city center—while soil samples from the Polesskoe, Chernobyl, and Ivankovo districts of the Kiev region registered contamination levels touching 20,000 μR/h (this is nearly 17,004 times the normal background). Upward of tenfold increases in gamma radiation backgrounds were also recorded in the Zhitomir, Lvov, Rovno, Kirovograd, and Cherkasy regions. The deputy minister, sending those secret data to the leadership of the republic's council of ministers, suggested notifying the public of radiation danger. Instead, Lyashko sent to the republic's television and radio outlets a false statement by the Ukrainian Council of Ministers approved by the Ukrainian Communist Party Central Committee. It assured the population that the radiation situation around the nuclear power plant and in the nearby villages had improved, and the radiation background in Kiev presented no hazard.

On April 30, 1986, Ukrainian Council of Ministers formed a task group for collecting information about Chernobyl as it came in from Ukraine's hydrometeorology committee, the health ministry, the Academy of Sciences, and other organizations. From May 1, 1986, on, a summary of their data was submitted daily to the republic's senior officials. Lyashko got himself a special map where radiation levels all over the republic were entered every day.

According to that data, background radiation in Kiev's various parts from May 1 to May 30, 1986, amounted to 1,500 μR/h. This is 125 times the natural background radiation. Kiev had turned into a lethal x-ray room where the May Day civil parade danced and marched to please the boss's fatherly eyes. As I have written before, the party bosses whisked their own children out of the city at once, out of harm's way. The overall beta activity in the Kiev reservoir that provided drinking water for the entire city was one thousand to five thousand times higher than the natural radioactivity background. Contamination of water reservoirs, wells, and also vegetables and milk was recorded in almost half of Ukraine's regions.

As early as May 6, 1986, the hospitals had admitted 1,560 persons for examination and treatment, according to the Central Committee secret minutes. Of these, 244 were children. Symptoms of radiation sickness were identified in 289 cases. All of that literally screamed of danger and cried out for instant protection for the people. But the nation's fathers were keeping their mouths firmly shut. On April 30, 1986, the USSR health minister, S. Burenkov, sent orders to the Ukrainian Health Ministry concerning provision of medical and sanitary services for the population in connection with the nuclear accident. He obligated the ministry, "in the event of recording excessive radiation contamination, to take urgent measures for protecting the public, particularly the children, against injury from radioiodine above all." If taken at once, stabilizing potassium–iodine tablets are known to reduce the total thyroid damage dose by 96 percent; within six hours, the dose may be halved; and after a delay of 24 hours, the whole thing is practically pointless.

On May 3, 1986, Romanenko, speaking at the meeting of the Ukrainian Politburo task group, recommended abstaining from administering iodine prophylaxis for Kiev residents. On the same day, he issued secret order no. 21-s that demanded "insuring non-disclosure of secret information about the accident."

On May 4, 1986, head of the health protection department at the Kiev City executive committee V. Didychenko sent Romanenko a letter in which he pointed out that, since April 28, his service had been raising the issue of protecting the Kiev residents, especially children, against radioiodine, and earnestly asked the minister for recommendations. The "recommendations" were duly given, the very next day. On May 5, 1986, Romanenko sent a secret letter to Ukraine's Communist Party Central Committee and Council of Ministers to inform them what exactly was to be done to keep the public from overexposure. This was the truth for the patricians at the top. As for the slaves, they were treated to three television addresses, on May 6, 8, and 21, 1986, which coolly misinformed them of the consequences of the accident. Each of the ministers' TV statements was invariably approved by Shcherbitsky, Shevchenko, and Lyashko.

On July 21, 1986, Ukraine's health minister Romanenko reported to the USSR Health Ministry that iodine prophylaxis in the republic had allegedly covered 3,000,427 adults and 676,000 children—in the Kiev, Zhitomir, and Chernigov regions, and in the capital.

On August 15, 1986, another of Romanenko's lies went to the central authority, this time alleging that in the same regions and in Kiev, 4.5 million people, including 1,038,000 children, had received prophylactic iodine treatment.

On December 5, 1986, Romanenko informed Moscow that the republic's entire population had been given prophylactic iodine tablets.

The global catastrophe required global lying and an available list of suspects. Moscow made full use of Ukraine's health minister, naturally, with his consent. Here is a sample of the Romanenko scenario in the appendix to the top-secret Politburo resolution ("On the Plan of Principal Propaganda Measures in Connection with the Anniversary of the Accident at the Chernobyl Nuclear Power Plant," dated April 10, 1987).

From the Main Editing Board for Union Information. (1) Place of birth, Chernobyl. In families evacuated from the dangerous areas

300 children have been born since the accident... no deviations from the norm have been detected; the children are developing normally. Reports from families, kindergartens and crèches. Commentary by the health minister of the Ukrainian Soviet Socialist Republic.

Within just the first four weeks after the accident, Romanenko and his deputy, Zelinsky, issued seven secret orders that they sent to regional public health departments and research centers, demanding that they classify information about the consequences of the accident, abstain from entering exposure doses in case histories, "encode" irradiation levels, and remove accident-related case records to a special archive that should be out of bounds to anyone without a special permit from the leadership of Ukraine's Health Ministry or a higher authority. (And Vakhtang Kipiani, editor of Ukraine's private 1 + 1 television channel, a man who claims to be a democrat, invites that criminal to appear in his programs as a Chernobyl expert!)

Having thus insured that the consequences of the Chernobyl disaster were shrouded in impenetrable secrecy, Romanenko, back in 1989, announced at the May plenary meeting of Ukraine's Communist Party Central Committee: "I can say, as someone who fully feels his responsibility, that apart from those who have fallen ill, of whom there are 209 persons, there are no people today whose ill health can or should be attributed to the effects of radiation." Well, what else could he say after all his previous misdeeds? He was echoed by a chorus of the entire servile party press (national, republic, and local), including the newspapers *Pravda Ukrainy, Radyanska Ukraina,* and *Radyanska Zhitomirshchina,* whose editor, Panchuk, later, when the people's deputies had finally broken the thick wall of Chernobyl lies, set up a Chernobyl Fund under the regional section of the Journalists Union, as though he had done nothing wrong. That lie is already being paid for by the current generations, but it will cost even more to the future ones.

Ukraine's prosecutor general's office paid no attention to the lame excuses by Shevchenko, Lyashko, and Romanenko to the effect that they had been unable to discharge their duties in terms of insuring the people's constitutional right to health protection because the Chernobyl nuclear power plant was exterritorial, and that once the USSR governmental commission and the Central Committee Politburo task group had been formed, decision-making and control over the situation were outside their scope. They had merely "complied with the provisions of Article 6 of the Ukrainian Constitution on the leading role of the party and with the requirements of secrecy laws, and they obeyed orders from state and party entities and departments." The public prosecutor's office stated harshly that they "were concerned about their own well-being and career," and "abused power and their official status, which entailed grave consequences" for the population. The verdict was thus: "the guilt of Shcherbitsky, Lyashko, Shevchenko and Romanenko has been proved." So the truth triumphed after all, and the guilty got their just deserts? Well no, oddly enough, this is precisely what the Ukrainian prosecutor general's office's decision does not suggest. After describing all the criminal offenses of the Ukrainian leadership, after delivering the guilty verdict, investigator of cases of special importance, A. Kuzmak, ruled: "[T]he case of the actions by Ukraine's officials during the accident at the Chernobyl nuclear power plant and elimination of its consequences is to be closed, of which the interested persons shall be informed." This is not a joke. This is the bitter truth. This is a slap in the face of the country and the world.

Ukraine's public prosecutor general's office found a really good reason for letting the guilty off lightly. The statute of limitations period was over! Oh yes, the party *nomenklatura* has always written criminal codes with an eye to its own interests. I do not doubt that the "interested persons" received the news with a feeling of deep satisfaction. Now try and imagine how it must have been received by those fathers and mothers whose children Chernobyl has taken away and continues to do so—or by the people whom Chernobyl has left disabled and left to wallow in their lifelong misery.

This official truth was squeezed out of the prosecutor general's office like toothpaste from a tube, by pressing sharply at both ends. The public pressing at one end, especially the Zeleny Svit ("Green World") movement which, way back in Soviet times, held a public trial and named the culprits and, at the other, the Chernobyl commission of Ukraine's Supreme Court, by its special ruling of December 6, 1991. But was the prosecutor general's office itself incapable of conducting its own investigation without waiting for pressure from the public and instructions from parliament seven years after the event? To all intents and purposes, it was guided by the same laws that Shevchenko, Lyashko, and Romanenko had cited—Article 6 of the Ukrainian Constitution on the party's leading role, and so on. After all, the public prosecutors themselves were members of party bureaus and the Central Committee. Was that not the reason why my deputy's inquiries about the responsibility of officials who had hushed up Chernobyl elicited nothing but meaningless verbiage from Ukraine's prosecutor general's office and its regional counterpart in Zhitomir? The party's minions securely guarded their masters' peace. Meanwhile, in any normal country and in a normal civil society, those prosecutors would themselves be in the dock after placidly looking on as the Chernobyl censors covered up the crimes. This way, one bunch of criminals was tried by another.

After the Soviet Union's collapse, the Communist Party was officially banned in Ukraine. But the has-beens still not continue their efforts to block the work of the prosecutor general's office. As the newspaper, *Kievskie vedomisti* (Kiev Gazette), reported, ex-prosecutor of Ukraine, Mikhail Potebenko, tried to intimidate investigator Alexander Kuzmak in charge of Chernobyl case no. 49-441. He advised the investigator to leave Romanenko out of the proceedings, hinting ominously that times have changed. Kuzmak himself mentioned that fact in his report to independent Ukraine's prosecutor general, V. Shishkin. Actually, I don't see the point of complaining when his resolution had saved them from a certain spell behind bars, thwarting the hopes of millions of people for people to lose faith in the justice system. But I suspect that there is more to it than meets the eye. Possibly, he was indeed intimidated. He may have feared for his family and took the line of least resistance. But at this point I am just guessing.

However, at that time the ex-prosecutor was not the only one to feel suddenly emboldened. Many of those who were, in effect, accomplices to the criminal withholding of information about the consequences of the Chernobyl disaster not only kept their jobs but were also promoted to ministerial ranks. For instance, Georgy Gotovchits, the one-time deputy chairman of the Zhitomir regional executive committee, became minister for the problems of Chernobyl. He was the one who had pressed forward with new housing construction for evacuees in obviously dangerous zones. His appointment took place after the whole country learned those facts from my articles in influential periodicals. And Romanenko's replacement as health minister (after he went to head the radiation center) was Spizhenko—the man who, in 1986, was the head of the public health department at the Zhitomir regional executive committee. He was one of the addressees of Romanenko's secret missives about the right way to dupe the people and as to what precisely should be classified and encoded. There had been no objections to these instructions. It was his childhood and motherhood protection section head, Victor Shatilo, I had come to see in search of truth about the condition of children in the stricken villages. And the answer I got then was all is well. Only later did it emerge that was one big lie.

The same thing happened in Russia. President Boris Yeltsin appointed Vasily Voznyak as head of the state committee for the problems of Chernobyl. His first deputy was Yuri Tsaturov. In 1989, after the First Congress of People's Deputies, the USSR Council of Ministers chairman, Nikolai Ryzhkov, ordered Vladimir Maryin, the then head of the fuel and energy resources bureau at the council of ministers, to reply to my deputy's inquiry about irradiation in the Narodichi District of the Zhitomir region. It was those two, Maryin and Voznyak, the latter then working under the former, who assured me, condescendingly, that all was well in the area where I came from. As they looked at my medical documents brought over from Narodichi, they said, "You have your documents, and we have ours." Yuri Tsaturov, as deputy chairman of the USSR committee on hydrometeorology, also used to send me insincere responses to my inquiries. The fact is six years after the accident it was finally revealed that sixteen regions in Russia were radioactively contaminated. Wasn't that a crime? Millions of unsuspecting Russians were exposed to radiation, and still are, every second.

Why did it have to be precisely these people, in the now independent states aspiring to the title of democracies, that were entrusted with helping the victims of Chernobyl? And which public prosecutor will finally make a statement about the criminal liability of the former leadership of the Communist Party Central Committee and the Soviet government? Despite all those high-sounding statements about "new thinking" and "perestroika," they cooked up a steady diet of lies and distortions, with lots of documents marked SECRET, TOP SECRET, SINGLE COPY, and NOT TO BE PUBLISHED that have already appeared in the press. So what more do the law-enforcement agencies want? Or has the statute of limitations expired—again?

However, some of the has-beens have already found the villain of the piece. "The emergence of glasnost and democracy has greatly exacerbated the already difficult situation," complained an ex-senior agriculture ministry bureaucrat, A. P. Povalyaev, at a seminar for young scientists held by the Academy of Sciences Institute of Nuclear Power Development Safety. (I am quoting from the report about the seminar "Radiation Protection: The Way It Was" published in *Spasenie*, no. 3, 2002.)

Many Ukrainian people's deputies then spoke out against the republic's prosecutor general's decision. The Chernobyl commission drafted a parliamentary resolution on amending the laws so that the Shevchenko, Lyashko, and Romanenko cases could be referred to court. But things are still right where they were then. If those who deceived their own people finally went on trial, it would mean a lot more to Ukraine than sorting out the Chernobyl problem. That would be a trial not only of individuals but also of the system they represented. After all, even in Bulgaria, the people who had tried to conceal the truth about the Chernobyl plume in their country ended up in the dock. They have already served their sentences and have been released. Now others will know better than to follow their act.

They say the blame lies squarely on the system. So it does. But the system is the handiwork of individual people. For many of us, this just trial is important for one more reason. Ukraine's Bolsheviks in parliament, taking their cue from Russia's, raised the issue of lifting the ban on the Communist Party. They had their way—the party has been legalized, and they are once more "fighting for the people's bright future," using their usual tired slogans. The refusal of the prosecutor general's office to refer the case to court of former top party and state leaders has inspirited advocates of Communism. They are already saying there hasn't been any Chernobyl problem. The democrats made it up to bring down the Soviet Union and ban Communism.

Will justice ever triumph and will this devastating truth about Chernobyl be laid bare? And not just in Ukraine either. It may be an impossible dream—to pry open this clamshell of lies. Guilty, but no trials!

20

Cesium, Curies, and Cover-up

The Soviet Union was steadily building up the capacity of its nuclear power plants; it had a stockpile of nuclear weapons, and it conducted numerous nuclear weapons tests, but it had no laws on the use of nuclear energy and/or nuclear safety. Meanwhile, other countries have long since adopted laws to that effect. France did so in 1945 and the United States and the UK in 1946. At present, all developed countries have nuclear legislation. In the Soviet Union, these laws were finally drafted—two years before the Chernobyl accident. Even after the horrendous catastrophe, the draft legislation was skillfully drowned in an ideological quagmire. Thousands of accidents that happened at Soviet nuclear facilities, both military and civilian, year in year out, including some with long-term consequences, as in the 1979 accident at the Leningrad Nuclear Power Plant, resulted in no legal consequences. Besides, all of these accidents were kept hidden under a shroud of secrecy. The Soviets wanted their nukes to be the most reliable in the world, even if it was only on paper!

Small wonder that after "the best of all possible reactors" blew up at the Chernobyl Nuclear Power Plant, neither the state nor the local authorities were prepared for a legal or political solution to environmental, social, and economic problems. The Soviet government did not have an existing legal framework to instantly render assistance to the victims, whether it was the plant personnel or army reservists and liquidators recruited for the cleanup, not to mention the hundreds of thousands who lived downwind. No law, no problem!

During the three-year period after the accident, the Supreme Soviet of the USSR, regardless of its ardently proclaimed glasnost and perestroika, did not even make an attempt to adopt a law that would protect the rights of citizens who suffered in the aftermath of the Chernobyl disaster. Immediate medical treatment and other essential benefits and compensation would not be available. Understandably, the totalitarian regime was laying down a smoke screen to keep information about the scale of contamination and the number of victims hidden under a lid of secrecy. Yet the global nature of the Chernobyl disaster was too obvious. Also, the changes in society had by then become irreversible. The matter was altogether impossible to hush up, even by the Politburo "gerontocrats." The population in contaminated areas was increasingly vociferous in demanding a solution to their health problems, a schedule for compensation and environmental rehabilitation.

The first attempts at a legal solution to Chernobyl's environmental and social problems came in the form of regulations approved jointly by the Central Committee of the Communist Party and the USSR Council of Ministers. In Soviet times that was the usual practice in the absence of regular legislation. The Central Committee was seen as the main organ of state power, the party's leading role being enshrined in the Brezhnev constitution. The first document to regulate the relationship between the state and the Chernobyl Nuclear Power Plant was the joint resolution by the Central Committee of the Communist Party and the council of ministers passed twelve days after the accident, on May 7, 1986. It bore the title "On Terms of Payment and Provision for the Personnel of Enterprises and Organizations in the Chernobyl Nuclear Power Plant Area."

In the first four years after the disaster, there were no laws covering it, just legal substitutes—various central committee resolutions that were sent to every Union republic-level and regional party organ. Not infrequently, they were classified or top secret. As for the resolutions that appeared in the press, they carried no facts about the scale of contamination, the number of victims, or a description of specific problems.

Inaction was the order of the day, with a once-potent political machine now hopelessly paralyzed. It was as if, just like the reactor, they too had broken down. Then they panicked. Everything the authorities did was improvised on the spur of the moment. They were utterly unprepared for a nuclear disaster of that magnitude. The Party apparatus did prepare them for survival—by lying on a grand scale. This is borne out, among other things, by the fact that the medical personnel failed to carry out iodine prophylaxis, so essential within the first eight days after any elevated radioactive exposure. The authorities even lied about this—to the whole civilized world. Even though chemical warfare and engineering units had been pressed into service to do the measuring and decontamination, along with the special equipment and machinery of the Soviet Ministry of Defense and Civil Defense Forces, the authorities failed to evacuate promptly and properly even the 116,000 people trapped within the 30-km "black zone" of Chernobyl's radioactive plume.

The expropriation of the land in the 30-km zone around the crippled reactor and resettlement of the villagers residing in that zone were done strictly on the basis of secret government and party resolutions. To an outsider that looked like some inexorable elemental force. No one explained anything to the people. The local bosses simply told them that they would have to leave their village for a while, two or three weeks perhaps, until it was safe to return. Although according to the heads of some contaminated districts, they did suspect that the villagers would never again see their native parts nor would they ever return to their houses flooded with radiation.

The actions of the government and the Politburo were neurotic, chaotic, and always performed in utmost secrecy. This is clear from the spirit and tone of their secret minutes. They were worried and scared, and the more scared they became, confronted with the uncontrolled chain reaction, the more secret documents they churned out. Until 1989, the government produced no properly researched special program of aid to the Chernobyl victims. This monumental failure to act was not due to a lack of Soviet scientific capacity. Rather, it was due to the fact that the USSR lacked freedom. The closed nature of society was ideologically incompatible with glasnost when applied to the Chernobyl events.

For almost four years, after the reactor exploded, all work on eliminating the consequences of the accident and helping the victims was run strictly by the party's vertical command-administrative management structure. To that end the Central Committee of the Communist Party set up a task group that acted in secrecy, gathering all reports from the governments of the republics and from defense ministries, health ministries, and other bodies. These reports by the task group members were heard and decisions were made on every issue for the innocent slaves of the system, including hospitalization, discharge, raising maximum permissible exposure doses for people, delivery of fruit and vegetables, resettlement or non-resettlement, re-evacuation of villagers, helping the nuclear plant personnel, specifying who gets compensation payments, medical care, and even bathing people. And all of it was done in a clever Orwellian fashion.

Secrecy and lack of coordination between various departments often resulted in mismanagement, confusion, and abuse of office. For instance, in the Narodichi District of the Zhitomir region, officials in charge of distributing accommodation for evacuees in other cities— Kiev, Lvov, Zhitomir, and so on—appropriated several apartments apiece, refusing those who really needed them. The beauty of this process was the fact that the people could not take these officials to court. After all, nothing untoward had happened in the country, had it? With no laws to restrain them, Soviet officials were having a field day.

In 1987–88, several joint resolutions by the USSR Communist Party Central Committee and Council of Ministers were passed, as well as resolutions by local leaderships in the affected republics. Typically, those were criminal decisions, such as those on housing construction for resettling people in areas just as badly contaminated as the ones from which they had been removed. Others were simply unworkable. For instance, there were resolutions prescribing "strict provision" of "clean foodstuffs" for residents of radiation-affected areas. In those times, the whole country endured food shortages, not just the people living in stricken villages, with exceptions for Moscow and Leningrad, the major foreign tourism centers. Thus, Central Committee resolutions on improved diets for the Chernobyl victims were altogether impracticable. The residents of contaminated villages who, under the secret decisions by the party and government, received thirty rubles in "coffin money" for "clean" food could not buy any in the village shop. The shops were practically empty. And anyway, the money they received was just peanuts.

On the positive side, the USSR finally established the ministry for atomic energy, the first time since the start of nuclear production. Previously, nuclear activities were hidden in the bowels of another ministry. Once the new ministry was there, the people had a legal entity that could be held responsible for what it did in handling the "peaceful atom," as nukes were generally referred to. Several years after the accident, two different and unrelated programs for eliminating the consequences of the Chernobyl disaster were drawn up, one for Ukraine, the other for Belorussia. As for Russia, where the Chernobyl blast had reverberated across sixteen regions, no program existed for dealing with the aftermath of the disaster. What Russia had was just a set of measures for eliminating the consequences of the accident in the Bryansk region, and then only for the period between 1988 and 1990. The only people aware of the documents' existence were the bureaucrats who had been involved in their writing. And, I mean, just writing, for there was no science-based work done on them. Not surprisingly, these documents proved to have very little bearing on the actual situation.

It was four years after the nuclear disaster, on April 25, 1990, when the first Chernobyl resolution was adopted by the country's reformed legislative body, the Gorbachev Supreme Soviet. The resolution, "On a Unified Program of Eliminating the Consequences of the Chernobyl Nuclear Power Plant Accident and the Ensuing Situation," approved the first state program at Union and republic levels to deal with urgent measures for 1990–92, aimed at eliminating the consequences of the accident on a national scale. That was the first instance in the whole nuclear history of the Soviet Union when we, the people's deputies, charged the government with "drafting a law on the Chernobyl disaster and submitting it to the USSR Supreme Soviet in the fourth quarter of 1990. The law is to define the legal status of victims of the nuclear disaster and participants in the cleanup, of people working within the contaminated zone, and also those subjected to forced resettlement, the legal regulations for the distress area, the procedure for people's residence and activities, for military service, the formation and functioning of local administrative bodies, and of public organizations in the affected areas."

Predictably, none of that was done on time. A year later, our next Supreme Soviet resolution of April 9, 1991, "On the Progress in Fulfilling the Resolution by the USSR Supreme Soviet of April 25, 1990 on a Unified Program of Eliminating the Consequences of the Chernobyl Nuclear Power Plant Accident and the Ensuing Situation," pointed out that "there has been a delay in submitting to the USSR Supreme Soviet the draft laws on the Chernobyl catastrophe and on use of nuclear energy and nuclear safety, which has made it impossible to pass them until the present moment." The government and its apparatus simply sabotaged the people's deputies' instructions.

Real Chernobyl legislation history had to wait till 1991. A whole five years had elapsed since the nuclear accident before the Soviet republics passed their first reasonably adequate laws regulating the state's responsibility for the damage inflicted on its citizens by the operation of a nuclear facility. There are three such laws: (1) the Belorussian Law on Social Protection for Individuals Who Suffered from the Accident at the Chernobyl Nuclear Power Plant, dated February 22, 1991; (2) the Ukrainian Law on the Status and Social Protection for Individuals Who Suffered from the Accident at the Chernobyl Nuclear Power Plant; and (3) the Russian Federation Law on Social Protection for Individuals Exposed to Radiation in the Aftermath of the Chernobyl Nuclear Disaster, dated May 15, 1991. In that same year, we also passed the first Union-level Law on Social Protection for Individuals Who Suffered in the Aftermath of the Chernobyl Disaster. As the names of the laws suggest, they applied to the afflicted population and the liquidators. The environmental issues and nuclear hazards were only indirectly involved. But even that, compared to the total legal vacuum in the nuclear sphere, was not just a major step forward, but a real revolution in lawmaking.

The scale of the Chernobyl disaster and of the environmental damage was the factor that provided the source material for scientists and jurists, that served as the basis for the first laws the republics finally adopted, requiring the social and environmental problems to be addressed. It was all the more important since no other country had ever dealt with anything remotely similar to this disaster since Hiroshima and Nagasaki. Dozens of other nuclear accidents, in the United States (the Three Mile Island plant), in the UK (at Windscale), and in other states, could not even begin to compare with the Chernobyl fallout. We Soviet lawmakers acquired our own unique experience of working on draft laws without any other model. We were very conscious of the responsibility that this fact imposed on us.

For the first time, The Law on the Legal Regulations for Territories Subjected to Radioactive Contamination in the Aftermath of the Chernobyl Nuclear Disaster put in effect in Ukraine on February 27, 1991 (with subsequent amendments and additions introduced by the Laws of December 17, 1991 and June 1, 1992), defined those territories. Under the law, the contaminated region was divided into four zones, depending on the landscape and geochemical features of the soil, the amount by which the pre-accident radionuclide levels were exceeded in the environment, potential harm to human health, and other factors. In the hard-hit Gomel region of Belarus, the resettlement process began in May 1986, but, in the new Maysky village (Cherikov District), settlers were allowed to raise produce on their old heavily contaminated land.

Zone One is the "alienated" area (code-named "black" in the party circles). This is the territory from which the population was evacuated in 1986. Then comes Zone Two, the zone of mandatory resettlement. (Shcherbitsky, first secretary of the Ukrainian Communist Party, referred to it as "red" in his correspondence with the Kremlin.) This is a territory intensely contaminated with long-life radionuclides and having the following contamination density in the soil above the pre-accident level: cesium isotopes, upward of 15 curies/km^2; strontium, upward of 3 Ci/km^2; plutonium, upward of 0.1 Ci/km^2, where the estimated effective equivalent exposure dose per person may exceed 0.5 rem a year over the pre-accident dosage. Zone Three is an area of guaranteed voluntary resettlement, with soil contamination density of 5–15 Ci/km^2 (cesium isotopes), 0.15–3 Ci/km^2 (strontium), or 0.01–0.1 Ci/km^2 (plutonium) above the pre-accident level. Here the estimated effective equivalent exposure dose per person may exceed by 1 rem a year the dose accumulated annually before the explosion. Finally comes Zone Four, increased radio-environmental monitoring. This is a territory with soil contamination density of 1–5 Ci/km^2 (cesium isotopes), 0.02–0.15 Ci/km^2 (strontium), or 0.005–0.01 Ci/km^2 (plutonium)—provided that the estimated effective equivalent exposure dose per person exceeds the pre-Chernobyl dosage by more than 0.05 rem a year.

On November 12, 1991, Belorussia passed a special law, "On the Legal Regulations for Territories Subjected to Radioactive Contamination in the Aftermath of the Accident at the Chernobyl Nuclear Power Plant." It was intended to lessen the radiation effect on the people and ecosystems, to stimulate environmental restoration and protection, as well as rational use of the territories' natural, economic, and scientific potential. The law regulated the new regime for radioactively contaminated areas and the conditions of residence as well as economic and scientific research and other activities. The Belorussian pattern of zonal division for contaminated areas differs from that in Ukraine. The Belorussian law defines zones in accordance with the environmental damage from the radioactive fallout. The Belorussian "zone" includes five types of territory.

The first one is the evacuation zone, the territory around the Chernobyl Nuclear Power Plant, from which the people were evacuated in 1986. This is a 30-km area whose population was resettled because the strontium-90 contamination density of the soil exceeded 3 Ci/km^2, and plutonium-238, -239, -240, and -241 levels were above 1 Ci/km^2. The second one is the immediate resettlement zone. It includes areas with soil contamination density upward of 40 Ci/km² for cesium-137, or of 3 Ci/km² and more for strontium-90, and plutonium-238, -239, -240, and -241. The next resettlement zone has soil contamination density of 15–40 Ci/km² for cesium-137, or up to 3 Ci/km² for strontium-90, or of 0.05–1 Ci/km² for plutonium-238, -239, -240, and -241, where the mean annual effective equivalent exposure dose may exceed 0.5 rem. (This also includes areas with a lower density of contamination by these radionuclides, where the mean annual effective equivalent exposure dose per person may likewise exceed 0.5 rem.) The fourth zone is where people have the right to resettlement. These are areas with soil contamination density of 5–15 Ci/km² for cesium-137, or of 0.5–1.25 Ci/km² for strontium-90, or of 0.02–0.05 Ci/km² for plutonium-238, -239, -240, and -241. Here the mean annual effective equivalent human exposure dose may exceed 0.1 rem. In the same category are the areas with lower contamination densities where the mean annual effective equivalent dose can also exceed 0.1 rem. And finally comes the least dangerous residential zone subject to periodical monitoring. These are areas with soil contamination density of 1–5 Ci/km² for cesium-137, or of 0.15–0.5 Ci/km² for strontium-90, or of 0.01–0.02 Ci/km² for plutonium-238, -239, -240, and -241. Here the mean annual effective equivalent human exposure dose must not exceed 0.1 rem. Although the environmental problems in the wake of Chernobyl involved sixteen regions of the Russian Federation, during the first years after the blast, the Russian Federation's program of dealing with the consequences of the accident mentioned no territories other than the Bryansk region, and later the so-called Kaluga-Tula-Orel plume.

The environmental problems of Russia's contaminated territories were legally regulated for the first time with the enforcement of the "Law on Social Protection for Individuals Exposed to Radiation in the Aftermath of the Nuclear Disaster at the Chernobyl Nuclear Power Plant," dated May 15, 1991. It is interesting to look at its section titled "The Regime and Environmental Recovery of Territories Subjected to Radioactive Contamination in the Aftermath of the Nuclear Accident at the Chernobyl Nuclear Power Plant." It shows that the Russian radioactive contamination zones differed from those in Belorussia and Ukraine. Each republic adopted its own set of legal standards depending on the scale of environmental damage. In Russia, four radioactive contamination zones have been defined—the evacuation zone, the zone of mandatory resettlement, and the right-to-resettlement zone and preferential-social-and-economic-status zones.

Article 7 of the law says that "the boundaries of these zones and the list of populated areas in them are established depending on changes in the radioactive situation and other factors and are to be revised at least once every five years." The "alienation" zone (in 1986–87, the party and government documents referred to it as the 30-km zone, while from 1988 on, until the Law was passed, it was known as the evacuation zone) includes the territory around the Chernobyl power plant and part of the territory contaminated with radioactive substances after the Chernobyl accident, from which the people were evacuated or resettled in 1986 and later. The mandatory resettlement zone is the section of the territory of the Russian Federation outside the alienation zone with the soil contamination density of over 15 Ci/km^2 for cesium-137, or over 3 Ci/km^2 for strontium-90, or over 0.1 Ci/km^2 for plutonium-239 and -240. The right-of-resettlement residential zone likewise regulates soil contamination levels. These are areas outside the alienation and mandatory resettlement zones that have soil contamination density of 5–15 Ci/km^2 for cesium-137. Additional criteria for determining the zone boundaries are established, depending on the radioactive contamination by other than cesium-137 radionuclides, by the government of the Russian Federation. Zone Four allows habitation with a preferential social and economic status. These are areas outside the alienation, mandatory resettlement and right-of-resettlement residential zones with soil radioactive contamination density of 1–5 Ci/km^2 for cesium-137.

Interestingly, the Chernobyl legislation in Ukraine, Russia, and Belorussia treats the global Chernobyl accident-related problems in two different ways. The first approach is territorial. It is based on the so-called territory zoning, defined above. The second approach is social. The laws aimed at social and economic protection of this country's citizens were adopted in the republics about a year before the Soviet Union's collapse. They complement the laws connected with the status of different territories. The benefits and compensation payments for Chernobyl victims take into account the level of radioactive contamination in the given area. Contamination by chemical or other toxic agents is ignored. The size of compensation and additional payments depends on different factors under the Chernobyl laws in Russia, Ukraine, and Belorussia: in Russia, the departure point is the minimum subsistence wage; in Belorussia, it is the monthly extra pay in absolute figures subject to subsequent indexing; in Ukraine, it is tied to the base wage rates and earnings. Some benefits and compensation payments are quite similar. In Ukraine, the people entitled to extra benefits are those employed in the health services, education, and culture. Estimates of compensation and additional payments in mandatory resettlement and right-of-resettlement zones suggest that under Russia's social protection system, moving people out of contaminated areas was taken more seriously than that under similar systems in Ukraine and Belorussia.

The Russian Federation's Law on Social Protection of Individuals Subjected to Radiation Exposure in the Aftermath of the Nuclear Disaster at the Chernobyl Nuclear Power Plant defines the status of such individuals. Section 3 of the Law names twelve categories of people entitled to compensation and benefits. The amounts of all such compensation payments and benefits are described in minute detail:

> (1) Individuals suffering from or cured of radiation sickness and other illnesses, as well as those disabled in the aftermath of the accident shall receive free medical care (in hospitals and out-patient departments), free medication as prescribed by the doctors, free dental care including artificial dentures, free annual treatment at sanatoriums and health resorts, or compensation for the price of the annual voucher, etc.; disabled persons who continue to work shall be paid temporary disability benefits for up to four months running, or up to five month in a calendar year equal to 100 percent of their average earnings; they are entitled to housing space with all modern amenities allocated free but only once, regardless of the length of residence in the given locality, within three months of the day of application, provided they have been found to be in need of housing improvement or living in communal apartments, and also to extra floor space in the form of a separate room; they are entitled to 50 percent reductions in rent payments, which also includes their family members living with them, and to 50 percent reductions in charges for use of the telephone, radio, collective television aerials and installation thereof; 50 percent reductions for use of gas, heating, running water and electricity; free travel on Russia's territory by every means of city and suburban transport, and also once a year throughout Russia; exemption from income tax payments, and from all other kinds of tax, etc.
>
> (2) Individuals permanently resident (working) on the territory of the right-of-resettlement zone can receive monthly compensation

depending on the length of residence period (in percentage terms against the minimum subsistence wage stipulated by the law): since April 26, 1986—40 percent; since January 1, 1987—30 percent; since January 1, 1991—20 percent.

The minimum subsistence wage in Russia was six hundred rubles. Thus people living within that zone, depending on the length of their sojourn, were entitled to a monthly extra pay of 240, 180, and 120 rubles. In dollar terms, it would amount to $8, $6, and $4, respectively. No comment.

Here is another legal norm. "Individuals permanently resident on resettlement territory prior to their re-housing in other areas can receive monthly compensation the size of which depends on the length of residence period (in percentage terms against the legally established minimum subsistence wage): since April 26, 1986—60 percent; since January 1, 1987—50 percent; since January 1, 1991—40 percent." This means that the monthly compensation for people who lived or worked in resettlement zones until being re-housed elsewhere, say, since January 1, 1987, amounted to 300 rubles, or just over $10.

Under the law, this category of people was also entitled to "increased monthly pensions and allowances for non-working retirees and disabled persons, and for disabled children regardless of the length of residence time (in percentage terms against the minimum old-age pensions and allowances): since April 26, 1986—300 percent; since January 1, 1987—200 percent; since January 1, 1991—100 percent."

Postgraduates and students at state primary, secondary, and higher vocational schools located on the resettlement zone territory were to be paid 100 percent grants. Students at state universities and colleges located on the resettlement zone territory were to get an eight hundred–ruble grant from the state ($25).

The law also provided for compensation payments (Section 5) for illnesses sustained in the aftermath of the Chernobyl accident. For instance, Group 1 and 2 disabled persons were entitled to an annual compensation for ruined health five times the minimum monthly subsistence wage. Thus, given the minimum subsistence wage of six hundred rubles a month, Group 1 and 2 disabled persons were to get three thousand rubles a year (roughly equivalent to $100), as compensation for ruined health. The law also provides for compensation payments to other categories of people whose health deteriorated as a result of the Chernobyl disaster.

In all fairness I must say that the Chernobyl laws helped in to improve the local health service in terms of funding and equipment, with a network of diagnostic and treatment-and-recuperation centers set up, medical staff retrained, and so on. The deputies and the public actually pressured the authorities into doing something useful. According to Russia's State Committee for eliminating the consequences of the Chernobyl accident, the monitoring of the health of the people living in contaminated areas within Russia was done not only by local medical institutions, but also by twenty-five leading research centers. Also, the Russian national medical-dosimetric register was created. Its database contains information about 137,600 people suffering from radiation exposure in the wake of the Chernobyl accident. This figure includes nearly ninety-seven thousand liquidators; about three thousand people evacuated from contaminated areas; over thirty-five thousand residents of radiation-affected areas; over twenty-six hundred children born to participants in the Chernobyl cleanup. Considering that there are at least 2 million people in Russia living in radioactively contaminated areas, the database appears woefully inadequate.

However, years after the Chernobyl accident, many scientists, experts, and ecologists, based on comprehensive research into the consequences of the disaster and damage compensation for the victims, started to question the merits of the Chernobyl laws passed by the three now independent states. A number of papers have subjected current activities to severe and justified criticism, particularly the system of social, economic, and medical protection. The stumbling block, predictably, is the issue of computing the average cumulative dose of persons living in contaminated zones, a measure that ought to serve as the basis for decisions about compensation and aid.

A closer look at the laws of Ukraine, Belarus, and Russia on social protection of individuals exposed to radiation shows that they fail to take into account certain important aspects of the problem, the basis for the entire Chernobyl legislation. This methodology used in computing accumulated dose and defining their consequences takes into account the specific features of the fallout and migration of radionuclides, time of exposure, dose rate, and so on. According to State Duma expert O. Yu. Tsitser, the calculation of doses on which the laws are based is deficient for a number of reasons. First, the radiation hazard for the population may vary by orders of magnitude. Second, attempts to compute the average individual dose within a population group will soon show that the spread in dose values is too great, thus the computed dose is largely a myth. Therefore, the number of tests per unit of territory should be increased. The third reason is the inadequate amounts of dosimetric and epidemiological data essential for parameter accuracy in the estimate model: distribution of exposure doses over various regions; parameters of socially significant biological effects, such as mortality rates; incidence of non-cancer diseases; and population classification in terms of sensitivity to radiation and radiation levels in the food. Here again the snag is the classified database gathered by the academician Ilyin and team. This last item is an extremely important constituent of the overall exposure picture in different areas. The proportion of people sensitive to radiation makes for an abnormally high morbidity rate, O. Yu. Tsitser believes.

Specialists conclude that basing estimates of territory contamination on radionuclide fallout density (and individual dosage as well), the so-called area approach, is an imperfect method, though lawmakers are still using it today, despite the fact that radionuclides tend to migrate, get absorbed, and transmute in a natural way, turning some into less harmful and others into considerably more dangerous elements. In accordance with the paper on the concept of radiation, medical, and social protection for the population exposed to radiation passed by the Russian Scientific Commission for Radiation Protection and recommended to the legislators by the government of the Russian Federation for revising and verifying the articles of the Chernobyl law, the current "area approach" was to be replaced by the dose-based method.

The issue of revision of Chernobyl legislation in the Russian Federation was also related to another important social factor. Several legislative acts and governmental resolutions adopted over the last few years deal with social protection in the country's various regions contaminated with radionuclides as a result of nuclear accidents at industrial and military facilities or in the wake of nuclear testing. They display an obvious tendency toward applying the Chernobyl law to those areas as well, such as the Urals, that suffered greatly from the activity of the Mayak Nuclear Facility, and also to Kazakhstan in the area of the Semipalatinsk test site. There, certain specific patterns of radioactive fallout and contamination are virtually ignored as is the nature of dose loads in the population. In fact, direct extrapolation of the Chernobyl law to those areas is misleading and inappropriate.

In 1994–95, the Russian State Duma fought a protracted battle with the government and President Yeltsin over the revision of the law on social protection for individuals residing in contaminated areas. Some deputies introduced amendments to the law that actually worsened the Chernobyl victims' situation even though they had promised those people their full support during the election campaign. Russia's president had to appeal to the RF Constitutional Court because the law passed by the Duma in 1995 infringed on people's constitutional rights and liberties. Actually, for all their imperfections, the Chernobyl laws could still provide some protection to both the accident victims and the liquidators, but they have one major flaw that cancels out their best merits. These laws have remained virtually inoperative for over a decade! The problem is that in the course of time the nuclear accident has lost its acuteness in the eyes of the authorities (and society at large), eclipsed as it was by numerous other issues emerging in the fledgling states born on the ruins of the Soviet Union. The new countries' economies were reoriented toward the so-called market, which in effect took the form of downright plunder of the people by the *nouveaux riche*. They don't spend time thinking about the fate of those long-suffering radiation victims.

Meanwhile, the scale of the Chernobyl disaster has not changed. It is such that compliance with the laws and the mechanism of dealing with the resulting environmental, social, and economic problems requires a good deal of money. For instance, in Belarus, a recent report found 80 percent of the budget went to Chernobyl-related expenditures. Russia and Ukraine have run up enormous arrears to the tune of billions of rubles. Chernobyl victims and liquidators in these countries have to wait years for their money. An important yardstick for assessing the success of the Chernobyl social laws and how well the state cares about its citizens living in contaminated areas is the target investment in housing the evacuees as well as production facilities to provide jobs. In each of the countries, the budget has a separate item for funding the elimination of the consequences of the Chernobyl accident, a reasonable tactic. Unfortunately, over the last few years, these sums have tended to shrink. The reason is rising inflation, recession, and other problems facing transitional economies.

According to the data obtained by Russians researchers A. Dumnov and Ye. Vosmirko, Chernobyl-related investment in each state's economy in comparable prices has been falling by about 10–30 percent a year. The actual volume of such investment has shrunk even more noticeably. In dollar terms, the Belarus Chernobyl-related investment in 1997 totaled $120 million dollars; in Russia, the figure was $60 million; and in Ukraine, $185 million. The overall reduction in the new housing construction for Chernobyl victims in the three states was 40 percent lower than the 1995 level. Russia commissioned a mere 27 percent of housing against the 1995 level; Belarus, 62 percent; and Ukraine, 75 percent. With the start of the second Chechnya military campaign, 150 houses under construction were mothballed in the Pochep District, Bryansk region (the town of Moskovsky), which the Moscow City government had been building under its charity program. During the last fifteen years, hardly any new health centers, outpatient clinics, and schools have been built for the resettled residents and others in contaminated zones. These are all vital infrastructure deficits.

One problem leads to another. The states' commitments with regard to resettlement are not being properly met. The resettlement of people in the so-called radioactive B Zones (in terms of the Chernobyl laws of Russia, Ukraine, and Belarus), where contamination levels are between 15 and 40 Ci/km^2 and higher, is proceeding at a snail's pace. In 1993, for example, 4,410 Belarus residents were moved out of the mandatory and guaranteed resettlement zones (in the Gomel and Mogilev regions). In 1995, the number dropped to 1,723. In Russia, 2,790 persons in similar zones (in the Bryansk, Kaluga, Tula, and Orel regions) were offered new accommodations in 1993, but that dropped to only 1,370 persons in 1995. The situation in Ukraine is much the same. By the beginning of 1997, Russia had 410,400 people living in contaminated areas in mandatory and guaranteed resettlement zones (in the Bryansk, Kaluga, and Tula regions); Belarus had 1,627,700; and Ukraine had 2,365,000 people living in such areas.

At present, all resettlement activity has practically disappeared. That means people being slowly killed by radiation may have to wait to be rehoused for decades. Twenty years has passed and the matter is still being debated! Worse yet, resettlement will never take place, a more likely result. As for the lucky ones who did settle in "clean" areas but failed to find a job, they too encounter problems awaiting legal regulation, and these problems just continue to snowball. No one bothers to create new jobs for resettled people. It is not unusual for those unable to adjust to the new living conditions to return to their "dirty" houses and "dirty" vegetable plots. Because of this, the Russian government passed a resolution, in January 1997, to devise a mechanism for getting back the housing money received by the resettled individuals if they leave the new place for home. Just great! And what about a mechanism for paying back the money that was stolen from the country by the party faithful?)

Budget difficulties arose in the rehabilitation of children, as well as of adults. In the Russian Federation, the "Children of Russia" special presidential program has been in effect for a number of years. One of its sections is named "The Children of Chernobyl." Despite its presidential status, even this program is severely underfunded—that in a country blessed with an abundance of natural wealth! Sadly, it has to be admitted that neither the Soviet government, nor the so-called democratic governments in the newly independent states have yet managed to meet even the barest minimum of commitments to their citizens provided for by the Chernobyl laws that were approved by their own parliaments.

In Russia, the 2005 situation was further exacerbated by the fact that the government announced the so-called monetization of benefits, also involving the Chernobyl victims. Instead of all that was specified by the law for their social protection, the government made these people, the disabled included, a generous offer of thousand rubles a month, by way of compensation. That is, slightly more than $30. This is expected to cover the cost of just about everything—transport fares, medication, food, and treatment. This move has been instantly nicknamed "Zurabovism," after health minister Zurabov, who is the cabinet member responsible for the monetization of benefits. In the wake of this measure, the country was swept by a tidal wave of rallies; strikes and mass protests spearheaded everywhere by Chernobyl victims.

21

"Curtains of Fog and Iron"

Less than five years after the "Wormwood Star" had turned the rivers around Chernobyl into low-grade radioactive liquid waste, almost the entire leadership of the country was suddenly preoccupied with the plight of the unfortunate people. You could not escape the buzzword—"benefits." One could expect them to begin offering perks! It turns out there are various classes of perks and benefits in this country. For businessmen who have passed through the revolving door into government "service," it is state-owned country dachas, free treatment in the country's best clinics, chauffeur-driven limos, and much else besides. Remember, that in the Soviet era they could also be sure of cast-iron immunity from prosecution plus hard currency from the budget for "establishing ties with fraternal communist parties." As for the ordinary mortals, the very right to life seems to be another privilege. Our government mocks the sensibilities of our long-suffering brothers and sisters when our leaders use such glowing terms as "benefits" for "coffin money," "clean" food, medical examination and treatment "for all who are in need," or "you can leave contaminated territory any time." Of course, none of these "benefits" have ever been fully implemented.

For all of two decades millions of people in contaminated areas have been fighting for this "privileged" life—and not in contaminated areas alone. Years after the accident, concerned citizens helped the government remember the six hundred thousand liquidators (the UN sets the figure at eight hundred thousand), the people who, in those dramatic hours, days, weeks, and months, faced imminent death to subdue the nuclear ogre and slow the spread of radiation all over the country. Whether it is six or eight hundred thousand, the figure is still only approximate. Who can tell now if there were more or fewer of them? It is common knowledge that records were slipshod at best. And if there were any accurate records kept, they are still classified. So those people, brown from "nuclear suntan," returned home to various parts of the huge country. The motherland had summoned them. The motherland has forgotten them. One does not bear a grudge against one's motherland, of course. One does against the authorities, the bureaucrats.

V. Kh. Doguzhiev, chairman of the state emergency commission for eliminating the consequences of natural phenomena and disasters: "The most important line in the work of public health agencies is improving medical service standards for the participants in the elimination of the consequences of the nuclear accident. The people who took part in the cleanup undoubtedly deserve both attention and respect. Unfortunately, in a vast majority of cases the medical staff of public health facilities proved unprepared for work with this category of patients."

In 1989, there was just one interdepartmental expert council in Kiev, and it was the only body authorized to establish the cause-and-effect relationship between a person's illness and his or her participation in the nuclear cleanup. Can you imagine that? Thousands of people came over from every corner of the country to be examined and to prove that they were ill, pointing out that they were unable to live normally after months of work in the radioactive inferno, but very few managed to prove it. After all, the interdepartmental expert council was based at the All-Union Research Center for Radiation Medicine where the director was—guess who?—Ukraine's health minister Anatoly Romanenko. That's right, the very man who, not so long ago, had been sending secret reports to Moscow on the sorry plight of radiation victims while assuring the public that there were no grounds for alarm. Indeed, how could Director Romanenko refute Minister Romanenko!

In a recent study by the European Committee on Radiation Risk (*Chernobyl: 20 Years On*), a paper by Prof. V. B. Nesterenko and A. V. Nesterenko, Institute of Radiation Safety in Belarus, noted that the government established a scientific and technical commission, and on May 3, 1986, the members went to the Chernobyl regions and then sent a letter to the government, requesting resettlement of the population living within a 100-km zone around the reactor. Coeditor A. V. Yablokov quoted two Russian scientists who estimated that, in 2002, 98–99 percent of all liquidators were ill from an assortment of serious diseases. What a heavy price to pay for their courage!

Small wonder that every government agency was swamped with complaints. People wrote that it was impossible to get their local authorities to provide not only decent medical treatment or food but even papers certifying their part in the cleanup or liquidator badges. I still receive similar letters and phone calls. People ask for an explanation as to what "benefits" they are entitled to. Even the staff of the Zhitomir regional sanitary and epidemiological service, themselves liquidators, could not get anywhere a coherent answer to their query: how could they obtain the liquidator certificate, if not much else? I had to apply to the Ukrainian government. The procedure, it turned out, was perfectly simple. One had to go to a regional Soviet executive committee and show it a document confirming the liquidator status. So why do the local authorities turn this straightforward procedure into an insurmountable hassle?

People ask me what class of receivers of benefits do servicemen engaged in decontamination belong to. Over four thousand eighteen-year-old soldiers ruined their health there. Their radioactive genes have already gone into our future or will do so presently. At the request of several mothers, my voters, I managed to tear their sons away from the lethal reactor. Here is a typical letter in my archives from Chernobyl veterans, liquidators:

> We appealed to Ryzhkov (head of the Soviet government) requesting a solution to our problems. There was no response. Some of our questions were brought to Gorbachev's attention. We were promised that the matter would be looked into. Three months later nothing changed. In the article entitled "This Is a Letter on an Urgent Issue. It Is Not to Be Published," in the daily *Izvestia*, we again listed our grievances. Someone from the USSR health ministry came and promised to send us written resolutions. Again, a wall of silence and secrecy. It is clear that the All-Union center for radiation medicine has been sabotaging the decisions by the health ministry board, denying hospitalization to Chernobyl nuclear power plant personnel for examination and treatment. Thus, laboratory assistant Belozertsev's request was turned down, and he died soon after, as did driver Nazarenko and many others. This is discrimination against active participants in the nuclear cleanup, a clear case of malpractice by the medics who should have provided treatment.

A bitter letter written several years after the accident reveals the extent of the problem:

> Under public pressure and in view of irrefutable facts, the central interdepartmental expert council started to grudgingly relate the numerous illnesses of cleanup participants to radiation. There arose

321

new problems. Even if such a link between radiation and illness is established, the expert council's decisions have no legal validity; they are not recognized anywhere, and are worse than useless to the person concerned. This is more traumatizing than radiation. Attempts to go to court were fiercely resented by the law-enforcing agencies of Kiev. Immorality and abuse of power at all levels are gathering momentum. The children of Pripyat have never received the kind of care they need. However, there is no shortage of statements by quasi-medical officials to the effect that all is well in this area. Kiev's local government organs still fail to deliver on decisions providing for . . . housing compensation to the evacuated population; the benefits that have been approved are kept secret and hidden from the public.

Here is what medical expert Ms. Gorbunova said at the parliamentary hearings:

> I am working on the Chernobyl problem and that of the liquidators. You should understand that basic morbidity will be naturally expected among the liquidators, and I was glad to hear our esteemed academician Leonid Andreevich Ilyin finally acknowledge that the expected increase in cancers may reach 10 percent. We, the local practicing doctors, observe a rise in cancer incidence. This has been recognized by the public. But try and look at the specialist medical press. Take the article "Chernobyl: Rumors and Facts." Believe it or not, in this All-Union Radiology Center article Comrade Romanenko [the center's director] denies any possibility of radiation-induced thyroid pathology. He tries to document the absence of any connection, although the report [Ilyin's] said in so many words that 1,600,000 children had absorbed the kind of radiation dose that required close attention.

The Chernobyl liquidators went to live all over the huge country, taking with them hundreds of thousands of mini-Chernobyls. They saved the world and the country from even more horrendous consequences at the cost of the most precious things they had, their life and health. They had every right to hope that the country would not forget them. But it turned out that rescuing a drowning man is the drowning man's own job, to quote the classic novel *Twelve Chairs* by Ilf and Petrov.

In September 1989, the Committee for Glasnost, Human Rights and Appeals received a copy of a letter addressed to "Secretary General of the CPSU Central Committee Comrade M.S. Gorbachev; Chairman of the USSR Council of Ministers Comrade N.I. Ryzhkov; Chairman of the All-Union Central Trade Union Council Comrade S.A. Shalaev; the television program Vzglyad (View)." Here is what it said:

> We differ in age, profession and social status, but we share a common misfortune. Not just our personal misfortune, but that of our whole vast country—the accident at the Chernobyl nuclear power plant. In 1986–87 we all had to take part in eliminating the consequences of the accident. We were not withdrawn from the danger area until we had absorbed certain doses of ionizing radiation. It has been more than once openly confirmed in the press that the persons who took part in the nuclear cleanup will enjoy certain benefits, including in matters of medical service. . . . Our illnesses are considered to be of a general occupational nature, and are not linked to our stay in the zone. When recruited for the cleanup, we underwent a medical examination and were pronounced fit.
>
> At present our health problems are affecting our work. We frequently go on lengthy sick leave, which is causing understandable resentment among our colleagues. We would dearly love to resume normal healthy life, enjoy work and leisure after working hours. However, we are regrettably denied this chance. Therefore, we are looked upon as the Soviet edition of "superfluous men." We are given Group 2 and 3 disability status for general occupational diseases and chucked overboard, so to speak. We know that a number of resolutions on benefits have been issued, but no factual information about that has come our way. Hasn't the experience of the Afghan veterans been lesson enough? Some of us have neither decent apartments nor telephone, and today no means of livelihood either. And many more are in for the same plight.

The letter was signed by dozens of people. The geographical range suggests that it must have been written in some clinic where all these people were being treated or else on the doorstep of the expert council in Kiev. Among the signatories were E. N. Kolesnikov of Tashkent, Uzbekistan; G. V. Gushcha of Dnepropetrovsk, Ukraine; V. Ye. Zieun of Donetsk, Ukraine; M. G. Danielyan of Spitak, Armenia; also people from Kiev, Kharkov, and Krivoy Rog in Ukraine, from Oktemberyan in Armenia, and many others.

The Zhitomir region has five thousand liquidators living in it. In the city of Zhitomir itself, there are nearly two thousand. This means they all need good food and medication. Where will it come from, if the government fails to allocate enough money? A most ingenious solution was found from the region's resources, that is, at the expense of the stricken locals who, in the northern parts of the region, did not get enough "clean" foodstuffs to go around anyway.

From the final report of the state expert commission for examining programs of eliminating the consequences of the Chernobyl nuclear accident:

> The programs do not deal with issues of medical monitoring and aid for persons that have left the contaminated area after absorbing considerable radiation doses in the thyroid and the entire body (evacuees and resettled individuals). Nor has the number of such persons resident on the republics' territories been verified. Medical aid is not envisaged for persons recruited for work in high-contamination areas during the cleanup at the Chernobyl plant itself, though these groups run into hundreds of thousands of people, and their exposure doses are on a biologically significant level.

Misinformation. Lies. Cover-ups. Indifference. Deception. It just could not go on much longer. As lies continued to accumulate, the fire of righteous indignation and rage started to smolder. The people realized that their letters were simply ignored. Their anger was vented in public protests, demos, and pickets by the premises of government agencies. Here is the chronicle of the Chernobyl popular unrest that started three years after the accident.

In 1989, the town of Narovlya, Belorussia, witnessed one of the country's first strikes by Chernobyl victims. The losses incurred as a result were estimated at over three hundred thousand rubles. It took the arrival of the republic's health minister, V. Ulashchik, and three high-ranking party functionaries—N. Dementei, Yu. Khusainov, and V. Yevtukh, and some fierce talk by the strikers, to defuse the situation. But the peace did not last long because the whole issue again petered out, resulting in nothing but empty promises. About the same time in the town of Cherikov, Belorussia, a protest rally was held in front of the district party committee building. People were beginning to wake up in protest from the official lies. The day chosen for the rally was symbolic—June 1, International Children's Day. Just then the first Congress of USSR People's Deputies was in progress, and a delegation from the rebellious town went to Moscow. There it joined the Belorussian people's deputies and was granted an audience with Nikolai I. Ryzhkov. The USSR chairman of the council of ministers, as the Belorussians said later, told them that a lot of what he had heard was news to him. It just doesn't wash. Obviously, Ryzhkov, who received detailed daily reports from hydrometeorology committee chairman Yuri Izrael and others, was kept well informed. I assume he was feigning ignorance because he feared the people would start a rebellion.

At the time Ryzhkov promised the people, now driven to despair, that an IAEA and WHO commission would work in Belorussia's afflicted areas in order to work out a safe residence plan jointly with our scientists. That was the same commission whose findings I have described earlier on. The result of its work is well known. It endorsed the lies of the official medical establishment while the people were sent packing. Protest rallies also swept the northern areas of the Zhitomir region. In June 1989, on the opening day of a regional Soviet session, a group of Zhitomir residents wanted to read a letter at that session in support of demands by the people in contaminated zones. But that proved quite difficult.

From the Zhitomir residents' letter:

> At the entrance to the regional executive committee premises we organized a picket with posters that read: "The Zhitomir treatment and sanatorium directorate for Narodichi children!" and "We demand evacuation from the radioactive zone!" We were not allowed to enter the assembly hall. So we remained on the steps by the entrance. People started gathering around us. Deputies were going inside for the session. Some stopped without a word, others assured us that they were for the Narodichi townspeople, still others told us to go to get out of there. But we did not answer back. Finally, a blonde came out and let us into the foyer of the Soviet building guarded by a policeman. Having inquired about the purpose of our visit, she graciously invited us into a room next door. Then she told us that we could not be present at the session, because there was no law that said we could. We were rank outsiders there.
>
> To deal with this awfully complex issue the regional executive committee leadership came out to see us. They tried to talk us into simply leaving the letter, which would be duly attended to afterwards. Knowing how letters from ordinary people were usually "attended to," we refused and stood our ground. To clinch their argument they asked us: "How will even a single deputy, shaken to the core by the tragedy of the northern areas (as though they had been innocent of all knowledge of the matter!) manage to go on working at the session?" Then the regional executive committee negotiators withdrew for consultations with their superiors. And finally, after the break, we were allowed into the hall. We declared that we did not trust the apparatchiks and therefore could not simply leave the letter and go away. We wanted it to be read out at the session in our presence. And if the apparatchiks did not agree, the picketing in front of the building would continue.

This was the beginning of glasnost, of openness about the aftermath of the accident! Here are some lines from an appeal to people's deputies by residents of the town of Korosten, Zhitomir region, who also decided to take protest action:

> We, the people of Korosten, are outraged by the state's attitude to the Chernobyl victims. This is a disaster on a global scale, and we have the right to demand aid from the whole of the country. Measly handouts of 15 rubles that won't buy you anything are nothing but a mockery. . . . We will be forced to fight for our children's life and health in a most resolute fashion, resorting to extreme economic and political measures.

In the fall of 1989, a hundred-thousand-strong rally gathered at a stadium in Kiev. The pictures of our numerous group from the Zhitomir region, holding up protest slogans, hit the front pages of national dailies and weeklies. Feelings ran high. Ukraine's health minister, A. Romanenko, received a unanimous vote of no confidence, and the session of the Kiev city Soviet passed a resolution declaring academician Ilyin persona non grata in Kiev. Thus, the public expressed its disagreement with the flood of lies about the real state of affairs in contaminated areas. People tried to protect themselves and their children as best they could.

On February 25, 1990, an environmentalist rally was held at the Zhitomir stadium, and it was packed with over twenty thousand participants. The rally was chaired by regional executive committee deputy head, G. A. Gotovchits, who was also chairman of the region's emergency commission. The speakers at the meeting included people from radioactively contaminated northern areas, members of Ukraine's first Zhitomir regional Civil Front for Promoting Perestroika (I was one of its cofounders), and members of the Rukh (Ukrainian People's Movement for Perestroika); also there were officials from the local government, USSR people's deputies, contenders for Ukraine's Supreme, and local Soviets (the whole thing was happening in the run-up to the election). Just before the rally, I had visited stricken villages, where I learned a great many shocking facts, so I had a few questions to put to the regional and national leadership. I was convinced that things could not go on like they had. Something had to be done. Therefore, at the end of my speech, I suggested tabling a motion of no confidence in Ukraine's government because of the post-Chernobyl situation, raising the issue of criminal liability for the republic-level and regional ex-leaders who had concealed information from us and misinformed the public, and I denounced the fallacious 35-rem-over-70-years conception. We raised the issue of immediate closure of the Chernobyl Nuclear Power Plant, giving a mandate to the newly elected Ukrainian Supreme Soviet deputies to pass laws on nuclear safety, on the status of territories subjected to radioactive contamination, and on the health of Chernobyl victims. The newly elected Supreme Soviet of Ukraine did carry out in part this latter mandate from the voters. Well into the fifth year after the accident Ukraine finally passed the vital laws protecting Chernobyl victims.

At the time, the more than twenty thousand Zhitomir residents endorsed the draft resolution of the rally, supplemented by other speakers' proposals, but the rally chair, head of the emergency commission, G. A. Gotovchits, tried to push through a compromise resolution his subordinate bureaucrats had drawn up in the seclusion of their offices. The people rejected it indignantly. Still, despite the insistent demands from the rally, Gotovchits did not put my resolution to the vote. It was done by a metal worker, Oleg Khamaidyuk, member of the board of the Civil Front for Promoting Perestroika, who resolutely took over the matter. He came up to the microphone in the center of the stadium, held up the sheet of paper with the text of the resolution, and without asking anyone's permission, loudly and clearly read it out once more. He then put it to the vote, and thousands of hands shot up in the air. Thus in full view of the astonished and scared authorities, the people's will was done as the resolution was voted on and passed.

Young perestroika fighter and sterling lad, Oleg Khamaidyuk, died a while later under mysterious circumstances. The lights suddenly went out on the shop floor where Oleg worked. Someone told him to go up some stairs to the loft, saying that something was wrong with the wiring. He climbed up but, in the dark, stumbled over some tube and fell to his death on the first-story floor. I refuse to believe that it was entirely accidental. His colleagues say that the wretched tube was usually safely closed, precisely to prevent people from falling into it. We think that it was revenge by the apparatchiks for the courage and fearlessness Oleg had displayed in fighting the totalitarian system.

A question arises. Why did local government officials try to publicly ignore the opinion of thousands of people on so painful an issue as political assessment of the Chernobyl disaster? However, the question is purely rhetorical. After the Zhitomir rally, a flood of letters hit every bureaucratic structure there was. This stand by the Belorussian authorities forced the deceived people in Narovlya and Minsk to resort to extreme measures to protect their right to life in habitable areas. They set up strike committees. Political freedoms became daily fighting tools to secure the people's right to life in ecologically favorable conditions. A political strike, where all sorts of things—yearning for freedom and passions about Chernobyl—were interwoven, also stirred up the city of Zhitomir. The story of its maturing is a graphic example of how people start seeing the light, rise from their knees, and become a nation.

I shall relate some of the particulars.

For years, whenever the talk turned to Chernobyl victims, evacuees, or liquidators, two hard-and-fast counterarguments were invariably cited by officials of different caliber. "There is no threat to children's health" and "There is no money." Let the business of classifying information about people's health lie heavy on the conscience of those who had the temerity to do so. God will give them their just desserts, or maybe at least one of the governments in the three republics will have the conscience and courage to open a case and bring it to the logical end. Or a group of enthusiasts will take the matter to the European Court. One thing is certain. The criminals in power will not get away with it. Could it be that there really was no emergency way out, some stopgap measure at least, until the sick children's problems and those of the radiation-scorched liquidators had been solved? But of course there was! For that, though, the authorities needed to see that way out. They had to exercise responsibility and concern and take a civic stand, but to do that they would have had to infringe on their own interests and well-being for the sake of someone else's children and someone else's lives.

One of the planks of my election program was the demand to make the exclusive party clinic and hospital available to Chernobyl children. For several years we fought to get this done in Zhitomir. And that was the proposal I sent to Vasily Kavun, Zhitomir's first party secretary. In his reply he wrote irritably that there was a parliamentary commission for perks and benefits, and the treatment and sanatorium directorate issue was within its province—as if the member of the CPSU Central Committee and first secretary of the regional party committee could not assume responsibility in the interests of the victims instead of waiting for orders from the Kremlin. That could have been redemption of sorts, albeit belatedly.

When the disaster struck at Chernobyl, many ordinary townspeople in Zhitomir had to forget about housewarming for quite a while. The city executive committee handed dozens of new apartments over to the people who had been moved out of the 30-km zone. Years after the accident some of the city's industrial enterprises were still waiting for the Chernobyl apartment debt to be repaid to them. At the same time an exclusive apartment block for party functionaries was completed in Zhitomir in the spring of 1986, built at the regional party committee's request by permission of A. Lyashko, Ukrainian Council of Ministers chairman. If you think the apparatchiks would give up a single apartment, you've got another think coming. It was the workers of the flax mill who, after a decade on the housing list, ceded their prospective accommodation to the victims. As for the party upper crust who had been living in pretty comfortable apartments anyway, they got brand-new luxury residences—in contravention of every Soviet law.

I wrote a satirical piece about the outrage, "Enter In and Dwell Here, Ye Sufferers," and took it to my daily *Radyanska Zhitomirshchina*. But it was never published, nor could it be. The party bigwigs who thought I was playing on their turf—regional party committee secretaries, the son-in-law of the regional executive committee chairman—were much too important. What was I to do? I wrote an article about this shameful fact, enclosed copies of documents to confirm it, and sent the envelope to Moscow, addressed to prominent *Pravda* journalist Viktor Kozhemyako. I liked his articles and his sincere stand on glasnost issues. At the time, the principal Communist daily, *Pravda*, formerly the boring thick-skinned sheet we all knew, was turning into a lively discussion club right before our very eyes. My article "A Feuilleton—in the Wastepaper Basket" was published without much delay. After my "Confession of a Provincial Journalist" in the national daily *Izvestia*, it became the second bombshell, both for my newspaper's management and for the party bosses, and not only in the region but in the republic as well. Today a younger reader would have trouble visualizing the ensuing hullabaloo in the high offices. That was not the sort of thing they were used to. "She's dishonored the region!" they hissed, for one was only allowed to glorify it. The common folk, on the other hand, were jubilant. People phoned me, came to my place, and sent letters of support from all over the country.

The sacred cows called an urgent meeting at the Zhitomir regional party committee and passed a resolution on me, a nonparty journalist, which they published in *Radyanska Zhitomirshchina*. In it they alleged, without turning a hair, that all of it was untrue and that I had misled the unsuspecting public. But the public was different now and refused to believe either the party bosses or the newspaper. Quite right, too. I went to Yakov Zaiko, my colleague at the regional press agency, Novini Zhitomirshchini, the only local journalist who had the courage to support me, and we used an ordinary typewriter to make copies of the documents I had obtained, by hook or by crook, for my article. We distributed the copies to the factories and research centers in the city. Activists hung them up in prominent places, and the people literally gloated over them.

Things were beginning to move. At rallies and staff meetings Zhitomir townspeople demanded that the posh apartments be instantly handed over to Chernobyl victims from the Narodichi District. V. Nikulin, deputy chairman of the city executive committee, trying to save the regional party committee's face, could think of nothing more intelligent than to announce at the city party committee plenary session that "the decision of the regional public prosecutor's office was revised by the regional TU council, which found that only four authorizations to apartments had been issued unlawfully." Since when had the pocket trade unions overturned decisions by public prosecutor's offices? When I asked him for a copy of the public prosecutor's office statement on checking the legality of apartment distribution, I got a gem of an answer: "The certificate you requested has arrived from the regional committee of the Communist Party of Ukraine marked "SECRET." Therefore letting you have a copy of the certificate was not deemed possible." Would anything like that be deemed possible in the civilized world? A member of the country's highest legislative body unable to get from a local clerk a copy of a statement on compliance with housing laws involving a single building somewhere in the provinces! Talk of radiation! The party nomenklatura's ambitions proved more powerful than that. The triumph of justice was taking longer than expected. Despite the intervention, at my request, of the USSR prosecutor general's office, the local party kingpins, who had unlawfully grabbed twenty-eight of the forty-four apartments, were never evicted, although these cases had been reviewed in court several times. The court rulings, whose copies I obtained, were verbatim replicas of one another. The message was this. Yes, indeed, the apartments had gone to those people illegally, but eviction was impossible—the three-year time limit, during which it could be done, was over. The infernal statute of limitations, again! Actually, regional public prosecutor, A. Dzyuba, candidate member of Ukraine's Communist Party regional committee bureau, had done his best to ensure that the nomenklatura stayed in their palatial quarters. When I first applied to him about the matter, justice had at least a year in which to do it.

But the decision was delayed until the law became powerless. The local party kingpins naturally lacked the decency to vacate the premises of their own accord. The apartments, so sorely needed by Chernobyl victims, remained property of high-ranking thieves, now on a seemingly legal basis.

Let's go back to the "no money" argument, that is, money for the Chernobyl victims. Public funds were always in such short supply, so the officials at the Zhitomir regional executive committee didn't give a thought to resettling the peasants from all the hundred and sixty radioactive villages. But then Yuri Tsavro, member of the USSR Supreme Soviet Commission for Privileges and Benefits, reported in the *Argumenty i fakty* weekly, no. 36, 1989, thus:

> In Yalta, the Chernomorsky sanatorium of the fourth directorate of Ukraine's health ministry (that directorate was in charge of Party nomenklatura vacationing and treatment) occupies 12.6 hectares. It is designed for only 64 clients. These clients, meanwhile, are served by a staff of 167. The full cost of a 24-day stay is over 1,000 rubles. They have started new construction on the premises, with a 0.78 hectares chunk of the strictly protected Nikitsky Botanical Gardens seized for the purpose. That was done in circumvention of the USSR Council of Ministers resolution.

What a spectacle! Apparently, money was no object in this particular case. When it comes to children in villages subject to strict radiation monitoring, children who faint from weakness, whose thyroid glands are diseased, who have leukemia and enjoy other gifts of post-Chernobyl life, and liquidators who are disabled, the authorities experience a catastrophic dearth of funds, medication, and accommodation in "clean" areas.

In the fall of 1989, as I was leaving for Moscow on people's deputy's business, the strike committee of several Zhitomir enterprises notified me of their demands to authorities for support of my program. Among the proposals was the demand for making immediately available to sick Narodichi children and young families from the region's contaminated areas the exclusive hospital and clinic as well as the twenty-eight unlawfully occupied apartments in the exclusive apartment block. To the authorities, accustomed as they were to ordinary folk who labored for their own well-being, this turn of events came as a nasty shock.

On September 25, 1989, the city witnessed a two-hour warning strike without stoppages. The workers who had done their shift held solidarity rallies right in the shops and yards of their factories to support the residents of contaminated areas and demanded the transfer of medical facilities and unlawfully occupied apartments. Indeed, when it came to their perks, the party apparatchiks were willing to fight tooth and nail—even against sick children.

Under the pressure of mounting protests, after we, the people's deputies in the Kremlin, managed by a simple vote to scrap the notorious Article 6 that described the Communist Party as the only leading force in society, the local party fortress fell as well. The Communist putsch, during which Gorbachev was locked up by his "comrades in arms" in the Crimean residence of Foros, fell through, thank God. My efforts and the strikers' insistent demands were finally fulfilled, and the region's exclusive party clinic was handed over to the children. The regional party committee premises were taken over by the courts, and the buildings of two district party committees likewise would serve the city.

From the final report of the state expert commission for examining programs for eliminating the consequences of the Chernobyl nuclear accident: "One of the consequences of social and psychological tension experienced by the population of contaminated areas is the emergence of a social–political movement that uses industrial action as one of its methods. Judging by the movement dynamics, it may soon assume very radical forms indeed, which is borne out by the active participation in it of Ukraine's Rukh and the Popular Front in Belorussia." The commission's prophecy was fulfilled 100 percent. The wave of protests not only swept across the contaminated areas but inexorably spread all over the country, tsunami-style, hitting the areas where the authorities had plans to build new reactors. In the summer of 1989, when the press had finally broken the Chernobyl taboo, a protest action was held in Tatarstan. For two days protesters camped out near the town of Kamskie Polyany, to campaign against the building of the Tatar Nuclear Power Plant. In that same year, a series of rallies took place in Ukraine's city of Cherkassy. The people protested against the construction of the Chigirin Nuclear Power Plant. And that was just the beginning.

Thanks to all those Chernobyl rallies, protests, and other forms of unrest, at long last, in the spring of 1990, the government decided to establish regional interdepartmental expert councils in Minsk, Kharkov, Chelyabinsk, Donetsk, Dnepropetrovsk, Voroshilovgrad, Moscow, Leningrad, and Kiev. It was extremely important to the liquidators who now would have to travel half way across the country to Kiev for a medical examination. Four years after the accident, following a public outcry, the government, jointly with the trade unions, adopted a resolution "On Measures to Improve the Medical Service and Social Security of Persons Involved in the Work to Eliminate the Consequences of the Chernobyl Accident." Albeit reluctantly, the authorities started to cede ground, thus admitting the seriousness of the Chernobyl releases. The position of Chernobyl victims and liquidators improved somewhat after the special Chernobyl laws had been enforced in the affected republics. Yet the Chernobyl victims never did benefit from them to the full.

Whereas in the first years after the laws were passed, there was some headway, the collapse of the Soviet Union brought the whole thing to a halt. In the independent states other problems hopelessly eclipsed the Chernobyl victims with their numerous health problems. True, everything was fine on paper—social benefits and guarantees, free medical aid in emergency, rehabilitation in sanatoriums, better housing, a new apartment within three months, and increased extra payments for pensioners. But in practice, it was a much different story.

In Russia the government had amended the Chernobyl law several times, and that only made things worse, both for the population and for the liquidators. The total inaction by Russian bureaucrats, who failed to comply with the law, so vital to several million people, has already resulted, and will result further, in terrible social consequences. This means sick people in contaminated zones living in abject poverty, and liquidators forced to the brink of survival throughout our vast country.

The Chernobyl death statistics seem to be again hidden under the SECRECY stamp. At present, liquidators tell of terrible ordeals. They say there is a secret order by the Russian Health Ministry not to connect their diseases to radiation exposure, followed by a refusal to provide them the status of Chernobyl invalids. Even twenty years after the accident doctors still tend to conceal from liquidators their real diagnoses. There are cases when only the post mortem revealed

333

the actual cause of a person's death, usually cancer, from which that person had suffered for many years. Chernobyl victims often told me, "We have to resort to subterfuges to prove we are ill. In the surgery we simply don't tell the doctor that we are liquidators because, at the mere sound of the words 'Chernobyl liquidator,' the doctors at specialized clinics where we are registered just see red."

Year in, year out, the authorities cut the already miserly benefits for Chernobyl invalids. The payments were supposed to be indexed to catch up with rising prices. But even that did not do much good. Over the last eight years, they have been indexed only once, by 19 percent. In the same years consumer prices in the country have grown by 800 percent, while housing rents have shot up by almost 1,400 percent. Hundreds of thousands of Chernobyl victims forced by officials into poverty and hopelessness across the CIS territory are learning anew to fight for their lawful right, the right to life. They have taken to going to court en masse.

In 1995, further draconian amendments to the Chernobyl law made the life of Chernobyl victims and liquidators still more difficult. In 1997, many of these people, having gone through the ordeal of our legal system, applied to the Constitutional Court, which, wonder of wonders, took their side. The court ruling of December 1, 1997, confirms that the victimized people's constitutional right to compensation for injury sustained as a result of state activity is unshakeable, and it also reiterates that providing full indemnity is the state's constitutional duty. Under the RF Constitution and the RF Law on the Constitutional Court of the Russian Federation, the state guarantees that laws abolishing or reducing the civil rights and freedoms of the individual shall not be issued in the Russian Federation and that a new legal order shall not cancel out the legal positions of the RF Constitutional Court. As it approved its basic law, the state acknowledged responsibility before the victims and liquidators of the Chernobyl disaster. The amount of indemnity recognized by the state must be unconditionally observed.

Unfortunately, even Russia's Constitutional Court proved unable to make the state abide by its laws. In desperation, Chernobyl victims turned to the European Human Rights Court. It, too, backed the people whose rights had been trampled upon and obligated Russia to pay back the arrears. Yet the bureaucrats are in no hurry to do even the European Court's bidding, although Russia has the legal duty to do so. Realizing that court rulings were poor substitutes for food, the victims of Chernobyl decided to try protest rallies and fatal hunger strikes as a last resort. The Chernobyl victims and liquidators had no alternative but to fight to the last. And the last was always certain death.

The sad chronicle of that deadly struggle for life over the past twenty years after the accident only proves that all things are in a state of flux throughout the world, but in this country nothing changes. In 1997, liquidators from Ivanovo, a city two hundred kilometers northeast of Moscow, having lost all faith in the state, decided to hold a protest action. I learned of it in a letter sent to me by the editor of the *Ivanovskaya gazeta* daily who was, at the time, a member of the regional council of the Chernobyl Union NGO, V. G. Sokolov. The government's debts to Ivanovo liquidators amounted to nearly 5 million rubles ($750,000 in one year). Pharmacies no longer gave them free medicines, and the local authorities stopped providing free accommodation at sanatoriums for them. Moreover, the social compensation department refused to pay sickness benefits to working liquidators.

On January 20, 1997, a rally was organized in Tula by the regional Chernobyl Union association. For several weeks fifty-five liquidators went on a hunger strike at the local Palace of Culture. They demanded to be paid twelve-month pension arrears. Nine of the hunger strikers were hospitalized because of a threat to their lives. In Ukraine the situation around benefits for Chernobyl victims and liquidators is hardly any better. Several years ago my sister, Natalya Kovalchuk, a lawyer in Zhitomir, defended twenty-five such unfortunates and won every case, but the courts simply refuse to consider their lawsuits against the state. According to the liquidators themselves, many of their fellow sufferers did not live to see their allowances indexed, so they were unable to pay for treatment and improve their health, ruined in the fight against the Chernobyl monster and the state. Very few who won their cases in court ever received money from the state.

On April 25, 1999, Ukraine's Chernobyl Union held an all-Ukrainian rally in Kiev. It started with a parade through the city's main streets to the music of a funeral march. The rally attracted almost six thousand people from all over the country. The spectacle was heartrending. Disabled liquidators in wheelchairs or hobbling on artificial legs, widows carrying their husbands' portraits with crape bands and Bibles, and sick women and children walked in silence. The participants in that rally demanded that their benefits be restored and social-benefit arrears paid (over 650 million hryvnias in 1998, and another 120 million in 1999). The protesters wanted regular preventive medical and sanatorium services free, the law on forming the fund for eliminating the consequences of the Chernobyl accident amended at once, and the disbanded parliamentary committee for Chernobyl reinstated. In its resolution the Chernobyl Union reserved for itself the right to resort to more drastic protest forms.

In Russia, too, protest passions were running high. In late 1999, several hundred liquidators in Rostov-on-Don burned the effigies of government leaders. Over a hundred people went on hunger strike. On October 19, 2000, grade 2 invalid Pyotr Lyubchenko, a fifty-year-old liquidator who had gone on an indefinite hunger-strike, died. According to his fellow hunger-strikers, he climbed out of the tent, where he was fasting, took a few steps, and collapsed. The ambulance could not save him. Lyubchenko had taken his life fighting against the government for his lawful rights. As chairman of the Chernobyl Union Rostov regional council, Alexander Filippenko said Russia's government was doing its utmost to drive liquidators to an early grave.

Eighteen months ago, following a letter by Russia's Labor and Social Development Ministry, the Chernobyl victims in Rostov-on-Don had their health compensatory relief cut. Dozens of trials they had won pronounced the "document" a mere recommendation and ruled that they be repaid. But the court decision remained on paper. The hunger strike of eighty liquidators from the town of Shakhty was joined by disabled Chernobyl victims in Rostov and other cities. This region has Russia's second largest group of disabled liquidators. Two thousand of them died before they could see the government deliver on its promises.

In early 2004, the Chernobyl victims' struggle for their rights took a new turn. The government and parliament promised the so-called monetization of benefits. That meant that all those entitled to benefits, such as free transport, medication, and sanatorium vouchers, would receive monetary compensation instead. The benefits of the Chernobyl victims were reduced to the same level.

On March 4, 2004, liquidators in Stary Oskol, Belgorod region, went on hunger strike. The reasons were the same as ever—delayed indexing of health-damage compensation benefits, failure to pay in full for sanatorium treatment, and delayed housing assignment for the disabled. On March 17, 2004, their counterparts in the Tula and Kurgan regions and in the town of Mikhailovskoe, Stavropol Territory, also went on hunger strike. They protested against the draft law on benefits monetization that infringed on their rights.

On July 26–29, 2004, the Chernobyl Union held an impressive all-Russia protest action against benefits monetization. Taking part in it were tens of thousands of surviving Chernobyl liquidators across the country. They converged on Moscow from various parts of Russia. They had formed columns near the parliament building, where they intended to hold a mass rally to call the government's attention to their grievances—years-long benefit arrears, nonindexing, no free housing assignment, and denial of free treatment and medication. The main reason for this protest was that the infamous monetization act was about to be considered in the Duma. The all-inclusive compensation of thousand rubles or so was a laugh. In a major city you spent that on a single visit to a supermarket. Besides, said the demonstrators, "If the benefits are renamed social welfare, in the cases of Chernobyl victims, this will mean that litigation will be out of the question." In short, the authorities devised an excellent trap for the "spongers" who, twenty years previously, had saved the country and the world from a nuclear nightmare. However, the all-Russia protest by disabled people going on foot or in wheelchairs, which was impossible to watch without tears, did nothing to make the deputies or the government backtrack on their plans.

On July 27, 2004, disabled Chernobyl liquidator Pyotr Budenny, who was on hunger strike, died in the town of Medvedkovskaya, Krasnodar Territory, at the age of 58. He had wanted the authorities to comply with the law and provide him with habitable accommodation. He started his hunger strike in early July in his clay-brick hut, where he lived with his wife. "After a week he felt bad and was rushed to the intensive care unit. The hospital treatment helped, but back home he resumed the hunger strike, and when several days later he was again put on a drip, it was too late," said Vyacheslav Grishin, president of the all-Russia Chernobyl Union. Chernobyl invalid Pyotr Budenny was forced to leave Kirghizia for his native Russia in 1998. He decided to settle in Krasnodar Territory. But his motherland proved just as harsh as Kirghizia. "Already in Kirghizia, circulatory disturbance, the commonest complaint among liquidators, cost him one leg. He was given Chernobyl grade 1 disability, but two years later the other leg had to be amputated," Grishin told the press. "Under the law, Chernobyl invalids are to be given accommodation within three months of joining the housing list, yet Budenny could not get an apartment for several years," he pointed out. "We begged him to halt his hunger strike and opened a special account to buy him an apartment, but we managed to collect only a few thousand rubles before he died." Even that appalling tragedy in the south of Russia failed to move the coldhearted troglodytes. In the fall of 2004, a dozen or so disabled liquidators in the city of Bryansk fasted on a hunger strike for twenty-six days. Seven of them had to be hospitalized.

Vyacheslav Kornyushin, chairman of the Bryansk regional organization of Russia's Chernobyl Union, reports that courts accepted the benefit scale factor claims of seven hundred Chernobyl invalids, but another two hundred people, for some reason that is not at all clear, were sent off with a lower coefficient. Besides, the extra money had not been paid for two years, and the federal budget owed in excess of 40 million rubles to the impoverished and sick heroes. The hunger strikers were backed by regional Duma deputies, in particular Lyudmila Komogortseva and Yuri Petrukhin, as well as by Vyacheslav Kobets, chairman of the regional social protection coordination committee for people affected by the Chernobyl nuclear accident. Appeals were sent to virtually every level of authority. A letter to the president of Russia was readdressed to the regional court and Mikhail Zurabov, Russia's health minister, the same person who was originally responsible for the benefits monetization scheme.

On December 4, 2004, fifty-six liquidators went on a hunger strike, by way of warning, in the town of Alexin, Tula region. They wanted the RF Supreme Court plenary session to speed up their lawsuit. The suit was over the fact that compensation sums were linked to the minimum subsistence wage. Over the last few years the minimum wage had been raised twice, yet Chernobyl payments remained the same. Thus, according to the local Chernobyl Union section, the government owed liquidators 5–6 billion rubles. The court dawdled over their claim consideration for two years. And then the people's patience ran out. On August 16, 2004, a hunger strike in the town of Gubkin, Belgorod region, was resumed after suspension. Six Chernobyl invalids wrote a desperate letter to the authorities. Here is what it said:

> At one time, when our common home that we call Motherland met with a disaster, we, young and healthy men, did our duty to our Motherland, our state, and our people. We sacrificed the most precious thing that we had, our health. And now, in these difficult, hard times, we, whose health has been ruined, are unable to work like other people, we cannot provide for our families as we would wish, cannot solve our housing problems, and constantly have to

overcome physical, moral and material difficulties. We, Chernobyl invalids, to whose heroism any European would take his hat off, expected our Motherland not to let us face our problems all on our own. Who is answerable for the lawlessness in our country? The last time a Chernobyl invalid was issued an apartment was in 2000 (according to the information of the Chernobyl Union Gubkin section), and even that was done at the expense of the local budget. The last apartment paid for from the federal budget was allocated in 1998. This is how our state honors its commitment to the liquidators of the consequences of the Chernobyl nuclear power plant accident. Will we live to see the promised housing?

Today we, distressed Chernobyl invalids, have to resort to extreme measures, going on an indefinite hunger strike, to force the state to remember its obligations and comply with its own laws. We went to Moscow, to Russia's emergency situations ministry, hoping to learn how the promises were being fulfilled. Ministry officials refused to receive us. The telegram we sent to the Belgorod region governor requesting a meeting with him remained unanswered. It was not 'til the last workday prior to our protest action that the regional and territorial administration heads invited us for talks. Again we heard nothing definite. Moreover, at present the RF government and the State Duma have passed a draft law on replacing the benefits we were entitled to under the aforementioned law by "monetary compensation." The very substitution of the phrase "social welfare measures" for the terms "compensation payments and benefits" violates the RF Constitution. If our state is law-based, then why are our constitutional and legal relations with the state being replaced by "social welfare measures," legally inferior in terms of social protection, in defiance of the people's opinion? Those measures depend on the will (good or evil, as the case may be) of the RF government. We are totally opposed to the idea of replacing the current benefits system by welfare payment schemes. The new draft law cancels many of the benefits and indemnity payments that are part of the compensation packet for Chernobyl liquidators.

Seeing that our problems are not being addressed, we have decided to resume our protest action, the indefinite hunger strike, at 10:00 hours on August 16, 2004, with all the original demands:

1. Immediate provision of housing for Chernobyl invalids registered with the housing department of the Gubkin city administration and Gubkin district, under Clause 3 of Article 14 of the RF Law on Social Protection for Individuals Exposed to Radiation in the Aftermath of the Accident at the Chernobyl Nuclear Power Plant.

2. Immediate compliance by the RF government, the construction department, transport department and housing and municipal department of the Belgorod region, with court

decisions on meeting the commitments to provide us, out of turn, with adequate accommodation.

3. A fresh account and indexing of all arrears and timely subsequent payment of all compensation for deteriorating health in the aftermath of the Chernobyl nuclear disaster.

4. Payment of compensation for sanatorium and spa treatment in full amount, which has been reduced through the fault of bureaucrats at the regional social insurance directorate.

5. Strict observance of norms and established time limits for cases brought by Chernobyl victims to court.

6. Rigorous compliance in future with the RF Law on Social Protection for Individuals Exposed to Radiation in the Aftermath of the Accident at the Chernobyl Nuclear Power Plant.

The list of liquidators taking part in the hunger strike: V. G. Burtsev, Group 2 invalid; A. I. Rakityansky, Group 2 invalid; A. A. Shokov, Group 3 invalid; V. A. Burtsev, Group 2 invalid; A. P. Kalyukin, Group 2 invalid; S. N. Obyedkov, Group 3 invalid.

After large-scale unrest throughout the country, amid an almost total information blackout and after the death of several hunger strikers, the government finally took notice of the Chernobyl victims' movement for their rights. The government singled them out among the body of people entitled to benefits by issuing a special resolution about them. But that did little to ease their plight. It was the government's resolution of December 27, 2004, "On Indexing in 2004 the Amount of Compensation and Other Payments to Individuals Exposed to Radiation in the Aftermath of the Accident at the Chernobyl Nuclear Power Plant," that prompted a new upsurge of indignation in the Chernobyl community. In fact, it left things largely unchanged.

The new protest action centered this time on Chernobyl veterans from Sestroretsk, not far from St. Petersburg. One of its organizers, Kulish, a disabled person, explained with bitterness what had forced them to resort to protests:

> The resolution provides for increasing payments by 38 percent over the last three years, while the prices in St. Petersburg have risen, by our estimate, by 350 percent in the same period of time. And if you take the last eight years, since they stopped indexing the sums paid to us in compensation for deterioration of health we sustained, the price rise has been about 1,800 percent. In all of these years, there was only one instance of indexing the payments, in 2001—by 19.7 percent. Add this to the 2004 indexing, and you will get some 65 percent. Meanwhile, the rents and utility rates have grown three or four times during these years, and will rise by another 30 percent

as of January 1. Public transport fares are constantly climbing (we have just been robbed of our right to free rides), and so are the prices of gasoline (which is very important to those of us, invalids, who own cars) and of food. Free medical checkups and treatment we are entitled to under the law is something we get only infrequently, and chargeable treatment costs a lot more than our compensation benefits.

On top of betrayal by their own state, they also had to face betrayal of their interests by the leaders of Russia's Chernobyl Union. The leadership of the union's Sestroretsk district branch wanted chief hunger-strike instigator Sergei Kulish stripped of his union membership. In the argument between disabled liquidators and the authorities, both Vladimir Dragush, head of the district branch, and president of the all-Russia Chernobyl Union Grishin took the side of the government and against the hunger strike. A similar thing, incidentally, happened in July 2004, when indignant liquidators marched on Moscow from across the country to take part in the mass rally in protest against privilege monetization. The Chernobyl Union leaders did their best to prevent the rally. Here is what Sergei Kulish said:

> They betrayed us by throwing their support, on behalf of Chernobyl victims, behind monetization which deprived us of most of the benefits (free treatment, sanatorium and spa provision, medication, prosthetic appliances, free urban and suburban transportation, provision of cars as medically indicated), in exchange for thousand rubles a month. For the vast majority of Chernobyl victims whose health has been irreparably ruined, this is a most inadequate exchange. Well, it seems we have no other means left to get ourselves heard except a hunger strike.

St. Petersburgers' protest action against benefits monetization was joined by invalids from Smolensk in western Russia, Pyatigorsk in the south, and other parts of the country. In early December 2004, St. Petersburg Chernobyl invalids who had gone on hunger strike demanded Russia's Supreme Court plenary session to be urgently convened, and launched a complaint about the unlawful nature of the government's resolution of December 27, 2004, "On Indexing in 2004 the Amount of Compensation and Other Payments to Individuals Exposed to Radiation in the Aftermath of the Accident at the Chernobyl Nuclear Power Plant."

The authorities' cynicism in this business of Chernobyl benefits was revealed by government actions at the height of all those hunger strikes and protests when, on December 3, 2004, it issued resolution no. 1562-r, in which we find paragraph 2 (I am quoting from the text published in the government's *Rossiyskaya gazeta* of December 9, 2004): "To use funds to the extent of 300 million rubles from the money in the Federal Budget saved while implementing the RF Law on Social Protection for Individuals Exposed to Radiation in the Aftermath of the Accident at the Chernobyl Nuclear Power Plant, for reimbursing the expenses of implementing in 2004 the RF Law on Rehabilitation of Victims of Political Reprisals by Russian Federation entities." What's that supposed to mean? A case of wicked baseness, setting one group of privilege-holders against another? A provocation? Consider that, by the end of 2004, the state had failed to pay some 1.5 billion rubles on just twenty-two thousand suits instigated by Chernobyl invalids!

Vladimir Kiveretsky, a St. Petersburg journalist, quotes on the Prima information agency Web site the hunger strikers in his city awaiting the Supreme Court session with this damning piece of evidence:

> The authorities have as good as killed us anyway; we won't live much longer now, so we have nothing to lose. All there was to lose we have lost already. All except human dignity. And our object now is to show the people of Russia where we made a mistake. We started fighting for our rights far too late. Our criminal rulers and the Chernobyl Union public organization that has sold itself to them were for years pulling the wool over our eyes, feeding us promises. And now we wish to tell the world: we have been purposefully bamboozled. In effect, it all boiled down to getting rid of us for good, to doing away with us for the sake of budget economy. We have gathered proof of deliberate extermination of Chernobyl invalids for The Hague Tribunal; there have been thousands of cases of Chernobyl's victims' deaths, repressive resolutions by the government, doctors' abuse of their position, the state's lies about our benefits, and finally this awful anticonstitutional decree by V. Putin cynically presented to us on April 26, for the nuclear disaster anniversary. This time around we will defend our rights more consistently, up to the international level. We must let the whole world know about the authorities' crimes against us. We have had enough!

Will the world heed this cry of despair? Why hasn't a single bureaucrat, senior or junior, answered yet for this monetization outrage? It seems the authorities have again dodged responsibility, as they did in the case of covering up the consequences of the accident. The latest Chernobyl law passed in the Russian Federation has Article 48, which says in the clearest possible terms, "Officials guilty of violating the aforementioned RF Law shall bear criminal, administrative, disciplinary, and material responsibility in accordance with RF legislation." Yet the law, which has been in effect for the last ten years, has worked hardly at all. Who has been punished for its most blatant violations that caused the death of Chernobyl invalids? No one. Chernobyl victims have won twenty-two thousand cases, but not one of the courts has issued even an intermediary order, to say nothing of applying to the prosecutor's office to launch action against officials violating the law. So the law intended to protect Chernobyl invalids actually protects the bureaucrats against them.

Rem, "roentgen equivalent man," is a term in physics. I would suggest an alternative interpretation. It is also a ruthlessness equivalent. And while the physical REM has an MPL, the maximum permissible level, the social REM seems to me to have UPL, unlimited permissible levels of ruthlessness.

Ukrainians started picketing their parliament, the Verkhovna Rada, on February 2, 2005, already after the Orange Revolution, as a solidarity action in support of Russian Chernobyl invalids. The picket organizer was the All-Ukraine Chernobyl People's Party. (See, they have even formed a party—it is easier to fight the bureaucrats' abuse of power this way.) The picketers carried these slogans for the benefit of the deputies and the apparatchiks: "Guaranteed medical treatment for Chernobyl victims," "Reliable social protection for Chernobyl children," "Chernobyl has taken our health, and the state is taking our life." The act was timed to coincide with Verkhovna Rada session that considered issues of their social protection.

On February 7, 2005, Chernobyl victims held a press conference in Kiev. It focused on the new program the "Orange" government had come up with. Liquidators announced that they had not seen anything in the program by the new president and government that would bear relation to their problems. "We will wait a while longer to see what steps they will take in this direction. If they do indeed cooperate, well and good, but if they don't, we will have to go onto the streets," said first deputy head of the All-Ukraine Chernobyl People's Party Vasily Gladky.

Chernobyl liquidators also told the journalists that even before the election they "tried to meet the incumbent, Victor Yushchenko, to tell him about our problems. The meeting took place. He showed concern, and we agreed on ways of cooperation." They hoped to see the then presidential candidate at the party congress, asking him to "speak there and look the Chernobyl liquidators in the eye. The congress has come and gone, and he never turned up. He showed himself to be a cheat," Gladky summed up harshly. Nor was the new "Orange" government spared. The Chernobyl Party leader said that "it was the wrong sort of people that got into it, such as Anatoly Kinakh who way back in 2002 signed the criminal resolution to cut the subsistence minimum for the Chernobyl victims down to 19.91 hryvnias. As for Mr. Pinzenik, he sent inflation into a spin and launched the 'shock therapy,' acting on orders from certain circles abroad."

Liquidators promised the country's new leadership nothing less than a Chernobyl revolution if the authorities forgot their duty to them. Today, two decades after that fateful spring night, it is abundantly clear that the governments of Russia, Ukraine, and Belarus have long since stopped noticing the heroes and victims of the twentieth century's worst disaster. They increasingly have to call the state's attention to themselves going on hunger strikes and industrial stoppages—to remind the authorities that not all of them have died yet, particularly liquidators, and that they need financial assistance from the state and its protection, for when the state asked them to sacrifice themselves in the Chernobyl cleanup, they did not set any conditions to anyone but without a moment's hesitation went right into the inferno.

Here is what the trusted party journalist Vladimir Gubarev of *Pravda* reported in his classified memo to the party's top body, enclosed with the top secret resolution by the CPSU Central Committee of May 22, 1986: "(2) Working in danger zones (within 800 meters of the reactor) were soldiers without individual protection means, as they unloaded lead and performed other tasks. They said, when I talked to them, that they had not been issued with this type of clothing. Helicopter pilots were in a similar situation." And another group of conscripts had to throw radioactive graphite off the reactor roof with their bare hands. Now, what if those people had refused to subdue the raging nuclear reactor and the other three Chernobyl reactors had blown up? Citizens of Russia, Europe, and the entire world owe these courageous cleanup soldiers a great debt of gratitude. It could have been much worse. The liquidators and their families deserve justice, but will the cries of protesters continue to fall on deaf ears, buried under "curtains of fog and iron" (a Churchillian phrase in another context).

22

Scientific Shell Game

The Chernobyl nuclear disaster became the acid test not only for politicians in power but also for scientists and doctors, worldwide. The penetrating radiation syndrome—that's a medical term—has turned into the penetrating official lie syndrome in the case of the country's ruling political and academic elite. The Chernobyl accident, like litmus paper supplied by history itself, tested that elite's conscience and ordinary human decency. Alas, the elite failed the test. Twenty years is quite long enough to start gathering stones in "our Chernobyl garden," or, more appropriately, "our garden of hell." The time is inexorably coming for counting the nuclear chickens, for they have hatched, all right. The numbers give mute testimony to the suffering of my townspeople, a painful personal reminder since I know many of the affected families.

In this chapter I survey official data on the changes in the health of 9 million Chernobyl victims over the two decades since the nuclear blast. They are still inhaling small doses of Chernobyl radiation. I will reveal the way the Chernobyl health data continued to change from official Kremlin lies to the current results at national research centers in independent states after the Soviet Union collapsed and the Kremlin lost its monopoly over the Chernobyl truth. To do it in the most graphic way possible, I reference, as background, the first public report by academician L. A. Ilyin, the man who is, quite rightly, associated with the highest potentates of power.

Ilyin's first public report, entitled "The Ecological Features and Medico-biological Consequences of the Accident at the Chernobyl Nuclear Power Plant" (I keep in my archives an almost seventy-page typewritten copy of it), was delivered at the session of the general assembly of the USSR Academy of Medical Sciences in Moscow on March 21–23, 1989. It is noteworthy that it happened three years after the accident. Undoubtedly, the academician had made a few reports before, during those three busy post-Chernobyl years, but not for the likes of you and me. They were intended for the Kremlin patricians and were therefore top secret. Now, what could have happened three years later to induce the academician to come into the open? Simply because the public report was to be delivered at the time of the first Congress of the USSR People's Deputies. It was not so much a scientific move as a preemptive political strike. The authorities knew that the Chernobyl issue would instantly be raised at the Congress, so they decided to cushion the blow of criticism.

Although the speaker was Ilyin, the report bore the signatures of twenty-three medical officials from Russia, Ukraine, and Belorussia—a sort of collective Ilyin. In this country responsibility has always been collective, never individual.

Note: The academician's report was news not only to the public (although, as far as I know, reporters never wrote about it as it is unlikely that they would have been allowed in the hall) but even to some uninitiated scientists, who found a lot of its points a revelation. Here is what the report said:

> The dosage load on the thyroid gland owing to radioiodine incorporation largely built up within a short period of time—10–12 weeks after the accident. Immediately, the USSR health ministry put in effect the previously devised emergency standard of maximum permissible concentration of iodine-131 in milk (3,700 Bq/l) that corresponded to the thyroid dose load of 0.3 Sv (30 rem) for children. According to preliminary estimates, the set of measures recommended by the USSR health ministry for short-term radiation protection of the people, which were aimed primarily at preventing or reducing the intake of radioiodine, helped reduce the potential dose loads by an average of 50 percent, and in some cases even by 80 percent.

This reminds me of other samples of the accuracy of our official medical establishment, such as "a set of protective measures has reduced 2 to 2.2 times the total dose in the population against the forecast levels." So what was compared with what, and what was forecast? That remained unsaid.

Now about Ilyin's assurances regarding "prevention or reduction of radioiodine intake." According to reports from the accident site and those of parliamentary experts, iodine prophylaxis was either omitted altogether or applied when it was no longer of any use. That was stated, both in the reply of the USSR prosecutor general's office to people's deputies and in the final report by Ukraine's prosecutor general. The

2004 research by a group of Belarusian scientists, headed by A. Ye. Okeanov, says that virtually the whole of Belarus was dusted with radioiodine. Only the northern section of the republic was relatively "clean." The rest of the territory was contaminated with the stuff at the level of 5–50, and even 300 Ci/km^2. Well, it was precisely in these parts that the iodine prophylaxis started ten days after the reactor exploded, by which time it was a totally useless procedure. The thyroid glands of the population (especially children) had already been crammed with dangerous radioiodine from unit 4. The same prophylaxis pattern was adhered to in the other contaminated areas. The whole thing was largely a deception or blatantly unprofessional and a perfect example of medical malpractice. Weren't the clinicians aware of that?

The authors of the report that Ilyin delivered assure us also that "specific values of radiation doses absorbed by the inhabitants of every locality in the permanently monitored areas over various periods of time after the accident have been established [computer-calculated]." Well, it was clear even at the time, and is known at present with complete certainty, that it was a garden-variety lie. Public prosecutors' investigations and reports cited in the previous chapters suggest that the medics did not manage to conduct even ordinary iodine prophylaxis (except on paper), and they did not keep specific dose records after the radiation impact and subsequent exposure of people trapped in the Chernobyl plume. That, incidentally, is also what the Politburo task group's secret minutes say. The authors further amplify the now-open record. Despite the fact that radiation "factors in diminished potential hazards of long-term consequences," it was that model they used, with this caveat—the "need for a balanced interpretation of the given data with the aforementioned extrapolative and other limitations taken into account."

What limitations do the authors mean? In their report they allege that "one of the main objections (to the no-threshold theory) lies in the fact that the numerical values of exposure risks (effect probability in relation to exposure dose unit), recommended for estimating slowly delivered low-power doses, were obtained in on-site research only for high doses and high-magnitude radiation effects." This brazen lie was exposed a year later, at the parliamentary hearings on nuclear accidents at the Mayak Production Facility that had repeatedly occurred in the Urals since 1949. All information about those accidents and their health effects was likewise classified. Ten thousand people were resettled; the country and the world were none the wiser. They were left to live along the Techa River banks where they have been absorbing those same small radiation doses ever since. Besides, we have recently learned that the Leningrad Nuclear Power Plant sustained a major accident that involved the same reactor type—years before the Chernobyl disaster. Those lies were told precisely in the hope that no one would ever learn the truth.

The next statement, "Stochastic (randomness in one or more of its variables) effects of a somatic and genetic nature in the given radiation dose range were simply not registered," is enough to shock not only experts but any reasonably well-educated laypersons interested in radiobiology. By the time the report was made, various outstanding scholars, such as John Gofman, Ralph Graeub, Abram Petkau, Ernest Sternglass, Rosalie Bertell, and many other researchers studying the impact of small radiation doses on health had already published their findings. Surely the academicians at the Kremlin court could have had those works translated for their edification! One is somehow reluctant to believe that the people who decided the fate of millions of Chernobyl victims (some still do) could be quite so unenlightened.

If they really had not read the works of their more advanced foreign colleagues, they must surely have known that the UNSCEAR Committee and ICRP had "legitimized" the linear no-threshold model, not the threshold model of the harmful effects from small radiation amounts. In so doing, it was definitely guided by ideological, political, or emotional considerations. Isn't that the reason why, albeit unwillingly, with reservations and explanations, the authors of the Ilyin report have to reckon with what to them is a calamity—the linear no-threshold theory? It appears that their own report refuted their position.

Grudgingly, after three years of ideological optimism, the Kremlin academicians gave their public "prognoses for three exposure levels sustained by the population at large, and separately by children under 7 at the moment of the accident":

1. For thirty-nine districts of nine regions, where radiation levels proved comparatively higher than elsewhere (total population, 1.5 million, including 158,000 children)
2. For the whole population of these areas (15.6 million people, including 1.66 million children under seven)
3. For residents of the central areas of the Soviet Union's European part (75 million people, including 8 million children under seven)

These mind-boggling statistics—particularly the 75 million people within the Chernobyl plume!—were then made public for the first time after the Chernobyl Nuclear Power Plant disaster, and only in narrow medical circles, at the time.

So what were those official prognoses?

> According to the linear no-threshold hypothesis, we can expect something like 90 cases of malignant thyroid tumors in children under seven within the next 30 years after the accident, 10 of them terminal. In all, the population of these areas (about 1.5 million people) may develop some 200 extra cases of thyroid cancer within the said period, without allowing for the accuracy of the hypothesis. Examination of the possible effect of radiation on thyroids for the entire population of the given regions (39 districts of 9 regions, although there are many more such areas), above all in the Kiev, Gomel, Bryansk and Zhitomir regions, suggests that within the 30-year period we should expect an incidence of malignant growths around 3.3×10^2, 3×10^1 of these incurable.

Prognoses for the population of the central European regions of the USSR, including the whole of Ukraine, Belarus, Moldova, and some areas in central Russia—a total of 75 million people, including 8 million children under seven—are as follows: "Based on available estimates, the following theoretically feasible number of thyroid cancers caused by radiation over the 30-year period after the Chernobyl nuclear power plant accident is suggested: up to 20 cases of incurable malignant tumors in children; and up to 50 cases in the population at large. As for curable malignant growths, there may be 170 and 400 cases, respectively." Bearing these statements in mind, it would be interesting to take another look at the secret correspondence between Ukraine's health minister, A. Ye. Romanenko, and USSR health minister Ye. I. Chazov. (Copies of the letters are in my archives.) Romanenko reports to Moscow:

> The areas with increased radiation levels in the Kiev, Zhitomir and Chernigov regions have a population of 215,000, including 74,600 children. 39,600 persons not previously registered have been found to be ill. Altogether, 20,200 persons have been hospitalized over a period of 12 months, about 6,000 of them children. Of those, 2,600 children (3.4 percent) were found to have an iodine radionuclide count exceeding 500 rem.

Where are they today, those 2,600 Ukrainian children referenced in the minister's secret letter? Who will answer this question? There is no answer. The Kremlin medical propagandists had known these terrible secrets two years before their collective report was delivered! Those statistics that the minister cites obviously came off the top of his head.

The report also predicts "potential long-term effects of total irradiation of various population groups in the Soviet Union in the aftermath of the Chernobyl nuclear accident," estimating exposure levels adjusted to the 35-rem conception of the USSR Health Ministry. (They still stick to their guns, regardless of the classified results of medical checkups known to none but themselves while ignoring the UN no-threshold model.) Relative to the population of permanently monitored zones, it is emphasized that "long-term effects were estimated on the basis of the actually computed dose accumulated over the first four years after the accident and its estimate out to 2060, given that in those areas, too, all restrictions on locally produced food consumption have been lifted." Two simple questions arise at this point. First, at the time when the report was made, three years had elapsed since the accident and very few doses were collected during that period. If this is no more than a bad mistake by the authors, it seems highly suggestive. A Freudian slip. And second, *who* actually computed the doses absorbed by the people in the first two or three months, and *when* did they do it?

The recently published book, *Chernobyl: 20 Years On: Health Effects of the Chernobyl Accident* (full text at the European Committee on Radiation Risk Web site, euradcom.org), reports 38.5 percent of 45,873 children surveyed in Ukraine, Belarus, and Russia, during the period 1987–96, had developed thyroid gland diseases (47 percent in the Gomel region). A 1997 paper by V. B. Nesterenko found, by 1992, that infant mortality in the heavily contaminated Gomel area was more than double the rate of that in Grodno, a relatively clean town. The author also tracked diseases in Belarus between the years 1988 and 1996 and noted that childhood cancers had multiplied 2.4 times; malignant tumors, 13 times; endocrine system diseases, up to 4.5 times; nervous and sense organs, 3.5 times; and blood circulation, 4 times; also, mortality from respiratory disease in under fourteen-year-olds had multiplied by 2.5. What a heavy burden the countless thousands of families have endured!

My analysis shows with perfect clarity what herculean efforts the authorities exerted to not only classify all information about the disaster but also destroy the primary medical documents that recorded precisely the real exposure doses (although inaccurate doses may have been the norm). Instead, the doctors were told to enter reduced doses in the medical records and put in any diagnosis as long as it did not bear any relation to radiation effects. Given all that, these seemingly serious people with their attractive academic titles invite their colleagues and the public at large to believe in their version of "real" dose estimates. Just how "real" those estimates were is graphically shown by the official secret documents of the USSR Academy of Medical Sciences in my archives, which suggest that in the Zhitomir region no autopsy was carried out on those dying after the accident, children included. If the authors of the report are sure of their facts, why weren't ordinary people and journalists who are interested in these matters given access to them so that the facts could be analyzed? Why are even professional experts denied such access? I have often heard both Russian and foreign scientists complain of that. Even after two decades the Chernobyl materials of Russia's Biophysics Institute of the Academy of Sciences are still inaccessible, apart from official abstracts. Why the secrecy now?

The authors' conclusion of the report made when predicting the future of the people in permanently monitored areas significantly understates the case. Note: "Despite the tendency toward rising spontaneous cancer morbidity and mortality rates recorded everywhere in the USSR, our calculations take these parameters as constant throughout the period under analysis (seventy years). Consequently, any extra proportion of surplus terminal tumors against the spontaneous level can be adjusted by reducing their incidence." The same idea recurs in the general conclusion: "The data cited in this work suggest that in the majority of cases predicted levels of the radiogenic effects of exposure under discussion, above all among the residents of areas placed under strict monitoring in the aftermath of the Chernobyl nuclear accident, are likely to stay within the range of percentages considerably smaller than standard fluctuation values of spontaneous levels recorded for corresponding pathology."

In other words, the people, first and foremost those living in strict-monitoring zones, who for decades have been exposed to radiation and its biological effects that remain toxic for centuries, are less likely to die of cancer than the population in other areas. In the case of thyroid tumors the authors are forced to conclude, "It is possible that the excess incidence of radiogenic cancers of this organ will be observed." But the odds are against it, apparently. Very reassuring! In short, give us more radiation; it'll do us good. That's the hormesis thesis, now promulgated by some pseudoscientists (a heavy dose is detrimental, but small doses are beneficial!). The true worth of all those statements and collective Soviet prognoses made on the basis of classified and distorted data was highlighted by those who have spent twenty years living in the Chernobyl radioactive oases.

This is what it was really like. It was the colleagues and fellow party members of Ilyin and his team who started to disprove (and even denounce) the torrents of lies that had inundated the country during the first three years after the accident. They had to do it, being cornered by public opinion and the media. Within a year of the infamous report at the USSR Supreme Soviet session, V. Kh. Doguzhiev, chairman of the government's commission for eliminating the consequences of the Chernobyl accident, made a statement that came as a shock for the country and the world: "Sixty-two percent of the population examined were found to have sustained exposure doses between 1 and 5 rem. For about 1.5 million people who, at the time of the accident, happened to live in areas with the highest radioiodine contamination levels, including 160,000 children under seven, thyroid irradiation doses will stay under 30 rem for 87 percent of the adults and 48 percent of the children. But it will reach 100 rem for 17 percent of the children there."

These official statistics are also based on secret reports preceded by equally secret orders not to enter real doses in the victims' medical records. That means that the figures have to be multiplied by an unknown number. The Ilyin team did not respond in any way to the Doguzhiev report. After all, the main thing in the official medical establishment is party discipline. Shortly before his sensational admission, Doguzhiev assured people's deputies, "The chief demographic indices—birth, death, and population growth rates in the contaminated areas of the Russian Federation, Belorussia and the Ukraine are on a par with the relevant indices throughout the country." By then I already had in hand a secret verdict by scientists from the USSR Academy of Medical Sciences, for internal use only, that stated the exact opposite: "Morbidity rates for the main classes of disease and mortality indicate an upward trend, particularly mortality rates among the adults and children in the Zhitomir region."

Finally, Ilyin himself was forced to reluctantly admit, at parliamentary hearings, that "a million six hundred thousand children have dose loads that are causing concern; we should now decide what to do next."

Squeezing out bits of information from party officials and medics about the health situation in radiation-affected zones was proving difficult three and four years after the accident. One had to do it, as Chekhov once advised, drop by drop. Thank God I had my own nuclear weapon, as it were, a people's deputy's mandate, that was like a red flag to those in authority. With the forced "go-ahead" from the top of the power pyramid, three years after the disaster and after lying to the whole world about its consequences, the government and ministers grudgingly started to give the people's deputies something remotely like the truth.

All this information ought to be correlated with the initial more or less public report by the official Ilyin team. The result would be a handbook on the big lies about the condition of Chernobyl victims, those that the authorities have been circulating for the last couple of decades. Ukraine's health minister Yu. P. Spizhenko, in reply to my inquiry (some four years after the accident), stated thus:

> The proportion of the population pronounced healthy upon examination within three years of the accident has dropped by an average of 27 percent, including by 18 percent among the liquidators; by 33 percent among the evacuees, and by 47 percent among the residents of contaminated areas. This points an actual decrease in health level indicators in the cohorts. The prevalent complaints among adults are disorders of the respiratory organs, circulation, nervous and endocrine systems, skin and subcutaneous fat diseases, and tumors. Diseases and disabilities were found to have been caused by participation in the Chernobyl cleanup in more than 2,000 cases.

These numbers are highly suspect.

Some villages in the Mogilev and Gomel regions of Belorussia, and in the Zhitomir region of Ukraine, have adults with an absorbed dose of 400 rem or more, just a few years after the Chernobyl accident. Those are lethal doses.

In the first ten years after the nuclear disaster, the health of radioactive-zone residents suffered severely. According to Russian researchers O. Yu. Tsitser and M. S. Malikov, analysis of cancer-related mortality rates in Ukraine's areas around the Chernobyl Nuclear Power Plant in the periods 1980–85 and 1986–91 suggests a significant increase in deaths from breast and prostate cancers. Independent Ukraine spokesmen, at the Columbia University conference dedicated to the tenth anniversary of the Chernobyl disaster, estimated 148,000 people had died in Ukraine by then in the aftermath of the accident.

Statistics do not impart the full impact of their awful significance, but they enlarge the scope of any study beyond the personal testimonials. Anyone with an interest in public health will find data on radiation to be most instructive, with credit to the Pediatrics, Obstetrics and Gynecology Research Center of Ukraine's Ministry of Health. The specialists believe that the accident has affected the country's entire genes pool. The birth rates have plummeted. This is not to be confused with the post-Soviet situation, when the impact of Chernobyl was compounded by the general "democratic" impoverishment of the people, a condition not exactly conducive to a baby boom. The contribution of Chernobyl to the dropping birth rates in Ukraine is as follows—from 15 percent in 1986 to 11.4 percent a decade later, while the mortality rate remained at 13.4 percent.

Examination of pregnant women from contaminated areas, according to the same research center, points to increased incidence of pregnancy complications and labor pathology. In the preaccident period unfavorable outcomes were registered in 9.6 cases per 100 pregnancies; after the accident this rate rose to 13.4 percent. The rate was found to depend to a considerable extent on the women's dose load. The incidence of anemia and risk of abortion has grown 1.5 to 2 times. (This has a direct bearing on the discussion, recorded in the secret minutes, on returning pregnant women and children, three months after the nuclear blast, to the places where they had absorbed 10 rem each within a single year.) Doctors are concerned about the rate of neonatal infant mortality (mortality within the first 28 days after birth) in increased radiation hazard areas. As both Russian and Western researchers note, this type of mortality has been steadily growing.

Prominent German scholar Dr. Alfred Korblein, of the Munich Environment Institute, published the results of his research into perinatal mortality in the post-Chernobyl period in the Kiev region, and in the cities of Kiev and Zhitomir. His research is based on the medical statistics of Ukraine's Health Ministry. He concluded that there was evidence of a certain impact of radioactive strontium in pregnant women's bodies on perinatal mortality in the Kiev region and Zhitomir. It peaked in April 1987 and has since followed seasonal fluctuations, with spring and autumn maximums. Korblein also cites as another reason the possible consumption of radioactive mushrooms and berries by pregnant women seven months previously, in August and September 1986. In his paper, published in the book *Chernobyl: 20 Years On*, Korblein found 431 excess prenatal deaths in Gomel, Belarus, 1987–98. He concludes, "The fetus seems much more vulnerable to ionizing radiation than generally believed," and his results contradict the widely accepted concept of a threshold dose for radiation damage during fetal development. This book, edited by UK physicist and ECRR Scientific Secretary Chris Busby and Russian biologist Alexey Yablokov, is the first to translate and reference hundreds of Russian studies that document cancer and noncancer health effects from the Chernobyl accident (full text, euradcom.org).

In his "Introduction," Busby refers to the revelation of "a simple and terrible new discovery: that the effects of low dose internal irradiation cause subtle changes in the genome that result in an increase in the general mutation rate." He indicates that low doses of ionizing radiation affect all species—animal, plant, and human. In his chapter on the health of the more than 740,000 workers (liquidators) who acted swiftly to limit exposures from the damaged reactor, coeditor Yablokov cites evidence demonstrating that, by 2002 (sixteen years after the accident), 99 percent of all liquidators had developed a wide range of diseases. Those identified as "priority" include digestive organ pathology, sensory organs, circulatory and neurological systems.

It is relevant to take yet another look at the manuscript of physicist Igor Gerashchenko, a Soviet émigré from Kiev, passed on to me in London in 1991. The manuscript, *Chernobyl's Missed Lessons*, reads, in part, thus:

> There are also Chernobyl victims no one has ever seen. They are young lives nipped in the bud. After the blast, doctors advised termination to pregnant women in Kiev and in other places as well. I know of several cases when fetuses were thus aborted into the sixth month of the term, perfectly officially, by doctors in clinics. Over the past year [the reference is to the first year after the Chernobyl accident], at least 20,000 pregnancies have been terminated because of the nuclear disaster. In Kiev alone! And what about the evacuated Pripyat women?

I haven't the slightest doubt on that score. Several months after the accident, I personally made rounds of contaminated villages in the Zhitomir region, where tearful women told me similar stories. Expectant mothers were insistently advised to terminate and warned not to talk to anyone about these recommendations.

On this subject A. P. Povalyaev offered up these words of wisdom at the 2002 seminar for young scientists held at the Institute of Safe Nuclear Power Engineering Development of the Russian Academy of Sciences: "This is sad business, abortions. Doctors recommended termination even when it was the woman's first pregnancy." Wasn't he the coauthor of numerous secret instructions for feeding the unsuspecting public radioactive meat and dairy products? This advice was dispensed immediately after the accident.

Twenty years on, we now find experts who note grave consequences of past terminations. This also confirms indirectly that no one really knows what doses the population, including women of reproductive age, actually absorbed in the first, most dangerous weeks and months after the Chernobyl explosion. We can only guess the dosage was considerable, judging by the consequences witnessed years later. Also disquieting is the number of congenital malformations in newborns in these areas. Zhitomir had until recently a secret laboratory that kept, preserved in alcohol, animal and human monsters born on radioactive territories, as recorded in the party minutes:

> SECRET. TO BE RETURNED TO THE SPECIAL SECTOR OF THE USSR COUNCIL OF MINISTERS ADMINISTRATION BOARD. Minutes No. 36. November 15, 1986. On Point 6. Alongside that, over the next 70 years we can expect 3,000 additional births with hereditary defects (the reference is only to the Gomel, Kiev, Zhitomir, and Chernigov regions. Prognosis for the 75 million people living in the Soviet Union's European part, where rises in the radioactive background were registered, is that over the next 70 years . . . the additional incidence of congenital malformations may reach 23,000 cases.

Judging by the information obtained by Adi Roche, the founder and international executive director of Chernobyl Children's Project International, the horrors of those long-term statistics have already manifested themselves to the full in Belarus, in less than twenty years.

The report by the Pediatrics, Obstetrics and Gynecology Research Center of Ukraine's Ministry of Public Health says that child morbidity rates in contaminated areas continue to rise against the preaccident period, while they have actually dropped by 6 percent in the rest of Ukraine. In some of the affected areas primary disease incidence in children grew 1.5–2 times within the first decade after the accident. The percentage of endocrine system disorders, blood and hemoplastic problems, congenital anomalies, and tumors has doubled and even trebled in areas with particularly high contamination levels. There are regions where these rates exceed Ukraine's national average 14–20 times! Whereas prior to 1986, only two or three cases of thyroid cancer in children were recorded annually, early in 1989 there were two hundred such cases.

The situation was especially depressing in the seventy-five strict radiation-monitoring areas, eleven specific regions, including Kiev, Zhitomir, and Chernihiv. Ten years after the accident, child mortality rates there were 1.6–2 times the national average. Children's health sharply deteriorated in Zhitomir. As head pediatrician V. I. Bashek told me, within eight years of the nuclear disaster every second child under twelve months had joined the risk group. Only 38 percent of the young survivors of the accident were pronounced healthy. But even among them the morbidity rate grew by 27 percent. The children of Kiev, Ukraine's capital, who also lived through the radiation shock, make up a special population group. Because the city is so near the damaged reactor, the consequences were, and still are, very sad indeed (although they are now adults). As Russian specialists O. Yu. Tsitser and M. S. Malikov write in their report, examination of 583 seven-year-olds in Kiev schools showed a significant number of severely retarded children in 1992 when compared with that in 1982. In short, not much cause for optimism. They then say that ten years after the accident 150,000 Ukrainian residents had absorbed tens or even hundreds of times more radioactivity in their thyroid glands than the human tolerance dose. In particular, 5,700 children had absorbed 200 rad, and 7,800 adults over 500 rad, while the established permissible dose in Ukraine is 5 rad over a lifetime.

In March 2002, the Ukrainian state press agency, citing official sources, reported that of the 3 million people in Ukraine exposed to radiation in the aftermath of the Chernobyl accident, 84 percent had been diagnosed with some disease, and 1 million of them were children. The deeper we delve into the medical and research reports by experts and scholars, free from Moscow's official control, the less optimistic we feel. However, bitter truth is preferable to comforting lies. The Chernobyl tragedy followed a scenario of its own in Belarus, where things are hardly any better than in Ukraine. At present, over 2 million people in Belarus, or 23 percent of the republic's population, live in areas with radioactive cesium contamination levels exceeding 1 Ci/km^2, while almost 8 percent of the territory registers 5 Ci/km^2.

Estimates of radioactive strontium-90 content in Belarusians' bodies after the Chernobyl accident, according to Russian researchers, showed that the absorbed doses for red bone marrow were in fact 2.5–3 times higher than in the preaccident period, and in 3 percent of the cases the average exceeded 4–8 times. Plutonium concentration in the hair of Gomel region residents was an order of magnitude higher than in the hair of Minsk dwellers.

According to national health ministry reports, a whole decade after the Chernobyl nuclear disaster, the general morbidity level in the most contaminated areas of the republic was 51 percent above that of the pre-Chernobyl period.

But the worst hazard of the first days was radioiodine, liberally sprinkled all over Belarus. Only its northern section could be described as "clean"—with reservations. In some areas its levels reached 300 Ci/km^2 and more. According to the latest data of a group of scientists at the Minsk Institute for Radiation Medicine and Endocrinology Research (A. Ye. Okeanov, Ye. Ya. Sosnovskaya, and O. P. Pryatkina), Belarus has had the world's highest incidence of thyroid cancers in adults since 1990. Before the Chernobyl reactor meltdown, that disease was a rarity. As for thyroid cancers in children, this has long ceased being debatable. Even the most hard-core pronuclear conformists have acknowledged the deplorable statistics. According to this group of scientists, cancer incidence in Belarus grew by nearly 40 percent between 1990 and 2000, against the preaccident level. The researchers used the data bank of the national cancer register kept in Belarus since 1973. In the Gomel region the figure is utterly stunning—about 52 percent. Prior to the accident this index was the lowest there. In the Minsk region, it is 49 percent; in the Grodno region, 44 percent; and in the Vitebsk region, 38 percent! The "collective Ilyin" crowd, with their "scientific" reports and prognostications, should be made to drink 300 Ci of radioactive iodine.

According to the same group of scientists, in 1980, thyroid cancer incidence among adults over thirty in Belarus was 1.24 per 100,000. In 2000 it grew to 5.67, and among liquidators it reached 24.4. In the worst contaminated Mogilev region cancer grew fifteen years "younger" than in Vitebsk. This is another peculiarity. Now it strikes women in the 45–49 age bracket. Cancer incidence is far higher in the Belarusian countryside than in cities. That is because the collective dose absorbed by villagers was twice the amount sustained by urbanites. The most common are cancers of the urinary system, colon, lungs, and thyroid. The scientists point out that thyroid cancers among Belarusian adults have grown more than fivefold. Although they sent their research reports on the matter to various international agencies, IAEA and UNSCEAR documents have still failed to acknowledge the Russian papers. Meanwhile, Okeanov and his colleagues are no laymen. Before taking a job with the Institute for Radiation Medicine and Endocrinology Research, Okeanov had for years been in charge of the national cancer register in Belarus. Also, the scientists' article was not published in some tabloid, but in *Swiss Medical Weekly,* a respected scientific journal. All contributions in that journal are subjected to a most thorough peer review, so neither the authors nor the publication can be suspected of quackery.

Nevertheless the UN scientific committee on the effects of atomic radiation had the nerve to make a shameless statement in 2000 to the effect that "14 years after the Chernobyl accident, there was no proof of the adverse influence on human health linked to ionizing radiation. Also, there was no rise in cancers or mortality rates that could be attributed to radioactive influence." This is followed by allegations altogether beyond the comprehension of normal individuals with normal humanitarian standards who are familiar with the way things are in the Chernobyl zones, to say nothing of those who have lived there for the last twenty years. A bunch of international bureaucrats, many of whom have no idea where some long-suffering Khoiniki or Polesskoe is, assure Chernobyl victims that their health will be all right in the future. Almost better, one assumes, than it could have been without Chernobyl.

The IAEA and the UN "nuclear" committee itself, even twenty-five years after the disaster, tirelessly repeat the same corporate mantra, already done to death: There are no Chernobyl victims, apart from thirty-one persons, chiefly firemen, and a handful of treatable child cancers.

This isn't even amusing. Let us leave that Soviet-style propaganda alone and continue our monitoring of the twenty-year Chernobyl radioactive marathon.

Already the first post-Chernobyl decade revealed an alarming tendency shared by the three countries involved—Ukraine, Belarus, and Russia: a rising incidence of thyroid cancers in children. The worst hit are Belarusian children. According to WHO data, there have been 379 such cases registered after 1986, against the twenty-one recorded between 1966 and 1985. Hundreds of children have had thyroid surgery.

In December 1995, 680 thyroid cancers were registered in children in Ukraine, Russia, and Belarus. According to the European Thyroid Association, this is just the thin end of the epidemic wedge, and within the next thirty years (the forecast was made in 1995), thousands of children will suffer from thyroid cancer.

But what really came as a shock to the public was the WHO report submitted to the UNO in April 2000. A group of WHO experts produced an even bleaker prognosis: according to them, the children and adolescents living in contaminated areas will develop 50,000 new cases of thyroid cancer. The worst situation is in Gomel. There, cancer is prognosticated for 36.4 percent of those who were under four years of age at the time of the accident. (As far as adults are concerned, the UN experts forecast cancer for 5 percent of the Mogilev region residents in Belarus.)

In Russia's three regions—Tula, Kaluga, and Orel—they expect to see 3699 cases of child cancers. That accounts for 1 percent of the area's entire child population.

UN experts conclude that the millions of people living in radioactive zones are in for serious trouble now, decades after the event. Speaking after the presentation of the report, UN Secretary General Kofi Annan said that we would never know the exact number of Chernobyl victims, but there were three million children in need of medical treatment and "many of them will die prematurely." You know, I have been studying the Chernobyl issue for almost twenty years, and myself lived with my family in Zhitomir for five years after the blast, but I have never heard anything nearly so compassionate about my fellow countrymen from our national leaders. Normally they just brush off the unfortunate blameless people like tiresome autumn flies.

It hurts one's national pride, of course, but there it is.

Prominent scholar Edmund Lengfelder, director of the Otto Hug Strahleninstitut in Munich, expert in radiology and Chernobyl-associated issues, speaks of 100,000 cases of thyroid pathology in all age groups. (Prof. Lengfelder works in cooperation with the thyroid center in Gomel.)

And this seems the right time and place for taking another look at the Ilyin report in which he alleged that "estimates allow us to forecast the following theoretically possible incidence of radiation-related malignant tumors of the thyroid gland within thirty years of the Chernobyl accident. Up to twenty cases of incurable cancers in children, and up to fifty such cases in the population on the whole. As for curable thyroid cancers, there may be up to 170 and 400 cases, respectively. " Let us leave these political rather than medical prognoses on the conscience of those twenty-three—I can't bring myself to say "scientists" —who signed that strictly party policy document. It bears little relation to real research and real medicine, which has been amply borne out by life itself in the affected areas. What is at issue is something else. Is not the price that Chernobyl victims are paying for such exercises by the upper echelons of the Kremlin court medical establishment rather too high? Isn't this worse than a mistake?

There is one more category of Chernobyl sufferers. These are the liquidators. (I vividly remember a Belarusian lady writer, who published a book of Chernobyl interviews eleven years after the accident, at the book launch in the French city of Caen in 2004. She was asked who liquidators were. The writer replied, through an interpreter, that being no physicist, she was not quite sure . . . I had to explain to the French audience what those people were, although I wasn't a physicist either, and anyway, what's physics got to do with it? I felt awfully embarrassed on her account: how can a person write about Chernobyl and not know that particular meaning of the word liquidator?)

According to WHO reports, morbidity and mortality rates among liquidators are steadily climbing. Their chief health problems are vegetovascular dystonia, lung cancer, heart and gastroenterological trouble, and leukemia.

According to official information in Ukraine, about 8000 liquidators died within the first decade of the accident.

As the research by Belarusian scholars at the Radiation Medicine and Endocrinology Research Institute A. Ye. Okeanov, Ye. Ya. Sosnovskaya, and O. P. Pryatkina shows, thyroid cancer incidence among Belarusian liquidators was 24.4 per 100,000 persons in the 1993–2000 period. This is nearly five times the incidence among residents of contaminated areas. (One hundred and twenty thousand Belarusians took part in the cleanup within the 30-km zone around the reactor.) The authors stress that it was the liquidator group that registered increased mortality from all kinds of cancer.

According to the Russian experts' official data, the number of Russian nationals whose death may be linked to their part in the nuclear cleanup is close to 7,000. (Press publications suggest the figure 50,000.) According to the same official data, some 20,000 liquidators have become disabled. One can only guess at the quality of their life (especially after 2005, when all Chernobyl benefits in Russia were exchanged for a pittance).

According to the public Liquidator Committee, in the years since the nuclear disaster at least 100,000 of the 800,000 have died. That number, the committee people explain, includes all liquidators whose death could be attributed to weakened immunity in the wake of the cleanup of the contaminated areas.

Recently, as I was going through my archives, I came across an article by Helen Ander, of June 7, 2002—about our Chernobyl in their Great Britain. Fifteen years after the accident, scientists from the UK and the Netherlands revised their estimates on how long it would take to eradicate radioactive contamination in Britain. By their estimate, Chernobyl radiation would affect the UK 100 times longer than forecast. The reference was to the hills and mountains of Wales, Scotland, and the north of England, where the sheep pastures were (so there too radiocesium had "fertilized" highland pastures). As a result, more than 230,000 sheep on nearly 400 sheep farms are now subject to restrictions for a further 10 to 15 years and must undergo continued testing for radiation before slaughter. Before ending up on the British dinner table, mutton must be pristinely free from Russian radiation.

We can only dream of such things. And we will go on dreaming of them for a long time to come. Ultimately, of course, it is human beings, not sheep, that are at the core of the issue.

Although, to all intents and purposes, the authorities in the West worry more about animals nibbling radioactive grass in the mountains than officials here do about children who have been suffering and dying in Chernobyl zones these last twenty-five years.

23

Who Stole Chernobyl's Green Meadows?

Like medieval French noblemen who gave their ladies gifts of potato flowers without suspecting that something more significant grew beneath the pink and white petals, many participants in the current discussion of nuclear energy fail to recall that Europe has been sitting on a nuclear bomb for twenty-five years: the Chernobyl sarcophagus. In 1986, the reactor went out of control and was hastily sealed away in this structure.

After Ukraine obtained its independence, the nation was stunned by evidence presented to the Ukrainian Supreme Soviet by the chairman of the parliament's Chernobyl committee. Earlier, in December 1991, both the government and parliament had issued decrees inviting engineering firms to participate in a tender to secure the reactor sleeping inside the sarcophagus. Ukraine's Chernobyl Ministry formed a steering committee and a jury for the tender under the direction of First Deputy Prime Minister Konstantin Masik. He became chairman of the steering committee.

Although the scientific and financial communities were informed of the tender by the Ukrainian government and many had begun to draw up their proposals, Masik dropped a note to the French engineering firm Bouygues asking it to save the Ukrainian people from a nuclear tragedy and construct a reliable cover for the exploded reactor. Later on, it became known that the director of Chernobyl Nuclear Power Plant, Mikhail Umanets, had already paid a visit to Bouygues. Naturally, he was received like a king.

The committee worked away, and the jury enthusiastically collected proposals and bids. None of that stopped Mr Umanets, operating on behalf of the independent Ukrainian government, from secretly signing an agreement with Jacques Gordon of Bouygues. The French company was granted rights to design and carry out all works to

363

secure the sarcophagus. One point from the agreement states: "This contract is of an exclusive nature, and the customer is obliged to name no other organisation to carry out the works defined in this contract." Pretty strong stuff.

Once this by-invitation-only spectacle had ended, the unsuspecting Ukrainian government issued another special decree (number 94 of February 24, 1992) ordering an international tender. Umanets himself, having signed the agreement with the French, was selected for both the steering committee and the jury. He enthusiastically distributed tender conditions and invitations to the world's best-known engineering firms. A date was set for a formal presentation.

But the wolf in sheep's clothing was revealed. The secret contract was discovered by the deceived Western companies, whose subsequent reaction to the Ukrainian government's invitation was predictable, since the contract with the tender winners had already been signed.

The young independent Ukrainian state had suffered a ringing blow delivered by its own national leadership. Only a few representatives of Western firms came for the governments' formal presentation of the tender. The presentation was a failure, although Mr Umanets declared his hospitable hosts from Bouygues the winners. The festivities were short.

When parliament received this shocking information, it voted to overturn Mr Umanets's secret protocol, which had compromised Ukraine in the eyes of the world.

Economic chaos, empty shop shelves, hitherto unseen inflation, the fight for personal power among the elite, and the common people's fight to survive overtook the problem of the sarcophagus.

But the nuclear caravan rolled on. The personal affairs of Ukraine's senior statesmen were publicized at home and abroad. In January 1993, the very same Deputy Prime Minister Konstantin Masik founded the Ukraine-Chernobyl Foundation. He named the late Georgy Gotovchits and Boris Prister as his deputies, and the team went to work. On the first deputy prime minister's orders, budget funds from the Chernobyl ministry were pumped into the newly minted fund. Were these funds intended to aid the victims in radioactive areas? Nothing is known about this. What is known is that the fund's charter specified that its financial resources were to be distributed, among other things, to the support of the families of the fund's founders, whose government perks were apparently inadequate. The founders' families were also to enjoy discounts on purchased goods. The founders did not forget to assign themselves the profits from any commercial activity conducted by the fund and—holy of holies—they granted the fund and its organizations tax-free status.

Documents detailing the activities of these people from the upper echelons of Ukrainian political life—the shameful tenders, the so-called Ukraine-Chernobyl Fund—were handed over to parliament, the prosecutor's office, and the press. How did the plot play out? Masik quietly resigned. The fund for the personal social security of the immortals in government just as quietly evaporated. Georgy Gotovchits continued to run the Chernobyl ministry as if nothing had happened, defending Chernobyl's millions of victims. Umanets retained charge of the state nuclear concern.

Who compensated the country for the damage inflicted on Ukraine by the activities of these statesmen? Millions of rubles raised for Chernobyl victims in a national charity telethon were spent on the so-called tender and siphoned into the fake Masik-Gotovchits fund. There was no compensation. Mere mortals were sent to prison for years for stealing a few kilos of sugar from a collective farm, while government bureaucrats who brazenly robbed the state were in clover. They had their own laws, were their own prosecutors, and were their own judges. This was Ukraine's long-awaited democracy.

Only the ardent promise of American President Bill Clinton and his European colleagues to secure the sarcophagus covering the exploded fourth reactor of Chernobyl Nuclear Power Plant, build a storage facility for the nuclear waste, and gradually take the other reactors out of service—practically transforming the ill-fated station into a green meadow—shone any light at the end of the tunnel. In December 2000, the West received a Christmas present from Ukraine in the form of a promise to close down Chernobyl Nuclear Power Plant.

That promise did not stop the flow of scandals which continued to shake Chernobyl NPP even after its ceremonial closure. Five years ago, Ukraine's public figures had informed the country and the world of cracks more than a meter and a half wide in the shaky, hastily assembled sarcophagus, and many in the West had tired of them. They don't tolerate surprises well. This was probably among the arguments used by the European Bank for Reconstruction and Development, which finally set aside money for the "cover," the bureaucrats' name for the sarcophagus in which the reactor had been buried alive for its murderous behavior.

"Money is the root of all evil," my mother said. New scandals came quickly.

On January 22, 2004, a group of deputies from the Supreme Rada went to the General Prosecutor's Office and Security Service to demand checks into abuses at Chernobyl. It turned out that Ukraine was running up against the same old obstacles—bureaucratic tyranny and corruption. This time, the role of French Bouygues was played by the enterprising people from Yuzhtoploenergomontazh, a construction firm that had already become notorious in Ukraine. They tried to receive and draw on money given by the EBRD—50 million hryvnias, or $10 million, no less—to construct "Sanpropusknik." Experts estimated this sum was around 75 percent more than necessary. But eating whets the appetite. The company demanded more and more. If the EBRD wouldn't give it, the government could—to the tune of 12 million hryvnias, or $2 million. Quite a racket.

So what about the tender? There could be no tender if every player at every level had his own selfish interests. In order to understand the dirty dancing that was happening alongside the Chernobyl cauldron, we have an inquiry by the Supreme Rada. (I retain the document's punctuation and style.)

> At this point he [the head of Chernobyl NPP supply service] is the real boss at the station and everyone understands that only he decides who will sell to the station (to put it simply, who gives the biggest bribe). All businessmen know the drop off point [for bribes] in the town of Slavutich, a cafe [the document lists the name of the cafe and its owner, who was openly called a mob boss by the deputies] . . . That meeting place doesn't change and only there is the fate of budget money decided, according to who gives the most. They give—they give so much that Mr. A. E. Smyshlyayev [the director of Chernobyl NPP] is selling a 2 million-hryvnia promissory note from Zaporozhe regional utility, which was to be paid immediately by Yuzhteploenergomontazh, according to a court order, for 100,000 hryvnias to a private fly-by-night firm. They have no sense of scale! . . . Under the illusion of pure competition for the tender, we are being shown another spectacle. How long can we stand it?

Remember, these are questions asked by parliamentarians. Their patience had finally snapped.

They had good reason. Of the three key projects at the station, the construction of a storage facility for nuclear waste, a processing plant for solid nuclear waste, and a complex for processing liquid waste, not one has been completed to this day, twenty years after the accident!

And where is the nuclear waste to go? Russia refuses to take back spent fuel it supplied in fresh form to Ukrainian nuclear power plants (it is choking on its own). Although the third quarter 2004 deadline for completing the new storage facility has long since passed, there is no light at the end of the tunnel. On this occasion, the row was between French Framatome, which was entrusted with this major project, and its Ukrainian partners. The reason was banal—a shortage of money again. The initial cost of the project was around 72–80 million dollars. Again, it was the EBRD that financed the project. About 90 million dollars was invested in the project, it remained unfinished, and there was no more money.

When, then, would such a seemingly respectable Western firm so severely miscalculate, then default on the project to the tune of the entire budget? Ukrainian experts nod in the direction of the French, saying they made disappointing mistakes in the planning stage and during construction of the storage facility. The French blame the station's management for providing incorrect data from the beginning. Each side has its own Waterloo.

The spent fuel is currently concentrated in a single aging storage facility, in cooling pools and in three reactors. It should all make its way to new premises for secure, long-term storage. When this will happen, God only knows.

Bear in mind that Ukraine's nuclear waste problem does not end with a failure to communicate between the Ukrainians and the French. Decades after the accident, the authorities cannot sort out all the haphazard radioactive burial sites. Ukraine has more than eight hundred such sites. Most of them were dug hastily in the months after the explosion. They can't legitimately be termed storage facilities. They are deep pits where radioactive soil and equipment were "temporarily" thrown in haste. Many of these temporary sites are lost forever.

The unfinished storage facility is holding up the full shutdown of the station itself. The reactors are not electric lamps to be switched on and off by pushing a button. To slow and completely stop the chain reaction is no less dangerous—and possibly more dangerous—than their everyday operation. The three Chernobyl reactors have not received their promised Caesarean section—four years after the official closure of the station, the nuclear fuel remains in their womb.

There is a Ukrainian saying: They danced and danced, but never took a bow. This is just such a case.

But the main issue of concern for Western society and donor nations who have poured money into the Chernobyl cleanup is: When will the long promised "green meadows" gladden the eye?

It is now clear to many of us that this was merely a myth that served as comfortable cover for moneygrubbers. The complete chaos surrounding the new nuclear security facilities and the new plan to close the station, approved in November 2004, only support this guess.

So what stood behind the fairy tale of the "green meadows," where the nuclear horror once stood? The sad truth is that there will be no full rehabilitation of the station in the foreseeable future. (The same is true for the contaminated areas where 9 million people live today. The half-life of uranium 235 is 704 million years. For uranium 238, it is 4.46 billion years.)

The fate of the station under the new plan is as follows: Experts estimate it will take eighty to one hundred years to cool the reactors. Then work on the forced circulation system will continue for another thirty to fifty years. Only then can the station be closed and dismantled once and for all.

For now, the reactor's burial vault continues to disintegrate amid a din of financial scandal. Western investors can only follow the advice of the Russian pop singer Zemfira and kiss all the cracks. We can only hope the so-called repairs will be finished by September 1, 2015. What could happen before then does not bear thinking about.

The head of Chernobyl NPP, Alexander Smyshlyayev, said at a press conference that "Here [at Chernobyl] we still have the threat of more accidents." It turns out that neither the Soviet Union, nor independent Ukraine, nor Europe could deal with the consequences of one single major nuclear accident. (We used to say we in the Soviet Union had the best of everything. We could even say we had the best accidents.) More recently, George Bush promised President Yushchenko he would help out a bit with money for the cleanup. What would happen to the world if not just one but several reactors blew up someplace else, as it has now happened in Japan?

For twenty-five years, the hard earned money of Soviet and later Ukrainian taxpayers and donor nations have been flowing into the hands of wheeler-dealers in the name of nuclear security and the phantom "green meadows." The latest news is that the Ukrainian state prosecutor has opened sixty-three criminal investigations into embezzlement at Chernobyl NPP. The state has suffered damages of more than $14 million, and Chernobyl victims and liquidators have been cheated of $170 million.

It appears that prolonging the aftermath of the Chernobyl catastrophe has been highly profitable for too many people. No one has thought of nuclear security for a while now.

Why think about it if all of the world and the European Union, to which authorities of the Ukraine so passionately aspires, just look on as the promise of "green meadows" is converted into greenbacks?

Epilogue

The Chernobyl nuclear disaster became the yardstick, which more dramatically than ever before, made humanity reconsider the universal issues of being. The most important of these issues concern life and man. These eternal philosophical categories have been perplexing ever since the times of cave paintings. Their perception and material embodiment in daily life are two inseparable sides of a single whole, like the two sides of a medal. And more often than not these two sides are extremely dissimilar.

In concluding our journey through one historical instance of human consciousness, through pain, suffering, lies and hopes, I am offering you, my patient reader, a brief excursus into the distant past. This is necessary for a better understanding of the post-Chernobyl present and for finding one's bearings regarding life's values. The global questions that Chernobyl raised before the world, and the answers to these questions, require approaches no less global. These refer above all to humanity and its life on Earth.

What is life as such? Scholarly works tell us that life is a form of the existence of matter that emerges inevitably under certain conditions as matter develops. It was life that changed our planet giving it a unique integument, the biosphere. Once the most perfect form of higher nervous activity evolved in our ancestors, life ascended to the social level, which involved the highest form of the movement of matter inherent only in man.

The issue of the essence of man as the highest stage in living organism development on Earth, his origin, purpose and place in the world—these are among the most important issues in the history of philosophy. Man stands in a certain relation to the cosmos, he is part of nature's uniform order—thus thought ancient Greek, Chinese, and Indian philosophers. Democritus called man a microcosm, a reflection of the universe—the macrocosm. Consisting of the body and the soul, man embodies all the main elements of cosmos, Aristotle believed.

The Indian philosophy of reincarnation does not draw a boundary between living beings, be they gods, human beings, animals or plants.

The Bible says that man was created in God's image. Man's divine and human nature is reflected in the historical person of Jesus Christ, God-Man, who is still at the center of fierce battles between various philosophers, theologians, and Marxists.

The Renaissance sang praises to man as a personality with an unlimited intellectual and creative potential. Remember Descartes? *Cogito, ergo sum.* I think, therefore I am. This idea formed the basis of new European rationalism that saw in reason alone the inimitable essence of man as the highest creature in life.

In the late eighteenth and early nineteenth centuries, German philosophy brought the concept of man back to the Renaissance context. Herder, Goethe, and the natural philosophy of Romanticism viewed Man as "Nature's first freedman." Man must mold himself by creating culture. Man is the carrier of consciousness, of the ideal element—spirit and reason.

In the nineteenth and twentieth centuries, conceptions of man in the framework of irrationalism was dominated by emotion, will, and sensation. Nietzsche defined man as the focus of volitions.

In the West, a naturalistic approach to man is also characteristic of traditional Freudianism and of many natural scientists of the twentieth century.

Such are the notions of man's ascendancy. That is one side of the coin. But what is the reality of it all?

Albert Schweitzer, one of humanity's geniuses, spoke of the high moral imperative of "reverence for life." I suppose this idea, if set against daily practice—the coin's other side, will be a perfect illustration of the enormous gap between the philosophic ideal of man and his purpose, on the one hand, and the actual state of affairs, on the other. The man-made (or anthropological, as a philosophical treatise would call it) Chernobyl disaster and its consequences for every individual shows how idealistic and romantic this maxim is. Extrapolating it onto Chernobyl victims brings nothing but sad thoughts. (Although this ideal formula is undoubtedly what we should seek to translate into practice.)

The global questions raised by Chernobyl in the environmental and humanitarian spheres are still without adequate global answers decades later. As the reader has already seen, they are buried under mountains of official lies by the powers that be and the corporate interests of transnational leviathans. After all, the Chernobyl disaster is but a link, however big, in the nuclear chain our planet is entangled in, like Apollo's priest Laocoon desperately trying to break out of the serpents' deadly coils.

And if we really mean to find answers to global "nuclear" questions and challenges, the search should be shifted to the plane of moral imperatives—a plane that has always been ignored by the powerful players on the nuclear turf. (Obviously, this kind of exploration and the results of such exploration are not in their egotistical interests.) The sufferers in this whole affair are invariably the innocent victims of nuclear developments. In the chapters of this book, I have already discussed how they suffered and who their offenders are. Let us now move up to a different, "macro" level of comprehending Chernobyl as a particular instance, and of life in the presence of the nuclear threat in general.

The face of the twentieth (and now the twenty-first) century, which revealed quite a lot of heroism and tragedy, has been disfigured by nuclear accidents and disasters that, along with other types of anthropogenic (human-related) activity, have pushed the world virtually to a point at which survival becomes a problem. Dangerous nuclear technologies have reached the level and scale in development and distribution that makes them transnational rather than national. This means that the nuclear threat is no respecter of frontiers and customs; it has no nationality, party membership, or religion. Nuclear facilities and technologies remain a hazard to humankind no matter whose territory they happen to be on. Chernobyl proves that beyond a shadow of a doubt.

The empirical and theoretical exploration of the scale and consequences of nuclear accidents and catastrophes, of their impact on ecosystems, the biological and social sphere, provide evidence of the global and universal nature of nuclear disasters for the planet.

Given the irreparable damage nuclear disasters inflict on all ecosystems, on the biosphere as the cradle of humanity, and on the human community at large, these catastrophes resulting from technological failures inevitably lead to global ecological ones. Many scholars—philosophers and ecologists—are asking themselves the question: how to determine which "of the global issues are immediate, urgent and calling for the attention of the whole humanity, and which can wait till tomorrow" (K. Kh. Delokarov). The debate concerns which nuclear events can be classed as global disasters, and which are local and regional.

Even though there is an international dimension to nuclear events, the governments of all countries where these incidents, accidents, and disasters happened invariably attempted a cover-up, concealing from their own people and the world community the truth about their consequences for man and the environment. With our Chernobyl nuclear disaster, this country is well ahead of the planet, as in so many other things.

It is the irreversible nature of the consequences of nuclear disasters, which alter the scientific picture of the world, that is the principal criterion for defining them as global. Global issues of nuclear safety cannot wait "till tomorrow" because they would at best turn into global issues of environmental danger, and at worst, "tomorrow" might never arrive. The latter necessarily follows from the former. And this is true not just of nuclear safety. In the classification of contemporary global challenges and dangers for humanity—nuclear, economic, social, and ecological—the first three definitely come before the ecological one. The combination of the first three inevitably leads to the global environmental crisis on the brink of which humanity found itself at the close of the twentieth century.

The report by the World Commission on Environment and Development (WCEP), *Our Common Future*, prepared in 1989 under the supervision of Norway's ex-prime minister Gro Harlem Brundtland, convincingly shows the cause-and-effect relationship between the environment and socioeconomic development. The conclusion about the global environmental crisis was also made by the world community at the UN conference on environment and development commonly known as the Earth Summit in Rio de Janeiro in 1992.

One of the conference's main conclusions is that the development pattern characteristic of the "golden billion" dozen of Western countries intent on unrestricted consumption has exhausted itself. The UN report's conclusion about it being a dead-end for humanity that spells disaster is seen as the guilty verdict for the resource-consumption development model.

Research works on issues of global nuclear accidents and catastrophes, their global consequences and nuclear safety look at the matter from a strictly technological vantage. And that is the whole point.

These definitions take into account only the technological aspects of nuclear safety, and none but the technological consequences of such accidents and catastrophes. As for the environmental aspect—the global radioactive contamination of ecosystems and the biosphere, or the social one—adversely affected human health, or the moral one that Academician Nikita Moiseev defined as "one group of people faced with the evil choice by another group of people who have power or weapons"—none of these have been taken into account yet.

This fact appears to epitomize the entire experience of humanity in the new times since the seventeenth century—of society dominated by positivist, technocratic approaches to issues of science and morality, to relations between the social domain and the biosphere. It is on the technocratic approach to the relationship within the nature—society system that the priority is denied of morality and spirituality in the development of humanity and civilization as a whole.

One of the main global responses to the global nuclear challenge to man is this: it is the environmental and moral imperatives that should be at the core of nuclear safety, not just its technological element—if society wishes in earnest to find a survival concept to preserve life on Earth.

The anthropocentric approach to the problems of man and society, so common in science, has drastically changed the moral priorities and values of society, pushing it to the point beyond which there may be no alternative to the destruction of modern civilization. This is a view shared by many scientists.

Outstanding natural scientists—like Albert Einstein, Norbert Wiener, Frederic Joliot-Curie, Max Born, Kliment Timiryazev—were the first to realize the supreme importance of morality in science. They came to the conclusion that ignoring the humanitarian, moral aspects in a scientist's creative work may have catastrophic consequences. One such consequence was the development of nuclear technologies for inhuman purposes—to destroy one's own kind. (Even animals do not destroy members of their own species!) What can be in store for us has been graphically shown in the "nuclear winter" theoretical scenarios worked out by Russian Academician Nikita Moiseev and American scholar Carl Sagan, who almost simultaneously modeled, each in his own country, the nuclear apocalypse technology.

The dramatic events at the Chernobyl nuclear power plant in 1986 were a practical demonstration of what a global nuclear catastrophe can be, and of the utter impotence of the powers that be, of science, and of society as a whole within the existing system of global nuclear safety and of the environmental and moral attitude toward it.

This raises the question of the moral integrity of scientists researching and creating anti-human high technologies that destroy the biosphere and the social world, including nuclear technologies expressly intended for such destruction. Scientists who deliberately deceive the public, who accept fundamentally false conceptions of safe habitation on radioactively contaminated territory after a global nuclear disaster, conceptions that are bound to bring about countless deaths and reduce the life expectancy and quality for millions of people—do such scientists experience moral problems?

Both science and society know of cases when great scientists, who had made important discoveries in nuclear physics and consciously participated in developing destructive nuclear technologies, later reversed themselves, exchanging their technocratic outlook for humanitarian ideas, and embraced the priorities of nuclear safety. But apparently it takes a truly great scientist to accomplish this transformation.

In their famous manifesto, Bertrand Russell and Albert Einstein thus addressed all humankind: "We appeal as human beings to human beings: Remember your humanity, and forget the rest."

A similar change of heart occurred in the life of Soviet physicist and Nobel Peace Prize winner Andrei Sakharov, who had created the first Soviet H-bomb on orders from Stalin and Beria. Years after he had personally took part in its testing at the Semipalatinsk test site, he started campaigning for such tests to be discontinued or limited. And it was his humanist position that won him the Nobel Peace Prize.

The outstanding British nuclear scientist Joseph Rothblat, after decades of nuclear research in laboratories, revised his ideas about the world and its values and headed the Pugwash Conference movement for peace. He too was awarded the Nobel Peace Prize for his dedicated work.

The issue of the relation between the ecological and moral elements, on the one hand, and purely technological ones, on the other, primarily in the areas of nuclear technologies and nuclear safety, provoked debates—it still does—not only among scientists, but also among philosophers and fiction writers.

The threat of civilization taking the path of technocratic development was criticized by the Russian existentialist thinkers Nikolai Berdyaev and Vladimir Solovyov, as well as by such Western counterparts like Martin Heidegger, Jean-Paul Sartre, and Albert Camus. They grasped the connection between the idea of existence and the possibility of a global catastrophe, should the world persist in its movement in that direction.

Research on the scientific and philosophical plane into the correlation between the technological, ecological, and moral aspects of nuclear safety suggests that in conditions of an impending global environmental crisis it is vital to provide a conceptual groundwork for ensuring the nuclear safety of the biosphere and of the social world. A unified strategy of this kind is yet to be worked out in Russia (or in the world, for that matter), nor is there a unity of scientific opinion on the issue. This concept of life, experts believe, should be based on the nuclear-facilities-ecosystems-biosphere-sociosphere system that would take into account nuclear safety not only in technological but also in environmental, social and moral terms.

Put more simply, nuclear safety is the condition of the nuclear-facilities-ecosystems-biosphere-sociosphere system that rules out destruction of ecosystems and the bio- and social spheres. Its chief distinctive feature is that man is its principal agent, both the object and the subject of providing nuclear safety.

The concept of nuclear safety is considerably narrower than that of environmental safety: the latter covers all risks created by man or by natural impact on the environment and the human community. Hence yet another distinctive feature of the concept of nuclear safety: it emerges exclusively as a result of human activity. But like the concept of environmental safety, it carries a powerful moral charge that can be positive or negative. The latter depends on the existential or positivist basis of the world outlook of scientists and politicians.

One of the fundamentals of nuclear safety in the present, hypertechnological world, one that represents the new element in the changing world outlook, is the notion of the culture and values of nuclear safety. It is gradually entering the vocabulary of not just scientists, philosophers, and ecologists, but also members of the domestic and international political, decision-making establishment. For the first time, the concept of the culture of nuclear safety oriented toward solving twenty-first-century security problems appeared in an international document at the Moscow Summit of April 20, 1996. The concept of nuclear safety culture is embodied in the declaration adopted by that summit.

The notion of nuclear safety culture as such already carries a moral charge aimed at a humanist solution to one of the most global anthropogenic problems of our century. Filled with philosophic and ecological content, it is becoming the cornerstone of changes in civilizational values: from superiority of force to superiority of reason.

I believe that this should be accompanied by the implementation of two more moral principles: prevention of nuclear danger before it can emerge and reduction of adverse effects for ecosystems and the biosphere, compensation not only for the material, but also for the moral damage in the social sphere.

The environmental and moral imperatives in matters of nuclear safety are closely linked with the notions of safe habitation, radiation monitoring, zone of super-strict radiation monitoring, risk, acceptable risk, and health.

The nuclear safety issue is connected especially closely with the problem and concept of risk. This category has several essential features—purely technological, environmental, and moral. When the technological element of the category of risk is dominant, none but the technical characteristics of nuclear disaster risks (e.g., the technical-economic losses from a nuclear disaster) are taken into account. The technological risk of a nuclear disaster at a nuclear facility or in nuclear production is factored in already at the design stage—although Andrei Sakharov warned years ago that "in reality it always happens so that accidents are far more numerous than the designers assume."

And since a nuclear accident has a negative, and occasionally a devastating effect on ecosystems, the biosphere, and the people, it would be natural to suppose that while factoring in technological risks, R&D specialists also factor in environmental risks. Yet this seemingly simple idea is proving slow to catch on.

The grasping of this fact will inevitably bring us to the realization of the moral essence of the risk category that is primarily associated with the nature-man system.

It is precisely this—what methodological basis the risk category should have and whether its ecological and moral aspects should be taken into account while computing risks—that is the subject of heated debates among scientists, engineers, biologists, radiobiologists, ecologists and philosophers. The discussions have grown particularly fierce since the disaster at the Chernobyl nuclear power plant.

Currently there are two diametrically opposed approaches to the issue of nuclear safety and the risks involved, which serve as a graphic illustration of the moral essence of the concept of risk.

The most fundamental point of the discussion is the question of radiation risk—threshold or no-threshold health effects of radiation.

One of the two possible approaches is based on the no-threshold methodology in treating the effects of radiation on man and society as a whole: it is assumed that any external radiation dose absorbed by a human being is a health hazard. Science has not proved yet that there exists some bottom threshold below which radiation is harmless. This theory, empirically confirmed by many Soviet, Russian, and Western scholars (Ye. B. Burlakova of Russia, Rosalie Bertell and Abram Petko of Canada, John Gofman and Arthur Tamplin of the U.S., Ralph Greyb of Switzerland, Roger Belbeoc of France) became known as the no-threshold radiation risk theory. (I wrote in greater detail about it in one of the preceding chapters.) This theory was accepted by the world radiobiological community on recommendations of the International Commission for Radiological Protection (ICRP) and the UN Scientific Committee for Atomic Radiation Effect (SCARE).

Obviously, this approach is based on the Schweitzer-type humanist "reverence for life" stance and on man's right to life, liberty and the pursuit of happiness—something that Thomas Jefferson, the third president of the United States, wrote about 200 years ago, around the time Rosalie of Chernobyl was guillotined in Paris by the Jacobins.

This scientific and at the same time profoundly moral, internationally accepted conception is opposed in this country's science, above all in official radiobiology, by the threshold concept of permissible radiation risk. (This, too, was discussed in detail in the previous chapters.)

Environmentally and morally oriented research into the impact of the scientific findings of different schools in radiobiology (quite apart from the matter of how accurate the results themselves may be) that are debating the essence of the two radiation risk concepts current in the world in connection with nuclear events, primarily with the Chernobyl disaster, suggest that each of the two rests on a certain world outlook.

While one of these, the internationally accepted no-threshold concept of radiation risk espouses "reverence for every human life, unique and inimitable," the other threshold concept, forced on Russian society by a small group of scientists heeded by those who take decisions, consciously accepts that there may be a certain "optimal" number of potential casualties "statistically negligible" in terms of the law of averages. I refer to this conception as the victims-among-strangers theory. I doubt that the authors of this conception or their friends and family would agree to be among that "optimal" and "statistically negligible" number of casualties.

379

In terms of the moral essence of the radiation risk models, the first one can be defined as a "casualty inadmissibility concept," and the second, as a "casualty admissibility concept." While the no-threshold radiation risk concept is based on the positive moral imperative, the threshold one rests on the pragmatic economic "profit-risk" system which, in its Soviet version, was in addition ideologically colored. The argument as to which is the highest boon—truth or gain—goes back to the time of Plato.

Scientists developing the "casualty admissibility concept" were reacting to orders from the state that placed the interests of ideology and economic expediency above science, ecology and morality. If the issue is formulated in some such terms as "society must weigh all the risks and all the benefits," the moral essence of the risk category clashes with the humanist-based ethics of science and thus goes beyond the limits of purely academic prerequisites.

Within each historical time space the genesis of the risk category depended on the level of development of science and technology and on worldview premises.

Until the 1970s, the Western and Soviet scientific outlook was dominated by the policy of ensuring man's technological security oriented toward achieving "absolute" security. That involved various technical devices and technologies, including nuclear ones. But the increasingly rapid progress in science and technology and the appearance of ever more complex machines and equipment induced scientists to question the feasibility of achieving "absolute" technological safety. This applies above all to nuclear safety.

It became socially imperative that the issue be addressed, because it affected the vital interests of society, on the one hand, and the corporate interests of scientists, manufacturers, and operators engaged in the R&D of hazardous devices, on the other. However, the simple solution prompted by common sense and the self-preservation instinct—to ban the use in industrial production of dangerous nuclear devices and technologies—was not accepted.

As a result, a kind of palliative emerged: if "absolute" technological safety was unattainable, if there existed a tangible threat of technological (including nuclear) danger that would eventually undermine the environment and adversely affect the human community, and if that worried society, then a certain conception should be devised that would take into account not only technological, but also ecological and social consequences of technological accidents, and reassure the public, while dangerous technologies continue to be built up.

The basis of the new policy was not a method that would rule out dangerous (above all nuclear) devices and technologies, but a certain palliative, a compromise between different interests. The disease was given a superficial treatment and driven inside.

The new policy was formulated within the framework of the new methodological approach to the safety issue, including nuclear safety, one that was based on the "acceptable risk" concept. At present, this concept is also actively incorporated into the legislation and value criteria in the United States, Japan, and Canada—countries with high levels of nuclear technologies in use.

It is assumed that the "acceptable risk" policy in the sphere of nuclear safety should include the following fundamental principles (based on the principles proposed by Russian scholars L.P. Feoktistov, I.I. Kuzmin and V.K. Popov):

- a new safety focus—improving the health of every individual, of society as a whole, and the state of the environment;
- development of methods for quantitative assessment of safety factors based on the risk methodology;
- development of methods for quantitative assessment of safety factors based on human health and state of the environment indices;
- development of methods for determining the acceptable balance between risks and benefits based on estimates of social preferences, society's economic potential, and impact on the environment.

Thus, the evolution of the technological risk category toward the "acceptable risk" category, which takes into account the impact on the environment and man, is perfectly obvious. (Traditional philosophy of science and technology ignored these problems altogether.) This evolution reveals a feeble attempt not so much at change, even, as at mere acknowledgement of the existence of the environmental and moral side to the worldview aspects of risk. It would be wrong to feel overoptimistic there for yet another reason: the problem, at least in the CIS countries and in Russia, has not been dealt with at all; it is conspicuously absent from Russian philosophic thought, and its nuances are somewhat obscure to everyman's consciousness—although its solution would be paramount to society, as it is directly connected with safety and survival.

A distinction should also be made between the category of "acceptable risk" in general and that of "acceptable risk" in nuclear safety.

The "acceptable risk" concept in nuclear safety officially admits, as it were, that the world has moved on to the stage of coexistence with extremely dangerous nuclear facilities and nuclear technology levels which inevitably jeopardize the stability of the society—nature system. (Scientists cannot guarantee that there will not be another disaster on the Chernobyl scale, or that some maniac terrorist will not make suicidal use of a nuclear power plant. Nuclear terrorism is looming ever more threateningly with every passing day as it becomes a new international factor of nuclear risk). Instead of giving up these technologies in the name of preserving life on the planet, society is forced to agree to live in the state of permanent "acceptable risks." In this way not only the risk itself is legitimized, but the degree of its acceptability is, too. What about human rights, then? The answer is deafening silence.

Scientists who suggest this kind of "contract" between state and society (their chief "scientific" argument being that the United States has been doing it for years!) overlook the fact that, owing to the global scale of civilization survival problems involved in nuclear risks and acceptable nuclear risks, these must be assessed not so much on the technological as on the ecological and philosophic-humanitarian dimension.

The degree of the danger depends on how hazardous the nuclear facility or technology may be, and also on the individual risk involved.

On the commonsense level the main psychological problem of the new value scheme embraced by several Western countries and aimed at grinding into the mass consciousness the "acceptable nuclear risk" category is that, when raised to the status of law, it leaves the public no freedom of choice, which is the highest value of human existence. If humanity voluntarily agrees to the new value precept of acceptable nuclear risk, then this will be its own conscious choice. If people are legally bound to submit to such a decision, then the "acceptable risk" category turns into the latest "forced risk" category, which is not at all the same thing.

A society of multiple risks and challenges does not yet fully understand and distinguish between the categories of risk and acceptable risk in a broad sense, and those of nuclear risk and acceptable nuclear risk. While in some ordinary non-nuclear facilities and technologies both these risk categories may have the right to coexist, in the sphere of extremely dangerous nuclear facilities and technologies fraught with global radioactive contamination of the environment and multiple kinds of harm to the population, application of these categories is doubtful to say the least.

The use of the acceptable nuclear risk category will tend to accumulate these "acceptable risks" turning them into "delayed risks" and ultimately, into "unacceptable risks" for the future generations of humanity that may cause its destruction.

It thus appears that the new meaning of the nuclear "acceptable risk" category recurs to the old philosophical essence of risk, a risk that jeopardizes life itself on Earth.

When nuclear weapons were used in Hiroshima and Nagasaki, and during military exercises in the USSR and U.S., with over 2,000 nuclear blasts, and major nuclear man-made disasters at civil and military nuclear facilities (Hanford in the United States, in 1944-1956; South Urals in the USSR, in 1949-1956, and in 1967; Windscale in the UK, in 1957; Three Mile Island in the U.S., in 1979; Chernobyl in the USSR, in 1986; Tomsk-7 in Russia, in 1993), hundreds of millions of people were subjected to the primary nuclear (radiation) shock. They are still living on contaminated territories in conditions of daily radiation hazard.

According to the latest data of the International Committee on Radiation Protection based on the UN exposure dosage statistics for the period between 1945 and 1989, 1,174,600 people have died from irradiation-induced cancer. The new research model of the European Committee on Radiation Risk forecast another 61,600,000 deaths from cancer, 1,600,000 deaths of newborns, and 1,900,000 other deaths.

What does a person feel, on receiving a primary radiation shock? Here are the main moral and psychological problems experienced by people who have lived through the risk of a primary radiation shock and continue to live in conditions of permanent daily radiation hazard (according to Russian experts' research):

- a sense of the futility of life, or total loss of purpose in life;
- a lack of empathy on the part of the authorities;
- a feeling of deprivation (isolation);
- a feeling of nostalgia;
- seeing oneself and one's family as guinea pigs sacrificed to science;
- fear for the health of one's children and of oneself;
- fear for the future of the children and grandchildren;
- despair from helplessness to change anything in the situation.

In the case of the Chernobyl nuclear accident, there is also the Chernobyl and post-Chernobyl syndromes of which the main element is the sense of unrelenting grief felt by the innocent victim.

One of the under-explored aspects of the post-Chernobyl syndrome is people turning to religion after their ordeal. Despairing of ever seeing their problems addressed by the authorities, these people, instead of trying to find a way out on their own and leave the contaminated areas, turn to God. They no longer demand from the authorities any benefits, "clean" food or medication, but campaign for churches to be restored or built anew. In their struggle for a chance to pray in churches on the same radioactive land, they appeal to the highest authorities—and not infrequently they get what they want.

The moral quintessence of this problem is contained in the utterance of L.P. Telyatnikov, a hero and at the same time a victim of the Chernobyl nuclear disaster: "It hurts me to see that Chernobyl has taught us nothing, though it is about time we learnt its lessons. . . . Future Chernobyls are therefore ripening within us, in our attitude to the world, to the people, and to ourselves . . ."

John Gofman offered his conclusion based on years of research into the health effects of radiation: those who think about the welfare of their descendants must avoid exposure to radiation.

The various risks building up over several centuries in a technology-based society had reached a critical mass by the end of the twentieth century. The biosphere that emerged 3.5 billion years ago and has since undergone complex evolutionary processes and transformations while preserving most of the life forms it contained throughout its history, has found itself at the mercy of the social sphere, which came into being far more recently.

As implements of labor improved and science and experimentation developed, the biosphere that produced man (or else provided a suitable cradle for human life introduced from the outside—a debatable issue both for natural sciences and for philosophy), was gradually conquered by man. In the process of industrial production the biosphere became an object of exploitation, a subsystem of the social sphere. The result was a crisis situation of reciprocal dangers: the danger of the social sphere destroying the biosphere, and that of the biosphere reciprocating by annihilating the social sphere, humanity in the first place. Thus the problem of survival moves from the purely mundane plane of everyday life to the planes of philosophy, ecology and morality.

Today we are already witnessing the biosphere punishing man, as countless environmental cataclysms are affecting the entire planet. Humanity is paying with millions of deaths for its senseless behavior.

There are most interesting theoretical and practical research projects (e.g., the work of Russian scientist A.V. Bykhovsky) that prove, relying on analyses of the Moissev-Sagan "nuclear winter" scenario and its aftermath, the fallacy of the traditional view on the planet's structure. Instead of anthropocentrism, they suggest a totally different approach based on biosphere-centrism.

Their point is that the biosphere possesses a mechanism of existential self-protection that human beings do not notice until "global evil" emerges. Yet changes in the structure of the biosphere at the existential level produce a boomerang effect: the biosphere altered through Man's anthropocentric activity responds in kind by exterminating humanity and the social sphere. The social sphere that threatens the existence of the biosphere ultimately puts in jeopardy its own survival, the existence of humankind. In other words, the biosphere can exist perfectly well without the social sphere, but the latter is dead without the former. It is like the embryo in the mother's womb: take it out, and it will die.

The runaway development of nuclear technologies that started in the 1940s—in conditions of dangerous experimentation that precedes the knowledge of its deadly effect on the biota and human communities—and nuclear testing in various parts of the planet, in the atmosphere, in space and under water (!), have become a kind of survival test to which human beings are subjecting the biosphere. Society engaged in all this failed to notice in time that it was also a test for its own survival.

During the Cold War, all those considerations—ecological, economic, moral, to say nothing of philosophical—were secondary to just one system of postulates—ideological. Humanity has already begun to pay for it with irreversible processes in the environment caused by thousands of nuclear tests, over a hundred accidents on nuclear submarines, hundreds of nuclear accidents and disasters at military and civil nuclear reactors.

The situation is exacerbated further by the fact that the world is yet to devise an optimal technology for processing and utilizing nuclear waste that is emitting billions of curies' worth of anthropogenic radioactivity all over the planet. Figuratively speaking, the nuclear genie released by scientists has become the decisive factor in humanity's survival within the multiple threat system. As Russian scientist Sergei Kapitsa rightly pointed out, "our entire planet, we all have become hostage to nuclear madness. . . . In other words, we are all facing a common danger, and we must join forces to look for ways of achieving common security."

Over the decades of life under the doctrine of nuclear possession, non-use and containment ("nuclear intimidation"), not only the environment, but also man's nature and psychology have undergone drastic change, possibly irreversible. The main "achievement" of "nuclear society" is man's psychological adjustment to the nuclear threat. People are used to that which is impossible to adjust to, for victims of nuclear disasters reach into millions, which jeopardizes mankind's gene pool—yet humanity does not seem to be overly concerned.

After nuclear disasters and nuclear testing, the biosphere went into a new, irreversible post-nuclear (post-Chernobyl) state.

The time has come for the human community to finally wake up to the crisis of old civilization values, try to revise them and work out a universal concept of survival in the nuclear world. And the first step should be gradual reorientation of industry toward alternative energy sources, considering the global consequences of the Chernobyl disaster. Some countries, such as Sweden, Switzerland, Germany, are already moving toward closing down nuclear power plants.

In his day and age the English philosopher John Locke proclaimed the right of every individual to life, freedom, and private property. In his famous Declaration of Independence Thomas Jefferson modified the Locke formula, replacing "property" with "the pursuit of happiness." And the Universal Declaration of Human Rights says, in Article 3: "Everyone has the right to life . . ."

What was happening twenty-five years ago, and is still happening in radioactive zones of Chernobyl, is a blatant violation of every law and every declaration of human rights. Millions of people are compelled to live on contaminated territories against their will, every day, every minute running nuclear risks. Yes, they seem to have their right to live. But is that life?

The idea of creating an independent body, as a counterweight to or replacement of the IAEA, has apparently long matured. The new body would conduct expert examination of all the reactors in operation not only in the ex-Soviet republics, but also throughout the world. It is likewise necessary to have a respected international committee on issues of environmental refugees and resettled people who are forced to live in radioactive areas—this relatively new variety of Homo sapiens, the "Chernobylites," largely the product of Homo sapiens himself and of his actions in the natural environment.

These independent committees should have the right to send inquiries to all governments and organizations, not excepting the IAEA and WHO; to get honest, competent and coherent replies unencumbered by pressure from the nuclear lobby; to make their own independent assessment of these answers; and to defend the interests and rights not of nuclear transnational corporations, but of their victims, the radiation-affected public. For it is the IAEA decisions that the leaders of the now independent states cite to justify their actions. And the IAEA decisions typically stem not from its own independent research, but from inaccurate and often frankly fraudulent data by the official Soviet medical establishment, concocted under the TOP SECRET sign at the Communist Party Central Committee and intended not for recording the truth, but for the exact opposite of it. These committees should have the right not only to give recommendations to governments within the framework of existing international law, but also to demand their implementation, not excepting appeals to the International Court of Justice in The Hague. In short, they should be a sort of fair international defender of all environmental—including nuclear—victims who have been vainly trying for decades to get their own bureaucrats to attend to their needs.

In light of world events in the twentieth century, and considering not only the problems of Chernobyl migrants and resettled villagers, but also those of victims of interethnic conflicts and occupation in various countries, it would be reasonable to also amend Article 3 of the Universal Declaration of Human Rights, giving it a more accurate wording: "Everyone has the right" not just "to life," but "to life worthy of Man."

Whereas only a short while ago the chief factor of humankind's survival was the termination of a dangerous standoff between two systems—the totalitarian Communist and the democratic one, now the main such factor is global environment (the biosphere is already punishing the foolhardy humanity with horrendous earthquakes and floods), as well as war and peace on various continents. The greatest danger to us all lies primarily in the fact that wars are being fought on territories peppered with nuclear power plants and crammed with nuclear weapons. The world—first and foremost, the world's politicians, but also the nations of the world—ought to see this at last.

And now last but not least. Even this one book cites enough materials and evidence, including the final report by the USSR public prosecutor's office and also the ruling of its Ukrainian counterpart, that prove the guilt of former high-ranking Party functionaries and politicians in hiding the truth about the Chernobyl nuclear disaster and its consequences for the former Soviet Union countries and the world. This should be enough for any international tribunal, like the European Court.

The corrupt Ukrainian prosecutor may cite the statute of limitation for this crime. But there is no time limitation for crimes against humanity!